James Bond
and Popular Culture

James Bond and Popular Culture

Essays on the Influence of the Fictional Superspy

Edited by MICHELE BRITTANY

McFarland & Company, Inc., Publishers

Jefferson, North Carolina

LIBRARY OF CONGRESS CATALOGUING-IN-PUBLICATION DATA

James Bond and popular culture : essays on the influence of
the fictional superspy / edited by Michele Brittany.
p.   cm.
Includes bibliographical references and index.

ISBN 978-0-7864-7793-7 (softcover : acid free paper) ∞
ISBN 978-1-4766-1821-0 (ebook)

1. Spy films—History and criticism.   2. James Bond films—
History and criticism.   3. Espionage in motion pictures.
4. Spy television programs—History and criticism.
5. Spies in literature.   6. Fleming, Ian, 1908–1964—
Characters—James Bond.   7. Bond, James (Fictitious
character)   I. Brittany, Michele, 1965– editor.
PN1995.9.S68J36 2014
791.43'6581—dc23   2014037052

BRITISH LIBRARY CATALOGUING DATA ARE AVAILABLE

On the cover: Sean Connery as James Bond in *Goldfinger*, 1964 UK
(United Artists/Photofest)

Printed in the United States of America

McFarland & Company, Inc., Publishers
Box 611, Jefferson, North Carolina 28640
www.mcfarlandpub.com

To fans of spyfi, espionage
and of course
James Bond aficionados everywhere...

Table of Contents

Part Three. Literature

Part Four. Lifestyle

Part Five. Reinterpretations

Acknowledgments

I could not have undertaken this endeavor without the support and friendship of a number of people along the way.

To Robert G. Weiner, who has been a steadfast friend and colleague among those of us who call ourselves independent scholars. The opportunities you have presented to me and your mentorship over the years has been invaluable. I have come a long way thanks to you ... and although you didn't mention all the hurdles I might face in the world of book writing and publishing, I now know it was because you knew all along that I could face the mountain of editing a collection and overcome the challenges that awaited me.

To the organizers of the Southwest Popular/American Culture Association's annual conference, which has been a forum for sharing ideas and networking with like-minded scholars via conversations focused on all things popular culture often lasting into the wee hours of the morning each year in a fascinating little city called Albuquerque.

To Stephanie Ogle, owner of a wonderful oasis known as Cinema Books in the U-District of Seattle. I loved spending hours in your store, chatting about all things films and otherwise. Thank you for your belief in me and always having words of encouragement when times were rough.

To Brian Garant for sharing the burden of reviewing and editing all the essays contained in this book. I'm not sure you knew what you were getting into when you said yes, but I think (and hope) you had fun.

To Nicholas Diak for his editing assistance too, often late into the night, especially as the deadline loomed near. However, more importantly, you have boosted my confidence and encouraged me to "go for it" and not let opportunities pass by. I could not have started or ended this if you had not been there by my side. And to my feline boys—Romeo, Caesar and Ashes—who always provided unconditional love and were looking to distract me just when I needed it most.

Lastly, to Dr. Phil Heldrich for first introducing me to the SWPACA conference—the path that led me here—and for his guidance as I traversed the trials and tribulations of a master's degree. Although Dr. Heldrich is no longer with us, I hope I have honored his legacy and been a torchbearer of knowledge and opportunity for others.

Foreword

ROBERT G. WEINER

The name's "Bond, James Bond." Well, no, it's not. It's Alan Cooper, Anthony Lawrence, Kelly, Napoleon Solo, Matt Helm, Lee Stetson, Quiller, Henry Lyme, Jim Phelps, Richard Hannay, Modesty Blaise, John Drake, Brodie, Archer, and so many others as this volume will attest. Sure, James Bond is without a doubt the most important and well known secret agent in the history of the world. One would be hard pressed to find someone from the age of 15 to 90 who has not heard of Britain's most famous secret agent (at least in most major urban centers). When Ian Fleming created the character of James Bond, he had no idea just how important his little "adolescent fantasy" would become to the world of popular culture. The writing of the character amused him and with his work in the British government he certainly understood how secret agents can and do work. It could be argued that he had this in mind when he gave Bond the code name 007 after the sixteenth-century British mystic John Dee who originally used the double digit code. With Bond, Fleming added style, violence, intrigue, adventure, panache, lovely women, compelling villains, and, frankly, good storytelling to craft a personality that became so much more than just an "adolescent fantasy." The films took this one step further and turned Fleming's "pubescent fictional" character into a superstar that took hold of popular culture like a fast-running train that never stops. We still love James Bond some 60 years after his literary debut and 50 years after the first feature film. Editor Michele Brittany's *James Bond and Popular Culture* reminds us that we also still love a good spy narrative whether or not it features James Bond.

I recently had a unique viewing experience watching the parody film *James Batman* (1966). It's an unauthorized mash-up from the Philippines featuring comedian Dolphy in both the James Bond and Batman roles. As the reader might imagine, *James Batman* is a completely silly film that makes the Adam West *Batman* show and the 1967 Bond parody *Casino Royale* seem as serious as *Citizen Kane*. Yes, the film suffers from bad editing, terrible acting, lousy subtitling, and poor sound (at least in the print I saw) and doesn't have much in the way of narrative continuity. Despite all this, the film does have its clever moments and at times is quite entertaining (for those who can appreciate such Z-grade entertainment). The film even features an evil organization, CLAW (think SPECTRE, QUANTUM, or SMERSH), and versions of the Penguin and Catwoman that will be familiar to most viewers. *James Batman* illustrates that "textual poaching" (a phrase made famous by the great theorist and aca-

Promotional poster for the Philipino *James Batman* film from 1966 and one of the strangest mash-ups in the history of cinema.

demic Henry Jenkins) is not a new phenomenon for modern media and the YouTube-style mash-up has been around for years. In addition, the film illustrates the power of media and literary creations like James Bond and Batman have on the worldwide psyche. It shows us that storylines featuring spies and costumed heroes (parody or not) are valued in all cultures. Keep in mind too, that in 1966 Bond and Bat mania was hitting their peak with the Adam West television show and feature film and the Sean Connery film series. "Spy" mania was too, as this book attests. Television shows, kid's toys (remember those decoder rings and X-ray glasses), novels, films, and comics featuring spy chronicles flooded the market during the 1960s.

The public's appetite for tales featuring intrigue, espionage, danger, mystery, death, and "secret agents" is not just for to those who save the world. Villains can be as compelling as heroes and this goes back to the silent era with films like *Fantomas* (1913), *Les Vampires* (1915), *Spiders* (1919), and the brilliant *Dr. Mabuse: The Gambler* (1922). (Let's not forget the wonderful Italian sequential art creation Diabolik [a jewel thief] or Mario Bavo's modest 1968 film *Danger Diabolik.*) These films feel like European spy films and viewers (and readers of the novels) are almost compelled to root for the main characters despite the fact that they are lawbreakers. These stories illustrate that the basic plot of the spy tale can be applied to villains and be structurally complex.

Ultimately, we want our "superspies" to save the world from the megalomaniacal individuals and organizations who would take our freedoms and those of others. Sure, we like our villains to be larger than life, the secret evil organization to "almost" have the upper hand against our superspy and wonder how he or she will get out of this mess. That is part of the fun of reading or watching a spy story. This brings us back to the content of this volume. Michele Brittany has brought together a variety of essays that go beyond James Bond to show how the spy tale has worldwide appeal from such diverse places as graphic novels, Bollywood, Italy, animation, television, music, and video games. The essays in this volume show us that spies in popular culture cross cultural boundaries and media formats (no small feat). Oh, and you'll find James Bond in here too. As you read, keep your mind alert, your gun handy, and your gadgets in working order.

Robert G. Weiner is an associate humanities librarian at Texas Tech University. He is the co-editor of *James Bond in World and Popular Culture: The Films Are Not Enough* (Cambridge Scholars, 2011) and has taught several courses related to James Bond in popular culture. He is the author of *Marvel Graphic Novels and Related Publications* (McFarland, 2008) and the editor of *Captain America and the Struggle of the Superhero* (McFarland, 2009) and *Graphic Novels and Comics in Libraries and Archives* (McFarland, 2010), among other works relating to comics, popular culture, film and music.

Introduction

Whiffs of expectation began to form on the horizon of popular culture in early 2012. Cinematic James Bond would be turning 50 and honoring him became a worldwide event. Even the 2012 Summer Olympics in London included a short film directed by Danny Boyle and starring HRH Queen Elizabeth II. Wearing his signature tuxedo, Daniel Craig arrives at Buckingham Palace to receive his mission: launch the games by parachuting into the Olympic stadium. It was a media sensation! Bond's cultural influence was further amplified by Sam Mendes, who shot much of the twenty-third Bond film, *Skyfall*, in London. The film premiered in October for Britons, November for Americans, receiving critical and commercial acclaim. It was a golden year for Bond and the media was in a frenzy. Tributes also appeared in many of the mainstream popular magazines that paid homage to Bond catch phrases, Bond fashion, Bond cars, and Bond girls. It seemed every aspect of Bond was examined and celebrated and a week did not go by that a facet of Bond made headlines. It was a fascinating phenomenon that interested the popular culture scholar in me and sparked the idea for this book.

In February 2013, I attended the annual Southwest Popular/American Culture Association's conference. It was my fourth year presenting and my second year serving as the James Bond, Espionage and Eurospy area chair. In all the panels I hosted, I witnessed how passionate Bond fans—casual fans, serious fans and academics alike—were to discuss all facets of Bond. Presentations evoked lively conversations and a common theme ran through all: each person had an opinion of his or her favorite Bond actor and favorite Bond film. Between the enthusiastic conversations in my conference panels and the media buzz that had taken place throughout the previous year, I decided to pursue my idea for a collection of essays that explored the influence of Bond on literature, film, television, video games, animation—truly anything that could be tied to James Bond.

Popular Culture, Shaken and Stirred

There are several insightful books available that analyze the phenomenon of James Bond, but they typically focus on Bond as the subject of analysis and his place in popular culture. Many revolve around the films because they have the greatest presence in society. Others have situated Bond as separate from the larger spy genre. However, it is rare to find books that look outward to society and pinpoint where the Bond phenomenon has inspired—directly or indirectly—our entertainment and lifestyle. The essays presented here take that approach and are divided into five parts: film, television, literature, lifestyle and reinterpretations.

Film is naturally where James Bond has been most influential, particularly in the 1960s. Audiences could not get enough of the suave British agent, so production companies around the world scrambled to fill the demand for Agent 007 to Agent 077 and all agents in between. In Japan, the spy genre was popularized by the successful series of films collectively known as *Nakano Spy School* that examined its country's colonial legacy after World War II and its place in the emerging Cold War. Italian production companies recognized a potentially easy market and quickly churned out spy movies that would come to be known as Eurospy or Bond knock-offs. However, taking a look at them as a group reveals a cycle of films nestled between the peplums and spaghetti westerns and they hence become important to the history of Italian cinema. These Bond-inspired films sought to emulate the Bond formula with rather comical results, however, some of the films subtly challenged the Bond tropes and narrative strategies with some surprising success. This part concludes with a historical perspective of the spy thriller in Bollywood.

Part Two delves into the smaller screen—television. While James Bond dominated the silver screen, Americans got to watch *The Man from U.N.C.L.E.* as its characters moved in the same circles as Bond—exotic locales, hobnobbing with people who have wealth and power, and triumphing over megalomaniacal villains proving the Bond formula could be just as successful weekly. The popularity of the show inspired decades of American spy television. *The Man from U.N.C.L.E.* also created a fascination with the enigmatic, Illya Kuryakin (David McCallum). By the 1970s, English television viewers were watching a little series called *Doctor Who*. At first glance, it would seem that Bond and the Doctor could not be more different, but the series was situated in contemporary Britain during Jon Pertwee's era, which gave the sci-fi series a way to incorporate Bond elements. By the 1980s, civilians were enlisted to assist begrudging spies complete their missions, week after week, such as in the series *Scarecrow and Mrs. King*.

Part Three returns to James Bond's roots—literature. Our cool, rational spy is turned on his ear in the critically-acclaimed *Mind MGMT*. This comic book thriller from writer/artist Matt Kindt applies Carl Jung's psychoanalytical theories presented in his final work, *The Undiscovered Self*. Then, in another twist, readers are given insight into the creative process of creating a female spy—

Chastity Flame—that James Bond would have loved to meet in some smoked-filled casino on the Riviera.

Part Four is about lifestyle. Most often, we associate the tuxedo with James Bond, but there are several other iconographic associations we can make: the Martini, Aston Martin DB5, watches, and, more recently, the smartphone and the beer (yes, I went there!). But, before the films, advertisers with only the Fleming books created their Bond to sell Courtelle clothing in the *Daily Express* in 1961. And as the old adage goes—a man's home is his castle—décor can reveal much. Bond's abode was seldom seen, but American spies Derek Flint and Matt Helm embodied the emerging playboy lifestyle and proudly displayed their bachelor pads in their respective films.

The last part considers Bond reinterpretations. Sterling Archer, from the hit cartoon *Archer* on FX, may look every bit the intrepid spy but he actually has several flaws stemming from fractured development and hearing loss sustained in the line of duty. In Activision's *007 Legends*, Daniel Craig's likeness as James Bond is ret-conned into pre–Craig era Bond films such as *On Her Majesty's Secret Service* and *Goldfinger* resulting in convoluted storytelling that left critics and fans disappointed.

These fourteen essays take a critical look at the phenomenal impact one British secret agent has had on popular culture for more than five decades. This book is a sample of a larger opportunity that exists to study this phenomenon and is by no means an exhaustive study of the subject. Hence we are at the beginning of a journey to discover and understand how James Bond has and will continue to influence all that defines and shapes us.

Part One

Film

Japan's 1960s Spy Boom
Bond Meets Imperial Nostalgia[1]

Michael Baskett

The Summer of '65: A World of Spies

In the summer of 1965, Japan was awash in spy fever. *Goldfinger* (1964, Guy Hamilton) had just been released in theaters, *The Man from U.N.C.L.E.* (1964–1968) debuted on the Nihon TV network, and the bestselling boy's manga *Shonen* (young men) published a special issue on spies featuring the child-friendly adventures of popular domestic spy *Hattori-kun the Ninja* together with an illustrated adaptation of the exploits of James Bond. This media frenzy was promptly dubbed the "spy boom" by pundits, but relatively little of it considered the nature of spycraft—why spies do what they do—so much as how spies looked and, most notably, what high-tech gadgets they used. Miniaturized technology was particularly resonant in 1960s Japan, which by mid-decade had already transformed its postwar image from that of a defeated nation into a model Cold War ally and leading international exporter of affordable transistorized technologies, mass-produced compact automobiles, and intricate mechanical toys. In Japan, toy manufacturers swiftly and effectively saturated the market with spy-related merchandise inviting a generation of prospective boy agents to become interactive participants in the boom through the consumption of shrewdly marketed "spy kits" containing disappearing ink, decoder books, badges, pipe periscopes, time bombs, electrified cigarette lighters, suitcase cameras, mini tape recorders, collapsible guns, etc.[2]

The spy boom also facilitated a rise in successful transmedia franchises including *Phantom Agents* (*Ninja Butai Gekko*, 1964–1967), *Cyborg 009* (1964–1968) and *Spycatcher J3* (1965–1967), and it motivated Toei Studios animation division to partner with Videocraft in the United States to co-produce the animated spy-themed children's program *Tom from T.H.U.M.B.* for export to the United States, Australia, Mexico, and Japan.[3] The sheer ubiquity of spies and their clandestine activities compelled parents to monitor their children's consumption of these products and, as a result, indirectly recruited parents as an unintended yet important secondary audience. As keepers of the household finances, parents often validated and even perpetuated the spy boom in subtle ways and through such seemingly mundane activities as buying their children *Get Smart* notebooks for school, 007-themed lunchboxes, or even by rearranging the presentation of traditional New Year's food to resemble Napoleon Solo's face.

Mass-produced media images of sophisticated, cosmopolitan, and sexualized spies encouraged a distinctly new type of star for teenagers and young adults to consume and emulate. Official and unofficial fan clubs for James Bond, John Drake, Napoleon Solo, Illya Kuryakin, April Dancer, and others proliferated literally overnight, providing dedicated members with a space in which they could passionately exchange knowledge about their favorite spies, trade goods, and create original stories, art, and newsletters.[4] Merchandising and media tie-ins were important ways in which these young consumers experienced the spy boom as they were often excluded from access to the more adult-themed James Bond films.

From this admittedly brief overview, the Japanese spy boom would appear to closely resemble other similar Bond phenomena occurring contemporaneously around the world. Yet, a closer inspection reveals several compelling areas where the 1960s Japanese spy boom differed significantly from the Bond phenomenon in other cultures. For instance, film critic Oka Toshio, writing in 1966 in Japan's leading film journal, *Kinema Junpo*, carefully reminded readers that their nation's current frenzy for spies was not simply the result of the popularity of the 007 franchise but had clear domestic precedents: "Before the appearance of 007, we [in Japan] were producing *ninja* films for quite some time."[5] Japan's ninja tradition was both an important precedent to the worldwide vogue for espionage as well as a crucial source of its inspiration, a notable example being Roald Dahl's screenplay for *You Only Live Twice* (1967, Lewis Gilbert). To a far greater degree than the Bond series, Japan's spy boom delineated a continuity between an imagined past and the Cold War present. The moral ambiguity of medieval Japan uncannily resembled that of the Cold War era in the narratives of *Samurai Spy* (*Ibun Sarutobi Sasuke*, 1965, Shinoda Masahiro), *Spy* (*Kancho*, 1964, Samajima Tadashi), and the long running *Shinobi no Mono* series (1962–1966, Daiei Studios) which invariably problematized notions of individual loyalty and identity as being perpetually contingent. The ninja in these films operated outside the conventions of social class or the *bushido* code of the samurai, as hired agents working on behalf of powerful rival organizations and often finding themselves irreconcilably caught between the two.[6]

Questions of individual identity overlapped with more general apprehensions about Japan's national identity in the contemporary spy films of this period.

Because spy narratives by their very nature question the notion of a stable identity, Japanese directors regarded espionage as an eminently relevant metaphor through which to explore their nation's ambivalent status within the Cold War order.[7] Neither a member nation of the North Atlantic Treaty Organization (NATO) nor of the U.N. Security Council, Japan nevertheless occupied a politically, economically, and culturally privileged position in Asia due to its proximity to the U.S. The nature of this liminal relationship not only enabled Japan's swift postwar economic recovery but was also the source of large-scale domestic protest movements against the U.S.–Japan Security Treaty. In the contemporary political thriller *The Proud Challenge* (*Hokoritakaki Chosen*, 1962, Fukasaku Kinji), an ex-communist Japanese journalist loses his job for uncovering a secret CIA plot to ship weapons throughout Southeast Asia. Dubious of the veracity of Japan's freedom of the press, this film also strongly criticizes institutionalized espionage as being fundamentally contrary to the basic democratic freedoms that the U.S. presumably sought to promote. Because the victims are Japanese—journalists and Japanese contract agents of the CIA—the film explicitly links their exploitation back onto the nation by intimating that this systemic victimization of Japan began with the United States occupation and continues into the present as a result of Japan's dependent geopolitical status within the Cold War order.

Finally, spy films enabled an examination of another sort of victimhood that originated within the nation itself, such as that portrayed in ex-communist director Yamamoto Satsuo's *Spy* (*Supai*, 1965), which offers a scathing critique of Japanese racial discrimination against Korean residents in 1960s Japan. Reminiscent of blacklisted leftwing writers in Hollywood who similarly advocated the need to depict the marginalized communities within U.S. society, Yamamoto's treatment of a police investigation into an influx of illegal foreign spies hiding in a resident Korean community in Japan, correlated the institutionalized violence against Korean-residents with the Cold War paranoia of communist infiltration. Thus, in this film, Japan's largest "hidden" ethnic minority performs a function similar to what Rosie White has described as the "doubly transgressive" nature of women spies who are similarly marginalized as objects and denied of their subjectivity.[8] Like their counterparts in mainstream Japanese cinema, these socially concerned spy dramas also situated the genre within a specific historical continuum that refused to interpret Japanese colonialism, official Japanese support of the Korean War, and ongoing Japanese support of U.S. military intervention in Vietnam as discontinuous historical "breaks" so much as a recognizable unified trajectory.

This essay explores how such issues of cultural specificity, identity, and history intersect with Japan's experience of the Cold War as seen in the successful five-film spy franchise *Nakano Spy School* (*Rikugun Nakano Gakko,* 1966–1968).

Produced at the height of the spy boom but set in the era leading up to the bombing of Pearl Harbor in 1941, *Nakano Spy School* integrated contemporary spy film conventions into the historical thriller thereby placing East-West tensions into a historical continuum.

The purpose of this analysis is twofold. First, by placing the *Nakano* series in dialog with key scholarship in James Bond studies[9] and Cold War culture studies[10] the spy genre provided Japanese filmmakers and critics with an opportune means by which to grapple with its indeterminate role in the Cold War order and its unresolved imperial legacy. Bond studies uniquely inform such a symbiotic relationship by their attention to the role of empire in analyzing Bond as a symbol of imperial decline. This study takes the work of Jeremy Black, Toby Miller, Michael Denning, Tony Bennett, and Janet Woollacott as crucial starting points from which to examine the different context in which Japan's empire intersected with the *Nakano* series. For instance, if the Bond forms are, as some have argued, "contributors to, and symptoms of, imperialism, sexism, Orientalism, class hierarchy, jingoism, and even mass pornography,"[11] then how might the ambiguous nature of Japanese colonialism as the only non–Western empire to colonize in Asia inform how Japanese spy films defined colonizers and colonized?[12] This research also seeks to contribute to a recent shift in Cold War studies towards a renewed assessment of the cultural as opposed to geopolitical or economic factors as well as a recognition of the relevance of the secondary powers in the Cold War order.[13]

Secondly, this essay responds to a general resistance among scholars of Japan and Japanese popular culture to examine this era beyond the dominant category of the "postwar." Because postwar studies tend to focus on Japan's domestic responses to defeat and reconstruction, and because many of those policies were initiated under U.S. military occupation, as a category, the postwar tends to over emphasize U.S.–Japan relations while obscuring those with other nations. More than just a simple matter of historical periodization, a paradigm shift from a postwar perspective to a Cold War framework reveals an entirely different set of geopolitical relationships than what we have been accustomed to. Specifically, what emerges are the historical and contemporary relationships between Japan and its former Asian colonies.

To that end, this analysis of the *Nakano Spy School* series is grouped into three specific areas, each of which examine the aforementioned themes through the intersection of ideology and the figure of the spy. The first area examines the ways in which Masumura Yasuzo and Hoshikawa Seiji, the director and screenwriter of the first film in the *Nakano* series, investigated the notion of "youth" (*seishun*) as a decisive stage in the development of the spy as an individual. Adapting Bennett and Woollacott's theories of the relation of fiction to ideology, the notion of youth serves as a region of ideology in which the various practices of indoctrinating spies while functioning within the dominant ideology also engage popular notions of individual agency, or choice. The notion of individual agency in the identity construction of spies marks a departure from conventional readings of what motivates spies to spy (e.g., Len Deighton's Harry Palmer) and at the same time challenges the orthodoxy of prevailing postwar discourses of Japanese victimization that claim the nation itself were helpless victims under a fascist wartime regime.

The second area builds on the discussion of ideology to examine how class differences are subsumed and at times violently eliminated during the training and subsequent missions of the Nakano agents. Following Denning's work on the imperial spy novel, this essay explores the ways in which representations of Nakano's spies are transformed from a privileged class of elite military officers into a group of faceless everymen through specialized and rigorous training.[14] The film problematizes the notion of a "classless society" prevalent in 1960s Japan. While the suppression of class difference among Nakano agents suggests an attempt to create a stable Japanese national identity through the lens of nostalgia for its lost empire, the ostentatious fashion of the agents challenges conventional notions of class orthodoxy. This ambiguity of a national/imperial identity read onto an imagined past correlates to Japan's enigmatic role in the Cold War order and simultaneously offers a form of resistance to that order by presenting a resurrected Japanese empire as the only viable form of regional security against U.S. militarism and Chinese communism.[15]

Finally, the third area extends the investigation of ideology and identity by analyzing the ways in which spies, through the act of disguising their ethnicity, question the malleable role of identity within the context of empire. The need for non–Japanese spies to disguise their ethnicity in these films is not only a matter of expediency or a tool of trade so much a symptom of empire. Thus, Chinese sleeper agents who pass undetected for Japanese citizens present a crisis in the ability of the ruling class to contain ethnicity and thus maintain a stable national identity. In contrast, when Nakano agents disguise their ethnicity, it is not presented as a crisis of identity but rather subsumed within a premodern tradition of *ninjutsu* thus codifying their *Japanese* identity as defenders of a "still-active" empire against the threat of invasion.

No Regrets for Our Youth: Ideology and Agency

Released on June 4, 1966, just seven weeks before Sean Connery and Eon Productions arrived in Japan to shoot *You Only Live Twice*, the first *Nakano Spy*

School film detailed the rigorous training of eighteen handpicked elite army officers at Japan's first spy school in the wake of the China Incident of 1937.[16] The narrative follows Lt. Miyoshi Jiro and eighteen other newly-commissioned army officers who are given orders to secretly assemble near the Yasukuni Shrine in Tokyo and tell no one of their activities. Once assembled, Lt. Major Kusanagi explains to puzzled recruits that the war with China has created an urgent need for reliable intelligence and they have been selected to give up their families, loved ones, and military commissions in order to undergo training at Japan's first spy school. Their first orders are to change from military uniforms into business suits, select new identities, and speak as only civilians avoiding any military jargon. Their curriculum is divided among theory (political science, economics, history, diplomacy, etc.) and practice (Judo, aviation, disguise, dance, safecracking, sexual seduction, etc.) with each topic taught by leading specialists in that field. Some agents distinguish themselves during the harsh training while others break under pressure. Lt. Maj. Kusanagi struggles to keep the Nakano School alive in the face of chronic underfunding and harsh factionalism among army leadership who see the school as unethical, overly expensive, and largely superfluous. Agent Miyoshi now known as Shiina distinguishes himself during his graduation mission by infiltrating the British embassy, microfilming a secret codebook, and returning it undetected. In the process, he manages to expose a foreign spy ring that had infiltrated the highest levels of the army and even involved his ex-fiancé. Thus having proved their loyalty, the film ends with Shiina and the other Nakano agents being deployed on secret assignments throughout Asia.

The initial impetus for the *Nakano Spy School* films came in the fall of 1965 when Hatakeyama Seiko, a popular writer of historical fiction, published a serialization on the actual Nakano School based on interviews conducted with many of its graduates. These former agents were anxious that their history not be forgotten but passed on to a generation that had not experienced war.[17] Using a pseudo-documentary style, Hatakeyama compiled a narrative based on the copious anecdotes and written materials of their wartime intelligence operations directed primarily against Soviet Russia.[18] Screenwriter Hoshikawa Seiji and director Masumura Yasuzo's final script utilized little from Hatakeyama's original novel but intriguingly relocated the target of the Nakano School's intelligence efforts from Russia to Asia, specifically mainland China.[19]

Masumura, however, maintained that the film's real focus was not on spies but the role of youth in the identity formation of the individual. Masumura, also a noted film critic, was unique among Japanese directors of that time in that he won a two-year scholarship to study in Rome at the Italian National Film School (Centro Sperimentale di Cinematografia). Reflecting on his time at the Center, Masumura speculated that the sum of his experience could be distilled into two realizations: "the first was that I was a solitary person born in a transitional period for whom neither Democracy nor Fascism held much appeal. Second, that humans are terribly powerless creatures who instantly weaken in the face of enormous organizations."[20] A director's comments, however, must always be viewed critically and although Masumura claimed that this film was not about spies, certainly notions of the interaction among ideology, the individual, and huge organizations spoke directly to the inherently conflicted nature of spies. Masumura elaborated on the complex interplay among youth, love, and loyalty in the process by which individuals become politically aware.

> Youth is ... to subjectively feel that one is part of something of immense value and to thoroughly love that something with all one's might. The object of that love may be human, an ideology, or the nation, but it is above calculated self-interest, something that one throws oneself entirely into to love. Why is it that such love is possible only during youth? Perhaps because ... the possibilities are limitless, one chooses something and loves it intensely precisely because one is alone; for when one has nothing it is easy to lose oneself for love... For my current film, *Nakano Spy School*, I met with several graduates from the school. They all said "Nakano School was my youth." It's fascinating to me that spies and youth share the same characteristics. Their job is dangerous and cruel with extremely little chance of success or of ever returning home. Most died unknown, like dogs. Rarely, if did one succeed, there was no glory or reward—they were doomed to wander in the shadows. This is true selflessness. Even if their eyes were gouged, tongues pulled out, ears torn off, hands and feet severed, they had keep on living to devote their very essence to the nation. How much greater must the effect of these unique conditions have been if one was a spy in one's youth? *Nakano Spy School* depicts the lives of 18 young men who fell in love with the outlook of a particular Lt. Major and thus devoted their lives to spying. In producing this film it wasn't my intention to portray spies, but rather youth.[21]

At a moment when the Bond phenomenon had all but redefined the spy genre in its own image and in the process drew fire from critics who lambasted it as sexist, racist, and reactionary, Masumura and Hoshikawa re-appropriated the genre as a way to interrogate the ways in which individuals might embrace an ideology without having to be coerced. Unlike Harry Palmer, the decidedly downbeat working-class protagonist of Len Deighton's *Ipcress File* (1962), who is blackmailed into servitude to the state to work off a prison sentence for black marketeering, Agent Shiina and the other Nakano officers are presented a choice of whether or not to spy. The narrative presents this as a philosophical dilemma during the first half of the film through a series of dialogue exchanges among the recruits over the nature of spies.

Their opinions on the relative merits or drawbacks to becoming a spy represent a variety of perspectives ranging from victimhood—"Now that we've given up our names, our loves, our futures, what will become of us?"—to opportunism—"Being a spy could be a damn sight more interesting than getting killed off on the frontline in Manchuria"—and even curiosity—"I heard that some are actually born with a natural predisposition toward becoming a spy."[22] Hoshikawa wrote that his intention was to capture the emotional realm of military experience as a form of indoctrination rather than a "so-called spy film."[23] In some respects, this echoes Hatakeyama and the Nakano School graduate's desire to educate postwar Japanese with an "authentic" account of the war. Yet the film does not align with reactionary rightists but considers the psychological power of ideologues on youth.[24]

For instance, after the recruits learn why they were gathered, they ask their superior officer why they were selected, why the school is even necessary, and whether or not they will be allowed to see their families. As a military commander, Kusanagi is uncharacteristically frank answering all of their questions and convincing them of the empire's need for spies: "Japan is already at war with China. War with the west appears imminent. I don't need to tell you all how vital spies are to the war effort. A single spy is worth twenty soldiers ... whether Japan prospers or perishes is up to you. I ask you to put everything behind you, join me, and become spies for the good of Japan."[25] Kusanagi emotionally admonishes his recruits that the true essence of a spy is "sincerity." According to Kusanagi, it was such purity of spirit that enabled Russo-Japanese War (1904–05) hero Capt. Akashi to infiltrate the communists, provide them with weapons, and pave the way for Japanese victory. In a voiceover, Agent Shiina directly addresses the audience explaining, "A solider doesn't disobey orders, but that wasn't why I agreed to join Kusanagi. I was overcome by his passion."[26]

The nature of this passion was a matter of concern among film critics, some of who were highly skeptical of what sort of message the film offered beyond a return to fascism. Shirai Yoshio, for example, criticized the film as ahistorical and that the idea of "sincerity" as portrayed in the film had anything to do with the focus of the real Nakano School which was about "safe-cracking, murder, and erotic seduction."[27] Yet even Shirai admitted to a certain pleasure in watching the process of the eighteen young officers, in the fanaticism of youth, alternately resisting and following their maverick leader down a gradually narrowing path. Masumura, who often meditated on the nature of fascism during his time in Italy, was well aware of the dangerous volatility of collectives such as this. When agent Tezuka becomes obsessed with a local geisha who was his partner for seduction training, he uses the methods of the school to steal from his classmates to make money for this woman. When he is caught by the local police he is temporarily returned to the school until the authorities can confirm his status as an officer in the army. Here the unintended consequences of decisions made in youth are depicted in their full horror.

NAKANO AGENTS. Do you think you're the only one suffering? We all want to sleep with women or be promoted. But we grit our teeth and bear it! Now [what you did] will come out in military court and stain the reputation of our school ... we won't have people mock Nakano, saying it's a school for thieves, not spies ... Die, Tezuka! Right here in front of us, and do it bravely![28]

TEZUKA. Fine! If you all want me to die that much, then I'll do it!

AGENT SHIINA. (*Voice over.*) There was no doubt that we all were responsible for killing Tezuka. But it was at that precise moment when we began to love the school. None of us could turn back now. Tezuka was reported as killed in action and his ashes were sent back to his family.[28]

Bennett and Woolacott remind us that popular narratives, including mainstream films, cannot simply impose the dominant ideology but must also make concessions to other ideologies in order to engage a variety of audiences.[29] The preceding scene is one of several in the film which seem to offer a critique of the totalitarian system to which Kusanagi's idealized spies must pledge their sincerity. Masumura rejects the facile interpretation that war is a faceless system under which everyone suffers equally, and instead turns his attention to the processes by which systems garner support from individuals. Such a standpoint was unique in the mainstream Japanese film industry at this time; Masumura demonstrated an awareness of the pleasures and power of ideology, particularly on the youth, but ultimately he places responsibility for those decisions not on undifferentiated social groups or vague ideologies, but rather on the agency of individuals.

"Me, or someone like me": Nakano Spies and the Myth of Classlessness

They are the ones of our middle class who have left home, spiritually as well as physically, to take the vows of organization life, and it is they who are the mind and soul of our great self-perpetrating institutions ... [they talk of] the inability to control one's direction. But they have no great sense of plight; between themselves and the organization they believe they see an ultimate harmony and ... they are building an ideology that will vouchsafe this trust.[30]

Every government has its secret service branch. America, it's CIA; France, Deuxième Bureau; England, MI5. A messy job? Well, that's when they usually call on me, or someone like me. Oh yes. My name is Drake, John Drake.[31]

One of the most distinct motifs of the 1960s spy boom was a fear of the loss of individual identity. Spy films and television programs obsessed over the anonymity of the individual in the face of vast multinational organizations, the replacement of personal names with numbers, coding and decoding, translations, and acronymic official and semi-official institutions. Not only spies but military servicemen, white-collared workers, scientists, doctors, lawyers, priests, students and others from nearly every walk of life seemed inexorably connected into networks of collectivization. Audiences recognized espionage organizations, both fictional and real, as stylized versions of familiar systems in part because most viewers shared some practical knowledge of the problems of collective work.[32]

In his study of the imperial spy novel, Michael Denning states that ideology turns precisely on the discourse of yet another collective, the nation. He argues that in spy thrillers, the needs of the ruling class are equated with those of the nation, thus any disturbances to the smooth business of that class, will inevitably generate disruption across the nation and often beyond its borders.[33] Bennett and Woollacott suggest that the ideological power of the imperial spy novel derives precisely from this alignment of the nation with the ruling class.[34] The agents of *Nakano Spy School* are directly equated with the ruling class of imperial Japan. In the first film, the young officers are all described as being university graduates (despite the fact that many actual Nakano agents were not) and most as desiring to become career army officers. This revisionism is less significant for any lack of historical authenticity than for what it tells us about the relation between class and spies in 1960s Japan.

By the mid–1960s, Japan had entered an era of high economic growth and the quality of life rose substantially as Japan shifted to a postindustrial society. Studies conducted by the Japan Sociological Society in the 1950s and 1960s, and later by the prime minister's office (1970), suggested that robust economic growth had inclined most respondents to identify themselves as the middle class regardless of whether or not they actually were.[35] Promoted by official institutions and widely commented on in the media, the notion of Japan as a classless society served the ruling class by establishing the image of a nation with few to minimal social divisions. The preeminent status of economic growth during this period imparted great importance to major organizations, especially corporations, whose aspirational goal, even if it did not reflect reality, was to put aside one's differences for the benefit of the organization—as in times of war.

The function of social class in the *Nakano Spy School* films is similarly ambiguous though always quite prominent; it is one of the first orders that the agents receive: to discard their former social positions, renounce their commissions, and interact among themselves without any trace of military hierarchy as though they were everyday civilians. Yet, as the *Nakano* films patently manifest, these agents are obviously not civilians nor does their superior officer, Lt. Maj. Kusanagi treat them as such. In the first film, he directly appeals to their sense of social class in order to convince the recruits to join the school: "Many of you would have become university presidents, CEOs, even government ministers. But we're asking you to give all of that up. Why? Because Japan is embroiled in a war with China and ... [the empire's] future prosperity rests squarely on your shoulders."[36] Despite being coded as part of the ruling class, the training these officer-spies receive requires them to become indistinguishable from the middle-class masses in order to operate freely and undetected among them. Narratively, the negation of their status as officer-spies and transformation into everymen-spies is a necessary prerequisite for their actions conducted on behalf of the nation, to acquire any meaning with popular audiences.

The physical appearance of the Nakano spies, and the resulting confusion it created, was an important motif throughout the series. In the second film, *Nakano Spy School: Cloud No. 1 Directive* (*Rikugun Nakano Gakko: Kumo Ichigo Shirei*, 1966, Mori Kazuo), Agent Shiina returns to Japan from his first mission in Beijing to investigate a series of sabotage attacks against Japanese freighter ships carrying secret weapons to the front. While investigating the crime site, Shiina is arrested by military police for suspicious behavior and taken to head-quarters for interrogation:

> INTERROGATING OFFICER. Sit. State your name and occupation.
> SHIINA. Shiina Jiro ... Imperial army officer.
> OFFICER. What? Who the hell do you think you're fooling?! (*He moves to hit Shiina.*)
> SHIINA. You wouldn't dare strike a superior officer.
> OFFICER. No one with hair that long could pass for an Army officer!
> SHIINA. Maybe not. Check and you'll find out.
> OFFICER. You're damn right I'll check. But you'd better prepare yourself.[37]

That actual Nakano spies dressed and acted like civilians was a happy coincidence for Daiei Studios producers desperate for ways to make their series set during the war, look like a modern spy film. This historical fact also lent a measure of plausibility as to why characters confused these spies' identities, a point that was exploited in nearly every subsequent film. But rather than functioning only as a class-cloaking device, the films narratively and visually celebrated this confusion over Nakano agents not "looking like their class" by contrasting their ostentatious fashion at a time when war mobilization campaigns proclaimed luxury and fashion the enemy of all good citizens. As with the Bond franchise, fashion and connoisseurship were intrinsic sources of the *Nakano* series appeal to audiences. For Japanese audiences, the visual gap separating Nakano agents dressed like 1960s spies versus imperial soldiers in vintage 1940s uniforms was infinitely greater, and hence more transgressive, than contemporary spies who looked like well-dressed, but ordinary, businessmen. Daiei Studios took meticulous care to photograph its star and co-stars as fashionably as possible, emphasizing the modern cut of their clothes and the coordination of their accessories. Even publicity materials (stills, posters, press sheets, etc.) for the film referenced design conventions consistent with other promotional campaigns for the Bond series in Japan as well as trends in fashion magazines.

This transgressive class-crossing appearance of the Nakano spies was further underscored by their unconventional behavior. In their capacity as everyman-spies, they frequented bars, hotels, dance halls, and even houses of prostitution—areas off limits to good officers. In this sense, the series tantalizingly appears to be at variance with the needs of the ruling class yet very much in synch with popular/middle-class expectations.

Despite their appearance as classless everymen, Nakano agents also represented the possibility of individual action in the face of inflexible, massive organizations. For example, Shiina functions as a popular hero defying the now-defunct Japanese military hierarchy just as surely as enemy spies and thus encouraged "middle-class" audiences in 1960s Japan to identify with spies rather than soldiers. In mission after mission, Shiina exposed Japan's military ruling class as thoroughly corrupt and as a result highly susceptible to enemy infiltration. The future of Japan, and by extension, the security of Asia, must not be left to the military. But what about Nakano's own status within this vast military industrial complex? How should we interpret these agents fighting so valiantly for a doomed empire?

If Bond is emblematic of a British empire in decline, Shiina is the symbol of an already lost empire. Some Japanese critics read Shiina as an anachronism much in the way that others in the West viewed Bond, however, they were less certain about the role that the Japanese empire played in these spy dramas in part because the real Nakano School legacy refused to die. Nakano graduates made newspaper headlines as "hold outs" hidden in old outposts of empire refusing to surrender or believe that the war had ended. Lt. Tanimoto Kikuo returned to Japan in 1954, after joining the Vietnamese independence struggle against the French as an advisor and commander. Nakano officer Lt. Onoda Hiro surrendered in 1974 only after his former commanding officer flew to the Philippines to relieve him of duty. The tenacity of these soldier-spies became fodder for American television programs at this time, but for Japanese audiences they presented nagging associations with Japanese defeat and questions about Japan's imperial legacy in Asia.

Imperial Masquerades: Disguising Ethnicity

[In the Bond novels] We move beyond the situation in which you only had to scratch a foreigner to find a villain, but you still don't need to scratch a villain to find a foreigner.[38]

It is a habit in all of us to make our cover stories, our assumed personae, at least parallel with the reality... We should take the opposition's cover stories more seriously... The more identities a man has, the more they express the person they conceal... Few men can resist expressing their appetites when they are making a fantasy about themselves.[39]

Returning Japanese imperial holdouts who fought alongside Asian independence armies raised questions as to whether Japan's empire truly had been a failed project. Returnees anxious to work through their experience of defeat and loss of their "youth" popularized a genre of nonfiction, known as "war record" (*senki*) literature in which authors lamented losing the war, but questioned whether their impact on anti-colonial movements throughout Southeast Asia after 1945 had not in fact resulted in the removal of Western colonists from the region.

For *Nakano Spy School*'s agents, to serve the empire meant to serve in Asia by exposing spies, preventing counterinsurgency, and promoting Pan-Asianism. Indeed, Kusanagi's initial appeal to the agents entreated them to sacrifice themselves in the same manner as their Russo-Japanese War heroes had in order to "become friends with the people in those territories, battle their corrupt governments and all invaders ... liberate the colonized territories and their people." When asked whether Japan itself was a colonizer of China, Kusanagi heartily agreed and cautioned that adventurism in Asia by "ignorant politicians and military leadership" had to be resisted in order to liberate the region from colonial domination.[40] Asia is represented as a region in perpetual crisis; first colonized by the West, then Japan, and thereafter becoming a battlefield in a proxy war between the superpowers—it was the only region where the Cold War turned hot.

Disrupting military adventurism, however, was not the sole province of Nakano agents—the various American, British, or Chinese resistance groups also carried out wide scale sabotage or counterintelligence activities in the colonies. Even Japanese port cities such as Kobe, Yokohama, and Nagasaki were susceptible to counterinsurgency due to their large foreign populations. This would seem to reinforce Kingsley's quote that "foreignness" and villainy were coequal in imperial Japan. In the *Nakano* series, non–Japanese women counteragents were especially plentiful yet they did not function as equivalents to the Bond girl. Despite his training in seduction, Shiina never gratuitously seduced or flirted with women. Thus, sexuality was never employed by the protagonist either to affect a political conversion or as a method by which to "turn" an enemy agent. Women counteragents, however, did use honey-traps throughout the series, but interracial sex was often represented as a lesser technique subordinated within the larger skill set of cultural assimilation.

A compelling example is found in *Cloud No. 1 Directive*, the second installment in the series, in which a Red Chinese agent passes as a Japanese geisha named Meika in order to gain access to a local military police officer. Her task is to transmit sensitive military intelligence to mainland China. This includes collecting information on the identities and operations of Nakano agents. This Chinese agent (we never learn her real name) escapes suspicion due to her mastery of the verbal and aesthetic skills appropriate to a high-level geisha. Her disguise is transgressive on several levels—the most unanticipated for the duped military policeman is the fact that a non–Japanese could ever assimilate to the point of becoming virtually indistinguishable from a "real" Japanese. Even after Shiina exposes her as a spy, the incredulous officer is unable to fathom that she was not Japanese and accuses her of treason to which she responds: "Perhaps, if I were Japanese. But I'm not. I'm a patriot for my homeland—a defender against Japanese aggression ... the unprincipled will always be deceived because they know neither freedom nor truth."[41]

In the third film, *Nakano Spy School: Dragon No. 3 Directive* (*Rikugun Nakano Gakko: Ryu Sango Shirei*, 1967, Tanaka Tokuzo), Chinese counteragent Shu Biran deploys a deception of another sort, not by disguising her ethnicity but by feigning to love a Japanese military police officer to gather intelligence. When her deception is discovered, Biran attacks her now ex-lover, shrieking: "Chinese women could never fall for scum like you even if we must sacrifice our bodies!"[42] This is a reference to the so-called "comfort women" system of Japanese military brothels, in which women, frequently Korean or Chinese, were deceived or forcibly abducted into service as sex slaves for Japanese soldiers fighting at the front.[43] The character of Biran, although not a comfort woman, does represent an idealized object of Japanese desire blending the lure of the exotic Other with the threat of danger and deceit; she is an Orientalist fantasy inscribed within a non–Western context.[44]

If non–Japanese women spies presented a threat to male Japanese agents, they also obliquely helped to establish recognition for the need for Nakano School itself through demonstrating the shocking degree to which the army administration was vulnerable to enemy infiltration. Women spies proved that without a systemized counterespionage organization like the Nakano School in place Japan was indeed at risk. At the same time, by exposing these unforeseen threats to the military ruling class (i.e., the nation), Nakano's agents demonstrated their usefulness and loyalty in the protection of the realm. In contrast to foreign women spies, male Nakano agent's (there were no women graduates) use of disguise served a markedly different function.

The role of agent Shiina was played by period film actor Ichikawa Raizo in one of his few contemporary roles. Japanese audiences in the 1960s would have known him best from starring in the eight-film *Shinobi no Mono* series, which was credited with helping to revitalize the ninja genre for a new generation of youthful viewers. In that series he played Ishikawa Goemon, a stellar ninja protégé of a secret style of *ninjutsu*. Much like Agent Shiina, Goemon is represented as an idealistic ninja who devotes himself to what he believes is a principled leader in a principled organization. But with each mission more dishonorable than the first, he gradually begins to grasp the full weight of the corruption of which he is now part. The *Shinobi no Mono* series significantly influenced the Bond franchise as well, reportedly inspiring the screenwriter of *You Only Live Twice* to include a cat-stroking villain, poisoning via a string, and the use of Japanese ninja.[45] Rooted as it was both of and in an imagined historical past, Ichikawa's star persona conjured up connotations of folkloric domestic espionage and ancient martial arts. In the *Nakano* series, Shiina's ability to disguise himself alternately as a second generation Canadian-Japanese tailor, a high-stakes Chinese gambler, or a Suzhou vagrant, invariably draw on his preexisting persona as a star in ninja films thus imparting him an air of authenticity denied other actors in Japan's spy boom. Ichikawa's authenticity reinforces Shiina colonial authority and stabilizes his distinctly *Japanese* identity regardless of which Asian ethnicity he is called on to adapt.

Yet some film critics found the all-too-stable identities of Nakano spies symptomatic of a larger problem with the series as a whole. Shirai writes, "Because it's virtually impossible to produce 007-style contemporary spy thrillers in Japan, the idea here appears to be that someone wanted to make a spy film that trades on nostalgia for the good old days. Perhaps the half-baked atmosphere of the setting made it feel anachronistic; like a wartime anti-spy film or a Yamanaka Minetaro spy novel for kids."[46] Likewise, Hayashi Tamaki, writing in *Kinema Junpo* later that year on *Cloud No. 1 Directive*, faulted the entire series as having little worthwhile to compare with the Bond franchise "even as action entertainment it comes up wanting." Beyond innumerable plot inconsistencies ("Meika confesses her fight against Japanese imperialism … a little too easily"), Hayashi called the use of Bond-like gadgets "laughable" inaccuracies for that period, and surmised that *Nakano*'s comparatively smaller scale and budget compared to that of the 007 series was a likely factor in the film's failure to produce any "real thrills."[47] Beyond these interminable questions over the *Nakano* series inauthenticity vis-à-vis the Bond series, not one observer asked why the Nakano spy school and the Japanese empire were being revived in the mid–1960s. Even politically oriented leftist film critics seemed less concerned by the obvious implications of a cinematic re-colonizing of Asia than by the question of "Why aren't our spies Bond?" By the third installment of the series in 1967, critics had apparently lost interest, as no major film journal carried any reviews of the series despite the fact that they represented some of the Daiei Studio's most successful products for those years.[48]

Conclusion: Boom and Bust

Shunned by critics as derivative and anachronistic yet embraced by audiences as exciting and relevant, we might ask, why do Nakano's spies matter at all? Lacking any comparable literary pedigree to that of the Fleming novels, Japan's Nakano spy school was however linked to specific and conflicted histories of empire. Unlike Britain who had come through World War II economically weakened but still a victor nation and major imperial power, Japan had been defeated, decolonized, and militarily occupied until 1952. Yet, the Japanese empire had also inalterably and profoundly changed assumptions about Western superiority throughout Asia, first by violently displacing it through military force, and then by influencing (directly and indirectly) nascent independence movements from 1945 onwards. As Jeremy Black points out, Bond's world was one of limited decolonization: along with the Dominions of Australia, New Zealand, and South Africa that had gained independence before the end of the war, India and Pakistan were ceded in 1947, Burma and Palestine in 1948, and Newfoundland in 1949.[49] For both Britain and Japan the postwar was a period of uneasy adjustment to the rise of American political, economic, and cultural preeminence across the globe.

The 1960s spy boom dovetailed with a period of unprecedented economic, technological, and cultural ascension in Japan. In May 1964, less than a month after the Japanese premiere of *From Russia with Love* (1963, Terrence Young), Japan National Railways debuted the first high-speed bullet train in anticipation of record international visitors for the first Olympics ever to be held in Tokyo that October. Color television coverage of the Olympics broadcast to the world images of a newly rebuilt modern nation. For many this was a symbolic end to the "postwar" and the beginning of a new age in which Japan could once again take its place among the leading industrialized nations of the world.[50] The spy boom embraced a similarly cosmopolitan view of the world in which agents, unimpeded by the limitations of race, class, or language, circulated freely throughout exotic locations on top secret missions. Meditating on the image of spies, and the espionage genre, Toby Miller suggests that much of their appeal and longevity derives from a malleability that is both changeable and consistent. "Part-individualist, part technocrat, spies are the ultimate empty signifier and susceptible to a wide range of ideological interpretations"[51] that also cross cultures and can be revived over time.

This essay has attempted to account for the ways in which the specificities of Japan's experience of empire, war, and the Cold War intersected with the global spy boom of the 1960s through an examination of the *Nakano Spy School*. The spy genre enabled a reexamination of the individual within the contexts fascism and colonialism during a highly ambiguous moment during the Cold War. *Nakano Spy School* illustrates the ways in which individuals intersected with ideologues, such as Lt. Maj. Kusanagi, as free agents rather than victims and also considered the devastating consequences of the decisions made in youth both on the individual and the collective.

Nakano Spy School addressed complexities of class discourse in 1960s Japan juxtaposing the needs of the ruling class against the possibility of individual action in the face of massive organizations. Nakano spies question our understanding of Japan as a classless society by the ostentatious fashions and behavior of Agent Shiina and the other Nakano agents. The timeliness of their fashion succinctly critiques the ruling class as represented by Japan's military administration as undifferentiated, thoroughly corrupt, and ultimately lost to history. The inability to rewrite history (i.e., Japan's defeat) parallels a more general sense of helplessness to function as a major player in the Cold War order. Finally, *Nakano Spy School* grapples with the legacy of Japanese imperialism in Asia examining fears of ethnic invasion by the Other. Shiina, as a *Japanese* spy regardless of which Asian ethnicity he may "pass" for minimizes Japanese fears of invasion by grounding his identity as a spy within a knowable domestic past. Implicit in the cinematic representations is a link to the legacy of the actual Nakano spy school and its graduates, which questions the ramifications of Japanese empire in Asia.

Neither another Bond nor a knockoff Bond, Shiina Jiro and the agents of Nakano are, however, similarly bound up in debates over the relevance of spies and history to our contemporary culture. Because they are popular forms, spy narratives engage a range of ideologies that call into question dominant perspectives or absolute definitions and instead highlight the ongoing struggle over cultural specificity, identity, and history.

Notes

1. In this essay, Japanese names appear according to Japanese convention: surname first, given name last.

2. Japanese toy manufacturer Sunstar released the popular *Supai techo* (literally, spy notebook or spy license) which it repackaged in various formats and titles between 1965 through the early 1970s. The overwhelming popularity of this spy kit spawned a hoard of imitators some of which can be seen online at http://homepage2.nifty.com/zenmaitarow/sab5.htm. On gadgets in a Western context see Danny Biederman, *The Incredible World of Spy-Fi: Wild and Crazy Spy Gadgets, Props and Artifacts from TV and the Movies* (San Francisco: Chronicle Books, 2004). On spy toys/games and their afterlife see Brian Paquette and Paul Howley, *The Toys from U.N.C.L.E. Memorabilia and Collectors Guide* (Worchester, MA: Entertainment, 1990).

3. Such programs build on the growing success of other Japanese animated television programs being exported primarily to the United States, Australia, New Zealand, and Mexico. Many non-spy programs included espionage-themed story arcs and characters acting as infor-

mal agents on behalf of or in opposition to governments such as *Gigantor* and *Marine Boy* as well as live-action programs including *Phantom Agents* (*Ninja Butai Gekko*) and *The Samurai* (*Onmitsu Kenshi*, 1964–1966, Senkosha Kikaku), a period program concerning a plot to use ninja spies to topple the shogun.

4. For a discussion of fans in a U.S. context, see Anthony Enns, "The Fans from U.N.C.L.E.: The Marketing and Reception of the Swinging '60s Spy Phenomenon," *Journal of Popular Film and Television* 28.3 (2000): 124–32.

5. Oka Toshio, "The Spy Film's Mad Dance" [*ranbu suru supai eiga sono keifu wo tadoru*], *Kinema Junpo*, July 1, 1966, 93.

6. For similar observations on Kurosawa Akira's *Yojimbo* (1961) see Marie Thorsten Morimoto, "The 'Peace Dividend' in Japanese Cinema: Metaphors of a Demilitarized Nation," in *Colonialism and Nationalism in Asian Cinema,* ed. Wimal Dissanayake (Bloomington: Indiana University Press, 1994), 11–29; and James Goodwin, *Akira Kurosawa and Intertextual Cinema* (Baltimore: Johns Hopkins University Press, 1994).

7. Virtually every major studio produced spy films set during the Pacific War including *Army Intelligence 33* (*Rikugun choho 33*, Kobayashi Tsuneo, Toei Studios, 1968) and *Miracle on Lubang Island: Nakano Military School* (*Rubang-to no kiseki: Rikugun Nakano gakko*, Sato Junya, Toei Studios, 1974). Others were contemporary set pieces featuring edgy Nakano-trained Cold Warriors retooled to defend Japan against the Communist threat throughout Asia. See *Nakano Spy School: Men Without Nationalities* (*Supai rikugun Nakano gakko: Kokuseki no nai otoko tachi*, Noguchi Haruyasu, Nikkatsu Studios, 1964) and the five-film *International Secret Police* series (*Kokusai himitsu keisatsu*, Toho Studios, 1964–1968).

8. Rosie White, *Violent Femmes: Women as Spies in Popular Culture* (London: Routledge, 2007), 3–4.

9. See for example, Tony Bennett and Janet Wollacott, *Bond and Beyond: The Political Career of a Popular Hero* (London: Macmillan Education, 1987); Jeremy Black, *The Politics of Bond: From Flemings Novels to the Big Screen* (Westport, CT: Praeger, 2000); James Chapman, *License to Thrill: A Cultural History of the James Bond Film* (London: I.B. Taurus, 2000); Toby Miller, *Spyscreen: Espionage on Film and TV from the 1930s to the 1960s* (Oxford: Oxford University Press, 2003); and Jeremy Packer, ed., *Secret Agents: Popular Agents Beyond James Bond* (New York: Peter Lang, 2009). In Japanese, Kinema Junposha, ed., *World Filmmakers 20: Masters of Spy Suspense* [*Sekai no eiga sakka 20 Supai sasupensu no kyoshotachi*] (Tokyo: Kinema Junposha, 1983).

10. Representative works include Tuong Vu and Wasana Wongsurawat, eds., *Dynamics of the Cold War in Asia: Ideology, Identity, and Culture* (New York: Palgrave Macmillan, 2009); Christopher E. Goscha and Christian F. Ostermann, eds., *Connecting Histories: Decolonization and the Cold War in Southeast Asia, 1945–1962* (Stanford: Stanford University Press, 2009); Zheng Yangwen, Hong Liu, and Michael Szonyi, eds., *The Cold War in Asia: The Battle for Hearts and Minds* (Leiden: Brill Academic, 2010); Tony Day and Maya HT Liem, eds., *Cultures at War: The Cold War and Cultural Expression in Southeast Asia* (Ithaca: Cornell University Southeast Asia Publications, 2010); Ann Sherif, *Japan's Cold War* (Columbia: Columbia University Press, 2008); and Hiroshi Kitamura, *Screening Enlightenment: Hollywood and the Cultural Reconstruction of Defeated Japan* (Ithaca: Cornell University Press, 2010). In Japanese, Komori Yoichi, ed., *Cold War Order and Capitalist Culture* [*Reisentaisei to Shihon Bunka*] *Kindai Nihon no Bunkashi 9* (Tokyo: Iwanami Shoten, 2002); Marukawa Tetsushi, *A Theory of Cold War Culture: The Reality of the Forgotten Ambivalent War* [*Reisen Bunkaron Wasurerareta Aimaina Senso no Genzonsei*] (Tokyo: Sofusha, 2005); and Takashi Toshihiko and Tsuchiya Yuka, eds., *The Era of the Cultural Cold War: America and Asia* [*Bunka Reisen no Jidai: Amerika to Ajia*] (Tokyo: Kokusai Shoin, 2009).

11. Michael Denning, "Licensed to Look: James Bond and the Heroism of Consumption," in *Contemporary Marxist Literary Criticism,* ed. Francis Mulhern (London: Longman, 1992), 225.

12. Recent journalistic interest in Eurospy and Asiaspy films has resulted in the programming of several retrospectives that question the imposed obscurity of non–Western spy films. See Richard Rhys Davies, ed., *Kiss Kiss Kill Kill: The Graphic Art and Forgotten Spy Films of Cold War Europe* (London: Picture and Sound, 2011); Marco Giusti, *007 all'italiana* (Roma: Isbn Edizoni, 2010); Daniele Magni, *Segretissimi: Guida agli spy-movie italiani anni '60* (Roma: Bloodbuster Edizioni, 2010); and Matt Blake and David Deal, *The Eurospy Guide* (Baltimore: The Luminary Press, 2004).

13. Vu and Wongsurawat, *Dynamics of the Cold War*, 3–4.

14. Black, *Politics of Bond*, 3–4.

15. Michael Denning, *Cover Stories: Narrative and Ideology in the British Spy Thriller* (London: Routledge and Kegan Paul, 1987).

16. The "China Incident," also known as the "Marco Polo Bridge Incident," occurred on the morning of July 8, 1937, when Japanese infantry troops attacked Chinese troops at the Marco Polo Bridge in China. Although a ceasefire was initially negotiated, heightened tensions on both sides led to increased violations of the ceasefire, a buildup of military forces, and eventually full scale war between Japan and China that would last for eight years. Referred to as an "incident" by the Japanese government at that time because neither government formally issued a declaration of war.

17. Hatakeyama's contribution is curiously uncredited in the final film although it is documented in Hosaka Masayasu Hatakeyama Seiko, "Secret Warriors-Nakano Spy School" [*Himitsu Senshi-Rikugun Nakano Gakko*] (Tokyo: Shukan Sankeisha, 1965). This was published in book form the following year, Hatakeyama Seiko, *Rikugun Nakano gakko* (Tokyo: Shinchosha, 1966).

18. Hatakeyama Seiko, *Secret History-Nakano Spy School* [*Hiroku Rikugun Nakano Gakko*] (Tokyo: Shinchosha, 1971).

19. Hoshikawa Seiji, "A Verbose Afterword" [*sakugo zeigen*] "Original Script: Nakano Spy School" [*orijinaru shinario Rikugun Nakano Gakko*] *Shinario* no. 216 (1966): 95.

20. Masumura Yasuzo, "My Discovery of the 'Individual' in Italy" [*Itaria de hakken shita "kojin"*] *The World of Film Director Masumura Yasuzo* [*Eiga Kantoku Masumura Yasuzo no Sekai*] (Tokyo: Waizu Shuppan, 1998), 59–60. For an introduction to Masumura in English see Jonathan Rosenbaum, "Enlightened Madness: A Maverick Subversive Loose in the Post-War Japanese Studio System, Yasuzo Masumura is Virtually Unknown in the U.S. What Have Been Missing?" *Film Comment* 38.5 (September–October 2002).

21. Masumura Yasuzo, "From the Set: Nakano Spy School" [*Satsueijo-Rikugun Nakano Gakko*], *Kinema Junpo*, May 15, 1966, 53.

22. Dialogue from *Nakano Spy School*, DVD, directed by Masumura Yasuzo (1966; Tokyo: Kadokawa Pictures, 2005).

23. Hoshikawa, "Verbose Afterword," 95.

24. James Orr, *The Victim as Hero: Ideologies of Peace and National Identity in Postwar Japan* (Honolulu: University of Hawaii Press, 2001).

25. Dialogue from *Nakano Spy School*.

26. Dialogue from *Nakano Spy School*.

27. Shirai further commented that "the scene where the cadets force one of their own to commit suicide is arguably the climax, but compared to Masumura's dynamic portrayal of the human conflict and inner workings of Imperial army in his previous film *Heitai Yakuza*, one realizes just how weak this film really is. At best this [film] recalls the mood of a fanatical system of a high school sports team." Shirai Yoshio, "*Rikugun Nakano Gakko,*" *Kinema Junpo*, July 15, 1966, 108–9.

28. Dialogue from *Nakano Spy School*.

29. Bennett and Wollacott, *Bond and Beyond*, 3–4.

30. William H. Whyte, Jr., *The Organization Man* (New York: Simon & Schuster, 1956), 4.

31. Voiceover opening narration from the first season of the British television series *Danger Man* produced by Incorporated Television Company (ITC), 1960–61 (New York: A&E Home Video, 2003). DVD.

32. Whyte, *Organization Man,* 4.

33. Denning, *Cover Stories,* 41–2, 74.

34. Bennett and Wollacott, *Bond and Beyond,* 97.

35. Odaka Kunio, "How Has Japan's Class Structure Changed? On Movements in the Middle Class" [*Nihon no kaikyu kozo wa do kawatta ka: Chukanso no ugoki wo chushin toshite*], *Jiyu* 7 (June 1960): 131–154; and Ishida Hiroshi, *Social Mobility in Contemporary Japan: Educational Credentials, Class and the Labor Market in Cross-National Perspective* (Stanford: Stanford University Press, 1993), 172, 238.

36. Dialogue from *Nakano Spy School.*

37. Dialogue from *Nakano Spy School: Cloud Directive No. 1,* DVD, directed by Mori Kazuo (1966; Tokyo: Kadokawa Pictures, 2005).

38. Amis Kingsley, *The James Bond Dossier* (London: Jonathan Cape, 1965), 86, cited in Bennett and Woollacott, *Bond and Beyond,* 97.

39. John Le Carré, *Tinker, Tailor, Soldier, Spy* (New York: Random House, 1974), 46.

40. Dialogue from *Nakano Spy School.*

41. Dialogue from *Cloud Directive No. 1.*

42. Dialogue from *Nakano Spy School Dragon No. 3 Directive,* DVD, directed by Tanaka Tokuzo (1967; Tokyo: Kadokawa Pictures, 2005).

43. Yoshimi Yoshiaki, *Comfort Women* (Columbia: Columbia University Press, 2002).

44. Hasegawa Kimiyuki, *Woman Gambler/Nakano Spy School* [*Onna Bakutoshi-Rikugun Nakano Gakko*] (Tokyo: Art Digest, 1994), 413. The trope of effortlessly being able to assume the identity of the Other is also a classical colonial archetype: in cinema stretching back at least to the silent era production of *The Four Feathers* (1929, Merian C. Cooper, Lothar Mendes, and Ernest B. Schoedsack). On imperial Japanese film culture and cultural passing see Michael Baskett, *Attractive Empire: Transnational Film Culture in Imperial Japan* (Honolulu: University of Hawaii Press, 2008).

45. Program Notes for *Shinobi no Mono* (Wilmington, NC: AnimEigo 2007). DVD. For more on Dahl's experiences in Japan see Roald Dahl, "007's Oriental Eyefuls," *Playboy,* June 1967, 86–91.

46. Shirai, "*Rikugun Nakano Gakko,*" 109.

47. Hayashi Tamaki, "Rikugun Nakano Gakko: Kumo Ichigo Shirei," *Kinema Junpo,* October 15, 1966, 63.

48. *Kinema Junpo* ran brief synopses of the film plots but without customary reviews. See *Dragon No. 3 Directive* [*Ryu Sango Shirei*], *Kinema Junpo,* February 15, 1967, 88; *Secret Orders* [*Mitsumei*], *Kinema Junpo,* June 1, 1967, 88–9; and *Eve of War* [*Kaisen Zenya*], *Kinema Junpo,* March 1, 1968, 90–1.

49. Black, *Politics of Bond,* 3–4.

50. William M. Tsutsui and Michael Baskett, eds., *The East Asian Olympiads: Building Bodies and Nations 1934–2008* (Leiden: Brill Academic, 2011).

51. Toby Miller, "Afterword: Why Won't Spies Go Away?" in *Secret Agents: Popular Icons Beyond James Bond,* ed. Jeremy Packer (New York: Peter Lang, 2009), 189–192.

Bibliography

Baskett, Michael. *Attractive Empire: Transnational Film Culture in Imperial Japan.* Honolulu: University of Hawaii Press, 2008.

Bennett, Tony, and Janet Wollacott. *Bond and Beyond: The Political Career of a Popular Hero.* London: Macmillan Education, 1987.

Biederman, Danny. *The Incredible World of Spy-Fi: Wild and Crazy Spy Gadgets, Props and Artifacts from TV and the Movies.* San Francisco: Chronicle Books, 2004.

Black, Jeremy. *The Politics of Bond: From Fleming's Novels to the Big Screen.* Westport, CT: Praeger, 2000.

Blake, Matt, and David Deal. *The Eurospy Guide.* Baltimore: The Luminary Press, 2004.

Chapman, James. *License to Thrill: A Cultural History of the James Bond.* London: I.B. Taurus, 2000.

Dahl, Roald. "007's Oriental Eyefuls." *Playboy,* June 1967, 86–91.

Danger Man. DVD. Produced by Incorporated Television Company (ITC). 1960–61; New York: A&E Home Video, 2003.

Day, Tony, and Maya HT Liem, eds. *Cultures at War: The Cold War and Cultural Expression in Southeast Asia.* Ithaca: Cornell University Southeast Asia Publications, 2010.

Denning, Michael. *Cover Stories: Narrative and Ideology in the British Spy Thriller.* London: Routledge and Kegan Paul, 1987.

_____. "Licensed to Look: James Bond and the Heroism of Consumption." In *Contemporary Marxist Literary Criticism,* edited by Francis Mulhern, 211–29. London: Longman, 1992.

"Dragon No. 3 Directive" [*Ryu Sango Shirei*]. *Kinema Junpo,* February 15, 1967, 88.

Enns, Anthony. "The Fans from U.N.C.L.E.: The Marketing and Reception of the Swinging '60s Spy Phenomenon." *Journal of Popular Film and Television* 28.3 (April 2, 2000): 124–32.

"Eve of War" [Kaisen Zenya]. *Kinema Junpo,* March 1, 1968, 90–1.

Giusti, Marco. *007 All'Italiana.* Roma: Isbn Edizoni, 2010.

Goodwin, James. *Akira Kurosawa and Intertextual Cinema.* Baltimore: Johns Hopkins University Press, 1994.

Goscha, Christopher E., and Christian F. Ostermann, eds. *Connecting Histories: Decolonization and the Cold War in Southeast Asia, 1945–1962.* Stanford: Stanford University Press, 2009.

Hasegawa, Kimiyuki. *Woman Gambler/Nakano Spy School [Onna Bakutoshi-Rikugun Nakano Gakko].* Tokyo: Art Digest, 1994.

Hatakeyama, Seiko. *Rikugun Nakano Gakko.* Tokyo: Shinchosha, 1966.

Hayashi, Tamaki. "Rikugun Nakano Gakko: Kumo Ichigo Shirei." *Kinema Junpo,* October 15, 1966, 63.

Hoshikawa, Seiji. "Original Script: *Nakano Spy School*" [*Orijinaru shinario Rikugun Nakano Gakko*], *Shinario* no. 216 (1966), 95.

Hiroshi, Ishida. *Social Mobility in Contemporary Japan: Educational Credentials, Class and the Labor Market in Cross-National Perspective.* Stanford: Stanford University Press, 1993.

Kitamura, Hiroshi. *Screen Enlightenment: Hollywood and the Cultural Reconstruction of Defeated Japan.* Ithaca: Cornell University Press, 2010.

Kunio, Odaka. "How Has Japan's Class Structure Changed? On Movements in the Middle Class" [Nihon No Kaikyu Kozo Wa Do Kawatta Ka: Chukanso No Ugoki Wo Chushin Toshite]. *Jiyu* 7 (June 1960): 131–54.

Le Carré, John. *Tinker, Tailor, Soldier, Spy.* New York: Random House, 1974.

Magni, Daniele. *Segretissimi: Guida agli Spy-movie Italiani Anni '60.* Roma: Bloodbuster Edizioni, 2010.

Masumura, Yasuzo. "From the Set: *Nakano Spy School*" [*Satsueijo-Rikugun Nakano Gakko*]. *Kinema Junpo,* May 15, 1966, 53.

_____. *The World of Film Director Masumura Yasuzo [Eiga Kantoku Masumura Yasuzo no Sekai].* Tokyo: Waizu Shuppan, 1998.

Miller, Toby. "Afterword: Why Won't Spies Go Away?" In *Secret Agents: Popular Icons Beyond James Bond,* edited by Jeremy Packer, 189–94. New York: Peter Lang, 2009.

_____. *Spyscreen: Espionage on Film and TV from the 1930s to the 1960s.* Oxford: Oxford University Press, 2003.

Nakano Spy School. DVD. Directed by Masumura Yasuzo. 1966; Tokyo: Kadokawa Pictures, 2005.

Nakano Spy School: Cloud Directive No. 1. DVD. Directed by Mori Kazuo. 1966; Tokyo: Kadokawa Pictures, 2005.

Nakano Spy School Dragon No. 3 Directive. DVD. Directed by Tanaka Tokuzo. 1967; Tokyo: Kadokawa Pictures, 2005.

Oka, Toshio. "The Spy Film's Mad Dance" [*Ranbu suru supai eiga sono keifu wo tadoru*]. *Kinema Junpo*, July 1, 1966, 93.

Orr, James. *The Victim as Hero: Ideologies of Peace and National Identity in Postwar Japan.* Honolulu: University of Hawaii Press, 2001.

Packer, Jeremy, ed. *Secret Agents: Popular Icons Beyond James Bond.* New York: Peter Lang, 2009.

Paquette, Brian, and Paul Howley. *The Toys from U.N.C.L.E.: Memorabilia and Collectors Guide.* Worcester, MA: Entertainment, 1990.

Rhys Davies, Richard, ed. *Kiss Kiss Kill Kill: The Graphic Art and Forgotten Spy Films of Cold War Europe.* London: Picture and Sound, 2011.

Rosenbaum, Jonathan. "Enlightened Madness: A Maverick Subversive Loose in The Post-War Japanese Studio System, Yasuzo Masumura is Virtually Unknown in the U.S. What Have We Been Missing?" *Film Comment* 38.5 (September–October 2002): 32, 35–9.

"Secret Orders" [*Mitsumei*]. *Kinema Junpo,* June 1, 1967, 88–9.

Seiko, Hatakeyama. *Secret History—Nakano Spy School [Hiroku Rikugun Nakano Gakko].* Tokyo: Shinchosha, 1971.

Sherif, Ann. *Japan's Cold War.* Columbia: Columbia University Press, 2008.

Shinobi no Mono. DVD. Wilmington, NC: AnimEigo, 2007.

Shirai, Yoshio. "*Rikugun Nakano Gakko.*" *Kinema Junpo*, July 15, 1966, 108–9.

Tetsuhi, Marukawa. *A Theory of Cold War Culture: The Reality of the Forgotten Ambivant War [Reisen Bunkaron Wasurerareta Aimaina Senso no Genzonsei].* Tokyo: Sofusha, 2005.

Thorsten Morimoto, Marie. "The 'Peace Dividend' in Japanese Cinema: Metaphors of a Demilitarized Nation." In *Colonialism and Nationalism in Asian Cinema*, edited by Wimal Dissanayake, 11–29. Bloomington: Indiana University Press, 1994.

Toshihiko, Takashi, and Tsuchiya Yuka, eds. *The Era of The Cultural Cold War: America and Asia [Bunka Reisen no Jida: Amerika to Ajia].* Tokyo: Kokusai Shoin, 2009.

Tsutsui, William M., and Michael Baskett, eds. *The East Asian Olympiads: Building Bodies and Nations 1934–2008.* Leiden: Brill Academic, 2011.

Vu, Tuong, and Wasana Wongsurawat, eds. *Dynamics of the Cold War in Asia: Ideology, Identity, and Culture.* New York: Palgrave Macmillan, 2009.

White, Rosie. *Violent Femmes: Women as Spies in Popular Culture.* London: Routledge, 2007.

Whyte, William H. Jr. *The Organization Man.* New York: Simon & Schuster, 1956.

Yangwen, Zheng, Hong Liu, and Michael Szonyi, eds. *The Cold War in Asia: The Battle for Hearts and Minds.* Leiden: Brill Academic, 2010.

Yoichi, Komori, ed. *Cold War Order and Capitalist Culture [Reisentaisei to Shihon Bunka].* Kindai Nihon no Bunkashi 9. Tokyo: Iwanami Shoten, 2002.

Yoshiaki, Yoshimi. *Comfort Women.* New York: Columbia University Press, 2002.

"Permission to kill"

Exploring Italy's 1960s Eurospy Phenomenon, Impact and Legacy

Nicholas Diak

With the release of *Goldfinger* (1964, Guy Hamilton) and its subsequent international success, the floodgates of James Bond imitators were unleashed. Various countries took to the formula, with output from Spain, Italy, France, and Germany. These Eurospy films sought to mirror the success of *Goldfinger* as cheaply and quickly as possible, with production companies churning out espionage themed films as fast as theatergoers would consume them.

Of the countries that contributed to the Eurospy genre of films, Italy was perhaps the most prolific and legendary in output. Despite their contribution, not much is understood about Italian Eurospy films, their importance to Italian film canon or their relationship to their source material. This essay will seek to rectify this knowledge gap. However, understanding an entire cycle of films with numerous entries and directors in its canon is way too much of a task for this one essay alone. Instead this essay will focus on creating a foundation for future scholars to start from by identifying key concepts, definitions and frameworks that are best taken into consideration when trying to analyze Italian Eurospy films.

First this essay will demonstrate the lack of authoritative texts on Italian Eurospy films by way of a literature review of primary texts of Italian film studies along with secondary sources. Secondly, the genre of Italian Eurospy films will be properly defined to take into consideration the unique attributes of the Italian film production phenomenon of the 1960s. Third, the argument for using vernacular cinema will be presented as the suggested framework for analyzing these films. Fourth, what types of films and how many entries make up the Italian Eurospy cycle will be discussed to aid in what films could be potential candidates for future analysis. And finally, the legacy and impact of these films will be presented to drive in the point that these are important movies with unique contributions to Italian film studies as well as James Bond studies. These films had a profound impact on the Italian production industry and their filmmakers, influences on other Italian film genres, as well as an interesting relationship with the James Bond movies proper by anticipating several Bond elements years before their realization.

Literature Review

There is a distinct lack of authoritative texts on the Italian Eurospy cycle of films. Primary texts on general Italian film history, such as Peter Bondanella's *A History of Italian Cinema* and *Italian Cinema: From Neorealism to the Present*, Mary Wood's *Italian Cinema*, Marcia Landy's *Italian Film*, Gian Piero Brunetta's *The History of Italian Cinema*, and Carlo Celli and Marga Cottino-Jones' *A New Guide to Italian Cinema* all omit references to the Italian Eurospy cycle, opting to jump from describing peplums to spaghetti westerns and focusing on *auteur* films from the likes of Visconti to Bertolluci.

Outside primary texts, references to Italian Eurospy films can be found in limited dosages. Texts on Italian genre directors may discuss an Italian Eurospy film if the director had contributed to their genesis. For example, in *Beyond Terror: The Films of Lucio Fulci*, Stephen Thrower devotes a few paragraphs to *Come rubammo la bomba atomica* (1967, Lucio Fulci), an Italian Eurospy/comedy directed by Fulci, a director more known for his gory horror films in the late 1970s and 1980s than his other genre output. Tim Lucas discusses at great length both *Dr. Goldfoot and the Girl Bombs* (1966, Mario Bava) and *Naked You Die* (1968, Antonio Margheriti) in his authoritative book *Mario Bava: All the Colors of the Dark*. These references are usually glorified film synopsis, but a few instances, such as Lucas' book, contain invaluable production information as well. However these texts rarely take the next step into scholarly dialog.

With the proliferation of social media, informal blogs that homage or honor cult and exploitation cinema have become commonplace online. Some of these blogs have carved out a niche by focusing Eurospy films (regardless of country) such as the *Double 0 Section*, the forums at *The Wild Eye* and *Permission to Kill*. With comments, reviews, news and articles, the dialog about these films remains active, but still stays confined to generalities without serious academic dialogue.

The most devoted text to Eurospy films, be it from Italy or other countries, is *The Eurospy Guide* by Matt Blake and David Deal. However, the book is far too colloquial and acts more as a general catalog of Eurospy films rather than a critical or serious discussion of them. The book provides an excellent index of nearly all the Eurospy films the authors could identify, peppered with their own musings. It is a good starting point for research, but it is not as authoritative as the cycle needs.

Taken as a whole, the literature available on Italian Eurospy films is not ideal. The most academic discussions about the cycle are missing from the major primary texts and relegated to small entries and footnotes in director specific books. Discussions are more abundant via the informal channels of online blogs, but they lack the authority and scholarship that primary texts would bestow.

Filones *and Vernacular Films*

The Italian Eurospy films take their cues from the spy genre of films, itself a subgenre of a juxtaposition of action and thriller films. Thematically, classifying Italian Eurospy films as a subset of the spy genre seems apropos, but it is not particularly constructive as it does not take into consideration many of the unique attributes of the Italian production system. During the economic boom years of the 1950s and 1960s, Italian producers turned to making large quantities of budget populist cinema, derivative of other films and genres whose success were easy to recreate. This concept, known as *filones*, is defined by Mary Wood as "a strand of similar films, rather than a genre. Trendspotting successful subjects, names, themes and stars resulted in quickly-made similar films, until public interest was seen to wane."[1]

Peter Bondanella highlights the impact of the *filone* phenomenon:

> The vogue of any genre *filone* (literally: "thread") was generally initially consumer-driven: audiences flocked to a few specific films that gave birth to the craze for such a film. Thus, when Francisci's *Hercules* and *Hercules Unchained* or Leone's *A Fistful of Dollars* made enormous and completely unexpected profits at first-run theaters—and continued to bring in revenue as they were recycled through the system—producers then sprang to imitate the trend, making dozens and even hundreds of imitations in the same genre, most of which were not masterpieces but many of which were quite respectable or even very good.[2]

There are many notable *filones* in Italy's film history. The peplums were a *filone* popular in the 1950s. These movies were set in ancient times, typically involving Hercules, gladiator combat, chariot racing, and vanquishing mythical beasts. The *giallos* were a *filone* that gained traction in the 1960s. The *giallos* were a type of horror film that usually featured a disguised individual in a wide brimmed hat and gloves dispatching as many nubile young women as gruesomely as possible. The *poliziotteschis* of the 1970s were a brief affair of police procedural movies inspired by the success of the *Dirty Harry* movies. The spaghetti westerns of the 1960s are perhaps the most well known *filone*, making Clint Eastwood and his Man with No Name character a cinema icon. The *filones* continued, albeit without any official names, after the advent of the blockbuster movie in the 1970s, with Italian producers releasing strings of movies that emulated films such as *Jaws* (1975, Steven Spielberg), *The Exorcist* (1973, William Friedkin), *First Blood* (1982, Ted Kotcheff), and *Raiders of the Lost Ark* (1981, Steven Spielberg) with fare such as *Devil Fish* (1984, Lamberto Bava), *Beyond the Door* (1974, Ovidio Assonitis), *Strike Commando* (1987, Bruno Mattei) and *Hunters of the Golden Cobra* (1982, Antonio Margheriti).

In this regard, it is best not to think of the Italian Eurospy films as a genre, but instead as its own *filone*, with a definite beginning and end, triggered by the massive success of *Goldfinger* and finally waned when successor *filones*, such as the *giallos* and the Italian sex comedies, became more popular and economically profitable.

Aside from viewing the Italian Eurospy genre as a *filone*, another facet for consideration is what lens to use to analyze them. There are many frameworks scholars could consider when diving in the realm of film studies with one of the most popular and versatile framework being *auteur* theory. Andrew Sarris describes *auteur* theory as having three characteristics: presence of technical competence, a director's personal style as criterion of value, and interior meaning derived from the tension between a director and his film.[3] In other words, the film demonstrates technical proficiency in its composition, has key elements in the *mise-en-scene* that are indicative of the director, and the film holds a particular agenda that the director wants to convey. *Auteur* theory provides a framework to identify what is significant in a film and ties it back to its director, such as reoccurring characters, themes, visual cues, repeating styles, and revisiting the same subject matter in multiple films. *Auteur* theory has been applied to Italian directors such Sergio Leone, Mario Bava, and Dario Argento in an attempt to analyze their films.

However the vast majority of directors of Italian Eurospy films are not *auteurs*. In fact most directors in any given Italian *filone* of populist cinema, from peplums to *giallos*, from mondo films to sex comedies are not *auteurs* but instead paycheck directors for hire by the different studios. While some of these directors may display technical acumen as required of an *auteur*, their general body of work is too idiosyncratic, jumping from genre to genre, to really allow a personal stamp to be created. Stephen Thrower underscores this problem of applying the *auteur* label to Italian genre directors as really a means to catalog and group their work, and

> as more information comes to light about the directors of Italian exploitation cinema, their roles often seem less and less like "auteurs"—they are more like superintendents, journeymen, supervisors, sometimes of a lax disorganized sort. The territory they

are responsible for superintending isn't their own (or anyone else's). Films made by directors like Bruno Mattei or Umberto Lenzi are like lazily marshaled sporting events played out on a genre pitch. Whilst there is certainly fun to be had in spectating, there is—to extend the metaphor—no evidence of the formulation of new or improvised game structures in their work.[4]

While diving into the world of the Italian *giallos*, British academian Mikel Koven developed his own framework to tackle the issues that Italian genre films were presenting. His vernacular film framework that he applied to understanding *giallos* is easily applied to any Italian *filone* and is extremely fitting for the Italian Eurospies. For Koven, applying *auteur* theory to these types of films is akin to fitting "square pegs into round (modernist) holes"[5] and instead calls to have Italian genre films examined at their own level.[6] Koven's vernacular framework encompasses several concepts. The first concept is in regards to the localized cinematic language[7] which for Italy would be the audience in the *terza visione* (third run theaters). This has parallels to the grindhouse theaters and the dollar theaters in the states. The audience for these types of theaters in Italy would be the blue-collar workers, gathering in a public places with their friends or other members of the community to socialize as well as be entertained by the ever changing stock of films being screened. The Italian film *Cinema Paradiso* (1988, Giuseppe Tornatore) depicts this dynamic flawlessly. The viewing practices of the *terza visione* theaters contrast with the *prima visione* (first run) theaters, which are synonymous with the more serious practice of sitting in a dark and silent theater with attention directed at the screen. The second concept of vernacular films explores the contrast between "high art" and common or folk art.[8] Vernacular cinema makes a clear distinction between *auteur* and populist or genre films. Lastly, vernacular films are made to be intentionally opposite of "high style."[9] They are meant to titillate, entertain, excite and exploit, but do not venture down the path of deeper meaning. Vernacular films wallow in their own acknowledgment of not being high art and do not care if an outsider understands or even views them.[10] The primary advantage of approaching Italian Eurospy films, as well as other Italian *filones*, with this framework is that it provides a means of analysis without relying on the "bourgeois criteria of classical narrative, intellectual abstraction, and elitist notions of the artistic."[11]

The Italian Eurospy films were cheaply and hastily made to capitalize on the spy film craze ushered in by *Goldfinger*. The directors were paycheck directors, the budgets low, and the films made to be quickly consumed by the *terza visione* audience. It is populist cinema, and any semblance of "high art" elements present in any film is coincidental. It is for these reasons and the tenants laid out by Koven that these films should be addressed with the vernacular cinema framework in mind.

The Canon of Eurospy Films

With the establishment that the Italian Eurospy film cycle is its own *filone* and that the films should be analyzed with the vernacular film framework, the next question becomes what movies constitute the Italian Eurospy *filone*.

The issue of identifying what films belong to the Italian Eurospy canon becomes problematic. *The Eurospy Guide* is a good starting point at listing Eurospy films across different countries, but the problem is that the book makes no distinction as to what an Italian Eurospy film is. While the book does state the directors of the films it catalogs, the various co-productions makes establishing a country of origin problematic. This makes evaluating the "Italianness" of a Eurospy film much more complex since there are instances of Italian films without an Italian director. Since the book concentrates on European films, American productions with Italian input would be absent from the book.

An example of this problem is with the film *The Venetian Affair* (1967, Jerry Thorpe), a spy film that straddles the line of being considered an Italian Eurospy film or not. The title is omitted from *The Eurospy Guide*, and for justifiable reasons. The film is directed by Jerry Thorpe who is mostly known for his television productions, particularly *The Untouchables* in the 1960s and *Kung Fu* in the 1970s. *The Venetian Affair* was also produced by Thorpe's own company along with MGM making this mostly an American spy movie, which is apropos. The film may not have been helmed by an Italian director, but there is enough input and contributions from the Italian production machine that this movie needs to be factored into Italian Eurospy canon. The obvious of course is the setting of the film being in Venice Italy, along with extras and actors (such as Fabrizio Mioni) and behind the scenes talent (the cinematographer for the Venice scenes was Enzo Serafin). These production aspects where no doubt brokered in cooperation with local studios and production companies which takes into consideration the production aspect of the *filone*. The presence of Italian actress Luciana Paluzzi provides the presence of a beautiful Italian starlet to the film, but also takes advantage of her marquee value of appearing in the James Bond film *Thunderball* (1965, Terence Young). This practice of using stars in this fashion is typical of the derivative nature of Italian *filones*.

These Italian co-productions are an important component of the Italian Eurospy *filone* because it ties directly into the production and money-making aspect of the cycle and demonstrates the complex partnerships Italian studios had with production companies in other countries. So regardless in the difficulty in establishing a true country of origin of these films, they should be considered part of the canon in understanding how the *filone* flourished.

The other issue when considering if a film is an Italian Eurospy film or not is the inherent nature of a *filone* to carry attributes from one cycle to the next. The tide pool of when one *filone* ends and another begins becomes nebulous, with both cycles taking on attributes of the each other. An excellent example is Antonio Margheriti's film *Naked You Die*. This film is first and foremost a *giallo* film, complete with a masked murderer terrorizing the young girls of a private school. However in the last few moments of the movie, the heroine rushes up to greet her father, a secret agent identified as Agent 009 complete with a sporty car outfitted with a phone. This final scene gives the *giallo* a slight Eurospy component and is an important demonstration of how aspects of one *filone* may feed into another *filone* and how derivative the cycles were. The movie as a whole may not be a spy film, but the inclusion of that scene makes it a good example at how the Italian Eurospy films are contextualized to other Italian genre cycles.

With this in mind, Italian Eurospy films can be divided into two broad categories: films directed by an Italian director and films not directed by an Italian director but have significant contributions from Italian production companies. Using *The Eurospy Guide* as a starting point, one can identify 104 films directed by an Italian director and 47 films that were only Italian co-produced. Adding titles not listed in the book, such as the Italian directed *Naked You Die*, *Come rubammo la bomba atomica*, and *The Spy Who Loved Flowers* (1966, Umberto Lenzi), along with the aforementioned co-produced *The Venetian Affair* brings the total projected entries in the Italian Eurospy *filone* to 155 films. This number is not infallible as other films can surface or be reclassified to fit the cycle.

The breakdown of these films by quantity in a chronological order juxtaposed against when the James Bond films were released is as follows:

Table 2.1 Italian Eurospy Chronological Breakdown

Year	Italian Dir.	Italian Prod.	Tot. Films	James Bond Film Release Year
1960		2	2	
1961				
1962	1	1	2	*Dr. No*
1963		3	3	*From Russia with Love*
1964	7	6	13	*Goldfinger*
1965	30	12	42	*Thunderball*
1966	33	11	44	
1967	29	8	37	*You Only Live Twice*
1968	6	3	9	
1969	1	2	3	*On Her Majesty's Secret Service*
	107	**48**	**155**	

Placed on a graph, the rise and fall of the Italian Eurospy cycle can be easily visualized:

Table 2.2 Italian Eurospy Cycle

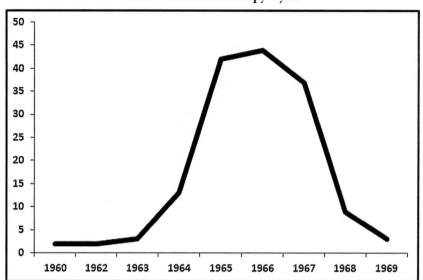

The genre cycle reached its zenith in the three years immediately following the release of *Goldfinger* where it abruptly tapered off. During this period, overt near-plagiarism of the Bond films was rampant. Many Italian Eurospy films were taglined or advertised with the codename "077," dangerously close to Bond's famous "007." Examples include *Agent 077—Mission Bloody Mary* (1965, Sergio Grieco), and *Agent 077 from the Orient with Fury* (1965, Sergio Grieco) which both use "077" in their titles, while movies like *Special Mission Lady Chaplin* (1966, Alberto De Martino and Sergio Grieco), *The Killers Are Challenged* (1966, Antonio Margheriti), *Secret Agent Fireball* (1965, Luciano Martino) and *Espionage in Lisbon* (1965, Federico Aicardi) all have their protagonists code-named "077." Sometimes the Bond references would stem from the literary world. In both *The Killers Are Challenged* and *Secret Agent Fireball*, the hero is played by Richard Harrison, and while his codename may be "077," his character's name is Bob Fleming, a lifting of Ian Fleming's name. The heroine of *Kiss the Girls and Make Them Die* (1966, Arduino Maiuri and Henry Levin) is named Susan Fleming, another overt reference to the author. While James Bond has been gifted with the famous phrase "a license to kill," Bob Fleming in *Killers Are Challenged* gets a similar but less impressive sounding "permission to kill." Both *Lightning Bolt* (1966, Antonio Margheriti) and *Secret Agent Fireball* have their titles play off of the title of *Thunderball*. The French/Italian coproduction of *The Spy I Love* (1964, Maurice Labro) takes its cue from the novel version of Fleming's *The Spy Who Loved Me* which was published in 1962. *Due Mafiosi*

contro Goldginger (1965, Giorgio Simonelli) has a title that takes its cue from *Goldfinger*, but its main villain is also named Dr. Goldginger, drawing from both *Goldfinger* and *Dr. No* (1962, Terrence Young) as well. *Dr. Goldfoot and the Girl Bombs* also has a slight nod to *Goldfinger*, with "foot" being a close facsimile to "finger." The list of plagiarisms is almost never ending.

As quickly as the Eurospy *filone* gained momentum, it would just as quickly fall. The later portion of the 1960s would see Italian production companies shift their attention to the *giallos*, the mondos, the spaghetti westerns, the macaroni combat films and the Italian sex comedies in search of the next popular film cycle to profit from.

Impact and Legacy

During its heyday and in the decades to come, the Italian Eurospy films had a profound impact in multiple capacities. Its legacy needs to be underscored in order solidify the *filone's* importance in cinema annals.

Firstly, as vernacular films, the Italian Eurospy cycle provided a guaranteed source of income to finance the larger budgeted, international films helmed by Italian *auteur* directors. In *Beyond Terror: The Films of Lucio Fulci*, Stephen Thrower states:

> It was this indigenous mainstream product that accounted for the industry's high level of activity. It also provided the financial security necessary to make Italy's 'art' cinema viable. Producers could afford to gamble on critically lauded but 'difficult' directors like Michelangelo Antonioni because the home market provided a steady flow of cash from the less esoteric, more populist entertainments.[12]

In *La Dolce Morte: Vernacular Cinema and the Italian Giallo Film*, Koven elaborates on Thrower's statement by positing:

> The only way an intellectual and critically acclaimed film culture can exist, particularly without complex studiolike systems like Hollywood, is through an exploitation and populist cinema. It is in this context that new filmmakers can gain experience, ideas can be explored (albeit oftentimes quite roughly and crudely), and revenues gained from "lower" films can be used to help finance more "prestige" pictures.[13]

The Italian Eurospy films fall into this camp of populist cinema and its commercial success would have been one of the avenues for production companies to fill their coffers and allow them to take chances with riskier endeavors. The cycle was also a breeding ground for Italian filmmakers early in their career to begin honing their craft. For example: Enzo G. Castellari, before he became a successful director of action movies and *Jaws* knock offs, was an assistant director for a plethora of genre movies in the 1960s, including the Italian Eurospy film *Special Mission Lady Chaplin*.

The Italian Eurospy films were important for their financial contributions to the Italian production system while being a proving ground for grooming directorial talent, but the *filone* was important for influencing other Italian genre cycles as well. In *Spaghetti Westerns: Cowboys and Europeans from Karl May to Sergio Leone* Sir Christopher Frayling illustrates the influence the Italian Eurospy films had on the spaghetti westerns:

> From the spy film, perhaps, the Westerns inherited an emphasis on the technology of death, on the anonymity of the central character (in the case of the spy films, lost in a vast bureaucracy), on the money-power equation (characteristically represented by 'The Organisation' our hero is set to infiltrate) and on flip 'asides' which release the audience's laughter after a sadistic interlude. (Sergio Leone has attributed the commercial success of the Bond films to the fact that 'out of sixty scenes, at least fifty ensnare the audience in suspense'; the low-budget Spaghettis were to rely even more on the impact of successive, noisy climaxes, usually taking the form of gun battles.)[14]

The technology of death aspect of Frayling's statement is easily illustrated with the advent of concealed weaponry and armor found in the spaghetti westerns. The Man with No Name creates a make shift bulletproof vest in *A Fistful of Dollars* (1964, Sergio Leone). The titular character in *Django* (1966, Sergio Corbucci) keeps a Gatling gun hidden inside a coffin that he drags around. Both of these examples of concealable armaments can be traced to the Italian Eurospy world of watches that double as Geiger counters such as in *Lightning Bolt* and pens with lasers such as in *Secret Agent Fireball*.

Unfortunately Sir Frayling is erroneous in his statement with regards to the anonymity of the Italian Eurospy protagonists translating to the spaghetti westerns. For practical purposes, a secret agent should be anonymous. But in the reality of these films, the agents are about nameless and anonymous as James Bond 007 himself. The heroes in the cycle certainly do have a plethora of code names: 077, S3S, FX-18, X-17 and so on. However their proper names are readily announced within the narrative: Bob Fleming, Walter Ross, Francis Coplan and Dick Malloy to name but a few. While the spaghetti westerns may have their "Man with No Name," the protagonists in the Italian Eurospy films are quite the opposite.

Sir Frayling is correct at proclaiming the fight sequences and gun battles that pepper the Italian Eurospy films are indeed replicated in the spaghetti westerns. Prolonged bar room brawl sequences can both be found in films such as *The Killers Are Challenged* and *Agent 077 from the Orient with Fury*. Matt Blake and David Deal support the similarities in the fight sequences in both genres. In *The Eurospy Guide*, they state that "the two genres both have their trademark elements (the bar-room brawl as opposed to the nightclub sequence, the gunfight as opposed to the cable car fight)."[15] They conclude their comparison with the apt statement "the spaghetti westerns were as much the children of James Bond as the spy films, albeit blessed with a slightly different visage."[16]

The spaghetti westerns were not the only Italian *filone* to be influenced by the Italian Eurospy films. A brief cycle of films exists in the late 1960s comprised of caped crusaders, masked avengers, super heroes and others of a similar ilk, drawn mostly from comic book sources. This cycle is called *cine-fumetti* (roughly "cinema comics") and includes films such as *Danger: Diabolik* (1968, Mario Bava), *Barbarella* (1968, Roger Vadim) and *Satanik* (1968, Piero Vivarelli). In these movies, the megalomaniacal villains with their over the top lairs and nefarious plans echo the villains and their lairs from the Eurospy films. Both genres also share a kinship with advanced technology. The concealed gadgets, hidden guns, lasers, and so on in the Italian Eurospy films were realized in the *cine-fumetti*. In *Fantastikal Diabolikal Supermen*, Matt Blake points out that the "stories often revolve around fantastical inventions," and "the characters make use of an assortment of supposedly high-tech devices, from Diabolik's sucker-climbers to the Three Fantastic Supermen's bullet-proof costumes."[17]

The protagonists are in essence the same in all aspects except in job description: from secret agent to masked crusader. Matt Blake posits the similarities between the super heroes in the *cine-fumetti*, Italian Eurospy, and spaghetti westerns as being

> pretty much the same despite their different costumes, they're usually anti-heroes, who operate outside the system, experts in their field, up to date with the latest gadgets and gizmos and with a certain anal quality, whether is be in wanting to plan the perfect robbery or bring the fastest gun in the west. Whether they had special, supernatural powers or not, these very different characters were all supermen in that they'd maximized their potential and become more than simply human, they'd become the Nietzschen *ubermensch*; arch individualists who operate according to their own value systems thanks to their own physical and intellectual strength.[18]

While linking Italian Eurospy films to these other Italian *filones* is easy, proving their influence the James Bond films proper is not. The Italian Eurospy films unashamedly lifted content from the Bond films as source material, but Bond films lifting material back is a hard case to prove. What can be shown however is the wide net cast by the Italian Eurospy films often times anticipated elements in future Bond films. With a canon of about 155 films, just by sheer probability the Italian Eurospy films were able to realize villains, plots, gadgets, gimmicks and other distinct details years if not decades before they were realized in the Bond films proper.

The examples are numerous. The scientist who gets gruesomely disintegrated while in suspended animation in *Lightning Bolt* anticipates the character of Krest exploding by decompression in a hyperbaric chamber in *Licence to Kill* (1989, John Glen). Bob Fleming is introduced as the hero via a failed training exercise in *Fury in Marrakech* (1966, Mino Loy and Luciano Martino) much in the same way that Sean Connery is re-introduced as James Bond in *Never Say Never Again* (1983, Irvin Kershner). The storyline of a formula that can make fossil fuels obsolete in *The Killers Are Challenged* predicts the energy crisis themes of *The Man with the Golden Gun* (1974, Guy Hamilton).

Perhaps the most notorious example of an Italian Eurospy film nailing key elements before a Bond film realized them is *Kiss the Girls and Make Them Die*. The similarities between this film and *Moonraker* (1979, Lewis Gilbert) are so numerous and precise, it almost seems like plagiarism. Both films take place in Rio de Janeiro (Bond does a little globetrotting before arriving in Brazil) and involve plots with a villain using satellites to neutralize Earth's population. In *Moonraker*, Hugo Drax has an elaborate space station designed to launch satellites that will cover the Earth in nerve gas, clearing the slate for a master race. In *Kiss the Girls and Make Them Die*, Mr. Ardonian is trying to launch a satellite from his base that will use radio waves to effectively sterilize the human race. Both villains have elaborate underground lairs in the Amazon rainforest and use orchids found in their locality for their various nefarious plans. The octagonal containers Ardonian uses to keep his harem of beautiful women in stasis anticipates the hexagonal Venini Glass containers that Drax stores his nerve gas in, both containers being integral to each villains' plot.

In both films, the lead female love interest are secret agents themselves: *Moonraker* has Bond girl Holly Goodhead as a CIA agent while *Kiss the Girls and Make Them Die* has Susan Fleming as a British agent. The protagonist in *Kiss the Girls and Make Them Die*, Kelly, is from the CIA, so both films have an American-British collaboration configuration. Both movies feature scenes of foreplay where concealed weapons are shown off. James Bond unearths Dr. Goodhead's poison injecting pen, dart-throwing dairy, flame throwing perfume and radio purse before getting down to intercourse proper. The equivalent scene in *Kiss the Girls and Make Them Die* steps up the flirtation a notch with both agents trying to outdo each other by showing off their gadgets. Kelly has a flashlight that shoots bullets and a shoe that shoots darts while Susan demonstrates her dart shooting cigarettes and poison tipped ring. Unlike the duo in *Moonraker*, Kelly's and Susan's romance is solidified later at the movie's end, but both scenes in their respective movies end with the two agents agreeing to work together.

While the similarities between *Moonraker* and *Kiss the Girls and Make Them Die* are striking, there are no direct or documented correlations to prove plagiarism or homage. There is one film series that does wear its homage and parody to the Eurospy films on its sleeve and that is the rebooted OSS 117 series: *OSS 117: Cairo, Nest of Spies* (2006, Michel Hazanavicius) and *OSS 117: Lost in Rio* (2009, Michel Hazanavicius). The original OSS 117 films were French Eurospy movies themselves and were contemporaries of the Italian Eurospy films of 1960s. The two new OSS 117 films draw much inspiration from Eurospy films of the 1960s, in both look and in filming technique, such as using rear projection to realize driving sequences. *OSS 117: Lost in Rio* has a climatic ending with a gunfight at the infamous Christ the Redeemer Statue in Rio de Janeiro, which is exactly how *Kiss the Girls and Make Them Die* begins. The pairing of OSS 117 with a female Israeli army colonel working with Mossad as a love interest mirrors other romantic team ups in other Italian Eurospy films such as *Kiss the Girls and Make Them Die* and *The Killers Are Challenged*. The outlandish plot of *OSS 117: Lost in Rio* of Nazis in hiding trying to establish a Fifth Reich (skipping the fourth) and employing luchador wrestlers as henchmen is about as over the top as any plot you could find in an Italian Eurospy film. Italian Eurospy films *Sicario 77, vivo o morto* (1966, Mino Guerrini) and *Our Agent Tiger* (1965, Claude Chabrol) both feature plots of Nazis trying to take over the world as well.

Conclusion

The Italian Eurospy cycle of films is a vast, multifaceted and complex cycle of films within Italy's film canon that exploded onto the scene during the spy craze of films in the 1960s. Despite being an important and popular trend of films, scholarly assessment of them remains elusive as is evident from their absence from primary texts in Italian film studies. The Italian Eurospy films should not to be viewed as a genre, but instead as a *filone*, since the concept of the *filone* takes into consideration the cycle's derivative nature as well as illustrating how the Italian production industry operated. Hence, these films cannot be viewed as high art or product of *auteurs* and instead a different framework is needed to analyze them. The vernacular cinema framework takes into account the unique attributes of Italy populist films and provides a method to look at Italian Eurospy films at their own level.

The Italian Eurospy film cycle had its heyday in the 1960s and saw around 155 entrants into its canon. Deciding what films fall into this canon becomes problematic due to the nature of complex Italian co-productions along with Eurospy elements appearing in films that are not necessarily Eurospy but are still important in demonstrating the nature of *filones*. During its lifespan the cycle had a profound impact within the Italian production industry. Monies earned from these derivative films provided the cash flow for production companies to take riskier endeavors while providing opportunities for Italian filmmakers and craftsmen to hone their skills. Italian Eurospy films also had an influence on other Italian film cycles, such as providing tropes and cues to spaghetti westerns and the comic book hero movies of the late 1960s. And finally these films often times were able to anticipate themes, tropes, situations and other elements years before their cinematic Bond counterparts were able to. Their importance would later be cemented via homage such as in the OSS-117 films, but additional scholarly and academic work would help underscore their legacy. It is the hope that this essay perpetuates the dialog and provides the tools to do so.

Notes

1. Mary P. Wood, *Italian Cinema* (Oxford: Berg, 2005), 11.
2. Peter Bondanella, *A History of Italian Cinema* (New York: Continuum, 2009), 178.
3. Andrew Sarris, "Notes on the Auteur Theory in 1962," in *Auteurs and Authorship: A Film Reader*, ed. Barry Keith Grant (Malden, MA: Blackwell, 2008), 42–3.
4. Stephen Thrower, *Beyond Terror: The Films of Lucio Fulci* (Guildford: FAB Press, 2002), 267.
5. Mikel J. Koven, *La Dolce Morte: Vernacular Cinema and the Italian Giallo Film* (Lanham, MD: Scarecrow Press, 2006), 22.
6. Ibid., 23.
7. Ibid., 28.
8. Ibid.
9. Ibid., 29.
10. Ibid., iv.
11. Ibid., 33.
12. Thrower, *Beyond Terror*, 42.
13. Koven, *La Dolce Morte*, 12.
14. Christopher Frayling, *Spaghetti Westerns: Cowboys and Europeans from Karl May to Sergio Leone* (London: I.B. Tauris, 2006), 92.
15. Matt Blake and David Deal, *The Eurospy Guide* (Baltimore: Luminary Press, 2004), 12.
16. Ibid.
17. Matt Blake, *Fantastikal Diabolikal Supermen* (East Sussex: TheWildEye Press, 2011), 7.
18. Ibid., 6.

Bibliography

Blake, Matt. *Fantastikal Diabolikal Supermen*. East Sussex: TheWildEye Press, 2011.
Blake, Matt, and David Deal. *The Eurospy Guide*. Baltimore: Luminary Press, 2004.
Bondanella, Peter. *A History of Italian Cinema*. New York: Continuum, 2009.
_____. *Italian Cinema: From Neorealism to the Present*. New York: Continuum, 2007.
Brunetta, Gian Piero. *The History of Italian Cinema: A Guide to Italian Film from Its Origins to the Twenty-First Century*. Princeton: Princeton University Press, 2009.
Frayling, Christopher. *Spaghetti Westerns: Cowboys and Europeans from Karl May to Sergio Leone*. London: I.B. Tauris, 2006.

Fury in Marrakesh. DVD. Directed by Luciano Martino and Mino Loy. 1966; Stockholm: Fin De Siècle Media, 2009.

Killers Are Challenged. DVD. Directed by Antonio Margheriti. 1966; Stockholm: Njuta Films, 2011.

"Kiss the Girls and Make Them Die—Dorothy Provine 1/4." 2013. Video Clip. YouTube. www.youtube.com, http://www.youtube.com/watch?v=bl3vQsIhkdI (accessed December 3, 2013).

"Kiss the Girls and Make Them Die—Dorothy Provine 2/4." 2013. Video Clip. YouTube. www.youtube.com, http://www.youtube.com/watch?v=B__osW7yxCk (accessed December 3, 2013).

"Kiss the Girls and Make Them Die—Dorothy Provine 3/4." 2013. Video Clip. YouTube. www.youtube.com, http://www.youtube.com/watch?v=kyh-jGU-rtc (accessed December 3, 2013).

"Kiss the Girls and Make Them Die—Dorothy Provine 4/4." 2013. Video Clip. YouTube. www.youtube.com, http://www.youtube.com/watch?v=al9HMZMhh28 (accessed December 3, 2013).

Koven, Mikel J. *La Dolce Morte: Vernacular Cinema and the Italian Giallo Film.* Lanham, MD: Scarecrow Press, 2006.

Landy, Marcia. *Italian Film.* Cambridge: Cambridge University Press, 2000.

Licence to Kill. DVD. Directed by John Glen. 1989; Beverly Hills: MGM DVD, 2006.

Lightning Bolt. DVD. Directed by Antonio Margheriti. 1966; New York: Rareflix, 2009.

Lucas, Tim. *Mario Bava: All the Colors of the Dark.* Cincinnati: Video Watchdog, 2007.

The Man with the Golden Gun. DVD. Directed by Guy Hamilton. 1974; Beverly Hills: MGM DVD, 2006.

Moonraker. DVD. Directed by Lewis Gilbert. 1979; Beverly Hills: MGM DVD, 2006.

Naked You Die. DVD. Directed by Antonio Margheriti. 1968; Orland Park: Dark Sky Films, 2007.

Never Say Never Again. DVD. Directed by Irvin Kershner. 1983; Beverly Hills: MGM DVD, 2005.

OSS 117: Cairo, Nest of Spies. DVD. Directed by Michel Hazanavicius. 2006; Chicago: Music Box Films, 2006.

OSS 117: Lost in Rio. DVD. Directed by Michel Hazanavicius. 2010; Chicago: Music Box Films, 2010.

Sarris, Andrew. "Notes on the Auteur Theory in 1962." In *Auteurs and Authorship: A Film Reader,* edited by Barry Keith Grant, 35–45. Malden, MA: Blackwell, 2008.

Secret Agent Fireball. DVD. Directed by Antonio Margheriti. 1965; Stockholm: Fin De Siècle Media, 2008.

Thrower, Stephen. *Beyond Terror: The Films of Lucio Fulci.* Guildford: FAB Press, 2002.

The Venetian Affair. DVD. Directed by Jerry Thorpe. 1966; Burbank: Time Warner Archive, 2011.

Wood, Mary. *Italian Cinema.* Oxford: Berg, 2005.

Subverting the Bond-Canon in *Madame Sin* and *Se tutte le donne del mondo*

FERNANDO GABRIEL PAGNONI BERNS

It is well known that film genres are created through a series of conventions or narrative characteristics that allow audiences immediate identification. Maria Pramaggiore and Tom Wallis state, "Despite the slipperiness of genre categories, film industry personnel, scholars, critics, and audiences inevitably begin any discussion of genre by considering conventions."[1] War films, horror films, comedies, dramas, westerns are all highly codified genres and recognizable by a series of visual and narrative strategies that make up the plot. These strategies construct genre and allow identifying it. Even from marketing genre is important because the films are sold to distributors as a "war film," "horror film," etc.[2]

These conventions create a rigid frame of reading. For example, in the western film the colors of the costumes are highly coded. The cowboys wearing black are always the villains, while those who wear light-colored clothes will be the heroes.[3] Of course, a film can break these codes with the explicit goal of putting that genre and its conventions under a critical eye. Continuing with the western, the appearance of the "countercultural" western by mid-sixties obliterates the (until then) clear difference between good and evil. The western had been for classic Hollywood one of the film genres that more heavily relied on a dichotomous basis between good/evil, heroes/villains, civilized/savage as a narrative core. The emergence of what Christopher Le Coney and Zoe Trodd calls "countercultural" western in which the myth of the West is revised and deconstructed to exhibit the genre's conventionalities play with the good/bad dichotomy in historical moments when the difference between good and bad was not so clear within America itself.[4]

Transgressing genres can be a risky matter. If the intention of the creators was to try to avoid excessive use of generic conventions to make something fairly "new," it will likely find some resistance by producers, distributors, marketing

47

and, of course, audiences. Even the countercultural western must use a number of conventions to be framed and read as a western film. Any film that transgresses too many of its own conventions will probably find a disappointed audience. This is especially true in highly codified genres.

The spy genre is not such a genre. The corpus of spy films is not so highly codified nor its imaginary crystallized in a package of always-present narrative codes. Many times, the genre brings together the conventions of action and the adventure film. However it is different for the James Bond franchise. In this case, the audience faces a kind of subgenre within the spy film, a highly codified one. Martinis, sports cars, exotic locations, car chases, beautiful women, gadgets, colorful villains and "Bond, James Bond" makes 007 a highly recognizable figure. The films of James Bond (or the subgenre of Bond-like spy films) are a good example of a conventionalized genre. The audience enjoys every conventionalized moment, every "shaken, not stirred" Martini, each "Bond, James Bond." To respect this tradition, some new ideas are allowed but to a certain extent, since breaking the rules of the genre "would be unthinkable in a straight secret agent story."[5] Any genre that wants to break many of its own rules would find many difficulties in finding an investor and studio for a film that "is but it is not" and therefore would be difficult to sell. In other words: a genre film can be as subversive as it wants only if it keeps intact at least some conventions and is economically viable because it can be classified as a certain genre of film. A cinematographic genre cannot break too many of its own rules without becoming another totally different genre.

The Eurospy or Bond-like films are more slippery since, while taking narrative strategies (some films take some, others almost all the whole "package") from the 007 films, the truth is that they are not 007 films. Sometimes these films can mimic the structure of a Bond film from start to finish with the lofty goal of being commercially viable. This is the case of the Agent 077's Italian productions, starting with opening credits that presents a series of female figures that recall the silhouettes of women in the opening sequences in the Bond franchise. These films opening title songs also recall the songs of the Bond films, with lyrics that often contain the film's title. For example, *Agente 077 Missione Bloody Mary* (1965, Sergio Grieco)[6] has an opening song sung by Maurizio Graf, who has a voice like that of Tom Jones, famous in the same year for his song for *Thunderball* (1965, Terence Young). With a smaller budget, this film follows the Bond formula with varying degrees of success.

The above case is a clear example of a film whose explicit intention is to fit into the Bond canon setting aside an identity of its own (which may seep in, but that was not intended neither for producers or directors). Instead, it is possible to find other films that under a Bondian structure lies elements which, while articulated with the main narrative, present developments regarding the canon. They can be elements absent in the canonical films. Pointing out those absences in two "Bond-like" films will be the purpose of this essay.

In *Madame Sin* (1972, David Greene), an unsold pilot for TV, Robert Wagner is the Bond-like agent who must face the Madame Sin (Bette Davis) of the title. While the film takes canonical strategies from the Bond films, nevertheless it offers a look at the good/evil dichotomy absent in the Bond films. Embodied in her own liminity (half Chinese, half American), Madame Sin calls into question the morality underlying an agent who has a "license to kill." With its downbeat ending and a gritty hero, the film can almost be read as a dark reflection of 007's canon.

More complex is the Italian production *Se tutte le donne del mondo* (*Kiss the Girls and Make Them Die*, 1966) by Henry Levin and Arduino Maiuri. As a film that apparently incorporates most of the Bond conventions, it hides a text that actually presents the "Bond girl" Susan Fleming (Dorothy Provine) as the true heroine of the film, to the detriment of the agent played by Mike Connors. However, the narrative conventions cleverly hide the fact that the film features a strong heroine that no Bond film has ever had.

The viewers of both films can relish upon the moments taken from a conventional 007 film (good-looking girls, gadgets, car chases, spies, treachery) completely unaware of the fact that, under those narrative conventions, has leaked a sensitivity that allows readings that even contradict the canons of the Bond films. It is possible to notice and point out these new elements or set them aside to enjoy a Bond film. These elements are not intrusive enough to ruin the experience of watching a film of adventures and spies. They are perfectly articulated with the Bondian conventions. But they can be critically accentuated with the intention of analyze how these new elements leave room for alternative readings, which are often critical of the canon, without falling necessarily within parody or irony (which would alienate the audiences that the creators want to reach: an audience who want to watch a Bond film even when there is not Bond).

This essay will analyze these subtexts present in two films that have not received any critical study and yet can be considered as intelligent subversions.

Madame Sin

Robert Wagner's Anthony Lawrence, an out-of-his-luck British agent, is kidnapped by the minions of a powerful woman who lives in a castle on an island, a woman who is only known as Madame Sin. She wants Lawrence's help in stealing a high-tech submarine called Starfish from an old friend of his, Commander Cavendish (Gordon Jackson). To do this, Madame Sin has advanced technology that brain-washes people and installs false memories. Lawrence cooperates with his captors, especially when he discovers that they have captive, his ex-wife Barbara (Catherine Schell), whom Lawrence believed was killed by enemy spies. With the plan successfully finalized, Lawrence will be betrayed twice before the film's ending, with no clear resolution. This is not surprising since *Madame Sin* was intended as a television pilot, which would have continued in subsequent episodes.

Despite appearances, the film is not camp. There is no attempt in the film, as Susan Sontag (1964) implies, to "dethrone the serious."[7] Even Davis as a kind of "super-villain" is restrained, which may disappoint many viewers who expected to see the diva's typical evil dame played to extreme. Obviously, there is a misreading about what is camp and what is not. The camp "misdirects and exaggerates to unveil pretense,"[8] showing that certain images are culturally constructed. It is important to emphasize this because in fact *Madame Sin* is far from camp, moving instead to a gritty, almost "realistic" version of the Bond's canon. Usually when the narrative conventionalities from a Bond film are taken to make a non–Bond film, this narrative adjustment necessarily involves the idea of parody or camp. Bond, as a subgenre within the spy genre, is so easily recognizable than any other film that attempts to emulates its imagery with a lower budget would always be camp.

Of course having Bette Davis, former diva of the golden age of classic Hollywood, as a character with qualities of "super-villain" (her nickname, her long black dress, her exaggerated makeup) also helps to read a priori *Madame Sin* as a camp film, especially to some who believe her antics to be camp already.[9] But none of this is really enough to consider the film as camp. In fact, everything in the film is very toned down and this will be the film's main axis, as *Madame Sin*, under its Bond-like appearance, hides facets absent in the 007's films. Of course, these characteristics are hidden within a generic framework that respects superficially the Bond canon, so there are fights, chases, gadgets, a powerful villain and beautiful women.

Wagner is a spy who does not have Bond's charm. A visual motif distinguishes Lawrence from his more famous counterpart: Robert Wagner almost never smiles during the entire film. He is a James Bond trapped in a depressing movie where evil can win. When the film begins, the camera follows Lawrence wandering aimlessly through the streets of London. He is thoughtful and downcast. This attitude has a reason. His wife, Susan, was recently killed. In this regard, *Madame Sin* could be read as a continuation of *On Her Majesty's Secret Service* (1969, Peter Hunt) after Bond (George Lazenby) loses his wife (Diana Rigg) at the end of the film, killed in an act of revenge.

Here appears a significant deviation from the Bondian canon: Anthony Lawrence is no longer working at "Her Majesty's Secret Service" because "Her Majesty's Secret Service" lets Barbara die. Lawrence, unlike Bond, has lost all sense of gratitude and belonging to the British intelligence service. Unlike Bond, who is always the first one to "embrace new trends, but, at the same time, he never loses sight of his motto 'For Queen and Country.'"[10] Lawrence is an agent with his own agenda, able to switch sides if there is enough at stake. Ideology is flexible and is patent to change, and with it, the hero becomes malleable, one who now responds to countercultural skepticism that put in crisis the simplistic dichotomy of good/evil.

If Lawrence would change his British service sympathy towards the sinister Madame Sin for money, his character would deviate from the Bondian mold. This would make him unrecognizable, and *Madame Sin* would not be a "Bond-like" film. But kinship between 007 and Lawrence are kept so the film does not stray too far from this label. The right hand of Madame Sin, Malcolm De Vere (Denholm Elliot) approaches Lawrence to ask for his help, a proposal that the agent rejects as Lawrence is no longer interested in working with anyone anymore. De Vere executes his Plan B and kidnaps Lawrence, in a sequence that is pure Bond: false nuns, quirky gadgets (ultrasound guns capable of destroying a brain), some comedic moments, and helicopters.

On Madame Sin's island, the agent initially balks at working for his new boss, until he is shown a film that depicts how Barbara was killed as part of a British government plan to deceive their enemies. Thus, the sympathies of our protagonist can turn towards Madame Sin without any financial reasons, which would make Lawrence an unacceptable hero. Being a mercenary for money breaks too many aspects of the genre, which the telefilm wants to adapt.

Lawrence finally agrees to stealing the Starfish for the simplest reason of all: it is an exciting mission, as he states in the film's only moment of voice over. Obviously, the director felt the need to make it clear that Lawrence did not accept the mission for economic reasons, so the director uses the most subjective resource of all, the main character's internal voice. The fact that Lawrence accepts the risks of the mission means he isn't straying too far from the Bond formula, even though Lawrence is, in fact, betraying his country and stealing a British submarine to be delivered to a suspiciously Fidel Castro–like commandant. At the end of the day, James Bond is an action hero and relates to Lawrence in his willingness to risk himself, in his taste for danger, in being a loner always "seeking confrontation and danger."[11] No reading about *Madame Sin* can ignore the simple fact that Lawrence is indeed betraying his country, a very uncharacteristic Bond action. Nor is Barbara mentioned in the voice over, as if the main reason for taking the mission was the excitement of getting into action. Too much emphasis on the figure of Barbara murdered by the government itself would foreground revenge, revenge to the country itself. This action would also take the risk of alienating Lawrence from the Bond mold.

By helping Madame Sin, Lawrence not only betrays his country, but also the friendship he has had with Cavendish for years. Only when Lawrence realizes he has been tricked, that Barbara is alive and that the film showing she is tortured is actually fake. Will he attempt to remedy what has been done, turning his sympathies to what is "correct," to his country that he has betrayed by his own interests (desire for action) and feelings (revenge)? But by then, Lawrence has already entered a gray area where differences between good and evil are blurred. Much of the film is devoted to Lawrence trying to fix what he caused. But sympathy for his character is fragile and malleable. From the start, the film puts into question the loyalty and the ideas of right and wrong from the moment the British government has (allegedly) decided to sacrifice Barbara to obtain a greater good (fool the enemy) while Lawrence agrees to work with Sin.

Lawrence enters a critical "grey area" area, but no one is more liminal than Madame Sin herself. Liminality comes from Latin and means "threshold."[12] It is not inside or out, one or the other, but rather right at the threshold, in the middle. This concept allows critiquing any binary axis. This "threshold area" is something that is presented as an alternative to the hegemonic, to the known and labeled. So it is dangerous, because it questions the naturalness of certain practices. As defined by Turner, ambiguous characters "slip trough the network of classifications that normally locate states and positions in cultural spaces. Liminal entities are neither here nor there."[13] Madame Sin is liminal since her hybrid nature between American and Asian, a construction that, like all hybrid identity, is a "combination of bothness and otherness,"[14] that creates a unique identity with no roots on either of the two nationalities.[15] Thus Sin does not belong to any nation: she lives in a remote and anonymous island far away from all nations. Not only has her national identity conformed her as a grey character, but she herself would make clear that serving an ideal of good deeds is useless because that ideal is simply a social construction. Any fact can be justified as good if this serves a purpose. The distinction of good/bad is just a social construct.

Madame Sin is a criminal and many of her assistants are people who have been previously brainwashed to instill loyalty and sympathy (the nature of loyalty is questioned once again, from the moment that it can be "indoctrinate"). One such assistant is Nikko (Pink-Sen), Sin's personal maid, a young Asian girl with whom experimental brainwashing has been regularly practiced. When Lawrence reproached this to Sin, she disarms her itching with the simple reply that Nikko's happy now. As a child, she was sold as a prostitute, and where in cruel brothels where Sin finds her. Now, with the memories of her terrible life erased by Sin's technology, the girl is happy, far from the horrors that her life as a "free" subject provides. Is it really that unethical if the experiment provides happiness to the subject, a happiness that the normal functioning of the world cannot bring? Sin complicates this issue even more when she mentions the hypocrisy inherent in the "license to kill" of certain agents (referring to Lawrence, but by extension, Bond). It is a license that allows the criminal action of killing (in fact, the most criminal of all), as entitled by law: killing is right if it is the enemy who is killed. Interestingly, the enemy thinks exactly the same thing. The state gives its agents "a right to act immorally."[16] Therefore, the true nature of good is compromised and becomes illusory.

This is replicated by various illusions of Madame Sin. With her ultrasound technology, Sin does not just wash brains and crush the spirit, but she can also create distort reality so her subjects think they see people who are really not there. Thus, the very nature of perception is questioned. This obfuscation of reality is seen again when Lawrence realizes that what he has seen in the film that documented the torture and death of Barbara was false. He believed in what he saw, in the objectivity of facts and images, but the documentary film, as well as three-dimensional images made with ultrasound, are proven false. So, reality is not unique thing to be feasibly comprehended, but a permanent construction of meanings.

Immateriality is present in Madame Sin herself: she is described as a myth. This conception of her identity serves Sin since no real power is readily apparent. Behind a public facade hides someone who manages him or her. Madame Sin is framed hidden in shadows[17] and within the shadows that efface her, she manages the world, without anyone suspecting that she is real. Only a tiny circle of people know that she is real, and that invisibility is what gives her global power. Carolyn Nordstrom (2004) calls "politics of invisibility"[18] the invisible structures in society that make money on wars and military confrontations between countries, structures whose power rests on "the optics of deception,"[19] i.e., their presence and purpose must remain undetected so they can extract money from the inequities of militarized violence. Madame Sin shows an astonished Lawrence all her technology and economic networks that allow her to stand as the center of power while remaining invisible. Madame Sin points that many of her companies are actually legal. Again, the distinction between bad/good is blurred, as many companies who make money are actually morally wrong but legally sustainable. Madame Sin is an all-seeing panopticon, but her power to be sustained, must remain invisible.

Madame Sin has cast doubt on the existence of a real distinction between good and evil, especially in the world of spies. Unfortunately, the series remained an unsold pilot, but still managed to foreground ethical issues that the blockbusters starring James Bond chose to leave out. And all that within a Bondian mold of exotic islands and fanciful plans. The only thing that perhaps is missing is more action, but there will be more than enough in *Se tutte le donne del mondo*, a film even more steeped in the Bond canon, but equally subversive.

Se tutte le donne del mondo

Unlike the previously discussed film, this Italian production starts off situated in the Bond canon, including an ad hoc song that mentions the film's title during the initial credit sequence, at least in the English subtitled version titled *Kiss the Girls and Make Them Die*. This fun and sexy spy adventure which, according to some critics, inspired *Moonraker*[20] (1979, Lewis Gilbert) a lot, begins with a prologue that sets the McGuffin: Lord Aldric (Terry-Thomas), a professor in the middle of the Amazon jungle, discovers a tribe performing a strange ritual. The professor is killed and his notebook is lost, triggering a race of spies who want to get the aforementioned notebook even without knowing exactly why.

Immediately the film assumes its Eurospy cannon. Mike Connors is Kelly, the Bond-like agent who must retrieve the notebook and who will carry the narrative, at least at first. The film opens with a spectacular fight at the Brazilian monument Jesus of Corcovado, which adheres faithfully to the Bond's formula: an exotic place, an impossible mission, a hero caught by a maniacal villain, adding a spectacular rescue by helicopter. The next scene shows the main villain, Mr. Ardonian (Raf Vallone) whose plans are, to that point, unclear. A parade of beautiful women ensues, including Susan Fleming (Dorothy Provine) who appears to be a naive blonde, but who will become the film's main Bond girl. So far, so good. Kelly saves the life of and subsequently seduces a lady who belongs to Ardonian's harem, thus calling the attention of Ardonian who decides that Kelly must be removed. From that moment begins a tense game of cat and mouse between the spy and the villain, with the notebook in the middle.

The film builds up to some extent from an exclusively male point of view. Kelly carries forward the story and it is his actions that advance the plot. The female roles respond to the classic mold of the Bond girl, extremely beautiful women who love dominant and economically powerful men. The typical Bond girl, especially the one who is paired with the villain, has a relationship with him more based in economic interest or fear about her life than love. This situation is enhanced in *Se tutte le donne del mondo*: in the classic Bondian mold, the villain has a partner who ultimately will choose Bond as lover, as a way to reinforce the masculinity of the British agent and redirect the bad girl nationality/ideology.[21] Ardonian, however, has not one consort but several, hence the film's title—*Kiss the Girls and Make Them Die*. If the Bond girls can be accused of being a mere decorative object, this position is exacerbated in a film where all women who have a relationship with Ardonian underlie the misogynistic traits in the Bond's films. All Ardonian's women seem to have only a financial interest in him. For example Sylvia (Nicoletta Machiavelli), one of his girls, is clearly cheating on him with a younger boy who poses as her "brother." Moreover, Ardonian keeps his women under close surveillance, ensuring that none of them have autonomy (an important issue in relationships between the villains and their sexual partners in the Bond's films). Ardonian's right hand, Omar (Sandro Dori) keeps a strict vigil on his boss's harem and the millionaire's expensive gifts that he gives to his female companions conceal hidden cameras that let him keep them under surveillance. So, Ardonian has in his office a wall covered with a large number of TV sets, each showcasing a different woman, all of them his lovers, as Silvia is, or prospective lovers, as is Susan.

In addition, the *mise-en-scène* plays with the misogynistic point-of-view that emphasizes the close-ups of female body parts that are re-converted into fetishes for the viewing pleasure of the (male) audience. Drops of water on a female back get a close-up for Ardonian's point of view, or a female's red lips magnified through a looking glass, are examples of playing with different ways of presenting female body parts that invite audience voyeurism thereby turning the girls into visual spectacle of comsumption.[22] The female's mouth is a representation by its very exaggeration and comic nature, of the artificial nature of these close-shots.

Now, with everything said so far, little room it would seem there is a subversive subtext in this film whose central axis is the submissive role of women around the main villain, who makes them fetishes and objects to be possessed. Like the enlarged shot of a woman's mouth within the diegesis, this misogynistic text in this film is actually more complex. First, the female presence is stronger because the villain has numerous partners. However, it is not just about the number of women. The entire plot revolves around the villain's need to subordinate women to his command. These women are not only a means of sexual exchange to underlie the heterosexuality of the main heroic character, but the engine of the action itself, as Ardonian's plan is based on his need to be alone with *Se tutte le donne del mondo*. They are not a minor part of the plan, *but the whole plan*. The dependence of the villain towards the feminine, then, puts a strain on a filmic text, which tries to coerce women into mere decorative roles. Part of Ardonian's plan is to eliminate the human race so only he remains with all the beautiful women he has previously frozen; turned into beautiful objects to be admired and, once awake, subsumed. But like the shot with the magnifying glass, which functions as a close-up of female parts, the film highlights the chauvinistic point of view and makes fun of it. Women are not just an ornament in the context of the film, but women as ornaments, is the main criticism that the film makes since turning women into objects of consumption is the primary purpose of the villain and the main narrative plot. Hence, what was subtext in the Bond films now becomes text.

This relationship, with the female subject becomes a subversive act by the intervention of Susan Fleming. A typical woman who is ignorant of what is happening around her, Susan is doubly revealed as a complex character. First, in the diegesis, Susan is discovered to be a British spy agent who, like Kelly, is on a mission to find the notebook. Her whole attitude of clueless blonde is just a charade to get close to Ardonian. Second, on a textual narrative level, once Susan is revealed as a spy agent, she gradually assumes the "Bond role" from Kelly. This conversion must be done gradually so the audience accepts this change of course in the narrative, to the extent that this movement is almost imperceptible. In *Madame Sin*, the ideas that challenge the Bond tropes must be inserted in a narrative of Bond-like adventures, thus avoiding the risk of alienating its market. It is not presented as a film with a female Bond, but a Eurospy *à la* Bond with comic overtones.

When the notebook, which contains information about an Amazonian tribe being used as guinea pigs for Ardonian's infertility experiments surfaces, it is Susan who manages to keep it. Kelly then must go to Susan to get the notebook. Both spies equilibrate each other, measuring themselves by the number of defenses that each of them has hidden in their clothing. This test ends in a tie, since both have the same amount of lethal defenses. Susan is revealed as a spy but more significantly, she is established as an equal to Kelly, a female counterpart with equal strength. However, Kelly, true to the Bond tradition, will try to seduce her, without success.

From that scene on, Susan will displace Kelly as the film's main character. She does this by taking on three exclusively Bondian (i.e., male) attributes: the gadgets, the final confrontation with the villain, and the escape from an impossible situation. All these attributes have been distinctly male, but is displaced to Susan when she is revealed as a spy.

Gadgets will become solely used onscreen by Susan and her phlegmatic English driver, James (Terry-Thomas).[23] Cars that camouflage themselves as advertising signs, pills placed in a car's radiator to cause it to disintegrate in minutes, or instruments that provide an escape disguised as harmless personal items are Bondian instruments with which Susan, not Kelly as the hero, has in her possession or control. It is thanks to the duo of Susan/James, and *their* gadgets, that the trio of heroes then overcomes several difficulties.

One of the moments that most strongly resonates with the Bondian imaginary is the hero's final confrontation with the villain. It is not about the physical battle, but the moment in which Ardonian explains in detail his plan to Bond and by extension, to the audience. However, instead of Kelly, this moment is exclusively Susan's. In face, Kelly did not even hear the plan from afar. She is the person occupying this predominantly male scene. From Ardonian's reveal of his plan to remove the sexual desire of mankind to bring about the extermination of the human race, keeping for himself all the beautiful women, Susan deduces the (rather obvious, everything has to be said) connection between the villain's plan and his sexual impotence. Thus, the phallic connection between the villain's desires and giant rockets in the Bond canon is parodied in this explicit link between erectile dysfunction and failed plan.

The physical showdown with Ardonian must be with Kelly, so as to not deviate too much from the Bond canon and alienate the intended audience. The audiences' expectation that Kelly defeat Ardonian is satisfied however; our American hero accidentally sits on the button that launches the rocket Susan was trapped in, apparently causing her death. Filled with anguish, Kelly watches helplessly as the rocket explodes. However, in a scene that explicitly presents Susan as the real protagonist of the film, she appears, without any harm, behind Kelly, smiling and triumphant. The scene in which she escapes from the interior of the rocket is not shown to the audience. The impossible escape is indeed so impossible[24] that the directors simply choose not to show it. Our hero Kelly, conceding that the film is no longer about him, states that he does not even ask how she got out of her predicament. This situation seems to make fun of the quasi-superhero canon of spy films and their impossible situations, while at the same time emphasizing the superiority of Susan over Kelly, since he accidentally sends her to her death but she manages to escape unaided by any male. Arguably, this narrative breaks too much with the Bond canon. However, there is still one last scene for Kelly to redeem himself into the hero role.

Kelly, completely in love with Susan, carries her in his arms to her car in the final scene, with Susan, coquettishly raising one leg in a clear female stereotype. This simple gesture seeks to restore the narrative topics to its "right" tracks, the familiar Bond formula. However, the exaggeration of her gesture stresses rather than cancels the absolute independence of Susan. She *only plays* the "fragile girl." This shot, like the others mentioned previously, spotlight the artificiality and conventionality. The audience already knows that Susan is not a girlish woman in need of a man, so this closing scene sharply contrasts with the previous moment, the impossible escape. While it is true that Susan, like all women spies in popular fiction, are rooted in patriarchy through her whiteness, heterosexuality and beauty, it is also true that[25] she challenges the established hegemony of male supremacy.

It is important to note, again, that this conversion of Susan into the film's hero has been a gradual one. Up to the film's middle, it is Kelly who carries the narrative with his heroic actions. The subversion of gender canons and spy genre has been so subtle that the audience can only accept it. Subversive elements have been inserted into a narrative that follows the mold to imitate the James Bond's films. *Madame Sin* tells how a spy must face the global threat of a picturesque villain, escapes death, engages in fist-fighting duels, high-speed races and is betrayed by a beautiful woman. Pure Bond mold. However, the Bond films do not end with the main character on the floor, deceived and poisoned by the woman he loves. The traditional Bond films do not have villains that raise questions about the nature of such concepts of good and evil, villains who in turn are liminal characters that refuse being labeled as simply "bad." However, these ideas that subvert expectations in this genre are subtly dispersed throughout the film, so the audience does not feel betrayed in their expectations of seeing a Eurospy, which twists the conventions of the James Bond movies.

Conclusion

In conclusion, let's go back to the expectations and audiences. *Se tutte le donne del mondo* could have arisen as a film starring a female Bond. After all, there are other films of that ilk already, such as *Modesty Blaise* (1966, Joseph Losey), with Monica Vitti. Yet, distributing the film as something "different" (a female Bond!), even as a spoof, runs the risk of alienating potential viewers. Viewers are familiar with spy tropes presented in the Bond films and that is what they have come to expect of spy oriented films. Being part of a genre or sub-genre involves respecting its rules and conventions, especially at the time of sale and commercial distribution. The posters advertising the film, both in Spain and in Italy, highlight Kelly, while Susan is just a face behind the figure of the male hero. Both posters also presented the film as a serious Eurospy and not as a camp effort. Only U.S. poster showcases Susan in full body, but tied up. None of the posters indicate that Susan will play a very important role within the film's narrative.

Maybe that's why *Madame Sin* did not work as a series and remained a telefilm, an unsold pilot. Perhaps its differences with the films it tried to imitate were too notorious, or the story was too depressing. *Se tutte le donne del mondo* was better formulated from its camp/spoof aesthetics and thus, it could be more subversive in its narration because camp allows the film to play with stereotypes.

The film is more successful, to the point of being considered Henry Levin's only good film.[26]

Madame Sin presents itself as a British televised Bond. Under the conventions lifted from its canonical model, it could be observed as reflections about the nature of evil and good, which is very interesting if we note that the spy films, especially the films of adventure and espionage, tend to work with binaries that frame and separate the good from the bad, both spheres clearly (and uncritically) defined. This film asks about the moral nature of the manipulation of memory, global business and the right to kill.

Se tutte le donne del mondo, meanwhile, has all the pop Bondian trappings, with its sexy blend of science fiction, adventure, humor, exoticism and espionage. But the masculine core will gradually shift to make room for a female character who is revealed gradually (to not alienate the audience), as the central character. If in the canonical Bond's films women are occasionally only props, misogyny here is playfully displaced so the story turns out guided by female agency.

With varying degrees of success and with different aesthetic and intentions, both films hid subversive elements and reflections within a genre mold. Noting there is much to read in the Eurospy films and in the films which take the spy genre as a model, it is a subgenre in need of critical examination. The two films examined in this essay has shown how the canon can be reconstructed without losing sight of the narrative strategies that made of Bond a cinematographic icon.

Notes

1. Maria Pramaggiore and Tom Wallis, *Film: A Critical Introduction* (London: Laurence King, 2005), 347.
2. To observe the different ways in which "genre" and its narrative works in the film industry, see Rick Altman, *Film/Genre* (London: BFI, 1999).
3. Philiph Skerry and Brenda Berstler, "You Are What You Wear: The Role of Western Costume in Film," in *Beyond the Stars: Studies in American Popular Films, Volume 3*, ed. Paul Loukides and Linda Fuller (Bowling Green, OH: Bowling Green University of Popular Press, 1993).
4. Christopher Le Coney and Zoe Trodd, "Straight Shooters, Stainless-Steel Stories, and Cowboy Codes: The Queer Frontier and American Identity in a Post-Western World," in *Queer Popular Culture: Literature, Media, Film, and Television*, ed. Thomas Peele (New York: Palgrave Macmillan, 2007).
5. James Chapman, "The Avengers: Television and Popular Culture During The 'High Sixties,'" in *Windows on the Sixties: Exploring Key Texts of Media and Culture,* ed. Anthony Aldgate, James Chapman, and Arthur Marwick (London: I.B. Tauris, 2000), 62.
6. Film co-produced by France, Italy and Spain.
7. Susan Sontag, "Notes on Camp," in *Against Interpretation: And Other Essays* (New York: Delta, 1966), 282.
8. Toby Johnson, *Gay Perspective: Things Our (Homo)Sexuality Tells Us About the Nature of God and the Universe* (Brooklyn: White Crane Institute, 2008), 66.

9. Ernest Mathijs and Jamie Sexton, *Cult Cinema* (Malden, MA: Wiley-Blackwell, 2011), 87.

10. Christine Berberich, *The Image of the English Gentleman in Twentieth Century Literature: Englishness and Nostalgia* (Hampshire: Ashgate, 2007), 163.

11. Andrew Spicer, *Typical Men: The Representation of Masculinity in Popular British Cinema* (London: I.B. Tauris, 2003), 65.

12. Victor Turner, *The Ritual Process: Structure and Anti-Structure* (Chicago: Aldine Transaction, 2008), 94.

13. Ibid., 95.

14. Khadidiatou Guèye, *Mapping the Liminal Identities of Mulattas in African, African America and Caribbean Literatures* (Ann Arbor: ProQuest, 2006), 10.

15. Sang Hyun Lee, *From a Liminal Place: An Asian American Theology* (Minneapolis: Fortress Press, 2010), 112.

16. Francis Sejersted, "Reflections on the Suspension of Ethics: Managers and Consultants as Manipulators," in *Ethics and Consultancy: European Perspectives*, ed. Heidi von Weltzien Hoivik and Andreas Føllesdal (Dordrecht: Kluwer Academic, 1995), 24.

17. Madame Sin is seen first with her figure silhouetted in shadows. Only after a few moments, she will come out to light while speaking to Lawrence.

18. Carolyn Nordstrom, *Shadows of War: Violence, Power, and International Profiteering in the Twenty-First Century* (Oakland: University of California Press, 2004), 34.

19. Ibid.

20. Wesley Alan Britton, *Beyond Bond: Spies in Fiction and Film* (Westport, CT: Praeger, 2005), 140.

21. And sometimes sexuality, as with Pussy Galore in *Goldfinger* (1964, Guy Hamilton), who undergoes a conversion from "amazonian lesbian private pilot and henchwoman to lover and loyal defender of the West after a roll in the hay with Bond." Shelton Waldrep, "Bond's Body: *Diamonds Are Forever, Casino Royale* and the Future Anterior," in *World Cinema and the Visual Arts*, ed. David Gallagher (London: Anthem Press, 2012), 43. Thus, the Bond girl is "put back into place within the regime of the phallus." Rosie White, *Violent Femmes: Women as Spies in Popular Culture* (New York: Routledge, 2007), 26.

22. White, *Violent Femmes*, 27.

23. It should be noted that the name James, with all semantic significance that it owns in spy films and moves to the figure of a driver, who retains the ownership of the Bond's gadgets. Moreover, James is Susan's driver/butler, then by displacement, the ownership of the gadgets remains on the female side.

24. The rocket was already separated from the stairs leading to it, so even if Susan managed to free herself from her bonds and somehow open the hatch, she would find the problem of the high altitude between the hatch and the ground.

25. White, *Violent Femmes*, 4.

26. Bertand Tavernier and Jean-Pierre Coursodon, *50 Años de Cine Norteamericano*, Volumen II (Madrid: Akal, 2006), 733.

Bibliography

Altman, Rick. *Film/Genre*. London: BFI, 1999.

Berberich, Christine. *The Image of the English Gentleman in Twentieth Century Literature: Englishness and Nostalgia*. Hampshire: Ashgate, 2007.

Britton, Wesley Alan. *Beyond Bond: Spies in Fiction and Film*. Westport, CT: Praeger, 2005.

Chapman, James. "The Avengers: Television and Popular Culture During The 'High Sixties.'" *Windows on the Sixties: Exploring Key Texts of Media and Culture,* edited by Anthony Aldgate, James Chapman, and Arthur Marwick, 37–69. London: I.B. Tauris, 2000.

Gueye, Khadidiatou. *Mapping the Liminal Identities of Mulattas in African, African America and Caribbean Literatures*. Ann Arbor: ProQuest, 2006.

Hyun Lee, Sang. *From a Liminal Place: An Asian American Theology*. Minneapolis: Fortress Press, 2010.

Johnson, Toby. *Gay Perspective: Things Our (Homo)Sexuality Tells Us About the Nature of God and the Universe*. Brooklyn: White Crane Institute, 2008.

Le Coney, Christopher, and Zoe Trodd. "Straight Shooters, Stainless-Steel Stories, and Cowboy Codes: The Queer Frontier and American Identity in a Post-Western World." *Queer Popular Culture: Literature, Media, Film, and Television*, edited by Thomas Peele, 151–67. New York: Palgrave Macmillan, 2007.

Madame Sin. Dir. David Greene. ABC, 1972. Telefilm.

Mathijs, Ernest, and Jamie Sexton. *Cult Cinema*. Malden, MA: Wiley-Blackwell, 2011.

Nordstrom, Carolyn. *Shadows of War: Violence, Power, and International Profiteering in the Twenty-First Century*. Oakland: University of California Press, 2004.

Pramaggiore, Maria, and Tom Wallis. *Film: A Critical Introduction*. London: Laurence King Publishing, 2005.

Se tutte le donne del mondo. Dir. Henry Levin, Arduino Maiuri. Dino de Laurentiis Cinematografica, Columbia Pictures, 1966. Film.

Sejersted, Francis. "Reflections on the Suspension of Ethics: Managers and Consultants as Manipulators." *Ethics and Consultancy: European Perspectives*, edited by Heidi von Weltzien Hoivik and Andreas Føllesdal, 7–26. Dordrecht: Kluwer Academic, 1995.

Skerry, Philiph, and Brenda Berstler. "You Are What You Wear: The Role of Western Costume in Film." In *Beyond the Stars: Studies in American Popular Films, Volume 3, The Material World in American Popular Film*, edited by Paul Loukides and Linda Fuller, 77–86. Bowling Green, OH: Bowling Green University of Popular Press, 1993.

Sontag, Susan. "Notes on Camp." *Against Interpretation: And Other Essays*. New York: Delta, 1966, 274–92.

Spicer, Andrew. *Typical Men: The Representation of Masculinity in Popular British Cinema*. London: I.B. Tauris, 2003.

Tavernier, Bertand, and Jean-Pierre Coursodon. *50 Años de Cine Norteamericano*, Volumen II. Madrid: Akal, 2006.

Turner, Victor. *The Ritual Process: Structure and Anti-Structure*. Chicago: Aldine Transaction, 2008.

Waldrep, Shelton. "Bond's Body: *Diamonds Are Forever, Casino Royale* and the Future Anterior." In *World Cinema and the Visual Arts*, edited by David Gallagher, 41–58. London: Anthem Press, 2012.

White, Rosie. *Violent Femmes: Women as Spies in Popular Culture*. New York: Routledge, 2007.

Nation and Action

The Case of the Bollywood[1] Spy Thriller

IPSHITA NATH AND ANUBHAV PRADHAN

Discourses on nationalism and nation-building, articulated through cinematic mediums, project concerns in territorialism, integration, historicity, identity and sovereignty; while providing as alternatives to mainstream history such narratives as make it heterogeneous, they often homogenize concepts of "Nation" and nationhood in patriotic imaginations. Indeed, construction of nationhood in films is an important instance of cultural/popular conceptualizations of the intersection of ruptures and stability, continuities and discontinuities, peace and violence, patriotism and sedition alternatively. Nationhood becomes a projected idea with its definitions in the rather variegated degrees of feelings of affiliation and loyalty—of an individual—towards the respective geographical space of the nation they may be residing in. Accordingly, the nation as an imagined community[2] within which emerges this 'imagined' sense of ownership, a feeling of identification and comradeship, that inspires attitudes of brotherhood, oneness, and unity in people, and allows them to cultivate ideas of self-sacrifice in the service of nation,[3] forms the essential link between such "imagined" ideals—common, perhaps, across cultures—and their filmic and textual depictions.

Memory in this way becomes an important medium of indoctrination. If nationalism is constructed from and through memories, then processes of integration of individuals into the circuit of patriotism (that emerge from the same concepts as in nationhood) arising during/due to exigencies become highly potent and effective. Times of crisis when there may be a threat to internal harmony accelerate, and give rise to, sentiments of unity and togetherness, which then take root in people's minds. This happens because the need for a common social sensibility that would encourage and valorize volunteer "saviors," and enable the negation of danger and threat, is felt most acutely in times of hardship. Hence, as world orders turn increasingly Manichean, such volunteer-saviors take the semblance of unifying forces or heroic entities which, assuming the mantle of the messiah, enact the restoration of that common sensibility which engenders the body politic.[4]

Such a cumulative, national condition that times of emergency and disaster, or even invasion, be it cultural or military, entail emerges from notions of territories: of the self and the other; the home and the enemy. In literary and cinematic articulations, such anxieties related to the invading alien get translated either into utopian visions of good (self) triumphing over evil (foreign), or cynicism and ambiguity prevailing in ways which reinforce a civic-patriotic ideal by highlighting deviations from it. These motifs can be observed in a range of cinematic texts across genres and schools since 1947[5]: while Raj in Raj Kapoor's 1955 *Shri 420* (*Mister 420*, or better yet, *The Swindler*) asserts his Indian identity despite being swamped by foreign influences,[6] Master in Raj Khosla's 1956 crime thriller *CID* cautions against the fickle trickiness of being in Bombay.[7] Thus, when boundaries of organic and wholesome as against foreign and diseased are sketched out clearly in people's imaginations, it becomes easy to generate meanings in signs and apply them to the available tools of semiotics, particularly in the case of nationalism where love for the nation and aversion to the "other"/alien must needs be simultaneously generated.

This chiaroscuro of violence and unity provides interesting entry points into the inter-textualities of war, violence, nationhood, cinema, and the battling hero of the society in the cinematic representations of these. Although attributing filmic narratives entirely to political contexts of production would not be critically conducive, especially to studies in and around Bombay cinema where the industry was supplying the audience with what it wanted, so that "the bigger the box office earnings, the more the films reflects the *zeitgeist*, conceived as 'what people want,'"[8] political upheavals and violence in/during the early and mid-twentieth century in India greatly informed narratives emerging from the film industry of South Asia. For instance, in the 1910s and the 1920s, British industrialization and colonial rule, along with poor technology hampered cinematic ventures,[9] and Dadasaheb Phalke found paltry business in mythological films such as the *Krishna* trilogy, and although these movies became popular if not profitable,[10] the movies reflected social realities even as they demonstrated the co-existence of modernity and tradition as "undiluted" polarities.[11]

Accordingly, the 1930s saw the emergence of the female hero-figure, "the fearless Nadia," created by J.B.H Wadia. Here, Indian action heroes and heroines, although heavily influence by their Western counterparts, were not merely products of the influence of American, or Italian films for that matter, as both were circulated widely in the subcontinent during this time. As Valentina Vitali in *Hindi Action Cinema: Industries, Narratives, Bodies* argues, even as audiences during the 1920s had access to movies featuring "muscular, athletic, acrobatic heroes"[12] such as *Attila il flagello di Dio (Attila the Scourge of the God*, 1918, Febo Mari) and *Samsone contro i Filistei (Samson amongst the Philistines*, 1918, Domenico Gaido), the appearance of someone like Ramamurthy, an Indian athlete[13] dubbed the "Indian Hercules," was not a simple borrowing from Western cinema but a reconfiguration of pre-existing stereotypes so as to create a different ideal-image of virile masculinity.[14] Hence, when locating cinematic texts within larger, overlapping frameworks, it is important to study what is borrowed in light of the choice of elements provided therein because these reflect the socioeconomic conditions and cultural inclinations of the receivers.

Vitali's arguments provide a basis for conceptualizing a symbiotic relationship between cinematic text and its socio-economic contexts in light of the "action ingredient" becoming more and more prominent in Bombay cinema of 1950s. This is so because the "action element" was part of the development of narratives of social conflict within and for the project of nation-building.[15] Of course, this "action ingredient" came to centrally inform Bombay cinema during the 1970s and 1980s, which seem to belong wholly to the "angry young man" who, characterized by Amitabh Bacchan,[16] reflects the frustrations and resentments prevalent in times of growing unemployment, rising crime, and greater corruption and inequity. Poor himself, this savior-hero selflessly took up the job of fighting against crime and injustice for the greater good, as, for instance, in Prakash Mehra's 1973 *Zanjeer*, wherein Inspector Vijay Khanna, played by Bacchan, is the ideal police inspector determined to fight crime and establish order, and is driven to undertake violent activities in order to fight back when circumstances compel him to avenge injustice. Yet, even in the 1950s,[17] despite the preponderance of melodrama in the mainstream, a strong undercurrent of 'action' marked the pulp so that the transition from fantastical hyper-action to socially pertinent action seems majorly a factor of the changing mood of the times. Hence, an argument like Koushik Banerjea's in "'Fight Club': Aesthetics, Hybridisation and the Construction of Rogue Masculinities in *Sholay* and *Deewar*," which conceptualizes the construction of male "avenging angels" who fight criminal forces not just in but also for the nation, can be persuasively linked to the presence of an undercurrent of virile, hyper-masculine pulp cinema in the 1950s, to growing political turbulence throughout the 1950s and 1960, and to greater incidents of crime and subterfuge in metropolitan life so as to consider the angry young men of the 1970s and 1980s spiritual inheritors of the virile Bhimas of earlier epochs.

It is in this transformation of the aggressive athletic male into the romanticized underdog-messiah that the patriotic operative may also be located. As Banerjea observes, with more and more films aiming to depict wishful defeats of the terrorist "other," one observes, the emergence and consolidation of a hybrid aesthetic within the commercial action genre reproduces the idea of nationhood as ambivalent text. In other words, the politics of surface which emerges in these films offers within its provisionality a critical grammar with which to explore the shifting parochialisms of culture and identity.[18]

In view of the growth of this parochialism, and the mainstreaming throughout the 1960s of the hyper-masculine male figure in cinema for the middle-classes, this essay will present a detailed explication of these motifs of masculine patriotism vis-à-vis the covert operative in Ravikant Nagaich's *Farz* (1967), Ramanand Sagar's *Aankhen* (1968), Deepak Bahry's *Agent Vinod* (1977), and Sriram Raghavan's *Agent Vinod* (2012). For before the young man became an "angry young man," the figure of the spy emerged on the Indian cinematic foray: the spy, similar to the later figure of the angry young man, was more a loyalist fighting external forces than an intelligence officer employed by the state to fight crime and terrorism. Ravikant Nagaich's 1967 *Farz* may be considered as one of the first Bombay cinema texts wherein the varying aesthetics of spy and *deshbhakt* (patriot) combine to engender a parochialism born out of tangible fears, and recent memories, of external aggression and sabotage. Accordingly, the figure of the spy in the Hindi films of the 1960s and the 1970s acquires a deeper significance, also as the possible origins of the figure of the "angry young man," and other such noble hero-figures of the cinema of later decades.

Farz, literally meaning duty, presents the dashing and dancing, flirtatious and ferocious Gopal, Agent 116 of the CID, whose mission to uncover the death of Agent 303 leads him to Damodar, a respectable Bombay businessman who also contrives bomb blasts, arranges murders and executes acts of infrastructural sabotage, such as blowing up trains and dams. Damodar is only a cover, for as Gopal's investigations uncover, he acts a puppet of a shadowy mastermind, the somewhat unimaginatively named Supremo. Of course, that he is shadowy is central, for it's not till the last forty-five minutes that one makes his acquaintance, which, once made, provides the movie its rationale. Promises of external aggressors, hints of conspiracy and sabotage get finally realized in the figure of the Supremo, a man with distinctly Mongoloid features dressed always in a sort of a Zhongshan, or Mao, suit and incapable totally of Hindustani[19]: as likely as not, Supremo is a caricature of the supreme leader of the Chinese people, Chairman Mao.[20]

Given textual evidences and contextual frameworks, this seems extremely possible. With political changes in the 1960s, especially the Sino-Indian War of 1962 which involved the shattering of Panchsheel, pressures on the carefully constructed notions of nationhood that had, throughout the struggles for independence from the British Raj during much of the first half of the twentieth century, helped India gain political independence, had begun to be felt. Despite the victory over Pakistan in 1965 the scars of 1962, the "Indian humiliation"[21] were still not healed, and presenting a Mongoloid megalomaniac bent on crippling India's infrastructure and agriculture—he's having poisonous vapor-based fertilizer researched in his factory—through proxy war, and thus destroying the country, would have struck a chord with the film's audiences. Supremo in *Farz* becomes the invading, humiliating alien embodied in flesh and blood, just as popular consciousness would've imagined him, and Gopal's success against him, and his traitorous Indian minions, appear cathartic in a way possible only in the 1960s.

The spy genre was new to the Indian silver screen, though James Bond had already made his appearance in 1962, so that Agent 116, like Agent 007, often appears dapper in black suits and ties. Like his British counterpart, he is quite the womanizer, calling every girl he meets *mohini* (enchantress), and reciting the same stock couplets to win her over, till, and this is unlike his British counterpart, he falls in love. Love is important here, not the least because romance lends space to motifs of family which make Gopal, like the murdered Agent 303, not simply a covert operative but also a healthy young man serving the nation, and looking forward to settling down to family life as a young patriotic bourgeois male may be expected to. In this way, love and Supremo made the movie a success: sufficiently bowled over, Gopal gives us memorable scores like "Mast baharon ka main aashiq" ("A lover I am of these pleasant spring-tides")[22] and "Hum toh tere aashiq hain" ("I am your lover")[23] and induces by virtue of his love for his daughter Sunita a change of heart in Damodar; sufficiently Mongoloid, Supremo fits the bill perfectly as the perverse, menacing outsider, necessitating a sweeping, onomatopoeic climax of guns, bombs and dynamite which any self-respecting subcontinental audience would expect. Between the two of them, they compensate splendidly for lapses in the plot, the cardinal one being that Supremo's diabolical plan is not exactly sketched out as one would expect it, for besides grunting monosyllabically, and generally exhorting his Indian commander to ruin India, he tells little of who he is, what he has in mind, and why he wishes to do whatever he wishes to do, his very being, a Mongoloid man in a Mao Suit being, apparently, sufficient to convey the grave threat to national sovereignty which he poses.

Farz worked despite this—and is a boon of its context. The mid 1960s, witness to escalating social tensions, border threats and fears of military takeover, gave such grand metanarratives of the vulnerable "home"/self being saved by socially invisible clandestine operatives a credence which might not have been found in the 1950s. Attacks on oneself must be fended off for self-preservation, particularly when violence occurs as power structures fail in their modes of coercion and bring about a sense of complacency, thereby leading to anomie.[24] The Indian spy can be considered a child of such patriotic self-defense, the reckless, devil-may-care, courageous young man devoted to his *farz*, duty to the motherland, a duty which comes more out of love for the country because it's one's job and must be performed. Gopal's outrage on being told about Agent 303's murder, his anger against traitors, his zeal in converting Damodar to the cause of the nation, these actions provide evidence that he is a *deshbhakt* (patriot) over and above a secret services operative—the fact that he is still Gopal, that he uses his name, and a very homely Hindustani name at that, in spite of being Agent 116 indicates that he is Indian first, and everything else later.

Memories of war and times of strife are one of the most effective metaphors for consolidation of nationhood. The outsider against whom figures like Gopal pitted their battles became emblematic of the political "other," and thus assumed monstrous proportions requiring incisive and sustained retaliatory action. This zealously defensive patriotism seems also to lie at the heart of the emergence of the patriotic vigilante, protectors as well as cleansers of the moral, military and economic framework of the motherland, operating on the peripheries of increasingly inactive and unreliable state apparatuses. Ramanand Sagar's 1968 production *Aankhen* is one of the foremost examples. Brought in a decade which saw armed aggression from powerful neighbors on the east and the west, in which a Prime Minister succumbed to death in foreign soil under mysterious circumstances, and which was witness to the crumbling of Nehruvian trickle-down socialism and the birth of Naxalism and insurgencies in many parts of the northeast—*Aankhen* generates a comprehensive picture of a nation at threat, involved in, as it were, cold war against enemies hollowing the fabric of the nation. Its opening credits underlie the acute sense of territorial threat and violation which inform the rationale of the movie:

A nation's borders cannot be attempted
If a nation's borders are guarded by eyes.[25]

The lyrical explication, which follows comes against the backdrop of a watchful sentinel hovering over the landmass of India, the all-encompassing secular fabric of which is actualized through the motif of a temple, the Taj Mahal and the Sanchi Stupa. These invest sight with penetratingly visionary qualities, and moves immediately upon a spectacle of what the failure in exercising these qualities leads to: destruction and death, as unknown enemies of the nation cripple its infrastructure and provoke internal strife—in this case through the blowing up of a railway line carrying supplies to armed forces stationed in the northeast.

The significance of this opening sequence is hard to miss, for after the wars of 1962 and 1965 India followed a more careful policy of border policing. Even more significantly, the 1960s witnessed increasing discontent. Areas like Manipur being under the draconian Armed Forces Special Powers Act (AFSPA) since as early as 1958, and military presence, and militarization, was viewed essential by not just the Indian state, but also the mainstream of the Indian people, the urban nationalist bourgeoisie, for such supposedly disturbed areas. Such positions are premised on an us against them axis, and preclude from their conceptual framework the possibility of discontent being not simply a consequence of external agencies provoking them but, as has been the case with many such insurgencies, a combination of various entrenched socio-historical factors slowly escalating into armed conflict, which then might draw, and receive, support from forces hostile to the nation. Thus, instead of being focused both introspectively inwards as well as attentively outwards, gaze, as is made abundantly clear from the striking opening shot, is to be directed outwards, scrutinizing the unknown unscrupulous other infiltrating and corrupting the motherland.

Such rhetoric consistently informs the action of *Aankhen*. Diwan Chand, leader of the vigilante[26] group sworn against "*mulk ke dushman*" ("enemies of the nation"), repeatedly harks back to the ideals of selfless service and sacrifice for the motherland instilled in him and other veterans of the group during the time served in Netaji Subhash Chandra Bose's Indian National Army. His son, Sunil, consistently puts *farz* (duty) before inclinations of private life and love, putting off the *ikrar-e-ishq* (declaration of love) to his lady love Meenakshi time and again with such statements as "Meenakshi, we're on a mission here, and can't afford the luxury of love and its games."[27] Love invades, and *ishq* (love) for the beloved, the *mashuqa*, fuses with *junoon*, passion, for the *matribhoomi*, the motherland, but in such a way that missions are not compromised, and the supposedly healthy balance of inner-outer, family-country, is finally realized in the concluding shot of the movie wherein Sunil and Meenakshi walk hand-in-hand into the sunset with "Love comes sparingly in life/Hearts get united sparingly in life"[28] playing apropos the earlier prophetic articulation of this happy ending.

The significance of this fusion cannot be overemphasized. Since the late nineteenth century, and increasingly throughout the twentieth, Indian nationalists of different hues and beliefs have conceptualized the nation as mother, Bharat Mata,[29] and seen themselves as its devoted sons. Impulses of a reinvigorated masculinity are not difficult to observe in this, for if the British emasculated most of their Indian subjects by dismissing them as inveterate and unsuited for action and enterprise, revivalists and reformists sought to instill a certain vigor and zest in the youth which would enable them, in their language, to free their mother, Bharat Mata, from shackles of foreign domination. The Indian male, his body a semiotic text, had to become manly in order to free India, and must remain manly to maintain that freedom. Hence, the contrast between the insipid Akram, so hopelessly prey to the charms of Lily—one of Doctor X's many female operatives expressly trained for the purpose of misleading men and then using them as moles—that he betrays his own brother to death. He also betrays the single-mindedly upright and zealous Sunil, whose charms unwittingly attract first Meenakshi and then Zehnab—another operative whose mission as femme fatale turns fateful for her as she falls in love with Sunil. Zehnab betrays the secrets of her gang and suffers death for it. Amongst the various plot twists, Sunil remains above love and worldly desires, going as far as staging his death for his father so as to better effect the capture of enemy gang in their hideout. Also apparent is the lack of familial ties amongst the enemy, Doctor X, Captain and Madam forming their own unit wherein the ties are not blood but of hatred for India, and monetary profit on the side form the basis for togetherness. Since this unit operates subterraneously, through an intricate network of underground tunnels, it further underscores the distinction between the healthy, normal world and lives of Diwan Chand, Sunil and Meenakshi, and the lurking, underground, rodent-like existence of Doctor X and his gang. The very appearance of Doctor X, dressed without fail, day or night, in a uniform loosely evocative of the uniforms of World War I and equipped with that mark of arch-villains, a monocle, invests him with an aura of military aggression that the patriots, defending from, and the core of their newly-found, multi-hued Indianized Modernity, clearly do not have.

The vigilante-spy[30] liquidates these margins: Sunil's job is to spy out these many *desh ke dushman* (enemy of the nation) from their various hideouts and to destroy them one by one. This takes him to Beirut, source of much of the arms and ammunition being smuggled into India, and from there the trail back to India is painstakingly exposed to sight. Of course, the enemies' gaze is on India, and this is nowhere more apparent than in the sequence when taking Captain around the secret hideout Doctor X takes him to the central observation post, the seat of a fake *sadhu* (religiously-minded mendicant), from where the gang keeps watch:

> The soldier in this post can see all around him. The enemy will never be able to take us by surprise. That stone quarry, there, it has many secret tunnels leading to our cellars. On the other side of that hill is the hospital from which you were brought. And from here we can see everything that goes on in the entire city. See, that's the harbour ... we watch each and every ship that comes and goes. And that's the aerodrome, there, and we immediately get to know whenever any flight, civil and military, is made.[31]

The metaphor of sight recurs continuously: Sunil, frustrating observation through a variety of disguises, consistently unearths secrets and sees through deceptions to flush out the enemy into the light of day. His gaze on and around India counters that of operatives like the Doctor, and successfully prevents its borders being breached, and proxy war being carried on. *Aankhen's* appeal seems to lie in exactly this, in banking upon existing societal tensions and widespread, territorial risk perceptions to present a spectacle of threat, aggression and subterfuge in which true, committed patriots transcend the inefficiencies of state to defend the motherland.

As the vigilante, so the spy: Agent Vinod of Deepak Bahry's 1977 *Agent Vinod* is just as patriotic as Gopal of *Farz* and Sunil of *Aankhen*, and fights to save home and hearth from threats external and internal, this time a gang of smugglers who also double up as blackmarketeers, counterfeiters and sabotagers. However, unlike the military minded Supremo of *Farz* and Doctor X of *Aankhen* respectively, JD of *Agent Vinod* is clearly a businessman[32] seeking profit any which way. He has Dr. Ashok Saxena—an Indian scientist who has invented a formula to neutralize radiation from nuclear bombs—kidnapped by his minion Madanlal so as to extract this formula and become the wealthiest man in the world. The ever-present yet invisible external agencies continue to exercise influence and guide action, for as Madanlal announces in the meeting held to plan Dr. Saxena's kidnapping, "Our job is to keep our foreign friends happy. And their express desire is to destroy this country."[33]

Even though the action of *Agent Vinod* is confined locally, specifically around Bombay, it asserts from the beginning that India's enemies are still other nations, external powers bent upon undoing not just the political but also the social and moral fabric of the nation. For if Doctor X planned communal riots, and Meenakshi and Mehmood, dressed as fakirs, going around Beirut singing a song of religious tolerance, JD, in the politically turbulent atmosphere of the mid 1970s, the Emergency years,[34] is content making fake medicines, distilling poisonous liquor,[35] black-marketing foodgrains and executing a few acts of infrastructural sabotage here and there, for the construction contracts to be gained consequently. This is not surprising, for more than a decade since 1965, and half a decade since 1971, the nation's priorities—and attitudes—had changed. The 1971 Indo-Pak War and the 1974 Pokhran test had instilled a confidence in India's capabilities to thwart external aggression, just as the devaluation of the rupee, the nationalization of banks and the crippling of industrial activities due to labor unrest had increased unemployment and given a fillip to the black market and gangsterism in urban centers and gaze now was turned inwards, towards splintering in the social fabric of the nation. The murmurs of the late 1960s were by now clear and loud voices, and as anger spilled onto the silver screen the enemies of the nation turned from grunting Chinamen and antiquated remnants of the Great War to respectably suited businessmen unscrupulously diversifying into all forms of manufacture to precipitate collapse through attrition.

This, then, is the mission Agent Vinod is entrusted with. He must rescue Dr. Saxena and prevent the formula from falling into the proverbial wrong hands. He must also strike a decisive blow to the enemy gang, and defeat their stated aim of destroying the nation. The traditional bogey of external agencies hostile to the nation combines with the increasingly apparent threat of internal dissolution, so that Dr. Saxena's fantastic invention, which would make nuclear power redundant, gets linked with JD's ambitions as a double-dealing gangster to present a believable whole of vulnerability against which zealous, patriotic operatives like Agent Vinod, and Zarina, must silently, invisibly function.

It might be tempting at this stage to consider Agent Vinod as Bond's mere shadow[36] but what gives him a distinctive substance of his own is his acute Indian-ness, a quality not to be found in his clothes or sexual mores or gadgetry, but in the motives of his operation. He iterates constantly, just like Gopal and Sunil, an abiding passion for *watan*, country. So does Zarina, the other secret agent, whose dying words express joy that her blood has been shed for the country, and on whose open grave, after Vinod has finished off Madanlal and gang, the camera zooms in as the following elegiac couplet plays in the background:

Around martyrs' shrines shall be held festivities every year,
For those who die for their country are to be remembered thus.[37]

Zarina is treated as *shaheed*, a martyr, just as Vinod is conceptualized as a son of the soil—flirtatious and reckless, but not so much that he would forget his essential, inerasable Indian-ness, sound loyalty to the motherland, and the values, which uphold its social framework. Thus, in tackling forces threatening the motherland, Vinod strays not too far from the route adopted by his precursor Gopal, whose playboy patriot image may be considered to be one of the inspirations for Vinod. Unlike Gopal and Sunil Vinod seems much less of a family man, the conclusion being a bit more open-ended than what it was for the other two, but the ideal of the patriot ever alert against enemies of the nation is sustained throughout.

Sustained, and carried forward to the next century by re-inventors of Vinod's legacy: Sriram Raghavan's 2012 *Agent Vinod* presents the familiar operative of the mid '70s in a much more cosmopolitan, international light. The movie starts with a pun on names, the first shot being an epigram made of a comment of Tuco Ramirez's, a character from Sergio Leone's 1966 classic *The Good, the Bad and the Ugly*: "One name is as good as another. Not wise to use your name."[38] It moves then to the Dasht-e-Margoh in Afghanistan, where our eponymous hero is imprisoned in a Taliban camp. From there the trail leads on to Russia, Morocco, Pakistan, India and England, as Agent Vinod unravels a conspiracy of almost impossible proportions. A suitcase nuclear bomb, international arms and drugs suppliers and Islamist fundamentalists, all combine to lend Vinod's mission a global aura, which many previous secret services agents lacked.

Nonetheless, the core of his mission is as local, central to the Indian nation-state, as it can be: Vinod has to prevent a nuclear explosion in the capital of the Indian state, New Delhi, and as he hunts down the bomb layers and layers of subterfuge unfold, and suave and alert though he is, the final truth startles him as well. The mastermind behind the conspiracy is none other than Sir Jagdishwar Metla, a multi-billionaire businessman of Indian origin part of a powerful group of financial tycoons and politicians, the Zeus Group, whose aim is to keep the profits rolling and achieve world domination through indirect financial coercion and shutdown. For them a small nuclear explosion would be the starting point towards a time of global peace and one government.

This Caesarian ambition is laid low by Vinod, who orchestrates Sir Metla's assassination by a suicide bomber of the Lashkar-e-Toiba, forestalling thus, even if temporarily, such manifestations of global power from precipitating nuclear war, and also extracting revenge for the chain of events which lead to so many deaths, that of his lady love included. Vinod is ruthless as a killing machine, but he has a heart as well, a heart which he loses without much compunction to a Pakistani doctor turned spy, and which at many other times shows him to be a more humane human at the core, not just a simple killing machine: in the final interview with Sir Metla, he cannot but be anguished as he confronts him with planning the death of millions just to achieve his desires.

In all of this the figure of Vinod per se, the man he is, does not appear as quintessentially Indian as his predecessors did. Unlike them, he does not wear his *deshbhaki* (patriotism) on his sleeve—he does go out to supposed death with a Jai Hind, but not for him the spontaneous bursts of patriotic fervor; again, his own identity remains undisclosed—"better not to use your own name," as the epigram advises. What makes him an appropriate part of this study, then, is not as much the man as his mission: like Gopal, Sunil and his namesake from the previous generation, Agent Vinod, he is exerting himself to save his country, India—that, and not global peace is his aim, though the latter is maintained in its precarious state consequently. The threat is still external, from an increasingly global network of adversaries, who in the post–1990 atmosphere are all unsurprisingly Muslim, with the inevitable, inescapable Pakistani and jihadi thrown in for good measure; the target still, as Diwan Chand had explained Sunil almost half a century ago, *"Hindustan ki democracy aur prajatantra"*[39] (India's democracy).

What makes *Agent Vinod* more intelligent than most other save-the-nation-from-Islamist-terrorist movies[40] is the depth which it displays in its conceptualizations of and engagements with the other, in this case the much hated, suspected Pakistani covert operative. Relations between India and Pakistan have been more or less strained since the beginning of militancy in the early 1990s, and a host of terror strikes in the past two decades, to say nothing of the Kargil War of 1999, have naturalized a suspicion and paranoia which considers the Pakistani as enemy, in much the same way the Chinese was in the 1960s. *Agent Vinod*, while presenting the enemy as consistently Muslim, and Pakistani, also humanizes that stereotype. First, Vinod falls in love with a Pakistani, so much so that he decides to leave secret services to realize her dream of a normal bourgeois life. Second, both Lt. Gen. Iftekhar Ahmed, the Director-General of Pakistan's intelligence gathering agency, the Inter-Services Intelligence, and Alay Khan, Pakistan's High Commissioner to India, are shown to be willing to cooperate with India in times of emergency, though the former is shot dead by his own staff for his sympathies. However, what is significant is that the enemy here is not one person, one group or one communal or ethnic identity: the agents might all be Muslims, but the mastermind, their supremo, is the unlikely aged multi-billionaire, and his other powerful friends of the Zeus Group. The fact that operatives like Abu Sayyed Nazer, David Kazan, and Jimmy are all Muslims, then, is not Islamophobia, not the text banking upon that for success; it is, instead, part of Sir Metla's "smart idea":

> The bomb blast in Delhi would've been your doing, but the world would've thought that terrorist groups like Laskhar were behind it. That's why Colonel used people like Abu, Kazan, Jimmy and Huzefa, got jihad stamped over all of this. You would've earned billions by starting war between the two countries [i.e., India and Pakistan].[41]

Fittingly, then, the enemy in this contemporary context of increasingly hegemonic business houses and monopolized finance capital is the businessman, not the ideologically driven religious fundamentalist. The target can be any other place, any other people, but Vinod's mission is India, his directive to protect the land from forces opposed to it, and not, as British and American spies often do, dabble in international affairs a bit far removed from homeland security. Thus, even if not as poetically inclined as his namesake, Vinod remains as much the son of the soil as he was in his previous avatar.

As established through these case studies, the Indian secret services operative is almost always cast in the role of the patriotic son of the soil whose exertions arise as much out of a sense of devotion to the motherland as duty to his agency. More contemporary figures like Agent Vinod of the 2012 *Agent Vinod* appear more detached from patriotic fervor as they exercise their license to kill, but their missions and exertions are all part of watching over, and protecting, the nation: the nature of the threat changes, as does its source and reach, but *watan* continues to be the guiding inspiration and object of one's *farz*. Relying on stock images and banking on the expected, these spies enliven the bourgeois nationalist's fantasy of masculine guardianship, channelizing successfully the anger of that class against failures of and corruptions within established state mechanisms into the patriotic machinations of healthy male bodies whose exertions as spy and vigilante rescue the body politic from dire, larger-than-life threats.

For even though the spy is part of the state, and working for the state, his invisibility within the state apparatus lends him an agency which can be utilized for the expenditure of that patriotic anger: of rescue, and establishment of orderly financial mobility and decency which, as hallmarks of bourgeois life, become the stamp of bourgeois nationhood and nationality as well. In as much as a nation is a community of objectivized, impersonalized individuals held together only by interests and ideals much more imagined and constructed than received and tangible in any sense, and that the discursive paraphernalia and apparatuses it consolidates and propagates itself with are necessarily top-heavy, the spy in Bombay cinema discursively reasserts not just the legitimacy, but also the expediency of these interests and ideals: to stay together, to fight for the nation not simply because survival necessitates it, but because patriotism demands it, and there can be no survival outside, or without, the existing nationalistic framework. Thus, the fear of decentralization or fragmentation vis-à-vis an ethos of risk and vulnerability of that which is being increasingly challenged by destabilizing, anarchic forces is addressed, and the legitimacy of the nation-state, as the only discourse capable of effectively ordering individual lives, vicariously established through spectacles of blood, subterfuge and eleventh-hour Samaritanism.

Notes

1. The usage of "Bollywood" here takes cognizance of the various contestations on the naming of the Bombay film industry, and is more a matter of convenience than a corollary of ignorance.

2. Benedict Anderson, *Imagined Communities: Reflections on the Origin and Spread of Nationalism* (New York: Verso, 2006), 7.

3. Wimal Dissanayake, "Introduction: Nationhood, History, and Cinema: Reflections on the Asian Scene," in *Colonialism and Nationalism in Asian Cinema* (Bloomington: Indiana University Press, 1994), xiii.

4. It therefore becomes essential that Spider Man lives up to his responsibilities as a super-hero because America needs him in times of peril. Similarly, Krissh in Mumbai must fight hoodlums and cleanse the city of evil forces lest crime and sin become rampant.

5. Raminder Kaur and Ajay J. Sinha, "Bollyworld: An Introduction to Popular Indian Cinema Through a Transnational Lens," in *Bollyworld: Popular Indian Cinema Through a Transnational Lens*, ed. by Raminder Kaur and Ajay J. Sinha (New Delhi: Sage, 2005), 12.

6. "*Mera joota hai Jaapani,/ Hai patloon inglistani,/ Sar pe lal topi Roosi,/ Phir bhi dil hai Hindustani*" ("My shoe is Japanese,/ These trousers English/ That cap on my head Russian/ Yet my heart remains Indian" [translation ours]). Shailendra, *Mera joota hai Jaapani*, Saregama CDF 120025 DP, 2012, compact disc. The concluding refrain of this verse, "*Phir bhi dil hai*

Hindustani," encapsulates the spirit of a core nationality of this nation-in-progress so well that it remains to date one of the most popular slogans of Indian-ness.

7. "*Zara hatt ke, zara bach ke/ Ye hai Bombay, meri jaan*" ("Be cautious, be aware/ This is Bombay, my dear"). Majrooh Sultanpuri, *Aye dil hai mushkil jeena yahan*, Ultra VCD No 2832, 2013, compact disc.

8. Valentina Vitali, *Hindi Action Cinema: Industries, Narratives, Bodies* (New Delhi: Oxford University Press, 2008), xviii.

9. Empire cinema is consciously skirted in this commentary; Prem Chowdhry's 2000 text on this aspect of Indian cinema provides interesting insights into the politics of cinematic texts imported to, as well as allowed in, colonial India.

10. Vitali, *Hindi Action Cinema*, 19–20.

11. Ibid., 11.

12. Ibid., 23.

13. Athleticism relates closely to images and ideals of nationhood and nation-building in the Indian subcontinent, for both reformists and revolutionaries sought to legitimize claims to self-sufficiency and freedom by presenting a pan–Indian hyper-masculinity as the appropriate response to the British dismissal of Indians as weak, feeble and dissolute.

14. Unsurprisingly, Ramamurthy himself preferred being styled as "the Modern Bhima," modeling himself on that enduring subcontinental ideal of super-human physical strength and manly boorishness, than on the Grecian Hercules. For more on this, refer to Vitali, *Hindi Action Cinema*, 27.

15. Vitali, *Hindi Action Cinema*, 119.

16. Koushik Banerjea, "'Fight Club': Aesthetics, Hybridisation and the Construction of Rogue Masculinities in *Sholay* and *Deewar*," in *Bollyworld: Popular Indian Cinema Through a Transnational Lens*, ed. by Raminder Kaur and Ajay J. Sinha (New Delhi: Sage, 2005), 163.

17. Vitali, *Hindi Action Cinema*, 123.

18. Banerjea, "'Fight Club,'" 165.

19. Hindustani here referring, generically, to the Hindavi language group whose many varieties are the lingua franca of much of the Indian subcontinent—and which has been the language of the Bombay industry.

20. The Zhongshan, or Mao, suit that Supremo is always seen to be attired in, combined with the recent memories of the dramatic loss of soldiers and territory to Mao's China, seems this the logical conclusion.

21. J.P. Dalvi, *Himalayan Blunder: The Curtain-raiser to the Sino-Indian War of 1962* (Bombay: Thacker & Company, 1969), i.

22. Anand Bakshi, *Mast baharon ka main aashiq*, Priya PVCD 978, 2013, compact disc.

23. Anand Bakshi, *Hum toh tere aashiq hain*, Priya PVCD 978, 2013, compact disc.

24. Swaralipi Nandi and Esha Chatterjee, "Introduction: Violence, Cinema and the Post-colonial Masculine," in *Spectacles of Blood: A Study of Masculinity and Violence in Post-Colonial Films* (New Delhi: Zubaan, 2012), 7.

25. Ramanand Sagar, "*Uss mulk ki sarhad ko koi chu nahi sakta/ Jiss mulk ki sarhad ki nighebaan hain aakheni.*" In *Aankhen*, DVD, directed by Ramanand Sagar (1968; New Delhi: Moser Baer, 2013).

26. The vigilante comes in many hues and forms, underlining a certain core of patriotic, nationalistic values, which state mechanisms, riddled with corruption, are not able to stay true to. The ordinary-man-turned-messiah Mr. India figure of Shekhar Kapur's 1987 *Mr. India* and the warrior-of-the-night Shahenshah figure of Tinnu Anand's 1988 *Shahenshah* are just two of many notable examples. In more recent times, The Common Man, enacted by Naseeruddin Shah, in Neeraj Pandey's 2008 *A Wednesday!* may be considered as evidence of the range and depth of the vigilante in Indian cinema.

27. Ramanand Sagar, "*Meenakshi, hum yahan mission par aaye hain. Na toh humare paas*

kisi ki mohabbat ka waqt hai, na hi kisi ki mohabbat pe jalne ka." In *Aankhen*, DVD, directed by Ramanand Sagar (1968; New Delhi: Moser Baer, 2013).

28. Sahir Ludhivani, *Milti hai zindagi mein mohabbat kabhi kabhi,/ Hoti hai dilbaron ki inayat kabhi kabhi,* Moser Baer PDVD A 009, 2013, compact disc.

29. The cult of Bharat Mata underwent a dramatic metamorphosis from her birth towards the closure of the nineteenth century, experiencing gradual deification with Abanindranath Tagore's iconic 1905 painting, and then progressively becoming the site of an aggressive nationalism with the rise of fundamentalist Hindu forces. *Aankhen* incorporates a secularism which gives no space to partisan sentiments of the religious kind, but references to motherland, and Diwan Chand and Sunil's unabated zeal, cannot but evoke the hyper-patriotic vocabulary of Bharat Mata.

30. Much of Bombay cinema presents this supposed genre muddle, of the operative being both vigilante and spy, and often being none and yet being as patriotic as both can be. *Jasoosi*, investigation, being part of what the spy does, a range of police officers, private detectives, army personnel, crime reporters have exercised their duty to the nation by intelligence gathering, surveillance and counter-surveillance, without institutionally being spies. Vijay Anand's 1967 *Jewel Thief,* Pachi's 1974 *International Crook* and Shakti Samanta's 1979 *The Great Gambler* are only some examples.

31. Ramanand Sagar, "*Iss chowki par baitha hua sipahi charon taraf dekh sakta hai. Dushman humpar kabhi bhi achanak humla nahi kar sakta. Yeh patthar torhne ki quaary hai, yahan bahut se khufiya raste humare tehkhane ki taraf jaate hain. Iss pahari ke peeche woh khairati haspatal hai, jahan se aap laaye gaye hain. Aur yahan se hum dekh sakte hain ke saare sheher mein kya ho raha hai. Woh bandargah ... hum har aane-jaane waale jahaz par poori-poori nazar rakh sakte hain. Woh hai hawai-adda, wahan se civil aur military ki jitni flights hoti hain, hume phauran pata chal jaata hai.*" In *Aankhen*, DVD, directed by Ramanand Sagar (1968; New Delhi: Moser Baer, 2013).

32. The villain in much of Indian cinema, particularly action thrillers, can be distinguished by the spectacular other-ness which his garb and personality enact, as well as the location of their hideouts, or headquarters, which are almost always subterranean, inaccessible, and outside the pale of the everyday bourgeois. Hence, JD, and later Sir Metla, being impeccably dressed in business suits, respectable members of the community operating out of feted financial districts lends the discovery of their villainy an added nefariousness which, by associative polarization, accords more virtue to the covert operative as the detector, and destroyer, of their plans. On a different note, more than Supremo and Doctor X, Shakal, the tech-savvy bald crime lord of Ramesh Sippy's 1980 *Shaan*, Mogambo, the militaristic megalomaniac of Shekhar Kapur's 1987 *Mr. India* and Kancha Cheena, bald, sadistic drug lord of Karan Malhotra's 2012 *Agneepath*, may be considered archetypes.

33. Girish, and Khalid Narvi, "*Humara maksad hai apne videshi doston ko khush rakhna. Aur unka maksad: Iss mulk ko tabha-o-barbaad karna.*" In *Agent Vinod,* VCD, directed by Deepak Bahry (1977; New Delhi: Moser Baer, 2013).

34. The nineteen-month-long National Emergency of 1975–77 had varying effects on Indian cinema, witnessing, most interestingly, an increase in the number of productions due to greater flow of finance in the black market, establishing smuggling and gang activities, and action melodramas, such as Yash Chopra's 1975 *Deewar*, as acceptable consumption for middle class audiences.

35. In Prakash Mehra's 1973 *Zanjeer*, De Silva becomes police informer to avenge the death of his three sons, who died on Christmas night by drinking illegally produced liquor, which turned out to be poisonous. Hence, as for Teja, so for JD—and so, too, for Agent Vinod, savior-vigilante à la Inspector Vijay Khanna.

36. Bond aficionados might be forgiven for doing so momentarily: Vinod has a girl hanging on his arm, but he sings, not sleeps, with her; then again, he breaks often—perhaps a bit too often—into *shayari*, to flirt or to affront, and it is difficult to imagine Bond composing cou-

plets spontaneously. There is also the typical high-speed car chase, but Vinod's car squirts water and smoke, with not a sign of missiles and bullets. Yet, *Agent Vinod* incorporates a self-reflexivity which comments on the Bond phenomenon, caricaturing him through Vinod's sidekick Chandu, who, as the country bumpkin, poses as 007, and which imparts Vinod a distinguishing distance from his slightly more famous British counterpart.

    37. Girish, and Khalid Narvi, "*Shaheedon ke mazaron par lagenge har baras mele,/ Watan pe mitne waalon ka yehi baaki nishaan hoga.*" In *Agent Vinod*, VCD, directed by Deepak Bahry (1977; New Delhi: Moser Baer, 2013).

    38. *The Good, the Bad and the Ugly*, DVD, directed by Sergio Leone (1966; Santa Monica: MGM Home Entertainment LLC, 2004).

    39. Ramanand Sagar, "*Hindustan ki democracy aur prajatantra.*" In *Aankhen*, DVD, directed by Ramanand Sagar (1968; New Delhi: Moser Baer, 2013).

    40. A sub-genre thickly populated with many dualistic, polarizing Sunny Deol starrers, *Indian* (2001), *Maa Tujhe Salaam* (2002) and *The Hero: Love Story of a Spy* (2003), being some of them.

    41. Arjit Biswas and Shriram Raghavan. "*Dilli mein bomb explode karte aap, aur duniya ko lagta ke Lashkar jaise kissi terrorist group ka kaam hai. Issi liye Colonel ne Abu, Kazan, Jimmy aur Huzefa jaise logon ka istamal kiya, har jagah jihad ka jhanda garha. Dono deshon ke beech jang cherh kar arbon kamate aap.*" *Agent Vinod*, DVD, directed by Sriram Raghavan (2012; Mumbai: Eros International, 2013).

Bibliography

Aankhen. DVD. Directed by Ramanand Sagar. 1968; New Delhi: Moser Baer, 2013.

Agent Vinod. VCD. Directed by Deepak Bahry. 1977; New Delhi: Moser Baer, 2013.

Agent Vinod. DVD. Directed by Sriram Raghavan. 2012; Mumbai: Eros International, 2013.

Anderson, Benedict. *Imagined Communities: Reflections on the Origin and Spread of Nationalism*. New York: Verso, 2006.

Bakshi, Anand. *Hum toh tere aashiq hain*. Priya PVCD 978, 2013, compact disc.

_____. *Mast baharon ka main aashiq*. Priya PVCD 978, 2013, compact disc.

Basu, Anustup. "The Geo-Televisual in the Age of the All-India Film (1947–88)." In *Bollywood in the Age of New Media: The Geo-televisual Aesthetic*, 54–70. Edinburgh: Edinburgh University Press, 2010.

Banerjea, Koushik. "'Fight Club': Aesthetics, Hybridisation and the Construction of Rogue Masculinities in *Sholay* and *Deewar*." In *Bollyworld: Popular Indian Cinema Through a Transnational Lens*, edited by Raminder Kaur and Ajay J. Sinha, 163–85. New Delhi: Sage, 2005.

Bhabha, Homi K. "DisseminNation: Time, Narrative, and the Margins of the Modern Nation." In *Nation and Narration*, edited by Homi K. Bhabha, 291–322. London: Routledge, 1990.

_____. "Introduction: Narrating the Nation." In *Nation and Narration*, edited by Homi K. Bhabha, 1–7. London: Routledge, 1990.

Chadha, Kalyani, and Anandam P. Kavoori. "Exoticized, Marginalised, Demonized: The Muslim 'Other' in Indian Cinema." In *Global Bollywood*, edited by Anandam P. Kavoori and Aswin Punathambekar, 131–45. New Delhi: Oxford University Press, 2008.

Chowdhry, Prem. "Introduction." In *Colonial India and the Making of Empire Cinema: Image, Ideology and Identity*, 1–28. New York: Manchester University Press, 2000.

Dalvi, J.P. *Himalayan Blunder: The Curtain-raiser to the Sino-Indian War of 1962*. Bombay: Thacker & Company, 1969.

Deshpande, Sudhanva. "The Consumable Hero of Globalised India." In *Bollyworld: Popular Indian Cinema Through a Transnational Lens*, edited by Raminder Kaur and Ajay J. Sinha, 186–203. New Delhi: Sage, 2005.

Dissanyake, Wimal. "Introduction: Nationhood, History, and Cinema: Reflections on the Asian Scene." In *Colonialism and Nationalism in Asian Cinema,* ix–xxix. Bloomington: Indiana University Press, 1994.

Farz. VCD. Directed by Ravikant Nagaich. 1967; New Delhi: Priya Video Private Limited, 2013.

Juluri, Vamsee. "Our Violence, Their Violence: Exploring the Emotional and Relational Matrix of Terrorist Cinema." In *Global Bollywood,* edited by Anandam P. Kavoori and Aswin Punathambekar, 117–30. New Delhi: Oxford University Press, 2008.

Kaur, Raminder, and Ajay J. Sinha. "Bollyworld: An Introduction to Popular Indian Cinema Through a Transnational Lens." In *Bollyworld: Popular Indian Cinema Through a Transnational Lens,* edited by Raminder Kaur and Ajay J. Sinha, 11–32. New Delhi: Sage, 2005.

Kesavan, Mukul. "Cine Qua Non: An Undergraduate History of Hindi Cinema." In *The Ugliness of the Indian Male and Other Propositions,* 9–18. Ranikhet: Permanent Black, 2008.

Ludhivani, Sahir. *Milti hai zindagi mein mohabbat kabhi kabhi.* Moser Baer PDVD A 009, 2013, compact disc.

Mitry, Jean. "The Image and Perceived Reality." In *Semiotics and the Analysis of Films,* translated by Christopher King, 37–58. London: The Athlone Press, 2000.

_____. "The Shot." In *Semiotics and the Analysis of Films,* translated by Christopher King, 59–90. London: The Athlone Press, 2000.

Nandi, Swaralipi, and Esha Chatterjee. "Introduction: Violence, Cinema and the Postcolonial Masculine." In *Spectacles of Blood: A Study of Masculinity and Violence in Post-Colonial Films,* edited by Swaralipi Nandi and Esha Chatterjee, 6–18. New Delhi: Zubaan, 2012.

Rajadhyaksha, Ashish. "The 'Bollywoodization' of the Indian Cinema: Cultural Nationalism in a Global Arena." In *City Flicks: Indian Cinema and the Urban Experience,* edited by Preben Kaarsholm, 113–39. Calcutta: Seagull Books, 2004.

Renan, Ernest. "What Is a Nation?" In *Nation and Narration,* edited by Homi K. Bhabha, 8–22. London: Routledge, 1991.

Satpati, Sayantani, and Samiparna Samanta. "Digging the Underworld Narrative: Revisiting Masculinity in Indian Films." In *Spectacles of Blood: A Study of Masculinity and Violence in Post-Colonial Films,* edited by Swaralipi Nandi and Esha Chatterjee, 126–44. New Delhi: Zubaan, 2012.

Schafer, David J., and Kavita Karan. "Introduction: Bollywood and Globalization: Researching Popular Hindi Cinema Through the Lens of Film Flows." In *Bollywood and Globalization: The Global Power of Popular Hindi Cinema,* edited by David J. Schaefer and Kavita Karan, 1–12. Abingdon: Routledge, 2013.

Shailendra. *Mera joota hai Jaapani.* Saregama CDF 120025 DP, 2012, compact disc.

Sultanpuri, Majrooh. *Aye dil hai mushkil jeena yahan.* Ultra VCD No 2832, 2013, compact disc.

The Good, the Bad and the Ugly. DVD. Directed by Sergio Leone. 1966; Santa Monica: MGM Home Entertainment LLC, 2004.

Thomas, Rosie. "Not Quite (Pearl) White: Fearless Nadia, Queen of the Stunts." In *Bollyworld: Popular Indian Cinema Through a Transnational Lens,* edited by Raminder Kaur and Ajay J. Sinha, 35–69. New Delhi: Sage, 2005.

Vasudevan, Ravi. "The Exhilaration of Dread: Genre, Narrative Form and Film Style in Contemporary Urban Action Films." In *City Flicks: Indian Cinema and the Urban Experience,* edited by Preben Kaarsholm, 223–36. Calcutta: Seagull Books, 2004.

_____. "The Meanings of 'Bollywood': The Many Forms of Hindi Cinema." In *Beyond the Boundaries of Bollywood,* edited by Rachel Dwyer and Jerry Pinto, 3–29. New Delhi: Oxford University Press, 2011.

Vitali, Valentina. *Hindi Action Cinema: Industries, Narratives, Bodies.* New Delhi: Oxford University Press, 2008.

Part Two

Television

Mr. Bond's Neighborhood

Domesticating the Superspy for American Television

Cynthia W. Walker

To domesticate: To train (someone) to behave in an appropriate way at home (such as by using good manners, being polite, being helpful, etc.); to make domestic: Fit for domestic life; to bring to the level of ordinary people.—Merriam-Webster online dictionary[1]

The Living Room Spy

It was the fall of 1965. A year earlier, the third James Bond film, *Goldfinger* (1964, Guy Hamilton), had appeared, breaking box office records and making Sean Connery a bona fide international star.[2] Now a fourth Bond film, *Thunderball* (1965, Terence Young), was just over the horizon. Bond's counterpart on U.S. television, *The Man from U.N.C.L.E.* (1964–1968), was also hitting its peak in popularity. Like the Bond films, the television series had built slowly after nearly suffering cancellation in the first half of its first season. However, as it began its second season on NBC on Fridays at 10 p.m. *The Man from U.N.C.L.E.* was a success story, earning a 44 share in the Nielsen ratings and attracting nearly half the audience tuned in at that time period.[3] The stars, Robert Vaughn who played Napoleon Solo, and David McCallum, who played his Russian sidekick, Illya Kuryakin, were mobbed by crowds of young fans everywhere they went. *TV Guide* proclaimed Illya "the greatest thing since peanut butter and jelly."[4] Even the visiting Beatles wanted to meet them.[5] "U.N.C.L.E.mania," along with the big-screen "Bondmania," was in full swing.

In the midst of what *Life* magazine called "the great spy scramble,"[6] *Photoplay* magazine published a fantasy wish-fulfillment article, pitting Sean Connery's "bedroom spy" against Robert Vaughn's "living room spy."[7] In the Connery/Bond section of the narrative, most of the action takes place, not surprisingly, in a bedroom. The emphasis is on sexuality and Connery's "diamond-in-the rough" dark, aggressive, and vaguely menacing masculinity. Connery enters with "the slim-hipped grace of a panther on the prowl." His eyebrows are "ferocious," his ears are "wolf-like," his hands are large, strong and "ham-sized,"[8] and there is a small scar on his left cheekbone, an echo of the facial scar of the literary Bond. The reaction of the fictional woman, an identity figure for the readers, is to first swallow a little scream, blush, experience a powerful heart flutter, and then to escape, if briefly, to the kitchen by volunteering to get Connery/Bond a beer. Even during the conversation that follows, Connery/Bond remains dominant and in control, polite, even occasionally warm, but distant and ultimately unattainable.

By comparison, Vaughn/Solo first meets the reader's identity figure in her own living room. Charming, witty, and intelligent, with Vaughn/Solo, the emphasis is on a kind of accommodating sophistication. He slips into the kitchen to prepare special sandwiches and vegetable juice cocktails, and then sits down companionably to talk about his life, past and present. Despite his difficult childhood and the fact that he's currently a swinging bachelor in Hollywood, Vaughn/Solo confides that he has plans to marry some day and have a family.

Judging from the photographs accompanying the article and the way the narratives are written, Vaughn apparently allowed the reporter far greater access to his home and himself than Connery did. The images of Connery/Bond are stock photos and the passages appear to be stitched together from scenes from Bond movies and old anecdotes. By contrast, Vaughn/Solo is photographed inside and outside his own home in the Hollywood Hills, and his passages seem to be based on information gathered during an actual interview.

Nevertheless, the fantasy scenarios placed side by side are revealing. Connery/Bond is formidable, even threatening, and larger-than-life. Vaughn/Solo is friendly and comfortable with an easy-going intimacy and an occasional hint of vulnerability. The contrast recalls the distinction that Marshall McLuhan made between "hot" and "cool" media. For McLuhan, film, like print, was "hot": all-encompassing and dream-like, a magic carpet of fantasy that cast a spell. "The business of the writer or the filmmaker," McLuhan wrote, "is to transfer the reader or viewer from one world, his own, to another, the world created by typography and film."[9] By comparison, television was "cool," a casual and intimate "close-up" environment that invited active participation and closure. McLuhan pointed out that movie stars, better suited to the "hot" medium of the big screen, did not do well on television. "Anybody whose appearance declares his role and status in life is wrong for TV," McLuhan observed. "Anybody who looks as if he might be a teacher, a doctor, a businessman, or any of a dozen other things all at the same time is right for TV."[10]

It would seem, then, that the fictional spy, who must look and act ordinary but is never quite what she or he appears to be, might be ideally suited to television. However, for a variety of reasons, this has generally not been the case. Despite some notable exceptions, spies and secret agents have never been as popular, successful, or ubiquitous on American television as cowboys, doctors, police officers and detectives.[11] Part of the problem is simply logistics. Until the suspension of the Code of Practices for Television Broadcasters in 1983 and the subsequent increase in competition from premium cable stations, it was difficult to adapt the sure-fire Bondian formula of "sex, snobbery and sadism"[12] to mainstream commercial programming. Limited budgets did not allow for lush, expensive, technologically impressive interiors like those designed for the Bond films by Ken Adam, nor for shooting in far-flung exotic locations. Some programs managed to adapt. For example, both *The Man* and *The Girl from U.N.C.L.E.* (1966–1967) and, more recently, *Alias* (2001–2006) took advantage of the standing sets of sprawling studio back lots and local sites in surrounding Los Angeles. In the early 1950s, *Foreign Intrigue* (1951–1955, also known as *Dateline Europe*) restricted itself to shooting in Stockholm with side trips to Paris. *I Spy* (1965–1968) traveled overseas as well, but filmed a number of episodes in each country it visited. *The Prisoner* (1967–1968) was shot at an actual resort village at the Hotel Portmeiron in North Wales. *Adderly* (1986–1988) and later *La Femme Nikita* (1997–2001) employed and redressed Canadian locations to mimic settings in the Soviet Union and other European countries.

The sex and sadism elements of the formula were more problematic. With sex, innuendo could be substituted for actual activity. Similarly, violence could be simulated or minimized through sleep darts and other devices substituting for bullets, weird Perils of Pauline–type torture set-ups, and elaborately choreographed and occasionally even humorous fight scenes, what George Gerbner called, "happy violence."[13]

Still, in the end, perhaps the problem lies in the character of the spy him (or her) self. John G. Cawelti and Bruce A. Rosenberg identify two breeds of spies, romantic and realistic,[14] a binary that has been more playfully labeled elsewhere as "tuxes" and "trench coats."[15] If McLuhan is correct, it is possible that the flamboyant, colorful, globe-trotting adventurer perfected by Ian Fleming is simply too incredible, too larger-than-life—too "hot"—for television, while the ordinary-looking, morally ambiguous "grey men" of Eric Ambler, Graham Green and John Le Carré may be so cool as to be, in the long haul, too boring and uninteresting.

In order for a television series to become successful, more than any other element, characterization is key. Viewers must be attracted to, and become invested in, the characters, and be willing to invite them every week into their living rooms.[16] In order for that to happen, over the years, creators of espionage-themed series have employed and perfected three main strategies: (1) blurring and even eliminating the boundaries between spying and everyday life, especially life set in suburbia; (2) featuring women in more prominent roles, not only as key or supporting characters, but as heroines in their own right; and (3) developing and emphasizing personal back stories and multiple relationships for the secret agents that often include complicated and dysfunctional families. It is these three strategies that have become more common to espionage stories on television than in either film or print, particularly in more recent years, and the details of how and the reasons why will be explored in this essay.

The Spies Next Door

Although the spy story in American literature is often traced back to James Fenimore Cooper's *The Spy* (1821), the modern espionage story really begins in the early 20th century with James Buchan, author of *The Thirty-Nine Steps*, (1915) and other "clubmen" writers, whose main characters were "talented amateurs," decent, honorable gentlemen caught up in what Rudyard Kipling called "the Great Game."[17] Their adversaries were, borrowing from the romantic adventure tradition, foreign in both race and culture, shadowy and exotic. With the rise of fascism and the coming of World War II, fictional spies became less romanticized, more realistic and more morally complex. However, after the war ended, Ian Fleming's James Bond arrived on the scene to reinvent the professional secret agent as a sexy, globe-trotting, Martini-drinking, tuxedo-wearing, technology-equipped superhero. As before, there was a rebalancing of fantasy and realism, and Mr. Kiss-Kiss Bang-Bang was soon joined by the anti–Bondian figures such as John Le Carré's Alex Limas and George Smiley.[18] On television, fictional spies have followed a similar trajectory. During the 1950s, the first spies to arrive on television were reminiscent of the early twentieth century clubmen. In *Passport to Danger* (1954–1955), Caesar Romero was a suave diplomatic courier. *Biff Baker* (1952–1953), played by Alan Hale, was a traveling import/export dealer. *The Hunter* (1952–1954) starred Barry Nelson as an American businessman with a talent for disguises. Nelson would also portray a brash, weirdly Americanized "Jimmy Bond" in a one-hour adaptation of Fleming's first novel, "Casino Royale," for *Climax Theater* (1954). With one exception (Biff Baker was married and traveled with his wife), all of these series featured single, attractive, financially secure white males who traveled for work and dabbled in espionage now and again. They chain-smoked and indulged in snappy patter much like the more familiar private eye, flirted with femme fatales and inhabited mostly static interiors with an occasional foray into foggy alleyways and dimly-lit streets. To give the episodes more of a gloss of authenticity, the action was sometimes enhanced with newsreel footage or hard-boiled narrative voiceover.

Sprinkled among these adventurous businessmen were a few professional agents. *Doorway to Danger* (1951–1953), *Dangerous Assignment* (1951–1952), *The Man Called X* (1955–1956), *Behind Closed Doors* (1958–1959), and an anthology series, *I Spy* (1955–56), hosted by Raymond Massey, all featured a quasi-documentary style and their 30-minute episodes drew from real-life espionage cases. But few of these series ever really connected with audiences and most were syndicated and short-lived, lasting an average of 39 episodes.[19]

The exception and the first hit series to feature an espionage theme was *I Led Three Lives* (1953–1956). Based on the true story of Herbert A. Philbrick, a Boston advertising executive who infiltrated the Communist party to provide information to the F.B.I., *I Led Three Lives* shared many of the motifs of the other spy series. It was shot in a black and white, had a quasi-documentary style and narrative voiceover. But unlike the other series, the outdoor locations were not only real, but recognizably average American streets and neighborhoods.[20] Philbrick, played by Richard Carlson, was neither a romantic amateur nor a traditionally trench-coated pro. He was a regular guy, a suburban dad with five children and a wife who cooked him dinners of "pot roast and brown potatoes."[21] Often on the verge of being exposed, Philbrick shared his thoughts in a first-person interior narrative that was a tremulous mix of angst and fortitude. Sometimes Philbrick bristled at his government handlers; other times, he dripped with disgust for the Reds and Commies who were threatening his family, his home, his country and his middle-class way of life. Philbrick's paranoia was intense but justified because the enemy was apparently everywhere. Communist spies could be anyone, from a telephone solicitor fronting a fake charity at Christmas to a visiting ten-year-old girl. By May 1954, the series was carried by 157 stations and was listed among the top ten television shows in the U.S. Fans ranged from J. Edgar Hoover to Lee Harvey Oswald.[22]

Six years later, when producer Norman Felton met with a group of advertising executives and was asked to come up with a James Bond–like series for television, he dreamed up a "mysterious man" who was average-looking but witty, intelligent and resourceful, an undercover superspy who reported to the Secretary General of the United Nations. To accomplish his missions (called "affairs"), this secret agent would recruit ordinary folks —"innocents"— folks not unlike Herbert Philbrick to aid him.[23]

The concept that would become *The Man from U.N.C.L.E.* went through many changes before it finally premiered in September 1964. For example, for a short time, Ian Fleming was involved, then sold his rights away for the sum of one pound.[24] Later, for legal reasons, producer/writer Sam Rolfe, who developed the series, changed the U.N. to a mythical international intelligence organization whose sprawling technologically advanced headquarters was tucked neatly behind the façade of a seedy tailor shop on the East Side of Manhattan. Nevertheless, from the pilot episode, "The Vulcan Affair," in which Robert Vaughn's Napoleon Solo teams up with an "ordinary housewife" played by Patricia Crowley, for the next three and a half years farm girls, school teachers, college students, stewardesses, librarians, secretaries, social workers, beauticians, nurses, and even a few children would be impressed into service to leave their humdrum lives behind and save the world. "If we were going to have a [hero] who was a superman," Felton explained in later years, "it was good to have someone the average person could identify with."[25] Of course, the world of *The Man from U.N.C.L.E.* was very different from the world of the 1950s spies. Indeed, it was different from that of other more serious espionage-themed shows of the time like *Danger Man* (1960–1962, renamed *Secret Agent* in the U.S., 1964–1968), *I Spy*, and *Mission: Impossible* (1966–1973). Notably, the Cold War and the threat of Communism was no longer a concern. The U.N.C.L.E. organization was multinational and Solo's partner, Illya Kuryakin, was a Russian. The pace was also faster, the images more colorful, youthful, and modern, with gadgets, gimmicks, and fashionable consumer products everywhere, positioning the show as part of the so-called "Pop" movement.[26]

Yet, despite the distinct and obvious differences in style and sensibility, *The Man from U.N.C.L.E.* and *I Led Three Lives* have, surprisingly, a number of elements in common. *U.N.C.L.E.*'s earliest episodes begin with a documentary-like prologue in which an authoritative narrator (not unlike the one at the opening of *I Led Three Lives*) explains the organization and takes us into the New York headquarters. Eventually, we meet Solo, Kuryakin, and their superior, Alexander Waverly, who break the fourth wall and introduce themselves, making a connection with the audience. Because outdoor and action scenes in the series were often photographed using a handheld Arriflex camera, the black and white episodes of the first season have a film noir quality much like the 1950s spy series. One of the more charming aspects of *U.N.C.L.E.* in all its seasons is that while the agents battle extraordinary, even campy threats like earthquake machines, deadly hiccup gas, and killer bees, they also discuss routine concerns like annual operating budgets, personal expense accounts, and health insurance.

Both series also invited viewers to imagine themselves as spies. As Cawelti and Rosenberg point out, clandestinity, which includes voyeurism, the ability to be invisible and hide in plain sight and the thrill of license, can be an appealing fantasy. There is also the powerful attraction of living in a secret liminal world that exists side by side with the so-called real one.[27] Taking their cue from the popularity of *U.N.C.L.E.*, other television shows began to portray their own characters becoming involved with spies. For example, popular situation comedies such as *The Beverly Hillbillies* (1962–1971) and *The Dick Van Dyke Show* (1961–1966) had spy-themed episodes. Vaughn and McCallum appeared as Solo and Kuryakin, albeit briefly, in an episode of *Please Don't Eat the Daisies* (1965–1967) which starred Pat Crowley who had paired with Vaughn in the U.N.C.L.E. pilot.[28] A new sitcom, *The Double Life of Henry Phyfe* (1966) offered Red Buttons as a mild-mannered accountant recruited to impersonate a dangerous now deceased operative, thus putting a comedic spin on the *I Led Three Lives* scenario. It survived less than a year. On the other hand, *Get Smart* (1965–1970) created by Mel Brooks and Buck Henry, spoofed *U.N.C.L.E.*'s complex organization, cleverly disguised gadgetry, and outrageous megalomaniac villains rather than the innocent/professional formula and enjoyed great success in its own right.

By the end of the dawn of the 1970s, the spy boom was over. Mimicking *U.N.C.L.E.* but without the innocents or the Pop aesthetic, spy series like *The Delphi Bureau* (1972–1973) and *Search* (1972–1973) and *A Man Called Sloane* (1979–1980), featured professional agents working for top secret, technologically-advanced organizations identified by acronyms. Audiences were largely unimpressed. Even a series like *Masquerade* (1983–1984), a sort of *U.N.C.L.E.* crossed with *The Love Boat* (1977–1986) in which a team of government agents recruited entire groups of average folks with specialized talents, failed to catch on and lasted barely four months.

It wasn't until a spy codenamed "Scarecrow" crossed paths at a commuter train station with a divorced soccer mom that viewers wanted once more to spy vicariously through the adventures of someone just like them. *Scarecrow and Mrs. King* (1983–1987) took the set-up of *U.N.C.L.E.*'s pilot and extended it through three more seasons.[29] Like *I Led Three Lives*, *Scarecrow and Mrs. King* was set in suburbia, this time just outside Washington, D.C. As Lee Stetson, aka "Scarecrow," Bruce Boxleitner mentored, partnered, and fell in love with Amanda King played by Kate Jackson. Eventually, they married although Amanda's involvement in the world of espionage remained a secret kept from her two sons and her live-in mother. The show made an impression, observed one fan, "because it proved that an ordinary citizen like Amanda King is able to participate and contribute something towards the greater good."[30]

If mundane folks could be dragged into the clandestine world, the process could also work in reverse. A superspy, fired, retired, or simply burnt out, might find himself marooned among non-spies where he would need to make a place for himself in the community. Most fared better than *The Prisoner*'s (1968–1969) poor Number Six who was trapped in "The Village" for 17 episodes, an

Orwellian vision of a small town as it might be imagined by Lewis Carroll. Top agent V.H. Adderly (1986–1989), lost his left hand in a mission and found himself reassigned to his agency's department of Miscellaneous Affairs, where he outmaneuvered his boss, Melville Greenspan, a penny-pinching petty bureaucrat; befriended secretary Mona Ellerby who was thirsting for adventure; and became involved with cases that always ended up more important than they first appeared.

By comparison, the retirement of another superspy, Robert McCall, was more voluntary but also more fraught. As *The Equalizer* (1985–1989) McCall donated his professional skills to defend the weak, the helpless, and the victimized—anyone who replied to his newspaper ad, "Odds against you? Need help? Call the Equalizer." A cross between James Bond and George Smiley with a bit of urban Robin Hood thrown in for good measure, the world-weary McCall was played by Edward Woodward. Woodward had also starred in *Callan* (1967–1973), an hour-long U. K. series about an solitary brooding assassin working for British Intelligence who was similarly dangerous, brooding and guilt-ridden.[31] Episodes in which McCall battled injustice for average folks aided by various fellow spies and contacts alternated with espionage stories in which we caught glimpses of McCall's "other life," often involving his old friend and ex-boss, Control, played by Robert Lansing.

The formula worked so well that it was revived almost 20 years later and moved from a bleak, crime-ridden Manhattan to a pastel-colored, sun-splashed Miami in *Burn Notice* (2007–2013). Like Adderly, top CIA operative Michael Westen (Jeffrey Donovan) is forcibly retired—"burned" in the spy parlance. Like McCall, Westen spends his spare time helping people in trouble (often at the request of his mother played by Sharon Gless). He, too, is aided by a group of friendly professionals including Fiona (Gabrielle Anwar), an ex–IRA ammunitions expert and his best friend, an ex–Navy seal with FBI contacts named Sam Axe (Bruce Campbell). However, unlike McCall, Westin isn't running away from his old bosses; he's running toward them. His long running espionage-themed arc chronicles his efforts to find the person who burned him so he can restart his failed career. One of the more interesting aspects of *Burn Notice* is Michael's often dryly humorous voiceover commentary, explaining to the audience the details of spy craft, what he's doing on a mission and why.

More recently, back in Manhattan, another brooding superspy seeking atonement, ex–CIA operative John Reese (Jim Caviezel) has taken over *The Equalizer*'s territory and mission. In *Person of Interest* (2011–present) Reese works with billionaire Harold Finch (Michael Emerson) and an omniscient computer called The Machine that was designed by Finch to prevent terrorist attacks but now pinpoints potential perpetrators of crimes and/or victims.

These days, it's odd to find a superspy restricted largely to the rarified world of jet set resorts, gold-domed casinos, and gourmet restaurants where you can order a Martini shaken not stirred. Like any other minority group, the superspies have been integrated into the general population and either through training or chance, anyone might become one. For example, *Chuck* (2007–2012), starring Zach Levi, reverses the *U.N.C.L.E./Scarecrow and Mrs. King* formula so that now the innocent is the protagonist. The veteran professionals protecting him (Yvonne Strahovski and Adam Baldwin representing the CIA and the NSA, respectively) are the sidekicks.

Chuck certainly required protection and tactical support, at least for a while. A computer nerd when the series begins, Chuck Bartowski accidentally downloads the Intersect, a huge database filled with government secrets into his brain and then spends the next five seasons evolving into a reasonable facsimile of a Bondian superspy. The change is marked not only by a growing proficiency with weapons and martial arts but also by better grooming, with his hair becoming shorter and his clothing, neater and more sophisticated. Chuck isn't the only one who undergoes a transformation, either. For a short period of time, his even nerdier best friend Morgan becomes one as well. By the end of the series, all of Chuck's family members and friends have taken part in several spy missions. Indeed, the barrier between the mundane and espionage worlds has become so permeable, that *Chuck*'s gleaming futuristic spy complex lies, not behind an out-of-the-way nondescript urban tailor shop, but under a big box store called the Buy More, located in the middle of a typical suburban shopping mall.

From Mata Hari to Spy Mom

There has never been a Bond movie without a Bond Girl. The women of Bond are as essential to the basic formula as the Walther PPK, the Aston Martin and that shaken not stirred Martini. Yet, despite the arrival of feminism, the Bond Girl has remained a limited character, an accessory not unlike the specialized guns and gadgets, and the fast, expensive cars. In a 2009 study entitled "Shaken and Stirred: A Content Analysis of Women's Portrayals in James Bond Films," the researchers performed a content analysis of 195 female characters in 20 Bond films found a trend over time toward more sexual activity and more violent behavior both from and against the women characters, but overall, no real differences in the stereotyped portrayals. Some were good girls, some bad, and some eminently disposable. Indeed, those ladies who threaten Bond are more likely to end up dead. But in the end, the Bond Girl remains an adjunct to Bond rather than a fully realized dimensional character in her own right, one who is unrealistically beautiful —"statuesque, very thin, small hipped"—or, in other words, likely to look good in a black leather catsuit.[32]

Although the catsuit remains the fashion choice for female spies on television as well, the situation has evolved rather differently on the small screen. While it is not entirely clear how much progress has been made in the nature and quality of the roles for women in espionage-themed programs,[33] there is no doubt there is at least a lot more of them.[34] Spying on television has become an equal opportunity profession and main characters are just as likely to be female as male, perhaps more so. For example, when *Chuck* producers Chris Fedak and Josh Schwartz were planning a new spy show, they did not automatically think of Scarecrow bumping into Mrs. King but, rather, *Alias'* Sydney Bristow walking into *The Office* (2005–2013) to kidnap Jim Halpert.[35]

This is rather noteworthy because despite the fact that adult women make up the largest portion of the television viewing[36]—and have for some time[37]—female characters have, historically, constituted only one third to one half of the total number of television characters.[38] The progress of women in the spy genre on television has been slow but steady. Biff Baker had his wife, Louise, who tagged along and lent an occasional hand, and Herbert Philbrick's wife, Eva, continued to keep the home fires burning. In general though, early spy heroes—all white males—were unmarried and largely unattached. Any women they came across fit into two categories: the "desirable girl," pretty but passive, and the more active, experienced, but ultimately evil woman, the so-called "femme fatale."[39]

Michael Kackman argues convincingly that *I Led Three Lives* was "a masculinist nationalism fantasy" where the "good" American women like Eva stayed home, docile, subservient, and therefore virtuous. Eva and others like her knew their place while the Communist women that Philbrick met and defeated did not. Those women were powerful bureaucrats and authority figures, often giving orders to men, women with agency, a rather diverse collection of "comrades" ranging from schoolmarm types to "ruby red vixens."[40]

As the spy game expanded into the domestic sphere and women characters began to appear working on the side of Good, the two categories expanded into four. In addition to the femme fatale and her variant, the "bad-girl-turned-good," there was also the helpful assistant and the innocent.[41]

All of these female characters, good and not so good, appeared in the three-and-a-half year run of *The Man from U.N.C.L.E.* Not only was U.N.C.L.E. HQ filled with attractive clerical types carrying handguns in the small of their backs, but it also featured an innocent or two (overwhelmingly female), who were dragged into the mission in every episode. Unlike the Bond Girl, though, the U.N.C.L.E. innocent was seldom personally familiar with, or dominated by, the villain, and was, in fact, shocked to discover what the bad guys were up to.

As either a wife/mother or an employed professional, such as schoolteacher, secretary or social worker, U.N.C.L.E.'s innocent took her duties very seriously. It was to this sense of responsibility that the agents often appealed when recruiting her. She also, incidentally and often accidentally, came through at crucial moments and often saved the agents' lives.[42] It was during the sixties era, of course, that the image of the tough chick or kick-ass spy girl—the heroic woman who looked and acted like a femme fatale —was defined for all time by the memorable and iconic Emma Peel. Played by Diana Rigg, Emma was more than simply physically active and sexually appealing. She was also a modern woman in the Pop sense as well: young, stylish, independent with a sense of humor.[43] She might know martial arts, she could take care of herself, and yes, she occasionally slipped into a black leather cat suits but she was also fun. It's interesting to note in passing that both Rigg and her predecessor in *The Avengers* (1966–1969), Honor Blackman, who played a similar character in Cathy Gale, both graduated to Bond Girl status on the big screen.

But for all of Emma's virtues and glamor, she was still a sidekick, a deliberate contrast to Patrick Macnee's more traditional gentlemanly bowler-hatted John Steed. Around the same time that *The Avengers* was imported to America, Anne Francis played the lead character in *Honey West* (1965–1966). Honey was actually a private detective with a male sidekick (John Erickson as Sam Bolt), but she sported the iconography of a spy girl. She was sexually liberated, she knew judo and jujitsu, and she kept a pet ocelot named Bruce. Critics greeted her as "Jane Blonde" and James Bond in skirts.[44]

Honey West episodes ran for just half an hour and so it was up to *The Man from U.N.C.L.E.* spin-off, *The Girl from U.N.C.L.E.*, to allow a woman to finally be featured as the main protagonist of an hour-long American action/adventure series. The idea of a female agent had existed from U.N.C.L.E.'s very beginning, but it kicked into high gear in 1965 when the wife of an NBC executive returning from London encouraged producer Norman Felton to create the American equivalent to Emma Peel. Felton wanted his version to be a more average and younger-appearing woman. The character, named April Dancer, first appeared in "The Moonglow Affair" (aired February 25, 1965) as an inexperienced field agent paired with a veteran, near-retirement older male agent. When the episode was expanded a year later into a series, the original actors cast as the leads, Mary Ann Mobley and Norman Fell, were replaced by Stefanie Powers and Noel Harrison who were thought to have more appeal with teen audiences.[45]

While athletic, competent, and fashionably dressed in mod style clothes, April Dancer was more of a "girl" than either Emma Peel or Honey West. She appeared virginal and seldom employed her sexual charms beyond mild flirtation to complete a mission. Because Felton didn't want even a hint of kinkiness, April was not allowed to fight hand-to-hand with male villains and as a result she was often in need of rescue by her male partner, Mark Slate. On the positive side, April had an equitable, easy-going relationship with Mark, largely free of sexual tension, but the overdependence on camp humor to replace any violent overtones probably doomed the show.[46] Like *Honey West*, it lasted just one season. Nevertheless, many of the female spies so popular today, characters like the 1990s USA Network's *La Femme Nikita*, *Alias*' Sydney Bristow, and Sarah Walker in *Chuck*, seem to be a combination of the sleek sexy aggression of Emma Peel and Honey West with the youth and girl-next-door vulnerability of April Dancer.

Perhaps because *Get Smart* was an exaggerated comedy, the influence of Barbara Feldon's Agent 99 is often minimized or ignored. Part of the joke of the series was that Maxwell Smart, played by Don Adams, wasn't very smart, and that his female partner was more intelligent, more competent and even taller than he was. Along with Cinnamon Carter, who was played by Barbara Bain who was part of the *Mission: Impossible* team in its early seasons, Emma Peel, Honey West, April Dancer and Agent 99 changed the expectations of how a female spy on the side of Good should look and act.[47]

But Agent 99 also has another distinction: she was the first spy mom. After marrying Max in fourth season, Agent 99 proceeded to combine her work with traditional mid–20th century domesticity. She decorated their apartment and learned gourmet cooking even as she contended with maids and nosy neighbors who turned out to be enemy agents. As she observed in one episode, "There are not enough hours in the day to be an efficient housewife and a good spy."[48] The work/family balance issue became even more difficult in the fifth season when in the opening episode Agent 99 announced to Max in the midst of a mission that she couldn't scale a wall because she was pregnant. After buying baby equipment and learning to knit, she finally gave birth to twins in an episode entitled "And Baby Makes Four."[49] Both the marriage and the birth were ploys to avoid cancellation, but as the series slid toward the concerns of a typical family sitcom, it finally ended in 1970. When *Get Smart* was revived some 25 years later, Max was the new chief of C.O.N.T.R.O.L, Agent 99 had moved into politics, and their son Zach, one of the twins, was an agent now teamed with another woman, Agent 66.

If both parents are working agents and they have children, the inevitable question occurs: Who is taking care of the kids? The next important spy mom, Amanda King, was lucky enough to have a live-in mother. The situation was a bit more complicated in *Under Cover* (1991), a far more realistic spy drama in which Anthony John Denison and Linda Purl starred as married spies living in suburbia and working for the National Intelligence Agency, the fictional equivalent of the CIA. Much has been made of how a nervous ABC network held back an episode and eventually canceled the series because of storylines that anticipated real events such as a SCUD missile attack on Israel by Iran during the Persian Gulf War.[50] What was even more fascinating about the series, however, was how the couple, particularly spy mom Kate Del'Amico, managed to juggle professional and family obligations in ways that viewers at home could recognize.

So what accounts for the increase in female protagonists in spy programs? As Sophia McDougall points out, for male heroes, strong and square-jawed can also mean boring and one-dimensional.[51] Female protagonists can be strong, but they are also more likely to express vulnerability with a wider emotional range. Going undercover allows them to be adaptable and take on multiple identities. They nearly always have love interests in their lives with some sort of romantic complications. Indeed, it's almost a requirement since female spies who don't are seen as cold-hearted and manipulative. "Today's TV Mata Hari," writes June Thomas, "is a superhero who appeals to both men and women—a toned and well-trained young woman who regularly outwits and outscraps brawny dudes."[52] Characterizing Sydney Bristow in *Alias*, Thomas jokes, "Danger, deception foreign travel, colorful hair—what's not to love?"[53]

Apparently, even the real CIA agreed and featured Jennifer Garner who played Sydney in an agency recruiting commercial.[54]

The Family That Spies Together

It seems inevitable that once the boundaries between the spy world and everyday domestic life began to blur, and women took on more prominent roles, the inclusion and expansion of familial relationships would result. At first, in the early days of television, male spies worked alone. Then, in the 1960s, in shows like *I Spy* and *The Wild Wild West* (1965–1969) they acquired male partners. In *The Man from U.N.C.L.E.*, Napoleon Solo was joined by Illya Kuryakin, but both agents also regularly received assistance from average folks and helpful organization support staff, all largely female. From *The Avengers* to *Scarecrow and Mrs. King*, male superspies began to be matched with talented female amateurs. The 1990s saw a natural evolution toward male/female teams and professional couples working together.

Then, in September 2001, just as the nation was reeling from the tragic events of 9/11, three espionage series premiered. The first, called *The Agency* (2001–2003), which ran on CBS, was a serious and fairly realistic portrayal of the CIA. The characters had back stories, but these were limited and mostly sacrificed to intricate plots emphasizing geopolitics and bureaucratic maneuvering in Washington, D.C. Because the CIA assisted in the series' production and even allowed access for filming at its actual facilities, some critics labeled the series propaganda.[55] Like *Under Cover* before it, *The Agency's* stories often came uncomfortably close to real life events. Of the three series that appeared together, it was the least popular and only survived two seasons.[56]

The second show was *Alias*, created by J.J. Abrams, who would go on to produce the cult favorite *Lost* (2004–2010) and several other espionage-themed programs including *Person of Interest*. Jennifer Garner's Sydney Bristow was a graduate student who actually worked for SD-6, a mythical black ops division of the CIA. Unlike *The Agency*, *Alias* was a spy-fi[57] thriller that became even more and more of a fantasy as it went along. Sydney battled all sorts of evil organizations behind bizarre arcane conspiracies, including SD-6 itself. Besides its unsettling atmosphere of paranoia and constant betrayal, however, what really distinguished *Alias* was its focus on Sydney's complicated relationships with her unsuspecting civilian friends, her colleagues at work and, most importantly, members of her family. These included father Jack Bristow (Victor Garber), a highly effective undercover CIA operative; mother Irina Derevko (Lena Olin), a dangerous and amoral ex–Soviet spy; Sydney's diabolical mentor, Arvin Sloane (Ron Rifkin) who'd had a brief affair with her mother; and finally, Nadia (Mía Maestro), her half-sister who had resulted from that union. The ABC series became a cult favorite and lasted five seasons.[58]

The third series, *24* (2001–2010), covered in real time 24 hours in the life of an anti-terrorist agent named Jack Bauer played by Keifer Sutherland. During the first season, which covered one night and a day, Bauer struggles to stop the assassination of a presidential candidate, Senator David Palmer, played by David Haysbert. In addition the unique race-against-the-clock structure, like Sydney Bristow in *Alias*, Jack is forced to juggle his family responsibilities with his professional ones. During the course of the evening, Jack's estranged wife Teri (Leslie Hope) and his teenage daughter Kim (Elisha Cuthbert) are constantly in and out of mortal danger. Teri is eventually and shockingly murdered by a mole within Jack's agency, but daughter Kim continues to be an important factor in Jack's life thought the series. Created by Joel Surnow, who was also involved in *The Equalizer* and the 1990s television version of *La Femme Nikita*, *24* enjoyed enormous popularity and continued on the Fox network for eight seasons.[59] Along with the millennium, the spy family had arrived.

Although James Bond never worried that one of his sexual encounters would result in a James Bond Jr. showing up one day on his doorstep, the life choices made by his more recent television superspy counterparts have not been quite so free of consequences. At least since the 1980s, the balance between personal and professional obligations has been a recurring and popular theme in espionage programs.

William Douglas points out that American families have always loved and enjoyed television[60] which probably explains why, as Ella Taylor observes, "the language and imagery of family break obsessively through the surface forms of all its genres."[61] Of course, the spy story, too, is similarly fluid, adapting itself and borrowing from various genres: danger and obstacles from adventure, intense emotions and moralistic assumptions from melodrama, decadence, wealth and living on the social margins from the hard-boiled detective, and gadgetry from science fiction.[62] It was only a matter of time before the spy genre and the domestic drama—particularly those concerning dysfunctional families—would find each other on television.

When espionage-themed programming turns its attention to the family, there are several common recurring themes. One is that spying tends to be a family business. For characters like Sydney Bristow and Chuck Bartowski, not only is dad involved in the Great Game, but mom is, too.[63] Children follow their parents into the profession as Jack Bauer's daughter does, and occasionally, the parents insure that this happens.[64] For example, during the first four seasons, *La Femme Nikita* tells a Pygmalion-type story shades with Nikita as a spy version of Eliza Doolittle and her unemotional and highly effective handler, Michael, serving as her Henry Higgins.[65] But in the fifth season, we discover that Nikita's father, played appropriately by the Equalizer himself, Edward Woodward, is the real "Mr. Jones," the chief and founder of her top secret Machiavellian-style agency. Everything she has been through, from being framed for murder to her recruitment and training, has been in preparation for her to succeed her father as head of the organization.

A second running theme is the sins of the parents—usually but not exclusively the father—and the resulting troubles. Back in the 1980s, Edward Woodward's Robert McCall was already trying to compensate for neglecting his son, Scott, and is hired to protect a young woman who turns out to be a daughter he never knew. Despite all the tough love and bad decision-making, spy parents are nevertheless dedicated to their children to the point of death. After making her promise to run his agency, Nikita's father dies so that her lover, Michael, and his own son may live. Jack Bristow sacrifices his own life to bring down his former friend and his daughter's nemesis, Arvin Sloane. Both of Chuck's parents go on the run in order to protect their small children. And, even though she is not a spy herself, at the end of the *Burn Notice's* long run, Madeline, Michael Westin's chain-smoking mother, stays behind to detonate an explosive so that her son and young nephew may escape to a better life.

Finally, spies seem to travel a trajectory from or to a domestic ending. Those, like Michael Westen and Sydney Bristow, who begin already working as professionals tend to end up retired, happily married to, and raising children with, their love interests. Conversely, those who are recruited from mundane everyday life like Nikita and Chuck Bartowski often find themselves as professionals with bittersweet conclusions.

Spies R Us

"The greatest thing would be if Felicity was recruited by the CIA," producer J.J. Abrams observed in describing how he came up with *Alias*.[66] Abrams never cast Keri Russell, the star of Abrams' college student series *Felicity* (1998–2002), as Sydney Bristow, but a more mature Russell recently appeared as one of the protagonists of the FX network's 2013 espionage series, *The Americans* (2013–present).

In many ways, *The Americans* is a culmination of all the trends in domesticating the spy genre for television. Set in the 1980s and the waning years of the Cold War, the series focuses on a family living in a middle class Virginia suburb just outside Washington, D.C. The family consists of a spy mom (played by Russell) who is actually more determined and ruthless than her spy husband (Matthew Rhys), and two children unaware of their parents' profession. There is also an added twist: the couple, Elizabeth and Phillip Jennings, are actually a pair of deep cover sleeper agents working for the Soviet KGB. "This is a show where the enemies are the heroes, with all the questions that come with that," explained series creator Joel Weisberg, who is also an ex–CIA case officer. "You couldn't do that right after the Cold War. But you can do it 30 years later."[67] In several interviews, Weisberg has also maintained that *The Americans* is as much about marriage and family secrets as about espionage and that Elizabeth and Phillip's evolving relationship lies at the heart of the series.[68]

So, in the end, Herb Philbrick was right after all. The folks next door *could* very well be Communist spies, although perhaps they and their children are more likely to be subverted and seduced by America's materialistic, consumerist culture than the reverse. But even more importantly, they have become the protagonists, and television audiences are being asked to empathize and identify with them as they grapple with familiar domestic issues of family and parenthood in their own critically acclaimed show.

Notes

1. *Merriam-Webster Online Dictionary*, http://www.merriam-webster.com/dictionary/domesticate (accessed November 13, 2013).
2. John Brosnan, *James Bond in the Cinema* (London: Tantivy Press, 1972).
3. *The Man from U.N.C.L.E.*, NBC, *09/22/64–01/15/68* (circa 1968), Nielsen Ratings Summary, Norman Felton Collection, University of Iowa Library, Iowa City, Iowa.

4. "The Quiet 'Man from U.N.C.L.E.,'" *TV Guide*, April 17, 1965, 6–9.

5. Robert Vaughn, interviewed for "Fandemonium" on *The Man from U.N.C.L.E. The Complete Series* DVD, Bonus Disc 1, Time Life/Warner Bros. Entertainment Inc., 2008.

6. "Great TV Spy Scramble," *Life*, October 1, 1965, 118–20.

7. Jim Hoffman, "Connery & Vaughn: Bedroom Spy vs. Living Room Spy," *Photoplay*, September 1965, 33–9, 70–1.

8. Ibid., 34–38.

9. Marshall McLuhan, *Understanding Media: The Extensions of Man: Critical Edition* (Berkeley, CA: Gingko Press, 2003), 384.

10. Ibid., 438.

11. Cynthia W. Walker, "Spy Programs," in *The Encyclopedia of Television*, 2d ed., ed. Horace Newcomb (Chicago: Fitzroy Dearborn, 2004), 2181–185.

12. First coined by Paul Johnson, "Sex, Snobbery and Sadism," *New Statesman*, April 5, 1958.

13. George Gerbner, "Television Violence: The Art of Asking the Wrong Question," in *The World and I: A Chronicle of Our Changing Era* (July 1, 1994): 385–97.

14. John G. Cawelti and Bruce A. Rosenberg, *The Spy Story* (Chicago: University of Chicago Press, 1987), 34–54.

15. "Spy Fiction," *TV Tropes*, which equates the "Tuxedo Approach" with "Martini Flavored" spy stories and the "Trench Coat Approach" with "Stale Beer Flavored," http://tvtropes.org/ pmwiki/ pmwiki.php/Main/SpyFiction.

16. See Ien Ang, *Watching Dallas: Soap Opera and the Melodramatic Imagination*, (New York: Methuen, 1985) who argues that character is key, the point of impact between text and reader.

17. Many authors and commentators of spy fiction have cited Kipling's term for geopolitics extended to espionage activities. See, for example, Cawelti and Rosenberg, *Spy Story*, 39. Also, Wesley Britton, *Beyond Bond: Spies in Fiction and Film* (Westport, CT: Praeger, 2005), 6.

18. Cawelti and Rosenberg, *Spy Story*, 34–54. See also Britton, *Beyond Bond*, 1–37.

19. For more background on early spy programs, see Wesley Britton, *Spy Television* (Westport, CT: Praeger, 2004).

20. Michael Kackman, "*Citizen, Communist, Counterspy: I Led 3 Lives and Television's Masculine Agent of History*," *Cinema Journal* 38, no. 1 (Fall 1998). Kackman points out that the series' documentary production style, shot on actual streets with minimal crew was also a cost-saving strategy.

21. Herbert Philbrick to his wife, Eva at the dinner table in *I Led Three Lives* "The Spy," Season 1, Episode 8, http://www.youtube.com/watch?v=oXSbatv0f4M (February 7, 2012). For detailed background on the series, see Martin Grams, Jr., *I Led 3 Lives: The True Story of Herbert A. Philbrick's Television Program* (Albany, GA: Bear Manor Media, 2007).

22. Grams Jr., *I Led 3 Lives*, 38.

23. The story of how *The Man from U.N.C.L.E.* was created has been chronicled numerous times over the years. For the latest analysis of its conception and development, see Cynthia W. Walker, *Work/Text: Investigating the Man from U.N.C.L.E.* (Cresskill, NJ: Hampton Press, 2013); and "The Cloak and Swagger Affair: The Untold History of The Man from U.N.C.L.E," *The Man from U.N.C.L.E. The Complete Series* DVD, Season 1, Disc 11 (Burbank: Warner Home Video, 2008).

24. The complete story of Ian Fleming's involvement with *The Man from U.N.C.L.E.* and the ties between Bond and U.N.C.L.E. is discussed in Cynthia W. Walker, "The Man from U.N.C.L.E.: Ian Fleming's Other Spy," in *James Bond and Popular Culture: The Films Are Not Enough*, 2d ed., eds. Robert G. Weiner, B. Lynn Whitfield, and Jack Becker (Newcastle: Cambridge Scholars, 2011).

25. *The Man from U.N.C.L.E.*, "The Vulcan Affair," September 22, 1964; Norman Felton, personal communication, October 2, 1995. Quoted in Walker, *Work/Text*, 103.

26. David Buxton, *From the Avengers to Miami Vice: Form and Ideology in Television Series* (Manchester: Manchester University Press, 1990) categorizes both *The Man from U.N.C.L.E.* and *The Avengers*, along with *Danger Man* and *The Prisoner* as "Pop" series which privilege style over content and emphasize modernity, technology, and conspicuous consumption.

27. Cawelti and Rosenberg, *The Spy Story*, 13–15. This blurring of boundaries between fantasy and reality in spy programs could also be seen as "Wainscot fantasy," defined in *The Encyclopedia of Fantasy*, ed. John Clute and John Grant (New York: St. Martin's, 1997), 991–92, as "invisible or undetected societies living in the interstices of the dominant world." See also Cynthia W. Walker, "The Future Just Beyond the Coat Hook: Technology, Politics and the Postmodern Sensibility in the *Man from U.N.C.L.E.*," in *Channeling the Future: Essays on Science Fiction and Fantasy Television*, ed. Lincoln Geraghty (Lanham, MD: Scarecrow Press, 2009), 41–58.

28. See *The Beverly Hillbillies*, "Double Naught Jethro," March 3, 1965, http://www.imdb.com/title/tt0522464/; *The Dick Van Dyke Show*, "The Man from My Uncle," April 20, 1966, http://www.imdb.com/title/tt0559833/; and *Please Don't Eat the Daisies*, "Say UNCLE," January 11, 1966, http://www.imdb.com/title/tt0675738/.

29. Britton, *Spy Television*, 205–07.

30. Julia Weingrad, "How 'Scarecrow and Mrs. King' Made an Impact Through '80s Television," *Yahoo Contributor Network*, http://voices.yahoo.com/how-scarecrow-mrs-king-made-impact-through-3914816.html?cat=2 (accessed July 29, 2009).

31. Cynthia W. Walker, "Edward Woodward," in *The Encyclopedia of Television*, 2d ed., ed. Horace Newcomb (Chicago: Fitzroy Dearborn, 2004), 2580–583.

32. Kimberly A. Neuendorf, Thomas D. Gore, Amy Dalessandro, Patricie Janstova, and Sharon Snyder-Suhy, "Shaken and Stirred: A Content Analysis of Women's Portrayals in James Bond Film," *Sex Roles* 62 (2010): 747–61.

33. Rosie White, *Violent Femmes: Women as Spies in Popular Culture* (London: Routledge, 2007).

34. June Thomas, "Secret Agent Woman: Why Are There So Many Female Spies on Television?" *Slate*, http://www.slate.com/articles/arts/culturebox/2011/11/covert_affairs_homeland_why_are_there_so_many_female_spies_on_television_.html (accessed November 17, 2011).

35. Chris Fedak in an interview in "Chuck: The Beginnings: The Flash That Launched a Hit Show," Special Features, *Chuck the Complete Fifth and Final Season*, DVD, Disc 3, (Burbank: Warner Home Video, 2012).

36. Ingrid Lunden, "Nielsen: Women Watch More TV Than Men, but Connected Games Consoles Are Changing That," *TechCrunch*, http://techcrunch.com/2012/10/05/nielsen-gaming-tv-console/ (accessed October 5, 2012).

37. See Aletha C. Huston, Edward Donnerstein, Halford Fairchild, Norma D. Feshbach, Phyllis A. Katz, John P. Murray, Eli A. Rubenstein, Brian L. Wilcox, and Diana M. Zuckerman, *Big World, Small Screen: The Role of Television in American Society* (Lincoln: University of Nebraska Press, 1992); and George Comstock, Steven Chaffee, Natan Katzman, Maxwell McCombs and Donald Roberts, *Television and Human Behavior* (New York: Columbia University Press, 1978).

38. Bradley S. Greenberg and Larry Collette, "The Changing Faces on TV: A Demographic Analysis of Network Television's New Seasons, 1966–1992," *Journal of Broadcasting & Electronic Media* 41, no. 1 (Winter 1997): 1–13.

39. White, *Violent Femmes*, 3

40. Kackman, *Citizen, Communist, Counterspy*, 99. See also Michael Kackman, *Citizen Spy: Television, Espionage and Cold War Culture* (Minneapolis: University of Minnesota Press, 2005), 26–48.

41. Tom Lisanti and Louis Paul, *Femme Fatales: Women in Espionage Films and Television 1962–1973* (Jefferson, NC: McFarland, 2002), 14–16.

42. Walker, "Fleming's Other Spy," 16.

43. See James Chapman, "The Avengers: Television and Popular Culture During the 'High Sixties,'" in *Windows on the Sixties: Exploring Key Texts of Media and Culture,* ed. Anthony Aldergate, James Chapman, and Arthur Marwick (New York: I.B. Tauris, 2000) 37–69; and James Chapman, *Saints and Avengers: British Adventure Series of the 1960s* (New York: I.B. Tauris, 2002). Also, Toby Miller, *The Avengers* (London: British Film Institute, 1997).

44. Julie D' Acci, "Nobody's Woman? Honey West and the New Sexuality," *The Revolution Wasn't Televised: Sixties Television and Social Conflict,* ed. Lynn Spigel and Michael Curtin (New York: Routledge, 1997), 81.

45. For the complete story of *The Girl from U.N.C.L.E.'s* conception, development and televised run, see Walker, *Work/Text,* 194–99, 235–48.

46. See Walker, *Work/Text.* Also Jon Heitland, *The Man from U.N.C.L.E. Book: Behind-the-Scenes Story of a Television Classic* (New York: St. Martin's, 1987), 187.

47. Susan M. Garrett, "You've Come a Long Way Baby: A Forty-Year Leap for the Spygirl From the Swingin' Sixties to the Naughty Oughties," in *Alias Assumed: Sex, Lies and SD-6,* eds. Kevin Weisman and Glenn Yeffeht (Dallas: Benbella, 2005), 191–98.

48. *Get Smart,* "The Laser Blazer," November 30, 1968, http://www.imdb.com/title/tt0587588/.

49. *Get Smart,* "Pheasant Under Glass," September, 26, 1969; *Get Smart,* "And Baby Makes Four: Part 2," November 14, 1969. Also see Britton, *Spy Television,* 170–72.

50. Britton, *Spy Television,* 217–18.

51. Sophia McDougall, "I Hate Strong Female Characters," *New Statesman,* http://www.newstatesman.com/culture/2013/08/i-hate-strong-female-characters (accessed August 15, 2013).

52. See Thomas, *Secret Agent Woman.* Also Kelsea Stahler, "Why Isn't There a Female Equivalent to James Bond?" *Hollywood,* http://www.hollywood.com/news/movies/43898798/why-isn-t-there-a-female-equivalent-of-james-bond (accessed November 9, 2012) par. 7.

53. Thomas, *Secret Agent Woman,* par. 1.

54. Tricia Jenkins, *The CIA in Hollywood: How the Agency Shapes Film and Television* (Austin: University of Texas Press, 2012), 74–7.

55. Lewis H. Lapham, "Notebook: The Boys Next Door," *Harper's,* July 2001, 10, 12–13.

56. For a discussion of the CIA's role in creating The Agency, see Jenkins, *CIA in Hollywood,* 54–72.

57. Danny Biederman, coined the term "spy-fi" in *The Incredible World of Spy-fi: Wild and Crazy Spy Gadgets, Props and Artifacts from TV and the Movies* (San Francisco: Chronicle Books, 2004).

58. For more on *Alias,* see *Alias Assumed: Investigating Alias: Secrets and Spies,* eds. Stacey Abbott and Simon Brown (New York: I.B. Tauris, 2007); and Miranda J. Brady, "The Well-Tempered Spy: Family, Nation, and the Female Secret Agent in *Alias,*" in *Secret Agents: Popular Icons Beyond James Bond,* ed. Jeremy Packer (New York: Peter Lang, 2009), 111–32.

59. For more on *24,* see Rod Brookes, "24," in *Fifty Key Television Programmes,* ed. Glen Creeber (London: Hodder Arnold, 2004), 1–5; and Alan Sepinwall, *The Revolution Was Televised: The Cops, Crooks, Slingers and Slayers Who Changed TV Drama Forever* (New York: Touchstone, 2013), 218–42.

60. William Douglas, *Television Families: Is Something Wrong in Suburbia?* (New York: Routledge, 2003), 7.

61. Ella Taylor, *Prime-Time Families: Television in Postwar America,* 2d ed. (Berkeley: University of California Press, 1991), 17.

62. See discussion in Cawelti and Rosenberg, *Spy Story,* 55–78.

63. Chuck's mom, Mary Elizabeth Bartowski, played by Linda Hamilton, is probably the first Spy Grandma, who must be reminded by her daughter, Ellie, not to pull her weapon in front of her grandchild.

64. In *Alias*, Jack Bristow entered his daughter in Project Christmas, a CIA program that trained children to be spies. See Paul Zinder, "Sydney Bristow's 'Full Disclosure': Mythic Structure and the Fear of Motherhood," in *Investigating Alias: Secrets and Spies*, ed. Stacey Abbott and Simon Brown (New York: I.B. Tauris, 2007), 40–53.

65. Laura Grindstaff, "A Pygmalion Tale Retold: Remaking La Femme Nikita," *Camera Obscura* 17, no. 16:2 (2001): 133–75.

66. Quoted in Thomas, *Secret Agent Woman*, par. 1.

67. Steven Zeitchik, "'The Americans' on FX Bets Viewers Will Warm up to Cold War," *Los Angeles Times*, January 26, 2013, http://articles.latimes.com/2013/jan/26/entertainment/la-et-st-the-americans-fx-keri-russell-matthew-rhys-20130127 (accessed November 7, 2013).

68. See Laura M. Holson, "The Dark Stuff, Distilled," *New York Times*, http://www.nytimes.com/2013/03/31/fashion/joseph-weisberg-uses-his-cia-time-in-the-americans.html (accessed March 29, 2013); and Olivia B. Waxman, "Q&A: The CIA Officer Behind the New Spy Drama The Americans," *Time*, http://entertainment.time.com/2013/01/30/qa-the-cia-officer-behind-the-new-spy-drama-the-americans/#ixzz2lhqMtcgU (accessed January 30, 2013).

Bibliography

Abbott, Stacey, and Brown, Simon. *Investigating Alias: Secrets and Spies*. New York: I.B. Tauris, 2007.

Ang, Ien. *Watching Dallas: Soap Opera and the Melodramatic Imagination*. New York: Methuen, 1985.

The Beverly Hillbillies. "Double Naught Jethro." Directed by Joseph Depew. Written by Paul Henning. CBS, March 3, 1965.

Biederman, Danny. *The Incredible World of Spy-fi: Wild and Crazy Spy Gadgets, Props and Artifacts from TV and the Movies*. San Francisco: Chronicle Books, 2004.

Brady, Miranda J. "The Well-Tempered Spy: Family, Nation, and the Female Secret Agent in *Alias*." In *Secret Agents: Popular Icons Beyond James Bond*, edited by Jeremy Packer, 111–32. New York: Peter Lang, 2009.

Britton, Wesley. *Beyond Bond: Spies in Fiction and Film*. Westport, CT: Praeger, 2005.

_____. *Spy Television*. Westport, CT: Praeger, 2004.

Brookes, Rod. "24." In *Fifty Key Television Programmes*, edited by Glen Creeber, 1–5. London: Hodder Arnold, 2004.

Brosnan, John. *James Bond in the Cinema*. London: Tantivy Press, 1972.

Buchan, John. *The Thirty-Nine Steps*. Edinburgh: William Blackwood and Sons, 1915.

Buxton, David. *From the Avengers to Miami Vice: Form and Ideology in Television Series*. Manchester: Manchester University Press, 1990.

Cawelti, John G., and Bruce A. Rosenberg. *The Spy Story*. Chicago: University of Chicago Press, 1987.

Chapman, James. "The Avengers: Television and Popular Culture During the 'High Sixties.'" In *Windows on the Sixties: Exploring Key Texts of Media and Culture*, edited by Anthony Aldergate, James Chapman, and Arthur Marwick, 37–69. New York: I.B. Tauris, 2000.

_____. *Saints and Avengers: British Adventure Series of the 1960s*. New York: I.B. Tauris, 2002.

"Chuck: the Beginnings: The Flash That Launched a Hit Show." Special Features, *Chuck the Complete Fifth and Final Season* DVD, Disc 3, Burbank: Warner Home Video, 2012.

"The Cloak and Swagger Affair: The Untold History of The Man from U.N.C.L.E." *The Man from U.N.C.L.E. The Complete Series* DVD. Season One, Disc 11. Burbank: Time Life/Warner Bros. Entertainment Inc., 2008.

Clute, John, and John Grant, eds. *The Encyclopedia of Fantasy*. New York: St. Martin's Press, 1997.

Comstock, George, Steven Chaffee, Natan Katzman, Maxwell McCombs, and Donald Roberts. *Television and Human Behavior.* New York: Columbia University Press, 1978.

D'Acci, Julie. "Nobody's Woman? Honey West and the New Sexuality." In *The Revolution Wasn't Televised: Sixties Television and Social Content,* edited by Lynn Spigel and Michael Curtin, 73–94. New York: Routledge, 1997.

The Dick Van Dyke Show, "The Man from My Uncle." Written by Garry Marshall and Jerry Belson. Directed by Jerry Paris. CBS, April 20, 1966.

Douglas, William. *Television Families: Is Something Wrong in Suburbia?* New York: Routledge, 2003.

"Fandemonium," *The Man from U.N.C.L.E. The Complete Series* DVD. Bonus Disc 1. Burbank: Time Life/Warner Bros. Entertainment Inc., 2008.

Garrett, Susan M. "You've Come a Long Way Baby: A Forty-Year Leap for the Spygirl from the Swingin' Sixties to the Naughty Oughties." In *Alias Assumed: Sex, Lies and SD-6,* edited by Kevin Weisman and Glenn Yeffeht, 191–98. Dallas: Benbella, 2005.

Gerbner, George. "Television Violence: The Art of Asking the Wrong Question." In *The World and I: A Chronicle of Our Changing Era* (July 1, 1994): 385–97.

Get Smart. "And Baby Makes Four: Part 2." Directed by Don Adams. Written by Arne Sultan, Chris Hayward. November 14, 1969.

Get Smart. "The Laser Blazer." Written by Mike Marmer, Mel Brooks. Directed by Jay Sandrich. NBC, November 30, 1968.

Get Smart. "Pheasant Under Glass." Written by Chris Hayward and Arne Sultan. Directed by Don Adams. CBS, September, 26, 1969.

Grams. Martin Jr. *I Led 3 Lives: The True Story of Herbert A. Philbrick's Television Program.* Albany, GA: Bear Manor Media, 2007

"Great TV Spy Scramble." *Life,* October 1, 1965, 118–20.

Greenberg, Bradley S., and Larry Collette. "The Changing Faces on TV: A Demographic Analysis of Network Television's New Seasons, 1966–1992." *Journal of Broadcasting & Electronic Media* 41, no. 1 (Winter 1997): 1–13.

Grindstaff, Laura. "A Pygmalion Tale Retold: Remaking La Femme Nikita." *Camera Obscura* 17, no. 16:2 (2001): 133–75.

Heitland, Jon. *The Man from U.N.C.L.E. Book: Behind-the-Scenes Story of a Television Classic.* New York: St. Martin's Press, 1987.

Hoffman, Jim. "Connery & Vaughn: Bedroom Spy vs. Living Room Spy." *Photoplay,* September 1965, 33–9, 70–1.

Holson, Laura M. "The Dark Stuff, Distilled." *New York Times.* http://www.nytimes.com/2013/03/31/fashion/joseph-weisberg-uses-his-cia-time-in-the-americans.html (accessed March 29, 2013).

Huston, Aletha C., Edward Donnerstein, Halford Fairchild, Norma D. Feshback, Phyllis A. Katz, John P. Murray, Eli A. Rubenstein, and Diana M. Zuckerman. *Big World, Small Screen: The Role of Television in American Society.* Lincoln: University of Nebraska Press, 1992.

I Led Three Lives. "The Spy." Season 1, Episode 8, October 16, 1955. YouTube. http://www.youtube.com/watch?v=oXSbatv0f4M (accessed February 7, 2012).

Jenkins, Tricia. *The CIA in Hollywood: How the Agency Shapes Film and Television.* Austin: University of Texas Press, 2012.

Johnson, Paul. "Sex, Snobbery and Sadism." *New Statesman,* April 5, 1958.

Kackman, Michael. "*Citizen, Communist, Counterspy: I Led 3 Lives and Television's Masculine Agent of History.*" *Cinema Journal* 38, no. 1 (Fall 1998): 98–114.

_____. *Citizen Spy: Television, Espionage and Cold War Culture,* Minneapolis: University of Minnesota Press, 2005.

Kipling, Rudyard. *Kim.* London: Macmillan, 1901.

Lapham, Lewis H. "Notebook: The Boys Next Door." *Harper's,* July 2001, 10, 12–13.

Lisanti, Tom, and Louis Paul. *Femme Fatales: Women in Espionage Films and Television, 1962–1973*. Jefferson, NC: McFarland, 2002.

Lunden, Ingrid. "Nielsen: Women Watch More TV Than Men, but Connected Games Consoles Are Changing That." *TechCrunch*. http://techcrunch.com/2012/10/05/nielsen-gaming-tv-console/ (accessed October 5, 2012).

The Man from U.N.C.L.E., NBC, 09/22/64–01/15/68. Nielsen Ratings Summary. Norman Felton Collection, University of Iowa Library, Iowa City, Iowa, circa 1968.

The Man from U.N.C.L.E. "The Vulcan Affair." Written by Sam Rolfe. Directed by Don Medford. NBC, September 22, 1964.

Merriam-Webster Online Dictionary, http://www.merriam-webster.com/dictionary/domesticate (accessed November 13, 2013).

McDougall, Sophia. "I Hate Strong Female Characters." *New Statesman*. http://www.newstatesman.com/culture/2013/08/i-hate-strong-female-characters (accessed August 15, 2013).

McLuhan, Marshall. *Understanding Media: The Extensions of Man: Critical Edition*. Berkeley, CA: Gingko Press, 2003.

Miller, Toby. *The Avengers*. London: British Film Institute, 1997.

Neuendorf, Kimberly A., Thomas D. Gore, Amy Dalessandro, Patricie Janstova, and Sharon Snyder-Suhy. "Shaken and Stirred: A Content Analysis of Women's Portrayals in James Bond Films." *Sex Roles* 62 (2010): 747–61.

Please Don't Eat the Daisies. "Say UNCLE." Written by Sidney Morse and Roy Kammerman. Directed by Alvin Ganzer. NBC, January 11, 1966.

"The Quiet 'Man from U.N.C.L.E.'" *TV Guide*, April 17, 1965, 6–9.

Sepinwall, Alan. *The Revolution Was Televised: The Cops, Crooks, Slingers and Slayers Who Changed TV Drama Forever*. New York: Touchstone, 2013.

"Spy Fiction." *TV Tropes*. http://tvtropes.org/pmwiki/pmwiki.php/Main/SpyFiction.

Stahler, Kelsea. "Why Isn't There a Female Equivalent to James Bond?" *Hollywood*. http://www.hollywood.com/news/movies/43898798/why-isn-t-there-a-female-equivalent-of-james-bond (accessed November 9, 2012).

Taylor, Ella. *Prime Time Families: Television in Postwar America*, 2d ed. Berkeley: University of California Press, 1991.

Thomas, June. "Secret Agent Woman: Why Are There So Many Female Spies on Television?" *Slate*. http://www.slate.com/articles/arts/culturebox/2011/11/covert_affairs_homeland_why_are_there_so_many_female_spies_on_television_.html (accessed November 17, 2011).

Walker, Cynthia W. "Edward Woodward." In *The Encyclopedia of Television*, 2d ed., edited by Horace Newcomb, 2580–583. Chicago: Fitzroy Dearborn, 2004.

_____. "The Future Just Beyond the Coat Hook: Technology, Politics and the Postmodern Sensibility in *The Man from U.N.C.L.E.*" In *Channeling the Future: Essays on Science Fiction and Fantasy Television*, edited by Lincoln Geraghty, 41–58. Lanham, MD: Scarecrow Press, 2009.

_____. "*The Man from U.N.C.L.E.*: Ian Fleming's Other Spy." In *James Bond and Popular Culture: The Films Are Not Enough*, 2d ed., edited by Robert G. Weiner, B. Lynn Whitfield, and Jack Becker, 239–56. Newcastle: Cambridge Scholars, 2011.

_____. "Spy Programs." In *The Encyclopedia of Television*, 2d ed., edited by Horace Newcomb, 2181–185. Chicago: Fitzroy Dearborn, 2004.

_____. *Work/Text: Investigating the Man from U.N.C.L.E.* Cresskill, NJ: Hampton Press, 2013.

Waxman, Olivia B. "Q&A: The CIA Officer Behind the New Spy Drama The Americans." *Time*. http://entertainment.time.com/2013/01/30/qa-the-cia-officer-behind-the-new-spy-drama-the-americans/#ixzz2lhqMtcgU (accessed January 30, 2013).

Weingrad, Julia. "How 'Scarecrow and Mrs. King' Made an Impact Through '80s Television."

Yahoo Contributor Network. http://voices.yahoo.com/how-scarecrow-mrs-king-made-impact-through-3914816.html?cat=2 (accessed July 29, 2009).

White, Rosie. *Violent Femmes: Women as Spies in Popular Culture.* London: Routledge, 2007.

Zeitchik, Steven. "'The Americans' on FX Bets Viewers Will Warm Up to Cold War." *Los Angeles Times.* January 26, 2013. http://articles.latimes.com/2013/jan/26/entertainment/la-et-st-the-americans-fx-keri-russell-matthew-rhys-20130127 (accessed November 7, 2013).

Zinder, Paul. "Sydney Bristow's 'Full Disclosure': Mythic Structure and the Fear of Motherhood." In *Investigating Alias: Secrets and Spies,* edited by Stacey Abbott and Simon Brown, 40–54. New York: I.B. Tauris, 2007.

The Undefined Agent, Illya Kuryakin

Making the Russian (In)Visible in The Man from U.N.C.L.E.

Thomas M. Barrett

"Dear Illya, you may be a Communist, but you're our Communist."—fan letter to David McCallum[1]

The most popular Russian character in the history of American popular culture was a Soviet spy, Illya Kuryakin in *The Man from U.N.C.L.E*, which ran on American television originally from 1964 to 1968. Previous scholarship on this show has focused on its groundbreaking marketing and merchandising,[2] internationalist and consumerist glamor,[3] and dismantling of the Manichean vision of the Cold War.[4] Perhaps the most stunning innovation of the show was its showcasing of a positive image of a Soviet Russian man, Illya Kuryakin, something that had never happened before to this degree in American popular culture. But, as this essay will show, the way in which this was accomplished, in the episodes of the show and intertextual material such as the contemporary spinoff novels, combined a reconstruction of the Russian/Soviet type with layers of typical Cold War imagery. Central to the success of this character was an elusive identity that connected Illya to longstanding tendencies in the depictions of Russians and Soviets in American culture, paradoxical since this character was such a new phenomenon.

For all of the fear generated by Soviet communism and the red scares in American culture, Russians remained remarkably absent during the Cold War. Because of the tendency to depict communism as a pathology rather than an alternate system, the overwhelming majority of communist evil doers in American culture tended to be Americans who had succumbed to the sickness, not Soviets. The Red Scare films of the 1940s and 1950s mostly focused on domestic communists, as did the most popular spy drama on American television before *U.N.C.L.E.*, *I Led Three Lives* (1953–56). Those Russians agents who did appear in American popular culture after World War II—and communists in general—lacked biography or any connection to Russian culture, society, or history; they were illegitimate blanks often with an American gangster-like veneer. For example, the background of Captain Scarface, the communist who hopes to blow up the Panama Canal in the eponymous 1953 film, is left blank; he speaks with a Bela Lugosi accent, has a grizzly scar on his face, and it's clear that he's a communist and linked to and possibly from the Soviet Union, but it's never stated. In *Big Jim McLain* (1952, Edward Ludwig), comrade Sturak comes to discipline the Hawaii (he pronounces it with a "v") cell after "illustrious services in many parts of the world."[5] He speaks with some type of European accent, but that's the only clue to his identity. In such films, the context was always lacking. This corresponded to what Richard Hofstadter called the "paranoid style in American politics" in which "the enemy is not caught in the toils of the vast mechanism of history.... He is a free, active, demonic agent."[6] K. A. Cuordileone has also described how communism in the 1950s "was now discussed less as a *system*, whose political economy was to be debated or critiqued, and more as a psychological *affliction*, born of man's neurosis, anxiety, fear of freedom or lack of self."[7] In his analysis of the vision of the enemy in Cold War films, Andrey Shcherbenok emphasizes the homogenization of Russian, Soviet, and communist characters who work to establish communism in the U.S. "not [as] a political goal ... but rather a sort of mass mental disorder" without "any political explanation of why the Soviet Union and its communist agents inside the USA want to destroy the American way of life."[8]

When the producers and writers of *U.N.C.L.E.* and the actor David McCallum started to create the character of Illya they had little to go on. As one of the creators of the show Sam Rolfe said that when he was developing the character, all he knew "was that he was a Russian, but it was a vague, smoky thing."[9] McCallum called the character "wonderfully enigmatic" and almost nothing was established about his biography over time.[10] Given the discursive context, how could it have been otherwise? A *New York Times* article quoted McCallum as saying that Illya was "a climate of negatives ... very much the enigmatic man because he's scrupulously undefined."[11] It was a conscious decision, he said, not to spell out his background, which was why "Illya's personal arrangements are as much an abstraction as the Russia he supposedly comes from."[12] His potency comes from, he said, "the avoidance of biography."[13] Since the character was originally conceived almost as a throwaway role—Napoleon Solo was *the* man from U.N.C.L.E. and in the pilot episode Kuryakin had only two brief scenes lasting less than one minute—McCallum had some freedom to shape the character as the show evolved. He did so by emphasizing the unknown. As he recalled, "whenever something specific arose, such as he was married, or had a family, or lived somewhere, or was educated, or whatever—whenever those arose, I took them out, with the permission of the writers. So in fact in the entire series there's nothing specific about the character of Illya Kuryakin."[14] If he was married, as was suggested by his wedding ring, nothing was ever learned of his wife or family. He may have had communist leanings since he occasionally used leftist terms. In "The Love Affair" episode, when visiting a well-heeled party at a sumptuous Long Island estate, he says, "Suddenly I feel very Russian," decrying the "blue bloods" and muttering about "revolution."[15] In "The Odd Man Affair" he calls pickpocketing a "bourgeois expression."[16] Yet in another episode he claims that he once was a gentleman.[17] Could he have still been working for the Soviet government? Rolfe said that he had originally conceived of Illya as a double-agent.[18] In "The Neptune Affair" he appears in a Soviet naval uniform off the northern coast of the U.S.S.R.[19] But no mention is ever made of his citizenship or nationality, and rarely of his ethnicity, not even in the one episode that came closest to any kind of Soviet reality, "The Jingle Bells Affair," in which a Khrushchev-like premier visits the U.S.[20] Was he instead a Ukrainian? An electronic thought translator reveals that he was a little boy in Kiev?[21] In the third season he claims that he attended the University of Georgia in the Ukraine, which makes no sense at all.[22] Could he have been Jewish? He sings "Hava Nagila" in "The Ultimate Computer Affair."[23] His first name and patronymic give no clue, especially since the name is inaccurately transliterated (it should have had only one "l") and the patronymic (Nickovetch) is an impossibility. If his father's name was Nikolai, it would be Nikolaievich; if perhaps he was a Greek named Nick, it would be Nikovich. Adding to the general confusion, in early episodes the other main characters in the show mispronounce his name as CURE-ii-ah-kin (rather than KOOR-ii-ah-kin). His accent was also difficult to pin down. McCallum said he aimed for a central European sound.[24] Some viewers thought it was really McCallum's way of speaking.[25] The *Newark Evening News* called it "hard to place" and one fan compared it to lisping, but others assumed it was Russian.[26] And in 1965 McCallum said that most women who wrote him letters thought that he was actually Russian or German.[27] The enigmatic approach maybe went too far: in the first season some reviewers seemed uncertain of Illya's origins, one saying nothing about Russia but mentioning that he "looks German or Scandinavian."[28] There was apparently enough confusion about the character still at the beginning of the third season that a newspaper syndicate television report ran a letter from a fan inquiring about his nationality.[29]

It makes little sense to hold the creators of the show to any kind of ethnically or culturally accurate standards and, regardless, the goal was to create an enigma. The continual masking of the character—he often disguised himself as Asian and European types and was set against his partner Napoleon Solo's occasional mask of a stereotypical American—also developed his inscrutability and embroidered on the longstanding uncertainty of Russia's place between west and east. His East European nature is emphasized with his expertise on Gypsies: such indigenous knowledge is crucial in "The Trebuf Affair" when he poses as a Bulgarian Gypsy and speaks their language.[30] At other times he is the western sophisticate, speaking French[31] and boasting of a Cambridge Ph.D. and post-graduate work at the Sorbonne.[32]

McCallum's notorious reticence about his status as a pop idol during the time, and the conflation of the character with the actor, further enhanced Illya's incoherence. Even though *17 Magazine* called him "the spy who'd rather not be known," much effort went into promoting the show and marketing Illya.[33] Besides the plethora of general *U.N.C.L.E.* merchandise, fans could purchase an Illya gun, game, doll, poster ("the eyebrows pulled together slightly, the brow lightly furrowed, the corners of the mouth turned up in an almost-smile"), Halloween mask, sweater, or fashion their hair in an Illya cut.[34] Smokers were asked to send in 25 cigar bands to a company in Philadelphia and receive a paperback fan book, *Illya: That Man from Uncle* (an expansion of an article published in *Look*); it is not known how well this promotion worked, but it complicates the assumption that Illya's fans were only teenage girls.[35]

Until the furor got overheated and McCallum felt the need to remove himself from the frenzy, articles and interviews stressed the similarity between actor and spy. McCallum often appeared and was presented in character. On the teen music show *Hullabaloo* he never once was called by name, coming instead as Illya in his trademark black turtleneck sweater.[36] A *Glamour* photo spread in June 1964 featured him and Robert Vaughn in character posing with guns and models on the streets of New York. His fans often greeted him with "All the Way with Illya K" signs.[37] Articles in fan magazines also conflated the actor with the spy, claiming that McCallum shared many traits with his television counterpart; he was quiet, "as befits secret agent Illya" he was secretive about his private life, had eyes that were cold and brooding, a pensive face, and was "dedicated to remaining a mystery man."[38] When asked if they shared traits, McCallum perpetuated the fuzziness with inconsistent answers. Sometimes he distanced himself from the character, insisting that Illya was fictional and quite apart; other times he'd draw closer, saying that he'd like to have him for a friend and that he added a lot of his real self into him.[39] Young people were understandably confused—national teen columnist for *Young Citizen* Susan Szekely wrote that when purchasing his posters, "David McCallum is more often referred to as 'the man from UNCLE' or Illya than by his real name."[40]

Continually mobbed by female fans whenever he made a press appearance, called a rival to Elvis and the Beatles, at the peak of the show's popularity McCallum received thousands of letters a week, more than any other star at MGM including Clark Gable at his most popular.[41] He was, in the words of the press, the new "tv idol," at the center of a "cult" of admirers.[42] Initially he seemed bemused by the adoration, calling it "disquieting," "baffling," intellectualizing its context, and pondering why youth needed idols, certainly one of the more brainy and distancing responses to popularity in the history of Hollywood.[43] (How many contemporary television stars would have agreed with McCallum that there's "no point in having an interview if there is nothing to talk about," as he said to *Teen Set* magazine?[44]) But after fans ran riot in Macy's on February 5, 1966, when a scheduled appearance had to be canceled because of the size of the crowd, McCallum attempted to reduce his visibility, declaring that he'd make no more personal appearances in the U.S.: "Such things simply can't be controlled any more. Why should I continue to run the risk of seeing people maimed and injured, including me?"[45] Another magazine quoted him as saying, "I can't stand my fans much longer," citing an incident when he was nearly crushed struggling through a mob of fans with the help of several policemen to get into a New York hotel.[46] He was, then, a fan-shy star making riotous public appearances, often showing up or being received in character—as a character about whom little specific was known except his ability to mask and obscure— from a show that balanced between parody and realism. No wonder some have called *U.N.C.L.E.* post-modern before the fact; the indeterminacy of the show, character, and actor all reinforced each other.[47]

With biography and history absent or uncertain, stereotype filled the void. Most importantly, Illya was portrayed, like a long line of Soviet communists in American popular culture, as emotionally reserved or gloomy, or as one fan magazine put it "that inscrutable man of few words with the Slavic look and the chilly eye."[48] This was demonstrated and described in various ways. He doesn't smile much, keeps an even temperament, and almost never gets involved in romance. Compare the look of Solo in the opening credits of Seasons 2 and 3, with his broad smile and a laugh, to Illya and his straight face, then just beginning to show a trace of a smile that is quickly suppressed. He is given to pessimistic sayings such as: "no man is free who has to work for a living,"[49] "a man must die a little every day,"[50] and "humor is the gadfly on the corpse of tragedy."[51] One character mentions his "brooding eyes ... like Dostoevskii."[52] The novels speak of his "dour Russian look," how his "enigmatic smiling hid all his emotions," and "the Russian side of his nature which tended toward gloomy prophecy."[53] In these novels the authors describe the reserve of the character in more extreme terms. In *The Mad Scientist Affair* he is called "that imperturbable and coldly efficient technologist and gatherer of unusual and useful information."[54] In *The Doomsday Affair* Harry Whittington puts it even more bluntly and refers to "the machinery of Kuryakin's unemotional mind."[55] When introducing the character, he writes, "It was easy to think that Illya was like a machine, computing danger and finding solutions for it, fashioned for this specific purpose."[56]

It was a staple of anti-communist rhetoric that communists lacked normal human emotions; this connected to their ability to perpetuate inhuman deeds or submit to party oppression. Harry and Bonaro Overstreet write in *What We Must Know About Communism* that "precisely as the individual is 'downgraded' in Communist theory and practice, so likewise are the emotions we have counted basic to sound human relationships."[57] W. Cleon Skousen called them "a regimented breed of Pavlovian men."[58] One also thinks of Ayn Rand's testimony before HUAC when she said that Russians don't smile, at least like humans do in America.[59]

Although male communists in American culture were usually coldly manipulative, Illya's emotional reserve connects him more strongly to communist analogues in cold war science fiction such as the emotionless human copies in *Invasion of the Body Snatchers* (1956, Don Siegel), the emotionally closed manipulated humans in *Invaders from Mars* (1953, William Cameron Menzies), and the cold and sterile counterfeit husband in *I Married a Monster from Outer Space* (1958, Gene Fowler, Jr.). It also gives his character, in the odd logic of anti–Soviet cinema, something of a (Soviet) female gloss. Ninotchka, the commissar rescued for the west through love and champagne in the 1939 film (Ernst Lubitsch) of the same name, is initially an emotional iceberg, speaking in monotones and lacking any interest in the passionate entireties of her suitor Leon or the beauty of Paris. In the remake *Silk Stockings* (1957, Rouben Mamoulian), Nina is equally cold, saying things like "music is essential for parades" and scowling at silk stockings.[60] The communist women in the television spy drama *I Led Three Lives* also often come across as emotionally closed, which desexualizes them.

Indeed, one of the genuine departures, and reasons for his popularity, was Illya's gendering, which moved him away from the typical macho masculine hero and towards the feminine. He was not muscle-bound but slight of build (a MGM press release put him at 5'8", 140 pounds); *Photoplay* magazine compared him to the Russian ballet dancer Rudolf Nureyev.[61] He wore long blonde hair and was complimented in one episode for the softness of his skin. Show writer Dean Hargrove claimed in an interview that NBC wanted to get rid of McCallum at first because he had long hair and they were afraid that he looked gay.[62] In the *New York Times*, Howard Thompson noted the sensitive face of a poet and "a crown of blonde hair that makes him look like a cherubic esthete."[63] His emotional reticence was perceived as a kind of vulnerability; one fan said that "he's so lonely you want to comfort him."[64] *Rave* called him sensitive and gorgeous;

Mr. Magazine expressed it in the opposite, saying he wasn't "homely in any rugged he-man way."[65] He seems annoyed and betrayed when Napoleon repeatedly hits on women and unlike the later he almost never does likewise and in fact often seems to avoid them. He is often wounded and rendered passive; as one fan magazine wrote, "Somehow Illya always manages to get stepped on. Everyone wants to help him up!"[66] He posed as a fashion designer once[67] and in the movie remake from 1983, *The Return of the Man from U.N.C.L.E.: The Fifteen Years Later Affair*, it turns out he quit the service to actually become a fashion designer. In the first U.N.C.L.E. book he's subordinate to Napoleon, almost a cipher, and can't help worrying about his fellow agent when he's out on assignment. As he paces in his Manhattan apartment he sounds almost like a housewife with a late husband: "Damn this infernal business of waiting, waiting, and waiting."[68] In one episode, when he and Napoleon create a cover as a suburban couple, Illya does the cooking.[69]

Again in the logic of communist-themed films, his braininess also genders him female. Male communists are usually rendered odd by making them goons; the women are made freakish with hyper-intelligence. Ninotchka masters the hypertrophied French legal code in days, Theodore (the communist streetcar driver in *Comrade X* [1940, King Vidor]) recites an entire book on capitalist overproduction in hours, and Vinka (*The Iron Petticoat* [1956, Ralph Thomas]) constantly spouts out Soviet statistics proving the rottenness of capitalism, driving her American companion to astonish, "I've never met a woman with a brain like yours."[70] In *U.N.C.L.E.*, Illya's extensive knowledge is a continual source of humor and sometimes annoyance to Napoleon; he has a Ph.D. in quantum mechanics,[71] is an expert in chemistry, physics,[72] and radio astronomy,[73] and speaks multiple languages. His foil, the more traditionally macho American Solo, on the other hand, demonstrates little formal education, but smiles a lot and has smooth ways with women.

Fans and critics fixed on Illya's blonde hair, black turtleneck, emotional reserve, and enigmatic brainy expressions as emblematic of some new "Moscow hip."[74] In one respect this was simply an antipode to the parade of previously chronically unhip Russian male characters in American culture, from the funny sounding and looking 1930s "mad Russian" type played by actors such as Bert Gordon and Mischa Auer, who acted in a socially inappropriate, extroverted, and comedic fashion, to the goons and creeps of various stripes played by actors such as Oscar Homolka and Bela Lugosi who populated horror, science fiction, and red scare films throughout the twentieth century. Part of it was, as McCallum himself acknowledged, a vogue for things European in American culture in the 1960s, such as the Beatles and Richard Burton. But it also derived from a contemporary curiosity about real Russians and their style during a period of unprecedented Soviet openness to the west and leadership in the most modern (space, nuclear) technologies. McCallum understood it this way: "Westerners are disturbed by the pall of the unknown that stretches over the Iron Curtain countries. Now here comes the mysterious and ominous Russian and he turns out to look like a customer at some Go-Go stompery, threatening nothing but the eardrums."[75] This hope and curiosity, for a short period, influenced spy culture. Appealingly (that is, not threateningly) sexy Russian spies working for us (or at least not against us) appeared in numerous novels and films during this period. However, they were almost always women, such as Vadya who helps Matt Helm eliminate a Nazi threat in South America in *The Ambushers*[76] and most famously Tatiana Romanova from the James Bond novel (1957) and film *From Russia with Love* (1963, Terence Young). As the sexy Soviet spy who is made safe for the west and consumerism through Bond's conquest, Romanova is the most direct precursor to Illya.[77]

The creators of the show continually reiterated that they wanted to completely avoid connecting the show to contemporary issues. Guidelines for episode writers put it plainly: "For obvious reason, neither U.N.C.L.E. nor its antagonists are involved in international politics or diplomacy, except in those occasions where wholly mythical countries are involved. U.N.C.L.E. does not serve interests that are peculiarly American. The Cold War or any of its ramifications do not exist for us."[78] But, despite the fictional nature of the U.N.C.L.E. organization and its antagonists, the parodic aspects of the show, and the often outlandish plots, it was impossible to make a spy television show at that time without some occasional connections, intentional, implied, or assumed, to the real world. For one, the western consumerist reimagining of the Soviet Union after the death of Stalin was a necessary precondition for the show.

The series emerged during a transitional period, when the Soviet Union was still emerging from the shadow of Stalin and embarking on a reform experiment that included peaceful engagement with the west and a new stress on consumerism. Soviet women especially were discovered during the late 1950s and 1960s, through travel accounts and magazine reportage and display, and reconstructed from an earlier image as unfashionable ("drab and shabby" in the words of one journalist) to objects of desire.[79] Shel Silverstein began an illustrated travelogue for *Playboy* in 1957 and one of his early stops was Moscow (March 1958), where he reported that "the girls are lovely"; one cartoon has him making love to a young woman with the caption, "Gee, Natasha—you mean you Russians invented *this*?"[80] Harrison Salisbury followed him in 1959 and conveyed similarly hopeful news that the Russian woman is going to claim "the heritage of her sex, the right and opportunity to look just as pretty as she wants to."[81] The evidence was everywhere including mobbed Christian Dior fashion shows, intense demand for nylon stockings, and spike heels.[82] Others too reported great changes: lipstick, wavy hair, jammed beauty shops, Italian hair styles, and window displays of strapless evening dresses and various colored nylon slips.[83] *From Russia with Love* helped advance this trend. The self-affirming trope of the beautiful, fashionable, consumerist, western-oriented Soviet woman proved potent and the phrase "from Russia with love" stuck and tantalized that desire, not just fears, could emanate from the Soviet Union. In the wake of the Bond film, and during the period of *U.N.C.L.E.*'s original airing, those open to the new possibilities from the U.S.S.R. could enjoy a *Playboy* expose on Soviet girls, sip Stolichnaya vodka (introduced in America in 1965 with the slogan "From Russia with Ice"), and wear a new Christian Dior theater coat called "From Russia with Love." Consciously or not, *U.N.C.L.E.* rode this wave, offering Illya—and his turtleneck, hairstyle, and merchandise—from Russia with love too.

A television series dealing with international conflicts and airing while the Vietnam War raged could hardly avoid some political aura. Although the meaning was unclear, a mother of two teen-aged fans from Kansas acknowledged that at least some received the show in this way when she reported that they had photos of McCallum and Vaughn in their room, along with Barry Goldwater and Werner von Braun.[84] The Soviets acknowledged it too; *Pravda* attacked the show and singled out "bloodthirsty, erotic and violent" Illya; picking up on the emotionless Russian stereotype, the article decried how he "works like a machine without reasoning and precisely executes the orders of Mr. Efficiency."[85] McCallum was never politically outspoken like Robert Vaughn (an anti–Vietnam War activist), but he made several statements about peaceful coexistence that sounded like something that could have come from an internationalist organization like U.N.C.L.E. He promoted the use of Esperanto as the official language of U.N.C.L.E. clubs all over the world, hoping that the spread of a universal language would bring people of "many different nationalities and backgrounds together and it could be the key to world peace."[86] He opined that if a universal language was taught in school across the world, "in one generation, there would be total verbal communication."[87] He took out American citizenship during the show's run (maybe that explains his photo next to Goldwater's), but made sure to tell *Motion Picture* magazine, which enthused over this ("in these times—when the U.S. is being blasted on every side, it's refreshing") that he was not narrowly nationalistic: "I don't believe in setting up barriers between people because they're born in this place or that and have this or that allegiance.... We should learn to live and love our neighbors as ourselves for the sake of peace and progress."[88]

U.N.C.L.E. certainly kept far away from reality when it ventured towards Eastern Europe; here venerable cultural tropes predominated: gypsies in the Balkans,[89] a Ruritania story,[90] and bats and a Dracula analogue in Transylvania (no mention of Romania, where the contemporary Transylvania is actually located).[91] "The Deadly Quest Affair" featured an East European accented Viktor Karmak and his pet jaguar hunting Solo through a twelve-block condemned area of Manhattan, obviously inspired by the 1924 Richard Connell story and 1932 move, *The Most Dangerous Game* (Irving Pichel and Ernest B. Schoedsack), in which a Russian count hunts humans for fun.[92] One early episode, "The Project Strigas Affair," featured Illya in a Trotsky-like disguise with a beard and round glasses and a warmongering Yugoslav leader.[93] Illya started to give him a communist tint comparing him to a Soviet bad guy: "one part Molotov" but then went on to generalize his nefarious nature "one part Von Ribbentrop, salt with Genghis Khan, and garlic with Machiavelli."[94] There were actually more Nazis in the four seasons of the show than commies.

The one episode that drew directly from contemporary Cold War history featured Russians and Communists (although never specifically mentioned them), but still in an evasive way that left Illya out in the cold. Akim Tamiroff guest starred in "The Jingle Bells Affair," which originally aired on 23 December 1966.[95] Tamiroff was the rare native Russian-speaking Armenian actor in Hollywood who was called on to play Russian roles. He had recently starred as the Soviet ambassador in *Romanoff and Juliet* (1961), directed by Peter Ustinov and based on his play of 1956. In the *U.N.C.L.E.* episode Tamiroff played Premier Georgi Koz who has come to the U.S. to promote his policy of peaceful coexistence and friendship with the west. He is never explicitly called Russian or communist—he's referred to in fact as "the bear of the Balkans"—but the hints are legion with references to vodka, "the exploitation of the masses," the working class, "imperialist lies," a "people's republic," and red flags on his car.[96] If viewers didn't get the connection to Nikita Khrushchev, the equally bald and rotund Tamiroff pounded it into their heads when he banged a desk with his shoe. He also mentioned security concerns regarding a visit to Disneyland, implicitly referencing Khrushchev's frustrated desire to see the Magic Kingdom during his 1959 trip. Koz arrives in Manhattan in the midst of the Macy's Thanksgiving parade, which Solo tells him is the beginning of the Christmas shopping season. Pointing to the consumerist fantasies regarding the Soviet Union, Koz tours Macy's with great interest, and selects a frilly black lace nightgown to take back home to his wife. It was just such an object of desire that turned Vinka in *The Iron Petticoat* towards the goodies of capitalism. Koz's security chief Maxim Radish is played by another native Russian speaker, Leon Belasco (who had a bit part in *Comrade X* and starred in the 1960 television version of *Ninotchka*). Radish, a committed communist, or as Koz puts it "a little too full of revolutionary zeal," tries to spoil the premier's charm offensive with fake and then real assassination attempts.[97] With things not going his way, and assuming a plot by

Americans, Koz becomes upset with his hosts, similar to Khrushchev's anger in Hollywood when he suspected plots to embarrass him. Koz survives one such attempt dressed as that avatar of American consumerism, Santa Claus; he is so effective and taken with this role that at the end of the episode he puts on the whiskers again and gives presents to children in a hospital, triumphing over Radish's attempts and his antagonistic view that Christmas is simply "an organized seduction of the children."[98]

Many of the show's aspects that swirled around the character of Kuryakin—peaceful coexistence, dreams of Soviet consumerism, a Russian friendly to the west—still had an essential absence at his center. There were ample opportunities for Illya to say a Russian word to his supposed comrades, for Koz to inquire about his service in the U.S., for Radish to update him on the class struggle, for Illya to inquire of the motherland. But this episode staunchly maintains Illya's blankness. He's just another U.N.C.L.E. agent, one of "those two nice guys" as Koz says, trying to protect the premier and uncover the plot.[99] Not a single mention is made of his Russianness (certainly Koz and Radish would have recognized it) and in this episode where we would most expect some details he remains "scrupulously undefined" as McCallum intended for the character from the start.[100] Just like all of the other Russian communists in American popular culture, he simply exists, without context and with a complete absence of biography and politics, although this time on the side of capitalist consumption.

Notes

1. Howard Thompson, "The Teenagers Cry 'U.N.C.L.E.,'" *New York Times,* June 20, 1965, x15.

2. Anthony Enns, "The Fans from U.N.C.L.E.: The Marketing and Reception of the Swinging '60s Spy Phenomenon," *Journal of Popular Film and Television* 28, no. 3 (Fall 2000): 124–33.

3. Michael Kackman, *Citizen Spy: Television, Espionage, and Cold War Culture* (Minneapolis: University of Minnesota Press, 2005), 79–98.

4. Rick Worland, "The Cold War Mannerists: *The Man from U.N.C.L.E.* and TV Espionage in the 1960s," *Journal of Popular Film and Television* 21, no. 4 (Winter 1994): 150–62.

5. *Big Jim McLain*, DVD, directed by Edward Ludwig (1952; Burbank: Warner Home Video, 2007).

6. Richard Hofstadter, *The Paranoid Style in American Politics and Other Essays* (New York: Alfred A. Knopf, 1966), 32.

7. K. A. Cuordileone, *Manhood and American Political Culture in the Cold War* (New York: Routledge, 2005), 101.

8. Andrey Shscherbenok, "Asymmetric Warfare: The Vision of the Enemy in American and Soviet Cold War Cinemas," *KinoKultura*, April 2010, http://www.kinokultura.com2010/28-shscherbenok.shtml (accessed May 12, 2010).

9. "The Quiet 'Man from U.N.C.L.E.,'" *TV Guide*, April 17, 1965, 6.

10. Jon Heitland, *The Man from U.N.C.L.E. Book: Behind-the-Scenes Story of a Television Classic* (New York: St. Martin's Press, 1987), 47.

11. Bernard Wolfe, "The Man Called I-l-l-y-a," *New York Times*, October 24, 1965, SM56.

12. Ibid.

13. Ibid.

14. Heitland, *The Man from U.N.C.L.E. Book*, 47.

15. "The Love Affair," Season 1, Disc 9, *The Man from U.N.C.L.E.* (March 29, 1965; Burbank: Warner Home Video, 2008), DVD.

16. "The Odd Man Affair," Season 1, Disc 10, *The Man from U.N.C.L.E.* (April 19, 1965; Burbank: Warner Home Video, 2008), DVD.

17. "The Fiddlesticks Affair," Season 1, Disc 6, *The Man from U.N.C.L.E.* (January 18, 1965; Burbank: Warner Home Video, 2008), DVD.

18. Heitland, *The Man from U.N.C.L.E. Book*, 27.

19. "The Neptune Affair," Season 1, Disc 4, *The Man from U.N.C.L.E.* (December 8, 1964; Burbank: Warner Home Video, 2008), DVD.

20. "The Jingle Bells Affair," Season 3, Disc 5, *The Man from U.N.C.L.E.* (December 23, 1966; Burbank: Warner Home Video, 2008), DVD.

21. "The Foxes and Hounds Affair," Season 2, Disc 2, *The Man from U.N.C.L.E.* (October 8, 1965; Burbank: Warner Home Video, 2008), DVD.

22. "The Hot Number Affair," Season 3, Disc 9, *The Man from U.N.C.L.E.* (March 10, 1967; Burbank: Warner Home Video, 2008), DVD.

23. "The Ultimate Computer Affair," Season 2, Disc 1, *The Man from U.N.C.L.E.* (October 1, 1965; Burbank: Warner Home Video, 2008), DVD.

24. "Ilya [sic] on Target," *McCallum & Vaughn—2 Magazines in One*, http://www.davidmccallumfansonline.com/target.htm (accessed May 21, 2013).

25. Steven H. Scheuer, "TV Mailbag," *San Antonio Light*, April 11, 1965, 10.

26. Tom Mackin, "McCallum Tailors Role to Himself," *Newark Evening News*, http:///www.davidmccallumfansonline.com/tailorsrole.htm (accessed May 21, 2013); Iris-Marie [Chandler] Brossard, *Illya That Man from U.N.C.L.E.* (New York: Pocket Books, 1966), n.p.; "If THRUSH Were After You, in Whose Arms Would You Want to Be Saved?" *Photoplay*, August 1965; and Thompson, "The Teenagers," x15.

27. "TV Boost Popularity of Actor," *Times Recorder* [Zanesville, OH], March 4, 1965, 6b.

28. "McCallum Is Hit," *San Antonio Light*, February 28, 1965, 10-tv.

29. "Illya's Background," *The Republican-Courier* [Finlay, OH], September 21, 1966, 4.

30. "The Terbuf Affair," Season 1, Disc 5, *The Man from U.N.C.L.E.* (December 29, 1964; Burbank: Warner Home Video, 2008), DVD.

31. "The Deadly Decoy Affair," Season 1, Disc 5, *The Man from U.N.C.L.E.* (January 11, 1965; Burbank: Warner Home Video, 2008), DVD; and "The Girls of Nazarone Affair," Season 1, Disc 10, *The Man from U.N.C.L.E.* (April 12, 1965; Burbank: Warner Home Video, 2008), DVD.

32. "The Her Master's Voice Affair," Season 3, Disc 1, *The Man from U.N.C.L.E.* (September 16, 1966; Burbank: Warner Home Video, 2008), DVD.

33. Edwin Miller, "The Spy Who'd Rather Not Be Known," *17 Magazine*, September 1965, 116.

34. Heitland, *The Man from U.N.C.L.E. Book*, 163–65; "Get a Free U.N.C.L.E. Card and an 'Illya' Sweater from David!" *16 Magazine,* October 1965; Susan Szekely, "Teen Idols Are Larger Than Life," *Tucson Daily Citizen*, January 25, 1967, 30; and Cynthia Lowry, "David McCallum Is Uncomfortable Center of Growing Cult of Admirers," *The Register* [Danville, VA], September 5, 1965, 6d.

35. "Cigar Smokers! Just Published ... Get 'Illya' Free," *San Antonio Light*, April 17, 1966, 13; and Heitland, *The Man from U.N.C.L.E. Book,* 164.

36. Heitland, *The Man from U.N.C.L.E.*, 53.

37. "The Quiet 'Man from U.N.C.L.E.'"; and "This Man, McCallum," *Rave*, June 1965.

38. "Television Is Ruining My Marriage," *Motion Picture Magazine*, February 1965; Vernon Scott, "Nontruth and Unreality," *Tucson Daily Citizen*, June 26, 1965, 29; "If THRUSH Were After You"; Gloria Stavers, "The Secret Life of David McCallum (Alias Illya Kuryakin)," *16 Magazine*, August 1965; and "Wanted for Stealing," *Romeo*, December 25, 1965.

39. "The Quiet 'Man from U.N.C.L.E.,'" 6; "This Man, McCallum"; Jack Ryan, "The Case of the Puzzled—and Puzzling—Romantic Idol," *Family Weekly*, September 26, 1965; Stavers, "The Secret Life"; "The Mystic Cult of Millions," *TV Guide*, March 19, 1966; and "Secret Side of a Secret Agent," *TV Week*, January 7, 1967, 12.

40. Szekley, "Teen Idols," 30.

41. Heitland, *The Man from U.N.C.L.E. Book*, 54. An MGM press release in 1966 claimed that he received 32,000 letters a month during the 1966–67 season, but studios tended to inflate such counts. "David McCallum," MGM press release for 1966–67 season, http://www.davidmccallumfansonline.com/mgmrelease2.htm (accessed May 21, 2013).

42. Chandler Brossard, "U.N.C.L.E.'s Illya: New Kind of TV Idol," *Look*, July 27, 1965; and Lowry, "David McCallum," 6d.

43. "The Quiet 'Man from U.N.C.L.E.'"; "This Man, McCallum"; Brossard, "U.N.C.L.E.'s Illya"; Ryan, "The Case of the Puzzled"; and Wolfe, "The Man Called I-l-l-y-a," SM 112, 117.

44. "David McCallum Goes on Record," *Teen Set,* November 1965.

45. Bob Thomas, "In Hollywood," *Jacksonville Journal* [Jacksonville, IL], May 28, 1966, 5.

46. Roger Elwood, "David McCallum—'I Can't Stand My Fans Much Longer!'" *Teen Circle*, June 1966, 23.

47. Toby Miller, *Spyscreen: Espionage on Film and TV from the 1930s to the 1960s* (Oxford: Oxford University Press, 2005), 108; Cynthia W. Walker, "The Future Just Beyond the Coat Hook: Technology, Politics, and the Postmodern Sensibility in *The Man from U.N.C.L.E.*," in *Channeling the Future: Essays on Science Fiction and Fantasy Television*, ed. Lincoln Geraghty (Lanham, MD: Scarecrow Press, 2009), 41–58.

48. "Wanted for Stealing."

49. "The Bow Wow Affair," Season 1, Disc 7, *The Man from U.N.CL.E.* (February 15, 1965; Burbank: Warner Home Video, 2008), DVD.

50. "The Secret Sceptre Affair," Season 1, Disc 7, *The Main from U.N.C.L.E.* (February 8, 1965; Burbank: Warner Home Video, 2008), DVD.

51. "The Pieces of Fate Affair," Season 3, Disc 8, *The Man from U.N.C.L.E.* (February 24, 1967; Burbank: Warner Home Video, 2008), DVD.

52. "The Pop Art Affair," Season 3, Disc 2, *The Man from U.N.C.L.E.* (October 21, 1966; Burbank: Warner Home Video, 2008), DVD.

53. David McDaniel, *The Dagger Affair. The Man from U.N.C.L.E. 4* (New York: Ace Books, 1965), 53; Harry Whittington, *The Doomsday Affair. The Man from U.N.C.L.E. 2* (New York: Ace Books, 1965), 10; and Michael Avallone, *The Man from U.N.C.L.E.* (New York: Ace Books, 1965), 127.

54. John T. Phillifent, *The Mad Scientist Affair. The Man from U.N.C.L.E. 5* (New York: Ace Books, 1966), 10.

55. Whittington, *Doomsday*, 42.

56. Ibid., 10.

57. Harry Overstreet and Bonaro Overstreet, *What We Must Know About Communism* (New York: W.W. Norton, 1958), 298.

58. W. Cleon Skousen, *The Naked Communist* (Salt Lake City: Ensign Publishing Co., 1961), 1.

59. Stephen J. Whitfield, *The Culture of the Cold War*, 2d ed. (Baltimore: Johns Hopkins University Press, 1996), 129–30.

60. *Silk Stockings*, DVD, directed by Rouben Mamoulian (1957; Burbank: Warner Home Video, 2003).

61. "If THRUSH Were After You"; and "McCallum Plays Kuryakin Kool, Man—But

Not When He's Rooting for Dodgers," Second Season Press Packet, http:///www.david mccallumfansonline.com/mgmrelease2.htm (accessed May 21, 2013).

62. Dean Hargrove, "Official Debriefings," Bonus Disc 1, *The Man from U.N.C.L.E.* (Burbank: Warner Home Video, 2008), DVD.

63. Thompson, "Teenagers Cry," x15.

64. Ibid.; and "This Man, McCallum."

65. "This Man, McCallum"; and Bernie Stiles, "U.N.C.L.E.'s Unlikely Sex Symbol," *Mr. Magazine*, 1966, http://www.davidmccallumfansonline.com/mr.magazine.htm (accessed on May 21, 2013).

66. "This Man, McCallum."

67. "The Hot Number Affair."

68. Avallone, *The Man U.N.C.L.E.*, 126–7.

69. "The Suburbia Affair," Season 3, Disc 6, *The Man from U.N.C.L.E.* (January 6, 1967; Burbank: Warner Home Video, 2008), DVD.

70. *The Iron Petticoat*, DVD, directed by Ralph Thomas (1956; Atlanta: Turner Vault Collection, 2013).

71. "The Her Master's Voice Affair."

72. "The Apple a Day Affair," Season 3, Disc 9, *The Man from U.N.C.L.E.* (March 24, 1967; Burbank: Warner Home Video, 2008), DVD.

73. "The Take Me to Your Leader Affair," Season 3, Disc 6, *The Man from U.N.C.L.E.* (December 30, 1966; Burbank: Warner Home Video, 2008), DVD.

74. Wolfe, "The Man Called I-l-l-y-a," SM 57.

75. Ibid., SM 112.

76. Donald Hamilton, *The Ambushers* (Greenwich, CT: Fawcett, 1963).

77. Thomas M. Barrett, "Desiring the Soviet Woman: Tatiana Romanova and *From Russia with Love*" (forthcoming).

78. "The Man from U.N.C.L.E.," Information for Writers, Research Files, Bonus Disc 2, *The Man from U.N.C.L.E.* (Burbank: Warner Home Video, 2008), DVD.

79. Louis Fischer, *Russia Revisited: A New Look at Russia and Her Satellites* (Garden City, NY: Doubleday, 1957), 17.

80. Shel Silverstein, *Playboy's Silverstein Around the World* (New York: Simon & Schuster, 2007), 50.

81. Harrison Salisbury, *To Moscow—And Beyond: A Reporter's Narrative* (New York: Harper, 1960), 46–8.

82. Ibid.

83. Howard Norton, *Only in Russia* (Princeton: D. Van Norstrand, 1961), 88–90; and Maurice Hindus, *House Without a Roof: Russia After Forty-Three Years of Revolution* (Garden City, NY: Doubleday, 1961), 13–16.

84. "Mystic Cult."

85. Vernon Scott, "Pravda Raps Mild Scotsman's Role," *Chronicle Telegram* [Elyria, OH], January 19, 1966, 19.

86. "World Peace," *Hutchinson News* [Hutchinson, KS], August 5, 1967, 7a.

87. "David McCallum," MGM press release for 1966–67 season.

88. Jane Ardmore, "Why I'm Becoming an American," *Motion Picture*, http:///www.davidmccallumfansonline.com/american.htm (accessed May 21, 2013).

89. "The Terbuf Affair."

90. "The Round Table Affair," Season 2, Disc 9, *The Man from U.N.C.L.E.* (March 25, 1966; Burbank: Warner Home Video, 2008), DVD.

91. "The Bat Cave Affair," Season 2, Disc 10, *The Man from U.N.C.L.E.* (April 1, 1966; Burbank: Warner Home Video, 2008), DVD.

92. "The Deadly Quest Affair," Season 4, Disc 3, *The Man from U.N.C.L.E.* (October 30, 1967; Burbank: Warner Home Video, 2008), DVD.

93. "The Project Strigas Affair," Season 1, Disc 3, *The Man from U.N.C.L.E.* (November 24, 1964; Burbank: Warner Home Video, 2008), DVD.
94. Ibid.
95. "The Jingle Bells Affair."
96. Ibid.
97. Ibid.
98. Ibid.
99. Ibid.
100. Wolfe, "The Man Called I-l-l-y-a."

Bibliography

Ardmore, Jane. "Why I'm Becoming an American." *Motion Picture.* http://www.david mccallumfansonline.com/american.htm.

Avallone, Michael. *The Man from U.N.C.L.E.* New York: Ace Books, 1965.

Barrett, Thomas M. "Desiring the Soviet Woman: Tatiana Romanova and *From Russia with Love.*" [Forthcoming.]

Big Jim McLain. DVD. Directed by Edward Ludwig. 1952. Burbank: Warner Home Video, 2007.

Brossard, Chandler. "U.N.C.L.E.'s Illya: New Kind of TV Idol." *Look,* July 27, 1965.

Brossard, Iris-Marie [Chandler]. *Illya, That Man from U.N.C.L.E.* New York: Pocket Books, 1966.

"Cigar Smokers! Just Published ... Get 'Illya' Free." *San Antonio Light,* April 17, 1966, 13.

Cuordileone, K.A. *Manhood and American Political Culture in the Cold War.* New York: Routledge, 2005.

"David McCallum." MGM Press Release. http://www.davidmccallumfansonline.com/mgmrelease2.htm.

"David McCallum Goes on Record." *Teen Set,* November 1965.

Elwood, Roger, "David McCallum—'I Can't Stand My Fans Much Longer!" *Teen Circle,* June 1966, 23.

Enns, Anthony. "The Fans from U.N.C.L.E. The Marketing and Reception of the Swinging '60s Spy Phenomenon." *Journal of Popular Film and Television* 28, no. 3 (Fall 2000): 124–32.

Fischer, Louis. *Russia Revisited: A New Look at Russia and Her Satellites.* Garden City, NY: Doubleday, 1957.

"Get a Free U.N.C.L.E. Card and an 'Illya' Sweater from David!" *16 Magazine,* October 1965.

Hamilton, Donald. *The Ambushers.* Greenwich, CT: Fawcett, 1963.

Hargrove, Dean. "Official Debriefings." Bonus Disc 1, *The Man from U.N.C.L.E.* Burbank: Warner Home Video, 2008.

Heitland, Jon. *The Man from U.N.C.L.E. Book: Behind-the-Scenes Story of a Television Classic.* New York: St. Martin's Press, 1987.

Hindus, Maurice. *House Without a Roof: Russia After Forty-Three Years of Revolution.* Garden City, NY: Doubleday, 1961.

Hofstadter, Richard. *The Paranoid Style in American Politics and Other Essays.* New York: Alfred A. Knopf, 1966.

"If THRUSH Were After You, in Whose Arms Would You Want to Be Saved?" *Photoplay,* August 1965.

"Ilya [sic] on Target." *McCallum & Vaughn—2 Magazines in One.* http://www.davidmccallum fansonline.com/target.htm.

"Illya's Background." *The Republican-Courier* [Finlay, OH], September 21, 1966, 4.

The Iron Petticoat. DVD. Directed by Ralph Thomas. 1956. Atlanta: Turner Vault Collection, 2013.

Kackman, Michael. *Citizen Spy: Television, Espionage, and Cold War Culture.* Minneapolis: University of Minnesota Press, 2005.

Lowry, Cynthia. "David McCallum Is Uncomfortable Center of Growing Cult of Admirers." *The Register* [Danville, VA], September 5, 1965, 6d.

Mackin, Tom. "McCallum Tailors Role to Himself." *Newark Evening News.* http://www. davidmccallumfansonline.com/tailorsrole.htm.

"The Man from U.N.C.L.E.," Information for Writers, Research Files, Bonus Disc 2, *The Man from U.N.C.L.E.* Burbank: Warner Home Video, 2008. DVD.

The Man from U.N.C.L.E. "The Apple a Day Affair," March 24, 1967. Burbank: Warner Home Video, 2008. Season 3, Disc 9. DVD.

_____. "The Bat Cave Affair," April 1, 1966. Burbank: Warner Home Video, 2008. Season 1, Disc 7, DVD.

_____. "The Bow Wow Affair," February 15, 1965. Burbank: Warner Home Video, 2008. Season 1, Disc 7. DVD.

_____. "The Deadly Decoy Affair," January 11, 1965. Burbank: Warner Home Video, 2008. Season 1, Disc 5. DVD.

_____. "The Deadly Quest Affair," October 30, 1967. Burbank: Warner Home Video, 2008. Season 4, Disc 3. DVD.

_____. "The Fiddlesticks Affair," January 18, 1965. Burbank: Warner Home Video, 2008. Season 1, Disc 6. DVD.

_____. "The Foxes and Hounds Affair," October 8, 1965. Burbank: Warner Home Video, 2008. Season 2, Disc 2. DVD.

_____. "The Girls of Nazarone Affair," April 12, 1965. Burbank: Warner Home Video 2008. Season 1, Disc 10. DVD.

_____. "The Her Master's Voice Affair," September 16, 1966. Burbank: Warner Home Video, 2008. Season 3, Disc 1. DVD.

_____. "The Hot Number Affair," March 10, 1967. Burbank: Warner Home Video, 2008. Season 3, Disc 9. DVD.

_____. "The Jingle Bells Affair," December 23, 1966. Burbank: Warner Home Video, 2008. Season 3, Disc 5. DVD.

_____. "The Love Affair," March 29, 1965. Burbank: Warner Home Video, 2008. Season 1, Disc 9. DVD.

_____. "The Neptune Affair," December 8, 1964. Burbank: Warner Home Video, 2008. Season 1, Disc 4. DVD.

_____. "The Odd Man Affair," April 19, 1965. Burbank: Warner Home Video, 2008. Season 1, Disc 10. DVD.

_____. "The Pieces of Fate Affair," February 24, 1967. Burbank: Warner Home Video, 2008. Season 3, Disc 8. DVD.

_____. "The Pop Art Affair," October 21, 1966. Burbank: Warner Home Video, 2008. Season 3, Disc 2. DVD.

_____. "The Project Strigas Affair, November 24, 1964. Burbank: Warner Home Video, 2008. Season 1, Disc 3. DVD.

_____. "The Round Table Affair," March 25, 1966. Burbank: Warner Home Video, 2008. Season 2, Disc 9. DVD.

_____. "The Secret Sceptre Affair," February 8, 1965. Burbank: Warner Home Video, 2008. Season 1, Disc 7. DVD.

_____. "The Suburbia Affair," January 6, 1967. Burbank: Warner Home Video, 2008. Season 3, Disc 6. DVD.

_____. "Take Me to Your Leader," December 30, 1966. Burbank: Warner Home Video, 2008. Season 3, Disc 6. DVD.

_____. "The Trebuf Affair," December 29, 1964. Burbank: Warner Home Video, 2008. Season 1, Disc 5. DVD.

_____. "The Ultimate Computer Affair," October 1, 1965. Burbank: Warner Home Video, 2008. Season 2, Disc 1. DVD.

"McCallum Is Hit." *San Antonio Light,* February 28, 1965, 10-tv.

"McCallum Plays Kuryakin Kool, Man—But Not When He's Rooting for Dodgers." *Second Season Press Packet.* http://www.davidmccallumfansonline.com/mgmrelease2.htm.

McDaniel, David. *The Dagger Affair. The Man from U.N.C.L.E. 4.* New York: Ace Books, 1965.

Miller, Edwin. "The Spy Who'd Rather Not Be Known," *17 Magazine,* September 1965, 116–17.

Miller, Toby. *Spyscreen: Espionage on Film and TV from the 1930s to the 1960s.* Oxford: Oxford University Press, 2005.

"The Mystic Cult of Millions." *TV Guide,* March 19, 1966.

Norton, Howard. *Only in Russia.* Princeton: D. Van Norstrand, 1961.

Overstreet, Harry, and Bonaro Overstreet. *What We Must Know about Communism.* New York: W.W. Norton, 1958.

Phillifent, John T. *The Mad Scientist Affair. The Man from U.N.C.L.E. 5.* New York: Ace Books, 1966.

"The Quiet 'Man from U.N.C.L.E.'" *TV Guide,* April 17, 1965, 6.

Ryan, Jack. "The Case of the Puzzled—and Puzzling—Romantic Idol." *Family Weekly,* September 26, 1965.

Salisbury, Harrison. *To Moscow—And Beyond: A Reporter's Narrative.* New York: Harper, 1960.

Scheuer, Steven H. "TV Mailbag." *San Antonio Light,* April 11, 1965, 10.

Scott, Vernon. "Nontruth and Unreality." *Tucson Daily Citizen,* June 26, 1965, 29.

_____. "Pravda Raps Mild Scotsman's Role." *Chronicle Telegram* [Elyria, OH], January 19, 1966, 19.

"Secret Side of a Secret Agent." *TV Week,* January 7, 1967, 12.

Shcherbenok, Anthony. "Asymmetric Warfare: The Vision of the Enemy in American and Soviet Cold War Cinemas." *KinoKultura,* April 2010. http://www.kinokultura.com.2010/28-shcherbenok.shtml (accessed May 12, 2010).

Silk Stockings. DVD. Directed by Rouben Mamoulian. 1957. Burbank: Warner Home Video, 2003.

Silverstein, Shel. *Playboy's Silverstein Around the World.* New York: Simon & Schuster, 2007.

Skousen, W. Cleon. *The Naked Communist.* Salt Lake City: Ensign, 1961.

Stavers, Gloria. "The Secret Life of David McCallum (Alias Illya Kuryakin)." *16 Magazine,* August 1965.

Stiles, Bernie. "U.N.C.L.E.'s Unlikely Sex Symbol." *Mr. Magazine,* 1966.

Szekely, Susan. "Teen Idols Are Larger Than Life." *Tucson Daily Citizen,* January 25, 1967, 30.

"Television Is Ruining My Marriage." *Motion Picture Magazine,* February 1965.

"This Man, McCallum." *Rave,* June 1965.

Thomas, Bob. "In Hollywood." *Jacksonville Journal* [Jacksonville, IL], May 28, 1966, 5.

Thompson, Howard. "The Teenagers Cry U.N.C.L.E." *New York Times,* June 20, 1965, x15.

"TV Boosts Popularity of Actor." *Times Recorder* [Zanesville, OH], March 4, 1965, 6B.

Walker, Cynthia W. "The Future from Just Beyond the Coat Hook: Technology, Politics, and the Postmodern Sensibility in *The Man from U.N.C.L.E.*" In *Channeling the Future: Essays on Science Fiction and Fantasy Television,* edited by Lincoln Geraghty, 41–58. Lanham, MD: Scarecrow Press, 2009.

"Wanted for Stealing." *Romeo,* December 25, 1965.

Whitfield, Stephen J. *The Culture of the Cold War,* 2d ed. Baltimore: Johns Hopkins University Press, 1996.

Whittington, Harry. *The Doomsday Affair. The Man from U.N.C.L.E. 2.* New York: Ace Books, 1965.

Wolfe, Bernard. "The Man Called I-l-l-y-a." *New York Times*, October 24, 1965, sm56.
"World Peace." *Hutchinson News* [Hutchinson, KS], August 5, 1967, 7a.
Worland, Rick. "The Cold War Mannerist: *The Man from U.N.C.L.E.* and TV Espionage in the 1960s." *Journal of Popular Film and Television* 21, no. 4 (Winter 1994): 150–61.

Who, Doctor Who

007's Influence on the
Pertwee Era of Doctor Who

John Vohlidka

At first glance, it may seem the only things spy film franchise James Bond and sci-fi television series *Doctor Who* have in common are that they are both British, the actor playing the lead character changes, and they are both roughly fifty years old. There is much more to it than this. The popularity of the Bond films made being British cool and portrayed England as the center of the world. Jon Pertwee is known as the "James Bond of *Doctor Who.*"[1] *Doctor Who* first aired on the BBC November 23, 1963. The main character, known simply as the Doctor, travels through time and space. To date, thirteen actors have played the Doctor in the television series. While the Doctor's title never changes in the context of the program, to clarify discussions, each actor is assigned a number. Jon Pertwee was the third actor to play the Doctor making him the Third Doctor. During his tenure (1970–1974), the series took a drastically different turn from the previous two Doctors. These changes can be seen as a legacy of the Bond films.

The Bond films were an attempt to retain Britain's status as a major power, at the time its empire was dissolving. By the early sixties, a large portion of the British Empire was gone with more of it disappearing. In the 1940s, Britain had an empire, which stretched around the world and had just defeated Germany. The 1950s saw de-colonization, a poor economy and rationing.[2] By the 1960s, a hungry public wanted to know what Britain's role would be in the world.[3] This would continue into the 1970s, exacerbated by social and political unrest.[4] The Bond films fed into the idea that the new Britain would still be a major player in global events.[5] Britain's 'greatness' in an age after empires was a conundrum in British popular culture. James Bond attempted to solve this by demonstrating British greatness in the form of Bond himself who embodied Britishness through the values of individuality and independence.[6] *Doctor Who* did the same, with the Doctor demonstrating those same British qualities to a more diverse audience on the small screen both at home and abroad. While Bond films were mainly for a grown-up movie going audience, *Doctor Who* was for all ages and broadcast right into their homes, making it more accessible and affordable to all classes, genders and peoples. By the time of the Third Doctor, the series was being broadcast around the world and growing in popularity.

Pertwee's Doctor was more action-oriented than his two predecessors and his time on the show saw fights, chase scenes, gadgets, super villains, and more. His Doctor was in fact a superhero of sorts, an individual with exceptional knowledge combined with superior fighting skills and a strong sense of right and wrong.[7] The template for the character comes from James Bond. While the Bond films stem from Ian Fleming's novels and feature British actors; they had a more American slant than the novels and 007 became more and more superhuman as the films went on.[8] Both the Bond films and *Doctor Who* were a response to the declining British Empire. The Third Doctor was influenced by the film Bond—a combination of the classic British hero of the Empire combined with the classic hero of America. This was demonstrated in the changes in *Doctor Who* and in its answer to a British public wondering about the continued relevance of their nation.

During the Pertwee years, the Doctor found himself more Earthbound in modern day Britain. While previously, he went back and forth in time and sort of fell into situations, it was now present day Earth, in most cases, facing danger. He would save the day, often from some megalomaniacal madman or other threats. There was a steady cast of supporting characters much like Bond had; these were military and official characters, like the Brigadier, Sergeant Benton and Captain Yates. Both James Bond and the Time Lord had gadgets and vehicles; the secret agent might have a magnetic watch and a car that doubled as a submarine, the Doctor had a sonic screwdriver and a car that could fly. In place of Bond's Blofeld, a recurring villain, the Master, was introduced on the television series. This Nehru jacket–clad master of disguise usually wanted to take over or destroy the world with some sort of super weapon. There were chases, fights, and daring feats. Still it was his intelligence, morals, sense of justice, and calm "Britishness" which made the Doctor, like James Bond, the hero of his series (or anti-hero in the case of Bond to some critics).

For an adversary, the Bond films focused on SPECTRE, a secret organization of evil geniuses and criminal networks.[9] Thus, James Bond's superhuman attributes were pitted against a super-organization of criminals. This superheroic nature was copied in *Doctor Who*. The Second Doctor was a clown who always knew more than he seemed. Pertwee's Doctor, with his flamboyant costume and cape (!), was every inch the superhero.[10] Bond was an expert in everything from Saki to microchips; the Doctor was an expert on vintage wines to the publications of prominent government ministers.

The Pertwee years marked a new direction for a television show that was already six years old. Instead of the cosmic hobo wandering through the universe, the Doctor was grounded, in more than one sense, in contemporary Britain. This grounding, as well as the new look of the show, was heavily influenced by the Bond films. In place of strange planets and aliens "with trees growing out of their ears," as producer Derrick Sherwin remarked, the Doctor would now face alien invaders and evil masterminds and there would be plenty of gadgets, quips and action.[11] Like the Bond films, *Doctor Who* would reinforce the concept that Britain was still a world leader during a time it had lost its empire.

History

Doctor Who began in 1963 as a science fiction serial aimed at a family audience. The central character, the Doctor, traveled through both time and space in his machine, the TARDIS, and he traveled with a variety of companions over the years. The original series ran from 1963 to 1989. It was revived in 2005 and is still going. This longevity was guaranteed in the show's third season when the lead actor, William Hartnell, was replaced by Patrick Troughton, establishing that the alien Doctor, a Time Lord from Gallifrey, could change his appearance and personality (regenerate) ensuring that the show could keep up with the times and actors wanting to leave.

When Troughton decided to leave the series in 1969, it was decided at the BBC to use this opportunity to change the style of the show. There would be fewer episodes per season, but they would be in color. The show would also skew towards an older audience and the Doctor would be more Earthbound.[12] These decisions were made by outgoing producer Derrick Sherwin and handed off to the new production staff, with Barry Letts becoming the new producer and Terrence Dicks hired as the new script editor. Trapping the Doctor on Earth was a decision they chafed at, but it was one with which they were stuck. The new lead actor chosen was Jon Pertwee, a well-known comic actor who had been in a number of the *Carry On* films and whose voice was familiar to listeners of the popular radio show *The Navy Lark* (1959–1977).

Jon Pertwee's life prepared him for his role. Coming from an acting family, he worked on stage and did some radio work before the start of the Second World War. During the war, he joined the navy where he worked in submarines and later on the *HMS Hood*. He had the extraordinary good fortune to be chosen as a cadet and was transferred off the *Hood* not long before that ship's fateful meeting with the *Bismarck*. He worked for Bond's creator, Ian Fleming, in Naval Intelligence (NID). There he did a number of things, including teaching commandos to use escapology equipment (gadgets) and working in the security staff.[13] His time in intelligence would help prepare him for his later role as the action-oriented Doctor. He even attended a number of Churchill's meetings (stealing Churchill's cigar butts to sell to American GIs).[14] Fearing that he would be sent to France as an agent (he came from a French Huguenot family), he deliberately flunked a French language test to avoid the mission, only to find out later from Fleming that the post was to be in Tahiti.[15] Hence, he was familiar with the world of espionage and with intelligence reports and gadgets.

After the war, Pertwee returned to stage work and did some very early and experimental television but spent most of the 1950s and 1960s doing parts in films and radio work. He turned down the lead role on the television series *Dad's Army* (1968–1977) to do a play on Broadway, but that play shut down and he returned to England and the radio. While on *The Navy Lark*, he was tapped to play the lead in *Doctor Who*, where he became a popular and well-known actor recognized by millions.

Pertwee, while primarily a comedic actor, desired to play the role straight. Although, it should be noted, the Doctor is serious about what he does, not how he does it. "I wanted to be the science fiction James Bond," Pertwee said.[16] His regeneration turned him into a suave, sophisticated, cool character as opposed to the grandfatherly or trampish previous two incarnations. Like Bond, he wore stylish clothes appropriate for the time (but which also referred back to Britain's early Imperial days),[17] as did his female companions who were all from present day as well.

UNIT

While Bond worked for MI-5, the Doctor worked for UNIT, the United Nations Intelligence Taskforce, a military intelligence organization, and the Time Lords, making him an agent who was sent on missions. The Doctor became the unofficial scientific advisor to UNIT, which had débuted during the Second Doctor's tenure. The Doctor thus became an unofficial part of a military organization and a number of militaristic regulars joined the show: Brigadier Alistair Gordon Lethbridge-Stewart, Captain Mike Yates, Sergeant Benton and the Doctor's assistants: Liz Shaw, Jo Grant, and Sarah Jane Smith.

James Bond was frequently assigned a female agent to help him on his missions. So too was the Doctor. His assistants (or companions) were meant to be a human link for the audience: characters for the girls watching to relate to, and something for the dads to look at. The Third Doctor's first companion was smart, sassy scientist, Liz Shaw. Liz could hold her own in the laboratory or in peril. In *The Ambassadors of Death*, her captor warns her not to try anything. She retorts, "Don't worry, I won't hurt you."[18] She shared the Doctor's love of science and helped him find cures and solutions for the various threats they faced. Even if the Doctor was captured, Liz would carry on. Despite her serious scientific position, her skirts got shorter as her time on the show went on.

Pertwee's second season saw the arrival of a new assistant, the quirky, bumbling Jo Grant. She possessed none of the advanced degrees of her predecessor. She only had UNIT training courses and an uncle at the United Nations who got her the job. Her escapology course came in handy as she was frequently captured and threatened with lethal gas, radiation, explosives, hypnosis, and human sacrifice. She escapes from handcuffs in *Colony in Space*, stops a prison riot in *The Mind of Evil*, crawls out a window and along a ledge in *The Curse of Peladon*, escapes through an air vent in *The Sea Devils,* and hits people on the head with a wine bottle (*Day of the Daleks*), tray (*The Mind of Evil*), and vase (*Terror of the Autons*). The final few stories of the Pertwee era introduced feisty feminist Sarah Jane Smith, a journalist, who stowed away on the TARDIS while she was working under cover. This independent journalist got into just as much trouble as her two predecessors as her investigative nature frequently put her in danger. While not a member of UNIT, she assisted the Doctor in his adventures. Sarah Jane stayed on with the Fourth Doctor and eventually had two spin-off series of her own.

The men of UNIT should not be ignored. The Brigadier served as an M figure in the series. While he answered to Geneva, instead of London, he still represented the old Imperial military might of Great Britain. His formal attitude and mustache were very British. When confronted by a living gargoyle in *The Daemons*, he remains unflappable and crisply orders a soldier, "Chap with the wings there. Five rounds rapid."[19] The security of the world was often in his hands and he relied on the Doctor to find solutions to the threats they faced. They did not always agree on what those solutions should be, as in *Doctor Who and the Silurians* where the Brigadier ordered the bombing of the caves killing the Silurians, a solution that infuriated the Doctor. The Brigadier did occasionally go under cover and get involved in some action, but he mainly dealt with trying to keep the Doctor under control.

His subordinates, Yates and Benton did most of the fieldwork and got involved in chases, gunfights, and other action. While they too were action heroes in the various stories, their main purpose was to support the Doctor or help stretch the story out. Yates flew helicopters and rode motorbikes in *The Daemons*. He went undercover and was brainwashed in *The Green Death*. In *The Mind of Evil*, he was shot and captured. Sadly, through misguided optimism, he ended up as one of the bad guys in *Invasion of the Dinosaurs*.

The loyal and loveable Sergeant Benton was always on the Doctor's side even when higher ups wanted the Doctor detained or did not trust him. He helped the Doctor escape in *Invasion of the Dinosaurs*. He often took a beating from the bad guys, such as in *The Daemons*. Benton did the grunt work. He manned the HQ, drove jeeps, tailed suspects, guarded prisoners, and stayed behind to mop up after UNIT raids. While he did not have a major role in the stories, Benton's unswerving dedication to the Doctor made him an integral part of the Pertwee Era.

The Nemesis

For the second season of Pertwee's tenure as the Doctor, Letts and Dicks decided to introduce a regular villain, a Moriarty to the Doctor's Holmes. The Master, a rival Time Lord, was introduced. Played by Roger Delgado, he was the main villain in every story that year: *Terror of the Autons*, *The Mind of Evil*, *The Claws of Axos*, *Colony in Space*, and *The Daemons*. He would also appear in two stories the following season: *The Sea Devils* and *The Time Monster* and the story *Frontier in Space* the season after that. Conceived as a foil who could match the Doctor in intelligence, Delgado's Master owed as much to Bond's villains as to Professor Moriarty. We can see parallels with Dr. No's scientific knowledge, Largo's cunning, and Blofeld's ruthlessness.[20] The Master killed without hesitation, used humans as pawns in his plans, and cared only about himself. In a few stories, he even helps the Doctor save Earth, not out of a change of heart, but because of his own strong sense of self-preservation. His degree in Cosmic Science was a higher class than the Doctor's. He knew a great deal about human and alien technology: he used shrink rays, built a machine to awaken the Sea Devils, and developed the TOMTIT machine. This device turned matter into light waves and transported it through time. He even preferred a Nehru jacket, as did a number of Bond villains (Blofeld and Dr. No). Delgado's performance as the Master even resembles how some of the villains in the early Bond films were portrayed. The black gloves worn by the Master mirror Dr. No's black hands. Pertwee said of Delgado's performance, "Roger understood that evil is best shown not by histrionics, but by being calm. Controlled. Cold, rigid evil."[21] This sounds very much like the portrayal of Dr. No, who, while he sat down to dinner with Bond, remained cold and emotionless.

Delgado's performance, ethnicity, and Nehru jacket, identified him as the Other, compared to Pertwee's Britishness. As with most of the Bond villains of that period, the Master was not British. Played by the half–Spanish Delgado, the Master's look connected with the Black Legend, a derogatory view of the

Spanish, which has persisted for over 500 years.[22] This negative view of the Spaniard appears to have started around the time of the Spanish Armada. Historian Eric Griffin dates the view to English polemicists who after the aborted invasion typified the Spanish as "cruel, duplicitous, arrogant, bestial, hypocritical, over-sexed, Antichristian, and ethnic."[23] This stereotypical view has persisted over the centuries. Delgado represented the Other in British society. Also, his Master generally attempted to destroy from within, disguising himself as a college professor in *The Time Monster*, or a vicar in *The Daemons*, not unlike various "yellow peril" storylines.[24] He therefore symbolized the dangerous non–Briton who threatened British society, an important point at a time of controversial immigration in Britain.[25]

The Master's arrival on Earth was in *Terror of the Autons*. He appears here as the well-dressed villain in either his Nehru jacket or suit and tie. He uses hypnosis to take control of a plastics factory to allow the Nestenes to invade the Earth. The Doctor receives an "M-like" briefing at the beginning of the story. A Time Lord, looking very conservative and British with his bowler hat and cane, warns and instructs the Doctor about the arrival of the Master on Earth. This rather informal briefing sets the stage for a number of other missions the Doctor would undertake on behalf of the Time Lords lasting right through the Tom Baker story *The Brain of Morbius*.

As did Bond's foes, the Master frequently told his plans to the hero and put off killing the Doctor, allowing time for an escape and the foiling of those plans. And what plans they were: from deadly plastic flowers (*Terror of the Autons*), to alien doomsday weapons (*Colony in Space*), to mind control and rockets (*The Mind of Evil*), and ancient demons (*The Daemons*) he tried everything to vanquish the human race. He was a master of disguise and dressed as adjudicators, vicars, businessmen, military personnel, phone repairmen, scientists, etc. The Master also had the power to hypnotize, and he had some gadgets of his own, including a laser gun, remote control death traps in his TARDIS, and even a machine for contacting the Sea Devils.

Villains and Plots

Although he did aid many of the Doctor's other foes (such as the Nestene, Axons, Daleks, and Sea Devils) for his own gain, the Master was not the only threat the Doctor faced. Plenty of aliens wanted to invade or destroy the Earth or humanity. Corporations, technology, and misguided idealism were also evils to be dealt with. The real threat these villains pose is similar to that of the Bond villains although in *Doctor Who* the threat seems more outlandish. Still in both, the villains are a threat to the status quo: the inhuman Daleks (*Day of the Daleks*) represent a fascist threat to liberal democracy; both the Axons (*The Claws of Axos*) and the Sea Devils (*The Sea Devils*) are a threat to the social order, as in their attempts to eradicate humanity they view all humans as the same; the giant maggots created by Global Chemicals (*The Green Death*) represent the threat of an excessive capitalist system against nature; even the giant spiders of Metebelis III (*Planet of the Spiders*) were villainous as they had taken control over humans, thereby upending the natural order. In other words, the threat this myriad of villains posed resembled those problems of the 1960s and 1970s (including decolonization, immigration, strikes, and modernization among others) that threatened to end the comfortable life that the viewer enjoyed.

Several of the Pertwee stories contain similar themes or motifs to the Bond films. In *Doctor Who and the Silurians*, the previous inhabitants of Earth, a reptilian species who had been in hibernation for centuries, awaken thanks to a nuclear reactor being built in the caves where they slept. The Silurians' plan to destroy humanity involved using a deadly virus that would be spread from person to person. This epidemic type weapon is similar to Blofeld's plan in *On Her Majesty's Secret Service* (1969, Peter Hunt).

The Mind of Evil borrows a similar motif from *Thunderball* (1965, Terrence Young). In *Thunderball*, Emilio Largo steals a NATO nuclear missile to blackmail nations and start a war. In *The Mind of Evil*, the Master steals a British nuclear missile to start a war. Both stories play into nuclear fears of the Cold War, where a resourceful maniac could tip the balance of power, leading to a nuclear confrontation.

Colony in Space borrows from *Dr. No* (1962, Terrence Young) with the Interplanetary Mining Corporation using a machine to play the role of monster to scare the colonists. Dr. No's security on Crab Key included a tank people thought was a dragon. Both use the motif of modern technology used against people's superstitions or fears. In *Dr. No*, the dragon tank kept superstitious islanders away from Dr. No's atomic reactor. In *Colony in Space*, IMC's monster machine plays on the colonists' fears of the unknown to drive them off the planet.

Gadgets and Vehicles

Pertwee had a fondness for gadgets and liked to incorporate them into the show whenever possible. The Doctor served as his own Q making many of his own gadgets. The sonic screwdriver was of course the most notable of all these. During his time as the Doctor, the use of the now iconic device became common on the show. This instrument was supplemented by a host of other mechanical devices including automatic door openers, homemade communicators, a TARDIS tracking device in his watch, explosives, and more.

For most incarnations of the Doctor, his most important and impressive vehicle is his TARDIS. This ship/time machine, which is bigger on the inside, is meant to disguise itself with the surroundings of wherever/whenever it lands. A broken circuit the Doctor never bothered to repair keeps it in the form of a British police box (underlying the essential Britishness of his character). In the Pertwee era, the Time Lords exiled him to Earth and took away his control of the TARDIS. He is only allowed to leave Earth when they decide to send him on missions and make his ship operational again. In the meantime, the Doctor had to find more modest means of transportation.

One of the first things the Doctor asked for when joining UNIT was a car. James Bond had his Aston-Martin; the Doctor had Bessie. This bright yellow Victorian-style roadster became highly identifiable with the Third Doctor. Bessie was involved in many chase and action scenes. In *The Green Death*, the Doctor and Benton throw dangerous fungus from Bessie to kill the giant maggots. Bad guys steal Bessie in *The Ambassadors of Death*, only to find she is equipped with an anti-theft device which causes them to be stuck to the car. The Doctor was frequently seen tinkering with his car. He tricked her out with gadgets that would make Q jealous. Some of the improvements he made included the antitheft device, a super-drive that allowed it to go at great speed, remote control (that the Doctor used to capture the Master), and brakes, which worked on the absorption of inertia.

For Pertwee's last season on the show, a futuristic car, the Whomobile was added. Pertwee designed the car himself and had it manufactured for his use. Producer Barry Letts asked if they could use it for the show. "I'll be brokenhearted if you don't!" responded Pertwee.[26] The vehicle only appeared in two stories: *Invasion of the Dinosaurs* and *Planet of the Spiders*. His regular car aside, the Doctor and other characters of the show used a variety of vehicles: motorbikes, choppers, mini-copters, army trucks, jeeps and a mobile HQ.

Action

The popularity of films such as the Bond series and the influx of American programs on British television, created an audience looking for action and excitement. As the audience for *Doctor Who* was now considered to be slightly older, the production team felt they could get away with more action. Fisticuffs and gunplay became a regular motif in the series as a backdrop to the Doctor's activities.

Just as in *Goldfinger* (1964, Guy Hamilton) and *On Her Majesty's Secret Service*, where climatic battle scenes occurred, UNIT soldiers were involved in quite a few shoot outs during Pertwee's years as the Doctor; and some of these shoot outs, like in *The Ambassadors of Death*, *The Mind of Evil*, or *Day of the Daleks*, could be quite extensive. Nevertheless, they were generally used as a method to help the Doctor defeat the villains. This does not mean the Doctor was unwilling or unable to fight his own battles. As Bond might personally battle opponents such as Oddjob or Mr. Wint and Mr. Kidd, the Third Doctor was no slouch in hand-to-hand combat.

Previous incarnations of the Doctor left the fight scenes to their younger male companions. The First Doctor's companion, Ian, fought Aztec warriors, Roman gladiators, and Daleks, while the Second Doctor's companion, Jamie, fought Cybermen and War Lords to name a few. Pertwee's Doctor took on the role of action hero himself and was a master of a fighting technique called Venusian Aikido. His Judo-like chops, flips, kicks, and the yelling of "Hi-Ya!" made short work of enemies. Private guards, soldiers and even alien thugs found themselves on the receiving end of the Doctor's martial ability. Usually, he would still get captured in the end allowing for an exciting escape scene later. *The Time Warrior* saw him swing on a chandelier, and have a sword fight while he was disguised as a robot. In *The Curse of Peladon*, he fights the king's champion in a pit with an axe and hand-to-hand combat.

The Doctor also shared James Bond's British sense of calm under pressure. Bond could calmly keep a villain like Red Grant talking in *From Russia with Love* (1963, Terrence Young) or make quips while being interrogated in *You Only Live Twice* (1967, Lewis Gilbert). The Doctor made jokes while captured and threatened in *Inferno*. While in a sword fight with the Master in *The Sea Devils*, he grabs a sandwich to eat because "violent exercise" makes him hungry.[27] When Jo knocks out an Ogron with a bottle of wine in *Day of the Daleks*, he says, "pity, it was a rather good vintage."[28] He also had a sense of humor about himself and his abilities. In *The Daemons*, the Brigadier asks, "do you know what you are doing?" the Doctor replies, "My dear chap, I can't wait to find out."[29]

The Chase

One of the cornerstone sequences in the Bond films is the chase scene. From *From Russia with Love*'s boat chase through *On Her Majesty's Secret Service*'s ski chase to *Live and Let Die*'s (1973, Guy Hamilton) speedboat chase, the chase scene became an integral part of the James Bond film experience. *Doctor Who* copied this idiom clearly. Although generally not as involved or as long (or expensive), there were a number of attempts to tap into the visual excitement of the chase scene. *The Daemons* saw the Doctor chased by a helicopter, which in turn was chased by Captain Yates on a motorcycle. In *Day of the Daleks*, the Doctor attempts to escape the Ogrons on an ATV (not unlike 007 in *Diamonds Are Forever* [1971, Guy Hamilton]). The Doctor went after the Master in a boat chase in *The Sea Devils*. In his first story, *Spearhead from Space*, Pertwee's Doctor makes his escape via wheelchair.

Chase scenes add a drop of excitement to a story and they appeared with a startling regularity on the show as compared to the previous years. Pertwee preferred to do a number of his own stunts on the show, although most of the stunts were done by his stunt double, Terry Walsh.[30] Many of the action sequences he did, however, involved chases with cars or motorbikes, as he felt it would look better with the lead clearly behind the wheel.[31]

The biggest and most Bond-like of all the chase sequences occurred in episode two of Pertwee's last story, *Planet of the Spiders*. This was arranged by the producer as a sort of going away present for Pertwee.[32] The villain, Lupton, flees UNIT headquarters, taking the Doctor's Whomobile. The Brigadier, Benton and Sarah Jane Smith give chase in the Doctor's roadster, Bessie. Meanwhile, the Doctor hops into a mini-copter to spy things out from above. Bessie chases the Whomobile through country roads (surprising a policeman) until Lupton stops in a field. The Doctor lands, and he and his UNIT companions search for Lupton who comes out of hiding and steals the mini-copter. The Doctor and Sarah Jane jump into the Whomobile, which can apparently fly. Now it is an aerial chase until Lupton lands when he is low on fuel. He scrambles down to a lake to steal a speedboat. The Doctor follows, borrowing a hovercraft and again gives chase over the lake (being able to keep up by going over land obstacles occasionally); he is just about to catch Lupton when the latter dematerializes into thin air, ending the episode in a cliffhanger.

This sequence took up almost the entirety of episode two of the story. It was filmed and edited well and keeps up its energy throughout; the only thing it was truly missing was some good action music like 007 had. Pertwee delighted in such chase scenes. This action packed send-off episode exemplifies what Pertwee envisioned in his desire to be the James Bond of *Doctor Who*.[33]

The East, the West and the Nuclear Age

Still to consider is the treatment of nuclear power. Science fiction films of Japan's Toho Studios warned repeatedly of the dangers of nuclear testing particularly in their Godzilla films. From the dark *Gojira* in 1954 (Ishiro Honda) to the lighter fare of 1975's *Mekagojira No Gyakushu* (Ishiro Honda) these films continually stressed the message of the dangers of the atomic age. In the West, however, the threat of the atom, while acknowledged, was not taken as seriously.[34] While fears of nuclear destruction were highlighted in films as *The Beast from 20,000 Fathoms* (1953, Eugène Lourié), where a dinosaur is woken by atomic testing, the same beast was destroyed by an atomic bomb. This film, as in others of the fifties and sixties, optimistically demonstrates that nuclear science solves the very problems it creates.[35] In *Dr. No*, nuclear energy appears to merely add a modern flavor to the story, but its ramifications are actually ignored. The somber scene of Bond and Honey being put through numerous showers to rid them of all traces of radiation is counterbalanced by the end of the film: where Dr. No's nuclear reactor blows up and destroys a Caribbean island, and no one seems particularly concerned about any radioactive fallout.[36]

This casual manner toward the nuclear age is copied in *Doctor Who*. The appearance of nuclear power in the show is also there to add flavor to the stories. In both *Doctor Who and the Siliurians* and *Inferno*, the action takes place at nuclear facilities. In *Doctor Who and the Siliurians* the reactor is established in caves close to where the underground race is hibernating. Subsequent trouble with the reactor is established to be the result of Silurian interference, not through human agency. Even at the story's climax, when the Silurians take over the reactor, they do not threaten humanity with any kind of nuclear destruction, but rather wish to use the reactor to power their own doomsday device. In fact, nuclear power is so safe one could access the uranium rods through a window in the control room.

While *The Mutants* is one of the few Pertwee stories to take place away from contemporary Earth, it still demonstrates a lax attitude towards radiation. While Jo, Sondergaard, Cotton, and Ky are put in the refueling chamber to be killed by the radiation, the humans suffer no ill effects once they are rescued. The radiation was enough to transform alien Ky into a super-being, but the others are barely impacted and require no medical attention.

The Ambassadors of Death is a rare story that sets radiation up as the danger. Contagious radiation is the weapon of choice. Even then, it is established, the danger comes from a single individual who is using the deadly radiation for his own purposes. The radioactive aliens themselves, are portrayed as being inherently peaceful and non-hostile, suggesting that nuclear radiation is not dangerous either.

The non-threatening nature of nuclear energy is again demonstrated in *Invasion of the Dinosaurs*, where Sarah Jane Smith discovers the villains' secret lair is a government base with its own nuclear reactor, directly under the heart of London. In *Doctor Who*, nuclear power is not the enemy (the Doctor rarely addresses the issue) but to what purposes that power is used. It is not the inventors of nuclear power who are the problem, but those who corrupt its purpose, as in interfering in the U.S. space program (*Dr. No*); cracking open the Earth's crust (*Inferno*) or rolling back time to the "golden age" (*Invasion of the Dinosaurs*). Nuclear power is not considered inherently evil; it is to what purposes it is used.

This relaxed attitude towards nuclear power during the Pertwee era also highlights Britain's role as an active and important participant in the nuclear age. In *Doctor Who and the Silurians*, the nuclear plant is experimental, suggesting that Britain is actively furthering the use of nuclear energy. In *The Mind of Evil*, UNIT is transporting a nuclear missile that is clearly understood to be British made, not American. The might and power of Britain in the world is showcased in these stories.

The New and Old Britain

The Bond films perpetuate a fantasy that Britain is still a world power. Often, it is up to the British agent to protect the civilized world. In *Dr. No*, it is Bond who saves the American space program. In *Goldfinger*, he saves the U.S.'s gold supply at Fort Knox. In *Thunderball*, he is the principal agent to protect NATO from SPECTRE's extortion. The semi-regular appearance of CIA agent Felix Leiter underscores this position. In the stories, Leiter aids Bond, not the other way around. When they first meet in *Dr. No*, it is revealed that Leiter is also investigating, but Bond quickly takes charge, relegating Leiter to the role of assistant.[37] By later films, Felix is reduced to simply cleaning up after Bond's messes. Thus, it is our British hero who saves America, while maintaining that "special relationship" between the two powers on a more or less equal footing.[38]

In *Diamonds Are Forever*, it is Bond who personally puts an end to Blofeld's scheme to blackmail the world. This comes after Blofeld's nasty comment that Bond's "pitiful little island" had not even been threatened.[39] The film shows Blofeld's defeat by Bond, not the Americans who come along later to clean things up.

The same occurs in *Doctor Who*. The Doctor was a member of UNIT, which was an international organization; but it was a very British international organization. The regular members of UNIT, the Brigadier, Captain Yates, Sergeant Benton, and Jo Grant were all white Britons. *Doctor Who* was arguing the importance of Britain being involved in the world, some of the stories were pro–NATO or pro–Europe, but also that the world needed British involvement. The Doctor's clothes and attitudes were symbolic of these feelings. The frilly shirt and tuxedo jacket signified that he was independent and individualistic as he did not dress in a uniform like most of the members of UNIT.[40] Also, his independent streak was a fixed feature of the show, as the Doctor frequently went off on his own to investigate or solve a perilous situation, much to the chagrin of the Brigadier.

This was a continuation of the old Imperialist view, that the British Empire was justified as the world needed the hard-working, inherently decent, Protestant British to administrate it.[41] By the 1960s, Britain had turned its interests from its collapsing empire (made more digestible to the public by the existence of the British Commonwealth) to joining the European Economic Community. Nevertheless, it remained a part of British political orthodoxy that Britain still had a hand in world affairs.[42] Applications to join the EEC were vetoed by Charles de Gaulle, but Britain formally joined the Union in January of 1973.[43] This was mirrored in *Doctor Who*, which tended to be pro–Europe in stories like *The Curse of Peladon*.

In *Doctor Who*, the world still needed Britain. It was up to the Doctor and the Brigadier's UNIT (and like Bond, the Doctor always takes charge) to defeat world invasions from the likes of the Axons, the Nestene, the Daleks and others. Indeed, even invaders from outer space recognized Britain's importance, by targeting it first for invasion. Axos chose Britain as the site to land, expecting that nation to be powerful enough to distribute the Axonite around the world. Clearly, Axos expected Britain to have the infrastructure and distribution ability to connect the world. Interestingly, none of these invaders chose the U.S. or the Soviet Union, but rather Britain, showing that Britain was where the action was.

Conclusion

The two franchises show very different characters; both fueled by a sense of duty and desire to help. Both are British heroes, but in very different ways. While James Bond is a rather brutal character, he shows little or no remorse killing bad guys in the line of duty, his knowledge and appreciation of culture and the finer things in life make him civilized. He is not English, nor are the majority of actors to portray him. He himself is a product and triumph of Empire. Everything he does is for queen and country.[44] The movies even make his vices seem classy and civilized. He knows the proper way to mix a drink. He gambles in fancy casinos and seduces women in evening gowns. He is what every British male wishes he was. Meanwhile, the Doctor is what every British male should be. While he is not human and therefore not British, he is, as J.P.C. Brown called him, "a very British alien."[45] While Bond's civility softens him and makes him more palatable to the audience, the Doctor's superior civility, including his intellect and morals (he shares none of Bond's human vices), is what gives him his strength. He is always the smartest and most civilized person in the room and has no problem letting others know that. His disdain for administrators and bureaucrats is rarely hidden. He does not kill his enemies, but those on the wrong side of what is right and just, usually get theirs in the end by some means. Some redeem themselves at the end, others do not, depending on what lesson the show wishes to impart in each story.

Yet, the two characters had a great deal in common as well. Both were action-oriented characters, more so than the traditional British hero, which tended to rely more on intelligence than physical confrontation. Both had a military connection, a nemesis to battle, gadgets and chases. Most importantly, both were symbolic of what it meant to be British during the twilight of the empire. *Doctor Who* and the Bond films hung on to the last vestiges of the British Empire, while setting the stage for what lay ahead. While they do show the decline of empire and the society which it fed, they also show the resilience of the British people and their own ability to regenerate to face the times and challenges ahead.

James Bond and *Doctor Who* are both known around the world today and are still in production. They are relevant not only to British audiences, but to those worldwide. They have changed with the times, not only keeping up with new actors and technology, but by carrying on fundamental values relevant to audiences. Both these franchises show Britain in the 1960s and 1970s was becoming a cultural power rather than military power. They were still leading a sort of cultural imperialism. The Beatles, Rolling Stones, James Bond, *Doctor Who*, just to name a few, were part of the "British Invasion" which sent their culture throughout the world. Britannia may no longer have ruled the waves of the seas with their once mighty navy, but they ruled the airwaves with their music, movies and television.

Notes

1. John Kenneth Muir, *A Critical History of Doctor Who on Television* (Jefferson, NC: McFarland, 2008), 21.
2. Cynthia Baron, "Doctor No: Bonding Britishness to Racial Sovereignty," *Spectator: USC Journal of Film and Television Criticism* 14 (1994): 71.
3. J.P.C. Brown, "Doctor Who: A Very British Alien," in *The Galaxy Is Rated G: Essays on Children's Science Fiction Film and Television*, ed. R.C. Neighbors and Sandy Rankin (Jefferson, NC: McFarland, 2011), 164.
4. Christine Cornea, "British Science Fiction Television in the Discursive Context of Second Wave Feminism," *Genders Online Journal* 54 (Summer 2011): 5, http://www.genders.org/g54/g54_cornea.html.
5. Tony Bennett and Janet Woolacott, "The Moments of Bond," in *The James Bond*

Phenomenon: A Critical Reader, ed. Christoph Linder (Manchester: Manchester University Press, 2003), 26.

6. James Chapman and Matthew Hilton, "From Sherlock Holmes to James Bond: Masculinity and National Identity in British Popular Fiction," in *Relocating Britishness*, ed. Stephen Caunce, Ewa Mazierska, Susan Sydney-Smith, and John K. Walton (Manchester: Manchester University Press, 2004), 143.

7. David Layton, "Male and Female Archetypes in *Doctor Who*," *Consciousness, Literature and the Arts* 11, no. 2 (August 2010): 23.

8. Marc DiPaolo, *War, Politics and Superheroes: Ethics and Propaganda in Comics and Film* (Jefferson, NC: McFarland, 2011), 2.

9. Klaus Dodds, "Screening Geopolitics: James Bond and the Early Cold War Films (1962–1967)," *Geopolitics* 10 (2005): 281.

10. Piers D. Britton and Simon J. Barker, *Reading Between Designs: Visual Imagery and the Generation of Meaning in* The Avengers, The Prisoner, *and* Doctor Who (Austin: University of Texas Press, 2003), 149.

11. David J. Howe, Mark Stammers, and Stephen James Walker, *Doctor Who: The Seventies* (London: Doctor Who Books, 1994), 7.

12. James Chapman, *Inside the TARDIS: The Worlds of Doctor Who* (New York: I.B. Tauris, 2006), 77.

13. Jon Pertwee, *Moon Boots and Dinner Suits* (London: Elm Tree Books, 1984), 194.

14. Jon Pertwee, "Interview with Jon Pertwee," by Matt Adams and David Southwell, *Doctor Who Magazine* 457 (February 4, 2013): 27.

15. Pertwee, "Interview," 25.

16. Jon Pertwee, interview by David Banks, *David Banks Talks with Jon Pertwee: The Classic Who Interview Pertwee in Person*, 10th Planet, April 19, 1990.

17. Britton and Barker, *Reading Between Designs*, 149.

18. *Doctor Who: The Ambassadors of Death*, DVD, directed by Michael Ferguson (1970; London: BBC, 2012).

19. *Doctor Who: The Daemons*, DVD, directed by Christopher Barry (1971; London: BBC, 2012).

20. Baron, "Doctor No," 72.

21. Pertwee, "Interview," 23.

22. Samuel Amago, "Why Spaniards Make Good Bad Guys: Sergi Lopez and the Persistence of the Black Legend in Contemporary European Cinema," *Film Criticism* 30, no. 1 (Fall 2005): 42.

23. Eric Griffin, "From Ethos to Ethnos: Hispanizing 'the Spaniard' in the Old World and the New," *The New Centennial Review* 2, no. 1 (2002): 95.

24. John W. Dower, *War Without Mercy: Race and Power in the Pacific War* (New York: Random House, 1993), 117.

25. Alan Sked and Chris Cook, *Post-War Britain: A Political History* (New York: Penguin, 1990), 232.

26. Pertwee, interview by David Banks.

27. *Doctor Who: The Sea Devils*, DVD, directed by Michael E. Briant (1972; London: BBC, 2008).

28. *Doctor Who: Day of the Daleks*, DVD, directed by Paul Bernard (1972; London: BBC, 2011).

29. *Doctor Who: The Daemons*.

30. Howe, Stammers, and Walker, *Doctor Who*, 15.

31. Pertwee, "Interview," 25.

32. Jon Pertwee and David J. Howe, *I Am the Doctor: Jon Pertwee's Final Memoir* (London: Doctor Who Books, 1996), 109.

33. Pertwee, interview by David Banks.

34. Chon Noriega, "Godzilla and the Japanese Nightmare: When *Them*! Is U.S.," in *Hibakusha Cinema: Hiroshima, Nagasaki and the Nuclear Image in Japanese Film*, ed. Mick Broderick (New York: Kegan Paul International, 1996), 59.

35. Noriega, "Godzilla and the Japanese Nightmare," 59.

36. Christoph Laucht, "Britannia Rules the Atom: The James Bond Phenomenon and Postwar British Nuclear Culture," *The Journal of Popular Culture* 46, no. 2 (2013): 360.

37. Jeffrey Richards, "Imperial Heroes for a Post-Imperial Age: Films and the End of the Empire," in *British Culture and the End of Empire*, ed. Stuart Ward (Manchester: Manchester University Press, 2002), 136.

38. James Chapman, "Bond and Britishness," in *Ian Fleming & James Bond: The Cultural Politics of 007*, ed. Edward P. Comentale, Stephen Watt, and Skip Willman (Bloomington: Indiana University Press, 2005), 139.

39. Jeremy Black, *The Politics of James Bond: From Fleming's Novels to the Big Screen* (Westport, CT: Praeger, 2001), 128.

40. Brown, "Doctor Who: A Very British Alien," 172.

41. David Marquand, "'Bursting with Skeletons': Britishness after Empire," in *Britishness: Perspectives on the British Question*, ed. Andrew Gamble and Tony Wright (Chichester: Wiley-Blackwell, 2009), 16.

42. Stuart Ward, "Introduction," in *British Culture and the End of Empire*, ed. Stuart Ward (Manchester: Manchester University Press, 2002), 7.

43. Black, *The Politics of James Bond*, 129.

44. Paul Stock, "Dial 'M' for Metonym: Universal Exports, M's Office Space and Empire," *National Identities* 2, no. 1 (August 18, 2000): 39.

45. Brown, "Doctor Who: A Very British Alien," 161–82.

Bibliography

Amago, Samuel. "Why Spaniards Make Good Bad Guys: Sergi Lopez and the Persistence of the Black Legend in Contemporary European Cinema." *Film Criticism* 30, no. 1 (Fall 2005): 41–63.

Baron, Cynthia. "Doctor No: Bonding Britishness to Racial Sovereignty." *Spectator: USC Journal of Film and Television Criticism* 14, no. 2 (1994): 69–81.

Bennett, Tony, and Janet Woolacott. "The Moments of Bond." In *The James Bond Phenomenon: A Critical Reader*, edited by Christoph Linder, 13–33. Manchester: Manchester University Press, 2003.

Black, Jeremy. *The Politics of James Bond: From Fleming's Novels to the Big Screen*. Westport: Praeger, 2001.

Britton, Piers D., and Simon J. Barker. *Reading Between Designs: Visual Imagery and the Generation of Meaning in* The Avengers, The Prisoner, *and* Doctor Who. Austin: University of Texas Press, 2003.

Brown, J.P.C. "Doctor Who: A Very British Alien." In *The Galaxy is Rated G: Essays on Children's Science Fiction Film and Television*, edited by R.C. Neighbors and Sandy Rankin, 161–82. Jefferson, NC: McFarland, 2011.

Chapman, James. "Bond and Britishness." In *Ian Fleming & James Bond: The Cultural Politics of 007*, edited by Edward P. Comentale, Stephen Watt, and Skip Willman, 129–43. Bloomington: Indiana University Press, 2005.

_____. *Inside the TARDIS: The Worlds of Doctor Who*. New York: I.B. Tauris, 2006.

Chapman, James, and Matthew Hilton. "From Sherlock Holmes to James Bond: Masculinity and National Identity in British Popular Fiction." In *Relocating Britishness*, edited by Stephen Caunce, Ewa Mazierska, Susan Sydney-Smith, and John K. Walton, 126–47. Manchester: Manchester University Press, 2004.

Cornea, Christine. "British Science Fiction Television in the Discursive Context of Second Wave Feminism." *Genders Online Journal* 54 (Summer 2011). http://www.genders.org/g54/g54_cornea.html.

Diamonds Are Forever. DVD. Directed by Guy Hamilton. 1971. Beverly Hills: Twentieth Century–Fox Home Entertainment, 2012.

DiPaolo, Marc. *War, Politics and Superheroes: Ethics and Propaganda in Comics and Film.* Jefferson, NC: McFarland, 2011.

Dr. No. DVD. Directed by Terence Young. 1962. Beverly Hills: Twentieth Century–Fox Home Entertainment, 2008.

Doctor Who and the Silurians. DVD. Directed by Timothy Combe. 1970. London: BBC, 2008.

Doctor Who: The Ambassadors of Death. DVD. Directed by Michael Ferguson. 1970. London: BBC, 2012.

Doctor Who: The Brain of Morbius. DVD. Directed by Christopher Barry. 1976. London: BBC, 2008.

Doctor Who: The Claws of Axos. DVD. Directed by Michael Ferguson. 1971. London: BBC, 2005.

Doctor Who: Colony in Space. DVD. Directed by Michael E. Briant. 1971. London: BBC, 2011.

Doctor Who: The Curse of Peladon. DVD. Directed by Lennie Mayne. 1972. London: BBC, 2010.

Doctor Who: The Daemons. DVD. Directed by Christopher Barry. 1971. London: BBC, 2012.

Doctor Who: Day of the Daleks. DVD. Directed by Paul Bernard. 1972. London: BBC, 2011.

Doctor Who: Frontier in Space. DVD. Directed by Paul Bernard. 1973. London: BBC, 2010.

Doctor Who: The Green Death. DVD. Directed by Michael E. Briant. 1973. London: BBC, 2005.

Doctor Who: Inferno. DVD. Directed by Douglas Camfield and Barry Letts. 1970. London: BBC, 2013.

Doctor Who: Invasion of the Dinosaurs. DVD. Directed by Paddy Russell. 1974. London: BBC, 2012.

Doctor Who: The Mind of Evil. DVD. Directed by Timothy Combe. 1971. London: BBC, 2013.

Doctor Who: The Mutants. DVD. Directed by Christopher Barry. 1972. London: BBC, 2011.

Doctor Who: Planet of the Spiders. DVD. Directed by Barry Letts. 1974. London: BBC, 2011.

Doctor Who: The Sea Devils. DVD. Directed by Michael E. Briant. 1972. London: BBC, 2008.

Doctor Who: Spearhead from Space. DVD. Directed by Derek Martinus. 1970. London: BBC, 2012.

Doctor Who: Terror of the Autons. DVD. Directed by Barry Letts. 1971. London: BBC, 2011.

Doctor Who: The Time Monster. DVD. Directed by Paul Bernard. 1972. London: BBC, 2010.

Dodds, Klaus. "Screening Geopolitics: James Bond and the Early Cold War Films (1962–1967)." *Geopolitics* 10 (2005): 266–89.

Dower, John W. *War Without Mercy: Race and Power in the Pacific War.* New York: Random House, 1993.

From Russia 2ith Love. DVD. Directed by Terence Young. 1963. Beverly Hills: Twentieth Century–Fox Home Entertainment, 2007.

Goldfinger. DVD. Directed by Guy Hamilton. 1964. Beverly Hills: Twentieth Century–Fox Home Entertainment, 2007.

Griffin, Eric. "From Ethos to Ethnos: Hispanizing 'the Spaniard' in the Old World and the New." *The New Centennial Review* 2, no. 1 (2002): 69–116.

Howe, David J., Mark Stammers, and Stephen James Walker. *Doctor Who: The Seventies.* London: Doctor Who Books, 1994.

Laucht, Christoph. "Britannia Rules the Atom: The James Bond Phenomenon and Postwar British Nuclear Culture." *The Journal of Popular Culture* 46, no. 2 (2013): 358–77.

Layton, David. "Male and Female Archetypes in *Doctor Who*." *Consciousness, Literature and the Arts* 11, no. 2 (August 2010): 1–29.

Live and Let Die. Blu-ray Disc. Directed by Guy Hamilton. 1973. Beverly Hills: Twentieth Century–Fox Home Entertainment, 2012.

Marquand, David. "'Bursting with Skeletons': Britishness after Empire." In *Britishness: Perspectives on the British Question,* edited by Andrew Gamble and Tony Wright, 10–20. Chichester: Wiley-Blackwell, 2009.

Muir, John Kenneth. *A Critical History of Doctor Who on Television.* Jefferson, NC: McFarland, 2008.

Noriega, Chon. "Godzilla and the Japanese Nightmare: When *Them*! Is U.S." In *Hibakusha Cinema: Hiroshima, Nagasaki and the Nuclear Image in Japanese Film,* edited by Mick Broderick, 54–74. New York: Kegan Paul International, 1996.

On Her Majesty's Secret Service. Blu-ray Disc. Directed by Peter Hunt. 1969. Beverly Hills: Twentieth Century–Fox Home Entertainment, 2012.

Pertwee, Jon. Interview with David Banks. *David Banks Talks with Jon Pertwee: The Classic Who Interview Pertwee in Person.* 10th Planet, April 19, 1990.

_____. "Interview with Jon Pertwee." By Matt Adams and David Southwell. *Doctor Who Magazine* 457 (February 4, 2013): 18–28.

_____. *Moon Boots and Dinner Suits.* London: Elm Tree Books, 1984.

Pertwee, Jon, and David J. Howe. *I am the Doctor: Jon Pertwee's Final Memoir.* London: Doctor Who Books, 1996.

Richards, Jeffrey. "Imperial Heroes for a Post-Imperial Age: Films and the End of Empire." In *British Culture and the End of Empire,* edited by Stuart Ward, 129–44. Manchester: Manchester University Press, 2002.

Sked, Alan, and Chris Cook. *Post-War Britain: A Political History.* New York: Penguin, 1990.

Stock, Paul. "Dial 'M' for Metonym: Universal Exports, M's Office Space and Empire." *National Identities* 2, no. 1 (August 18, 2000): 35–47.

Thunderball. DVD. Directed by Terence Young. 1965. Beverly Hills: Twentieth Century–Fox Home Entertainment, 2012.

Ward, Stuart. "Introduction." In *British Culture and the End of Empire,* edited by Stuart Ward,1–20. Manchester: Manchester University Press, 2002.

You Only Live Twice. DVD. Directed by Lewis Gilbert. 1967. Beverly Hills: Twentieth Century–Fox Home Entertainment, 2012.

Refashioning James Bond as an American Secret Agent

Scarecrow and Mrs. King, *1983–1987*

Christine D. Myers

In October 1983, CBS introduced a new spy in the family-friendly series *Scarecrow and Mrs. King* starring Bruce Boxleitner and Kate Jackson.[1] Although comparisons can be made between the program and any previous spy movies or television shows, direct inspiration taken from James Bond is visible throughout the four-year run of *Scarecrow and Mrs. King*.[2] The premise of the series, in which a divorced mother of two (Amanda King) is swept up in the work of a covert government agency by Lee "Scarecrow" Stetson, differs from James Bond, and yet her "real world" character has seen the Bond films and refers to them from time to time. During the first season she admits to having fantasies about secret agents[3] and even compliments Lee at one point by quoting the theme song from *The Spy Who Loved Me* (1977, Lewis Gilbert), by telling him: "And nobody does it better. Nobody."[4] Episode titles, plotlines, and dialogue were often inspired by the Bond films because they were familiar to audiences and increased the espionage credentials of the program. Despite the show's popularity, *Scarecrow and Mrs. King* (hereafter referred to as *SMK*) received only cursory coverage in books like Wesley Britton's *Spy Television* and Michael Kackman's *Citizen Spy: Television, Espionage and Cold War Culture*, and is often overlooked when studying espionage in Hollywood productions.[5] This essay will examine both direct and subtle Bond references used during the four seasons of *SMK* and argue that their use impacted the trajectory of the series, thereby establishing the extent to which the '80s show was inspired by 007.

In 1976 Drew Moniot wrote an article titled "James Bond and America in the Sixties: An Investigation of the Formula Film in Popular Culture." His analysis practically laid out a roadmap for the writers and producers of *SMK* in the following decade.[6] Moniot provides a list of "the ingredients of the Bond formula" which "included more than just sex, gadgets, and violence."[7] The aspects reused in establishing James Bond's character in each film, for the benefit of new audience members, were so familiar to American TV audiences by the 1980s that they were "a sure-fire premise for a successful television series."[8] Although Moniot criticizes "the Bond imitators" of the 1960s for failing to use this formula successfully, some of the additional aspects of Bond films that the creators of *SMK* were able to incorporate include "the choice of an actor as excellently suited to the role as Sean Connery" in the attractive and charismatic Bruce Boxleitner and "technical aspects ... such as the cinematography, editing, musical scoring [that] were executed with an air of true professionalism."[9] These technical aspects were one of the keys to the success of *SMK*, which won an Emmy Award in 1986 for its music (composed by Arthur B. Rubenstein), and earned nominations for cinematography in 1985 and costume design in 1985 and 1986.[10] The skill with which those off-screen did their work explains how the show was able to captivate audiences, just as the Bond films did, "but it would seem that the predictability of these devices (such as the fight and chase sequences) would tend to dull their effect in time." Moniot continues, "Why then have the audiences returned again and again to see the same well worn formula adventure?"[11] Similarly, why did viewers of *SMK* tune in week after week for four seasons?[12]

What Makes a Spy?

The most obvious comparison between James Bond and *SMK* is the character of Lee Stetson, who is presented as a charming, suave, well dressed ladies' man with "a bachelor's taste for freedom" in need of reform, often using women as a means of obtaining information needed for a case.[13] The Agency, for which Lee and Amanda work, refers to this sort of espionage as a "Peacock Dance" in which agents form a relationship in order to give false information to or acquire good intelligence from an enemy.[14] Lee was both the subject of such a situation and the one executing the scenario in various episodes during the four-year run of *SMK*, since his enemies knew that beautiful women were a weakness for him. Early in the series Scarecrow's womanizing ways are summed up visually when Amanda finds a pair of robes with "Lee" and "She" embroidered on them at his apartment.[15] Later in the first season Amanda runs into one of his neighbors who assumes Amanda is the latest in a long line of women with whom Lee has been spending time. His doorman also calls him a "degenerate."[16] Lee's romantic past remained a main theme of *SMK* throughout the series, especially once he decides to give up that lifestyle in order to commit to Amanda. Her ability to get past his reputation with the ladies is akin to Teresa di Vicenzo falling in love with, and marrying, James Bond in *On Her Majesty's Secret Service* (1969, Peter Hunt).[17]

A repeated piece of gossip that Amanda endured hearing about as her romantic relationship with Lee began to develop in the third and fourth seasons of *SMK* was that Lee had various liaisons with female circus performers. In "A Lovely Little Affair" a congresswoman on a budget oversight committee questions him about Hungarian trapeze artists, who were a pair of twin sisters and their mother, known as "the Flying Federovas."[18] In another episode viewers hear a passing reference to a case involving the Russian circus when Lee was assigned to a "Bulgarian sword swallower" named Svetlana, though he corrects the record and says she was "a juggler."[19] Then, in Season 4's "Need to Know," Amanda refers to "a couple of tumblers from the Moscow Circus" who Lee says were "the Petrovich twins."[20] It is unclear if these were meant to refer to the same story from Lee's past or several similar situations. Amanda's mother, Dotty West, who does not know her daughter is a spy, even makes her own connection between espionage and the circus when explaining the plot of a book she is reading about a Soviet defector who falls in love with a tightrope walker.[21] Many viewers may not have perceived the James Bond connection in these references, but the fact that *Octopussy* (1983, John Glen) was released in June 1983, just before *SMK* debuted in October of that year, makes the circus-spy connection more clear because the title character in that film used a traveling circus as her cover.[22]

Lee Stetson is also similar to James Bond in the fact that both characters are orphans who put service to their country ahead of making emotional connections with the people around them. This prototype of a womanizing loner making for a good spy holds true in the minds of many audience members, but adding a sad childhood is a way of softening this characterization and making the spy in question more likeable. As Roger Moore notes in his book *Bond on Bond: Reflections on 50 Years of James Bond Movies,* "Jimmy was an orphan. Poor Jimmy."[23] *SMK* viewers first learn that Lee is an orphan in the Season 1 episode "The Long Christmas Eve," but that part of his back story is not developed further until the following season. In "A Relative Situation" viewers have the chance to meet Lee's uncle, Colonel Clayton, who raised him after his parents were killed in a car crash when Lee was five.[24] Bond's parents, as established in the novel *You Only Live Twice,* died in a climbing accident when James was 11.[25] The creation of a back story for Lee that was so similar to James Bond's past is no coincidence, as it was sure to resonate with audiences who had seen Bond films or, as James Brand comments, has "read the books."[26]

Later in the same episode, *SMK* viewers learn that when Lee was seven, he got in a fight to protect his girlfriend, Alice. His uncle further explained that he had instructed Lee not to cry after this incident, because that was not a manly response to being upset about something. This anecdote was beneficial because it explained why Lee was so seemingly detached from those around him, while at the same time being highly protective of Amanda. The Colonel also told Lee, upon being introduced to Amanda, that his "taste is improving" with the assumption being that Lee's other female friends have been less classy in nature. The final piece of Lee Stetson's character that viewers hear from his uncle is the assertion that Lee has been "playing secret agent" for too long. At this point, just before the denouement of "A Relative Situation," both men are tied to chairs with no apparent means of escape, yet Lee's complete confidence that they'll be free in time to save the day is irksome to his uncle.[27] Allan Hepburn notes that "spies routinely find themselves bound, gagged, lassoed, or otherwise immobilized,"[28] a fact which the Colonel undoubtedly knew. And because this is common knowledge, the almost postmodern line of dialogue from the uncle, questioning the bravado of a spy in a spy show, further enhances the Bond-like qualities of *SMK*.[29]

Much of this bravado comes through in the characters of James Bond and Lee Stetson when they had a drink in their hand.[30] In the Season 1 episode "The Long Christmas Eve" when Lee and Amanda are stranded in a cabin with two KGB agents and an American double agent, some vodka is shared by one and all. Lee's comment when he is first offered a drink is "You got any vermouth? We could make a Martini."[31] Unlike James Bond, Martinis were not usually the drink of choice for Scarecrow or Mrs. King. Instead the characters on *SMK* preferred beer, champagne, and wine, with hard liquor typically reserved for the more stressful and dramatic episodes. Much of the alcohol consumption happened at embassy parties or other occasions when having a drink in one's hand enabled the characters to have a greater chance of gathering intelligence. Drinks, whether alcoholic or not, could also be used to subdue an enemy agent or asset. In "The Three Faces of Emily" in Season 2, Lee puts a knockout drug in the champagne of a British man who works for the KGB.[32] Similarly, in *Dr. No* (1962, Terrence Young), James Bond and Honey Ryder were drugged by way of their coffee, another favorite beverage on *SMK*.[33]

Romance and marriage between spies became another way that the writers of *SMK* took their lead from James Bond. Allan Hepburn argues that "American writers typically represent espionage narratives as romance to insert distance between individuals and ideologies."[34] He sees this as a contrast to British spy fiction, but there is a resemblance between the Bond films and *SMK* when talking about love and marriage. Watching *On Her Majesty's Secret Service*, when James Bond and Contessa di Vicenzo meet and fall in love, one can see many similarities between their relationship and that of Amanda King and Lee Stetson. After Bond escapes from Blofeld's clinic, he accidentally runs into Teresa (Tracy).

She helps him evade the henchmen and they are forced to spend the night in a barn. This plotline is used to some extent in "Utopia Now" in the third season of *SMK* and in "Night Crawler" in the fourth season. In the earlier episode, when Lee and Amanda spend the night in a swamp, they have a discussion with dialogue highly influenced by *On Her Majesty's Secret Service* about not having any regrets.[35] In the film Bond proposes to Tracy spontaneously, despite (or because of) the fact that they are in peril at the time. Lee proposes to Amanda in Season 4's "Night Crawler" while they are being held captive and, like Tracy, Amanda asks Lee if he's sure he wants to marry her before accepting the offer. Both women are not entirely convinced that their ladies' man is being completely serious with them.

SMK took further inspiration from the Bonds' marriage later in the fourth season. When Kate Jackson's treatment for breast cancer meant she needed to reduce her time filming, her absence from the storyline in the episode "Mission of Gold" had to be explained in some manner.[36] This script change was potentially challenging because the episode featured Lee and Amanda's honeymoon. Looking to James Bond for an idea, the writers chose to have Amanda shot at the start of the episode. At the end of *On Her Majesty's Secret Service* when James and Tracy were headed for their honeymoon he leaves her briefly in the car, only to have her shot through the windshield. The same premise is used in *SMK*, with Lee leaving Amanda in their rental car at the start of their honeymoon in California. Unlike Tracy Bond, Amanda didn't die from her wounds, but the motivation given to Lee and James to exact revenge for the crimes against their brides was considerable. The lack of family each orphaned spy began with was altered when they finally entered into a serious romantic relationship.[37] This transformation from being emotionless to being consumed with a need to avenge an attack on a loved one enables viewers to excuse any subsequent violence by the hero as being done "through sheer perseverance and the moral rightness of his cause."[38]

Dealing with Danger

The choice of enemy is also as varied in *SMK* as it is in James Bond movies. The Cold War backdrop, whether Moscow-based or not, made for a convenient premise for tales of espionage, but it was not overused in either the films or television series.[39] An occasional defection was practically a prerequisite to being considered a viable part of the spy community, and both Bond and Scarecrow use their skills to help women escape from their Soviet keepers. In *From Russia with Love* (1963, Terrence Young) the woman in question is Tatiana Romanova, a "cipher clerk" who works at the embassy in Turkey.[40] Her *SMK* equivalent is Magda Petrak, who works for the "Hungarian Cultural Mission" in Washington, D.C.[41] The key contrast between these characters is that Magda is not seduced by Stetson like Tatiana is by Bond. Both women do share a love of Western consumerism because anyone living under a totalitarian regime was invariably "very drawn to the luxuries of the free market system."[42] Though no one knew when the show premiered in 1983 that the Cold War would be over in less than ten years, it was a wise move on the part of the powers that be to not make Eastern Bloc operatives the exclusive foe for Scarecrow and Mrs. King.[43] The Bond movies had passed this cliché by the end of Connery's time in the role, after "a gradual de-emphasis of the Russians-as-villains ... a trend which reflects a similar shift in the international politics and public opinion of those years."[44] This variety in adversary was essential in a television series that needed to come up with many storylines in quick succession.[45]

Another parallel between James Bond and Lee Stetson are the cover stories they use in their dealings with both allies and enemies. Bond works for Universal Exports, the "corporate front for the British Secret Service."[46] Lee and Amanda work for "the Agency" (which, it should be noted, is not the CIA, but is simply referred to as the Agency). Just as Bond's MI-6 had a civilian cover for agents to use, the Agency used International Federal Films, or IFF, as theirs. Bond flirting with Miss Moneypenny when she's placing folders in a filing cabinet is as familiar a sight as Lee doing the same with Amanda in the Q Bureau once they begin dating partway through the series.[47] In both settings the spies have desks in offices and have an aversion to doing paperwork, preferring to be in the field doing something more exciting.[48] The duality of the spy community is mirrored in the villains' world, with many appearing to be respectable businessmen who are actually hiding in plain sight; "we live in a world of avarice and deceit."[49]

One of the key evil business deals in *SMK* takes place in the Season 1 episode "Service Above and Beyond." In this episode an American fast food tycoon is being pressured by an East German villain to use his contacts in Washington to acquire "Pershing missile intelligence."[50] Along with the similarity in characterization to Bond villains, there is a noteworthy connection that was made in the casting of Walter Gotell as the archetypal Eastern Bloc threat. The actor had appeared in five Bond films by the time his guest appearance on *SMK* aired.[51] As James Chapman notes, Gotell's repeated appearances are "an example of how the Bond films at this time maintained continuity with their predecessors."[52] In turn, *SMK* was able to us an actor known to Bond fans to help establish its own legitimacy among other productions in the spy genre.

At times Lee is more susceptible to the evil doings of his enemies than Bond. In the third episode of the series, "If Thoughts Could Kill," Lee is brainwashed while in the hospital to be treated for an injured knee. In *On Her Majesty's Secret Service* Blofeld brainwashes the young ladies who have come to his Swiss clinic to be treated for their allergies. In both instances, the subjects of the brainwashing are given a "prettily wrapped present" that contains an innocuous object that will cause them to do the villain's dirty work.[53] The trigger from Blofeld is a compact, while in *SMK* a stuffed toy called Lester the Duck is used instead. Upon hearing the voice of the person who brainwashed them, the young ladies and Lee Stetson are all prepared to take someone's life, until stopped by the intervention of Bond and Amanda respectively.

Bond films are also known for their tongue-in-cheek dialogue and double entendres, from character names to sexual innuendo, what Drew Moniot refers to as "verbal fencing" between characters.[54] These remarks were often said in the midst of dramatic scenes to break the tension, or "diffuse a serious situation," like preventing a bomb from exploding.[55] In a classic, harrowing situation arranged to kill James Bond in *Goldfinger* (1964, Guy Hamilton), Auric Goldfinger even admonishes him, "Choose you next witticism carefully, Mr. Bond. It may be your last."[56] The writers on *SMK* followed suit, lacing their own scripts with puns and other plays on words in the same way as their big screen counterparts. It was a family show, so character names in *SMK* were never overtly sexual like Pussy Galore, but in "The Long Christmas Eve" the primary guest character was named Rudolph, a fact that would not have gone unnoticed with even the younger viewers of the program.[57]

Characters were also written out of episodes with clever dialogue. In Season 2 Lee was dating someone named Margo who viewers never meet because she "took off with an airline pilot."[58] Where James Bond would comment that something was "shocking, positively shocking" or a character "blew a fuse" after they were electrocuted,[59] Lee Stetson and his boss, Billy Melrose, had the following conversation:

> BILLY. Martinez has surfaced.
> LEE. Where?
> BILLY. The Potomac.[60]

Such simple witticisms were sometimes accompanied by sexual banter or euphemisms. Lee and a co-worker, Francine Desmond, stop short of openly discussing their past sexual relationship by calling it "playing backgammon" instead.[61] Amanda's purer persona is also drawn into similar puns on occasion. In "Charity Begins at Home" Lee instructs her to disrobe an unconscious security guard. Her response

> AMANDA. I'll do everything except the pants.
> LEE. Suit yourself.[62]

These innuendos and plays on words would have been caught by the sharp adult viewers of the program, but were probably seen as innocent exchanges by children in the audience who would not be as likely to pick up on the double meanings of the dialogue.

Wit and charm would only get spies so far against the villains. On both the large and small screen secret agents need to have a wide range of skills, never knowing what they might have to do in the course of an investigation. Along with being good with weapons, from firing guns to disarming bombs, a secret agent also needs to be agile and athletic. Both Scarecrow and 007 were adept at golf, and both used their ability in the game as a way of getting close to a suspect they were investigating. James Bond's golf match with Auric Goldfinger is similar in many respects to Lee Stetson's with Gordon Standish in the episode "Magic Bus," with both pairs sizing each other up while playing a round on the links.[63] Fencing and hand-to-hand combat are also necessary and utilized by both Bond and Stetson with relative frequency.[64] Horsemanship, another key skill for spies, was particularly popular in the 1980s, with exciting horse chases being filmed for *A View to a Kill* (1985, John Glen), "Affair at Bromfield Hall," and "Do You Take This Spy?"[65] Scuba diving was more common in the Bond films, but Lee Stetson tries his hand at it in "Mission of Gold" in the fourth season, when he sneaks on to the villain's yacht to search for evidence, a visible nod to the spy genre.[66]

A related aspect of the James Bond franchise that *SMK* incorporated on a regular basis was the elaborate methods of death concocted for Lee and Amanda by the villains.[67] In "Vigilante Mothers" Amanda's hands are tied to a dry cleaner's conveyer system by the villain, so that she will wind up being killed by the machinery.[68] Of course, this dramatic set-up only provides time for Lee to arrive and rescue her before apprehending the bad guy in the following scene. More dramatically, in "You Only Die Twice," whose title was as Bond-inspired as one can get, Amanda finds herself tied in a quarry where a bulldozer is poised to push rocks over a cliff and crush her.[69] In "The Legend of Das Geisterschloss" the bad guys are disgruntled Brits who are spying on NATO "missile deployment talks."[70] They plan to kill Amanda, Lee, and their allies from MI-6 and Austrian intelligence by locking them in a room in a castle with a bomb hanging from a beam overhead that will bring the structure down around them. And the classic *Goldfinger* ploy of loading tanks of poison gas on an airplane to be dispersed and kill those below is used in "I Am Not Now, Nor Have I Ever Been ... a Spy."[71]

Gadgets and Quartermasters

Gadgets were not front-and-center in *SMK*, but they were utilized at key points in many episodes. As Allan Hepburn comments in his book *Intrigue:*

Espionage and Culture, "The spy enhances his masculinity and invincibility with technology."[72] So to not have technology would make one a less effective spy. The gadget aspect was common on both sides of the actual Cold War, and was therefore paramount to movie and television portrayals during the era. Computers were at the forefront of espionage stories, and *SMK* made a point to utilize similar graphics when identifying suspects that Bond was using in films in the 1980s.[73] Helicopters were used frequently in *SMK* starting in the pilot episode, when Lee and Amanda are forced to escape in one.[74] Later in the season there is a long action sequence with Lee dangling from the skids of a helicopter much like Roger Moore does in the opening of *For Your Eyes Only* (1981, John Glen).[75] In the second season episode "You Only Die Twice," Lee dons a black jumpsuit and repels from a helicopter onto a rooftop in order to infiltrate the villains' headquarters.[76] He looks through the air vents of the building, just as Bond does in *Goldfinger*. In both situations the hero winds up having to save the damsel they did not know was in distress.[77]

The sequence also requires Lee to attach a device to a lock in order to scan it for the correct access code. Similar technology is employed in other episodes to go beyond the standard lock picking that was a regular feature in *SMK*. Other standard spy gear in the program included binoculars, cordless/mobile phones, crossbows with grappling hooks, hidden transmitters, homing devices, infrared technology, listening devices, microdots, microfilm, miniature cameras, tools for safe cracking, two-way radios, and sports cars for the requisite chase sequences, all of which made Lee "less vulnerable to enemy intrusions."[78] The pilot episode of *SMK*, "The First Time," featured a music box that held the clue to plugging a leak within the Agency. Inspiration for this prop may have come from *The Spy Who Loved Me* in which the KGB contacted their operative, Anya Amasova, by way of a music box transmitter.[79] Atomizers are also featured in both James Bond and *SMK*. In *On Her Majesty's Secret Service* a virus is going to be spread by way of atomizers given to the patients in Blofeld's allergy clinic and in "A Relative Situation" viewers find out that Lee borrows Amanda's atomizer on a job.[80] One of the last and most memorable gadgets featured in *SMK* was a "gyrocopter" Lee steals from an Agency assault team to use in Season 4's "Promises to Keep" that was a knock off of the "auto-gyro" in *You Only Live Twice*.[81]

Starting in the third season, the series had its own quartermaster in an attempt to appeal to viewers familiar with the concept from the Bond films. In *SMK* the quartermaster was Leatherneck, a Vietnam veteran, who had an office in the Agency, but also spent a good deal of his time running the motor pool repairing cars damaged in the line of duty. Leatherneck's primary responsibilities, unlike Q in the Bond series, were helping to train agents in basic skills like using firearms or picking locks.[82] He also issued the items needed to establish an agent's cover story on a mission.[83] The one episode when Leatherneck's knowledge of gadgetry is most called upon is "Santa's Got a Brand New Bag" in the fourth season. The plot revolves around a toy company using their research and development team to create military-grade weapons, rather than toys for children. Instead of having Leatherneck analyzing the weapons, however, the writers used his character's know-how to ascertain that the toys produced by the company were "very low tech" and not dangerous at all.[84] Despite the limited role provided for *SMK*'s quartermaster, he remains one of the show's most memorable characters, just like Desmond Llewelyn's Q.[85] Both actors were given some of the best one-liners of their respective series, fixing them in the minds of the viewers regardless of the number of minutes they spent on screen. In his first episode, "Over the Limit," Leatherneck tries to teach Amanda how to shoot by using a video simulation training program. When Amanda fires her gun at the ceiling at the end of the scenario Leatherneck tells her the "ceiling's on our side," his wit calling to mind the banter between Q and Bond.[86]

Whether the quartermaster made an appearance in an episode or not, the existence of such a character caused an increase in the number and creativity of the gadgets in *SMK*. In the fourth season, despite Leatherneck only featuring in one storyline, viewers are shown a pen containing acid ink that was now "standard Agency issue"[87] and "thermite wire" concealed in Lee's shirt collar that can be detonated by the buttons on his cuffs.[88] All of these new gadgets were used to either enable Lee and Amanda to break in to or out of secure facilities. Late in Season 4 Lee and Amanda's colleague, Francine Desmond, is caught by one of the bad guys and locked in a crate on a cargo plane. Thanks to the new emphasis on spy gadgetry in *SMK* she is able to free herself with some explosives that were hidden in her high-heeled shoe.[89] These similarities between Bond and *SMK* were much more apparent in the final two seasons of the series than they had been in the first two following the addition of a quartermaster to the supporting cast. Lee and Amanda's enemies also attempted to use Bond villain tactics, like those in "Need to Know" who planned to contaminate "the free world's stockpile of tri-tanium" with radioactive material, much like Goldfinger planned to do to the U.S. gold reserves at Fort Knox.[90]

Familiar Tales

By the time the third season of *SMK* started in the fall of 1985 the writers had two additional James Bond films to take inspiration from—*Never Say Never Again* (1983, Irvin Kershner) and *A View to a Kill*.[91] Plotlines and technology in *SMK* began drawing from these big screen spy stories soon after. In "The Eyes Have It" Lee begins the episode by tracking down a pair of contact lenses that contain sensitive data only to have them stolen, resulting in a need to recover them a second time.[92] The use of contact lenses was somewhat different in this story and *Never Say Never Again*, when a contact lens is used to cover up a false eye.[93] *SMK* did something similar in the second season episode "Brunettes Are In" by having the villain in that episode, played by Robert Pine, wear fake contact lenses so he could appear to be blind.[94] The many potential uses for this type of technology in espionage were undeniable.

Specific episodes highlighted the Bond connection in more pronounced ways than others, in particular two episodes from the second season that were filmed in England.[95] Having Lee and Amanda working on cases alongside members of the British intelligence community practically required them to make references to the Bond films, and to feature locations that appeared to be "right out of the pages of a tourist brochure" of Europe providing an "atmosphere of beauty and underlying intrigue."[96] In "To Catch a Mongoose" Lee and Amanda are supposed to make contact with someone in a casino and wind up encountering the episode's villain instead. This setting is quintessentially Bond, since the first Bond novel was *Casino Royale* and the first scene in the long-running film franchise, *Dr. No* (1962, Terrence Young), is set in Les Ambassadeurs Casino in London.[97] The estate featured in "Affair at Bromfield Hall" has many similarities in layout to the golf club in *Goldfinger*, and one can't help but be reminded of that fact when someone attempts to kill Lee with a stone urn causing a crash that sounds a great deal like Oddjob's hat decapitating the statue.[98]

The most obvious homage to James Bond in *Scarecrow and Mrs. King* was the Season 3 episode "Welcome to America, Mr. Brand."[99] It featured a James Bond wannabe and accountant for MI-6, James Brand, who helps crack a case while visiting Washington, D.C. Through much of the episode the references to Bond are veiled, as though the characters were not allowed to use the iconic spy's name for legal reasons. For example, Mr. Brand's first bit of dialogue takes place in a restaurant where he orders "a Martini, very cold, stirred, not shaken with a twist." The twist, no doubt, being that the spy he was trying to emulate prefers his Martinis "shaken, not stirred."[100] When waiting in the Agency to find out background information on the investigation, Brand tries, several times, to toss his hat onto a coat rack in true Bond fashion, eventually succeeding.[101] Furthermore, Brand's explanation of the schemes undertaken by the villain in the episode, who specializes in "economic chaos" just as Auric Goldfinger did, is not unlike the briefing Bond receives over dinner with his superiors in the same film. Eventually Lee does say that Mr. Brand "is an accountant who thinks he's bloody James Bond," a comment that spurs Brand to try to capture the villain on his own without Lee's assistance.[102]

If the character's name and comparisons to James Bond in the dialogue and storyline were not explicit enough, at various points during the episode the show's theme music was altered to resemble the Bond theme originally composed by John Barry.[103] Mr. Brand also claims to have many Q-style gadgets, like tear gas in his attaché case or an Aston Martin complete with an ejection seat.[104] Not only were all of these were shown in Q's scene with 007 in *Goldfinger*, Brand's explanation of the features in his car is entirely reminiscent of Q's explanation to Bond, complete with a warning not to push the ejector seat button.[105] Not surprisingly, Brand's gadgets are as non-existent as his credentials as a spy, but he does wind up helping Lee solve the case, while at the same time furthering the Bond-style "elements of entertainment and escape" in the minds of *SMK* viewers.[106]

Two side stories are also given a good amount of screen time in "Welcome to America, Mr. Brand." First, Amanda's mother, Dotty, is working on tracing their family tree, which is apparently "crawling with" British ancestors, "thank goodness."[107] It is possible to see this pedigree as more than just a convenient conversation piece for a supporting character; the British heritage can also be seen as a connection to James Bond's legacy for spies, further emphasized in the series by the fact that Lee Stetson's mother was British and became a spy herself during World War II.[108] Second, Lee needs to re-qualify in hand-to-hand combat with the Agency's martial arts expert, Stanley Chow (referred to by the agents as "Dr. Pain").[109] Despite Lee's normally successful fight sequences in *SMK*, he is not able to subdue "Dr. Pain" without using advice he received earlier in the episode from James Brand. The otherwise bumbling Mr. Brand happened to provide this and other valuable suggestions in the episode, simply because he was British and worked for MI-6; those facts being enough to qualify him as a spy.

Following the Formula

While *Scarecrow and Mrs. King* is but one of the many "variants of 'formulaic' spy fiction," it provides excellent insight into the lasting impact of the James Bond franchise on American popular culture.[110] Although one of the classic lines from *SMK* is that agents should "expect the unexpected," the very fact that this quote was taken from James Bond in *The Man with the Golden Gun* (1974, Guy Hamilton) illustrates the extent to which more recent spy programs are composed of recognizable elements.[111] The increase in television shows centering on espionage in the decades since *SMK* was on the air owe at least some of their success to all their predecessors, not just Bond himself. As Drew Moniot observed, "the Bond imitations [of the 1960s] flourished briefly and then died, though some lingered on longer than others."[112] *Scarecrow and Mrs. King* did outlive many of these earlier attempts at using James Bond's "foolproof formula" on the small screen, and continues to have fans to this day because it blended all the elements of that formula in a fun and pleasing way.[113] As with the Bond films themselves, *SMK* viewers having the "knowledge of practically everything that will happen ... serves to enhance the audience's participation since they already have an understanding of the star players, team strategies, handicaps, and ground rules as well as the ultimate object of the game."[114] Maintaining this familiarity on a weekly basis, over the course of four seasons, *SMK* gave audiences something to look forward to, just as Bond fans eagerly await the latest installment of that secret agent's exploits in the cinema. Despite the fact that *Scarecrow and Mrs. King* will never have the cultural cachet of James Bond, it remains a worthy addition to the family of espionage productions headed by 007.

Notes

1. *Scarecrow and Mrs. King*, Warner Bros. Television and Shoot the Moon Productions, 1983–1987. The series has been released on DVD by Warner Bros. 2010–2013 and is also available on Amazon and iTunes. Initial analysis of the series was posted by the author at the *Scarecrow and Mrs. King* Forum on Yuku in the Episode Discussion section, http://scarecrowandmrskingforum.yuku.com/forums/18/Episode-Discussions (accessed October 31, 2013).

2. It is, perhaps, fitting that the first ever production of James Bond was the 1954 adaptation of *Casino Royale* on CBS. See James Chapman, *Licence to Thrill: A Cultural History of the James Bond Films* (London: I. B. Tauris, 2007), 34; and Jason Mulvihill, "The Golden Age of Bond: Creation of a Cold War Popular Hero (1962–1965) Part II," *International Journal of Instructional Media* 28, no. 4 (2001): 341.

3. "Service Above and Beyond," Season 1, Disc 2, *Scarecrow and Mrs. King* (November 21, 1983; Burbank: Warner Home Video, 2010), DVD.

4. "The Artful Dodger," Season 1, Disc 4, *Scarecrow and Mrs. King* (March 5, 1984; Burbank: Warner Home Video, 2010), DVD. The Carly Simon theme song from *The Spy Who Loved Me* in 1977 was possibly more memorable than the film itself. Carly Simon and Marvin Hamlish, *The Spy Who Loved Me* (Los Angeles: EMI Records USA, 2007).

5. Wesley Britton, *Spy Television* (Westport, CT: Praeger, 2004), 259; and Michael Kackman, *Citizen Spy: Television, Espionage, and Cold War Culture* (Minneapolis: University of Minnesota Press, 2005), 179. *SMK* is not mentioned at all in Jeremy Packer's edited collection *Secret Agents: Popular Icons Beyond James Bond* (New York: Peter Lang, 2009) or Danny Biederman, *The Incredible World of Spy-Fi: Wild and Crazy Spy Gadgets, Props, and Artifacts from TV and the Movies* (San Francisco: Chronicle Books, 2004), 152.

6. Drew Moniot, "James Bond and America in the Sixties: An Investigation of the Formula Film in Popular Culture," *Journal of the University Film Association* 28, no. 3 (Summer 1976): 25–33.

7. Ibid., 26.

8. Ibid.

9. Ibid. See also Jeff Smith, "Creating a Bond Market: Selling John Barry's Soundtracks and Theme Songs," in *The James Bond Phenomenon: A Critical Reader,* 2d ed., ed. Christoph Lindner (Manchester: Manchester University Press, 2009), 147.

10. "We're Off to See the Wizard," Season 3, Disc 1, *Scarecrow and Mrs. King* (September 23, 1985; Burbank: Warner Home Video, 2012), DVD. See *Scarecrow and Mrs. King,* Academy of Television Arts & Sciences, http://www.emmys.com/shows/scarecrow-and-mrs-king (accessed October 25, 2013).

11. Moniot, "James Bond and America in the Sixties," 28.

12. There were 88 episodes of *Scarecrow and Mrs. King* in total.

13. *On Her Majesty's Secret Service,* DVD, directed by Peter Hunt (1969; Santa Monica: MGM Home Entertainment, 2000). See also Allan Hepburn, *Intrigue: Espionage and Culture* (New Haven: Yale University Press, 2005), 71, 190, and 290; Moniot, "James Bond and America in the Sixties," 27; and Mark Moss, *The Media and the Models of Masculinity* (Lanham, MD: Lexington, 2006), 41–2.

14. "Stemwinder: Part I," Season 4, Disc 1, *Scarecrow and Mrs. King* (November 19, 1986; Burbank: Warner Home Video, 2013), DVD.

15. "Saved by the Bells," Season 1, Disc 2, *Scarecrow and Mrs. King* (November 28, 1983; Burbank: Warner Home Video, 2010), DVD.

16. "Remembrance of Things Past," Season 1, Disc 3, *Scarecrow and Mrs. King* (January 9, 1984; Burbank: Warner Home Video, 2010), DVD.

17. *On Her Majesty's Secret Service.*

18. "A Lovely Little Affair," Season 3, Disc 1, *Scarecrow and Mrs. King* (September 23, 1985; Burbank: Warner Home Video, 2012), DVD.

19. "Over the Limit," Season 3, Disc 1, *Scarecrow and Mrs. King* (October 7, 1985; Burbank: Warner Home Video, 2012), DVD.

20. "Need to Know," Season 4, Disc 2, *Scarecrow and Mrs. King* (December 5, 1986; Burbank: Warner Home Video, 2013), DVD.

21. "One Bear Dances, One Bear Doesn't," Season 3, Disc 3, *Scarecrow and Mrs. King* (January 6, 1986; Burbank: Warner Home Video, 2012), DVD.

22. *Octopussy,* DVD, directed by John Glen (1983; Beverly Hills: Twentieth Century–Fox Home Entertainment, 2007). Francisco Scaramanga, the assassin in *The Man with the Golden Gun,* was raised in a circus as well. *The Man with the Golden Gun,* DVD, directed by Guy Hamilton (1974; Culver City, CA: Sony Pictures Home Entertainment, 2005).

23. Roger Moore, *Bond on Bond: Reflections on 50 Years of James Bond Movies* (Guilford, CT: Lyons Press, 2012), 20.

24. "A Relative Situation," Season 2, Disc 3, *Scarecrow and Mrs. King* (February 11, 1985; Burbank: Warner Home Video, 2011), DVD.

25. Ian Fleming, *You Only Live Twice* (London: Jonathan Cape and Ian Fleming Publications Ltd., 1964, and Las Vegas: Thomas & Mercer, 2012), 203–04. Bond was raised by his aunt, Charmian, in the following years.

26. "Welcome to America, Mr. Brand," Season 3, Disc 1, *Scarecrow and Mrs. King* (October 21, 1985; Burbank: Warner Home Video, 2012), DVD.

27. "A Relative Situation."

28. Hepburn, *Intrigue: Espionage and Culture,* 90.

29. "A Relative Situation."

30. Craig N. Owens, "The Bond Market," in *Ian Fleming and James Bond: The Cultural Politics of 007,* ed. Edward P. Comentale, Stephen Watt, and Skip Willman (Bloomington: Indiana University Press, 2005), 107–08.

31. "The Long Christmas Eve," Season 1, Disc 3, *Scarecrow and Mrs. King* (December 19, 1983; Burbank: Warner Home Video, 2010), DVD.

32. "The Three Faces of Emily," Season 2, Disc 3, *Scarecrow and Mrs. King* (December 31, 1984; Burbank: Warner Home Video, 2011), DVD.

33. *Dr. No,* DVD, directed by Terrence Young (1962; Santa Monica: MGM Home Entertainment, 2007).

34. Hepburn, *Intrigue: Espionage and Culture,* 241.

35. Tracy, in a conversation with her father, says, "Whatever happens, there will be no regrets." Amanda assures Lee in their conversation that she has none about the time she has spent with him.

36. The original script, by Lynne Kelsey, was called "Mystery in a Minor Key" and the "Shooting Final" version is dated January 9, 1987. And added Bond touch in this episode was a talking parrot reminiscent of the one in *For Your Eyes Only.*

37. Kackman, *Citizen Spy,* 179.

38. "Night Crawler," Season 4, Disc 2, *Scarecrow and Mrs. King* (October 31, 1986; Burbank: Warner Home Video, 2013), DVD; and Moniot, "James Bond and America in the Sixties," 32. Bond did not get his revenge for Tracy's death on screen until the opening sequence of *For Your Eyes Only,* DVD, directed by John Glen (1981; Beverly Hills: Twentieth Century–Fox Home Entertainment LLC, 2012).

39. Kackman, *Citizen Spy,* 179; and Chapman, *Licence to Thrill,* 26, 32.

40. Mulvihill, "The Golden Age of Bond," 343, 348.

41. "Dead Ringer," Season 1, Disc 4, *Scarecrow and Mrs. King* (February 6, 1984; Burbank: Warner Home Video, 2010), DVD. Coincidentally, there is a character named Magda in *Octopussy.*

42. Mulvihill, "The Golden Age of Bond," 348. Magda Petrak's character goes on to open a dress shop, solidifying her love of Western materialism in "Night Crawler."

43. Tony Bennett and Janet Woollacott, "The Moments of Bond," in *The James Bond Phenomenon: A Critical Reader. Second Edition,* ed. Christoph Lindner (Manchester: Manchester University Press, 2009), 30.

44. Moniot, "James Bond and America in the Sixties," 27. See also David C. Earnest and James N. Rosenau, "The Spy Who Loved Globalization," *Foreign Policy* no. 120 (Sept.-Oct. 2000): 89.

45. Hepburn, *Intrigue: Espionage and Culture,* 60.

46. Moniot, "James Bond and America in the Sixties," 31.

47. *For Your Eyes Only.* The Q Bureau, which was introduced in the third season of *SMK,* was Lee and Amanda's office. Q, in this case, stood for "question" rather than quartermaster. "Tail of the Dancing Weasel," Season 3, Disc 1, *Scarecrow and Mrs. King* (October 14, 1985; Burbank: Warner Home Video, 2012), DVD.

48. Moniot, "James Bond and America in the Sixties," 30–31.

49. James Bond in *On Her Majesty's Secret Service.*

50. "Service Above and Beyond."

51. Gotell played Soviet General Gogol in *The Spy Who Loved Me, Moonraker, For Your Eyes Only,* and *Octopussy* and would play the character twice more in *A View to a Kill* and *Licence to Kill.* Gotell had previously played Morzeny in *From Russia with Love* and also had roles in other spy productions like *The Spy Who Came in from the Cold* and Roger Moore's *The Saint.* See Christoph Laucht, "Britannia Rules the Atom: The James Bond Phenomenon and Postwar British Nuclear Culture," *The Journal of Popular Culture* 46, no. 2 (2013): 362; Chapman, *Licence to Thrill,* 190, 272, 278–81, 283–84; and Walter Gotell, *Internet Movie Database,* http://www.imdb.com/name/nm0331770/?ref_=nv_sr_1 (accessed October 31, 2013).

52. Chapman, *Licence to Thrill,* 175.

53. Blofeld in *On Her Majesty's Secret Service.*

54. Moniot, "James Bond and America in the Sixties," 31; and Moss, *The Media and the Models of Masculinity,* 41.

55. Laucht, "Britannia Rules the Atom," 369.

56. *Goldfinger,* VHS, directed by Guy Hamilton (1964; Santa Monica: MGM/UA Home Video, 1995).

57. *Goldfinger* and "The Long Christmas Eve."

58. "The Three Faces of Emily."

59. Moniot, "James Bond and America in the Sixties," 28.

60. "I Am Not Now, Nor Have I Ever Been ... a Spy," Season 1, Disc 3, *Scarecrow and Mrs. King* (January 30, 1984; Burbank: Warner Home Video, 2010), DVD.

61. "Remembrance of Things Past."

62. "Charity Begins at Home," Season 2, Disc 1, *Scarecrow and Mrs. King* (October 29, 1984; Burbank: Warner Home Video, 2011), DVD.

63. *Goldfinger,* and "Magic Bus," Season 1, Disc 1, *Scarecrow and Mrs. King* (October 24, 1983; Burbank: Warner Home Video, 2010), DVD.

64. "Remembrance of Things Past,"; "A Class Act," Season 2, Disc 2, *Scarecrow and Mrs. King* (December 3, 1984; Burbank: Warner Home Video, 2011), DVD; and "Welcome to America, Mr. Brand."

65. *A View to a Kill*, DVD, directed by John Glen (1985; Beverly Hills: Twentieth Century–Fox Home Entertainment LLC, 2012); "Affair at Bromfield Hall," Season 2, Disc 2, *Scarecrow and Mrs. King* (November 26, 1984; Burbank: Warner Home Video, 2011), DVD; and "Do You Take This Spy?" Season 4, Disc 4, *Scarecrow and Mrs. King* (February 13, 1987; Burbank: Warner Home Video, 2013), DVD.

66. "Mission of Gold," Season 4, Disc 4, *Scarecrow and Mrs. King* (February 20, 1987; Burbank: Warner Home Video, 2013), DVD.

67. Moniot, "James Bond and America in the Sixties," 28.

68. "Vigilante Mothers," Season 2, Disc 5, *Scarecrow and Mrs. King* (May 13, 1985; Burbank: Warner Home Video, 2011), DVD. Just as Goldfinger says Mr. Solo "has a pressing engagement" when he is about to die, the villain in "Vigilante Mothers" says the same thing about Amanda in this scene.

69. "You Only Die Twice," Season 2, Disc 4, *Scarecrow and Mrs. King* (April 1, 1985; Burbank: Warner Home Video, 2011), DVD.

70. "The Legend of Das Geisterschloss," Season 2, Disc 1, *Scarecrow and Mrs. King* (October 22, 1984; Burbank: Warner Home Video, 2011), DVD.

71. "I Am Not Now, Nor Have I Ever Been ... a Spy."

72. Hepburn, *Intrigue: Espionage and Culture*, 15. See also Moss, *The Media and the Models of Masculinity*, 41.

73. *For Your Eyes Only*; and "Fearless Dotty," Season 1, Disc 5, *Scarecrow and Mrs. King* (March 26, 1984; Burbank: Warner Home Video, 2010), DVD.

74. "The First Time," Season 1, Disc 1, *Scarecrow and Mrs. King* (October 3, 1983; Burbank: Warner Home Video, 2010), DVD.

75. *For Your Eyes Only.*

76. "You Only Die Twice."

77. *Goldfinger.*

78. Hepburn, *Intrigue: Espionage and Culture*, 16.

79. James Bond Multimedia, "Gadgets," http://www.jamesbondmm.co.uk/gadgets/kgb-music-box-radio (accessed September 12, 2013).

80. *On Her Majesty's Secret Service* and "A Relative Situation."

81. "Promises to Keep," Season 4, Disc 3, *Scarecrow and Mrs. King* (January 9, 1987; Burbank: Warner Home Video, 2013), DVD; *You Only Live Twice*, DVD, directed by Lewis Gilbert (1967; Beverly Hills: Twentieth Century, 2007); Moniot, "James Bond and America in the Sixties," 27; and MI-6: The Home of James Bond, "Allies: Q (Desmond Llewelyn)," http://www.mi6-hq.com/sections/allies/q.php3 (accessed September 12, 2013).

82. "Over the Limit" and "All the World's a Stage," Season 3, Disc 5, *Scarecrow and Mrs. King* (May 12, 1986; Burbank: Warner Home Video, 2013), DVD. In the script for "Over the Limit" Leatherneck's last name is given as Nelson. Tom Ropelewski, "Over the Limit" (Warner Bros. Television, Warner Bros. Inc., Rev. Shooting Final, July 15, 1985), 51.

83. "The Wrong Way Home," Season 3, Disc 3, *Scarecrow and Mrs. King* (December 2, 1985; Burbank: Warner Home Video, 2012), DVD. See also Moniot, "James Bond and America in the Sixties," 27.

84. "Santa's Got a Brand New Bag," Season 4, Disc 3, *Scarecrow and Mrs. King* (December 19, 1986; Burbank: Warner Home Video, 2013), DVD.

85. Q being short for quartermaster, of course. The character's name was in fact Major Boothroyd. See MI-6: The Home of James Bond, "Allies: Q (Desmond Llewelyn)"; Chapman, *Licence to Thrill*, 180, 187; and Moniot, "James Bond and America in the Sixties," 29.

86. "Over the Limit."

87. "One Flew East," Season 4, Disc 4, *Scarecrow and Mrs. King* (February 27, 1987; Burbank: Warner Home Video, 2013), DVD. James Bond had such a pen in *Octopussy*.

88. "Bad Timing," Season 4, Disc 3, *Scarecrow and Mrs. King* (February 6, 1987; Burbank: Warner Home Video, 2013), DVD.

89. "Suitable for Framing," Season 4, Disc 4, *Scarecrow and Mrs. King* (May 14, 1987; Burbank: Warner Home Video, 2013), DVD.

90. "Need to Know"; Mulvihill, "The Golden Age of Bond," 345, 347; Chapman, *Licence to Thrill*, 80; Moniot, "James Bond and America in the Sixties," 27; and Laucht, "Britannia Rules the Atom," 367.

91. *Never Say Never Again*, DVD, directed by Irvin Kershner (1983; Beverly Hills: Twentieth Century–Fox Home Entertainment LLC, 2009); and *A View to a Kill*. See also Laucht, "Britannia Rules the Atom," 368–69.

92. "The Eyes Have It," Season 3, Disc 4, *Scarecrow and Mrs. King* (February 17, 1986; Warner Home Video, 2012), DVD.

93. *Never Say Never Again*.

94. "Brunettes Are In," Season 2, Disc 2, *Scarecrow and Mrs. King* (November 12, 1984; Burbank: Warner Home Video, 2011), DVD.

95. Production moved from California to Europe in the summer of 1984 to avoid the Olympic Games. In total five episodes of *SMK* were filmed overseas; two in England, two in Germany, and one in Austria. See Greg Morton, *Lifting a Foot Forward: A Lesson in Balance* (Glendora, CA: Morton Design Works, 2012), 14.

96. Moniot, "James Bond and America in the Sixties," 28–29.

97. Mulvihill, "The Golden Age of Bond," 346; and Moniot, "James Bond and America in the Sixties," 27. See also John Brosnan, *James Bond in the Cinema* (New York: A.S. Barnes, 1972), 14; and Moss, *The Media and the Models of Masculinity*, 42.

98. "Affair at Bromfield Hall" and *Goldfinger*. The golf club featured in *Goldfinger* is Stoke Park House in Buckinghamshire, while the estate in *SMK* is Wrotham Park in Hertfordshire. For more on Bond filming locations see The Worldwide Guide to Movie Locations: Goldfinger Film Locations, http://www.movie-locations.com/movies/g/goldfinger.html (accessed October 26, 2013). For more on the filming locations *Scarecrow and Mrs. King* used in England see SMK in London, http://www.zeemaps.com/SMK_in_London (accessed October 26, 2013).

99. "Welcome to America, Mr. Brand."

100. John M. Diamond, *The CIA and the Culture of Failure: U.S. Intelligence from the End of the Cold War to the Invasion of Iraq* (Stanford: Stanford University Press, 2008), 207–08.

101. Bond does this when entering Miss Moneypenny's office. Moniot, "James Bond and America in the Sixties," 31.

102. James Bond actually delivers the line about Goldfinger's plan to cause "economic chaos in the West." In *Scarecrow and Mrs. King*, the way American currency will be devalued will not be a contamination of the gold supply, but contamination with disappearing ink. See also Mulvihill, "The Golden Age of Bond," 342, 349.

103. Jon Burlingame, *The Music of James Bond* (Oxford: Oxford University Press, 2012),

2; Smith, "Creating a Bond Market," 147; and Kevin J. Hagopian, "Flint and Satyriasis: The Bond Parodies of the 1960s," in *Secret Agents: Popular Icons Beyond James Bond,* ed. Jeremy Packer (New York: Peter Lang, 2009), 42.

104. Moniot, "James Bond and America in the Sixties," 26; and Claire Hines, "'Entertainment for Men': Uncovering the *Playboy* Bond," in *The James Bond Phenomenon: A Critical Reader,* 2d ed., ed. Christoph Lindner (Manchester: Manchester University Press, 2009), 97.

105. "Welcome to America, Mr. Brand."

106. Moniot, "James Bond and America in the Sixties," 29.

107. "Welcome to America, Mr. Brand."

108. "Unfinished Business," Season 4, Disc 1, *Scarecrow and Mrs. King* (October 3, 1986; Burbank: Warner Home Video, 2013), DVD.

109. "Welcome to America, Mr. Brand."

110. Hepburn, *Intrigue: Espionage and Culture,* 60.

111. *The Man with the Golden Gun.*

112. Moniot, "James Bond and America in the Sixties," 26.

113. Ibid., 25.

114. Ibid., 29.

Bibliography

"Affair at Bromfield Hall." Season 2, Disc 2, *Scarecrow and Mrs. King.* November 26, 1984; Burbank: Warner Home Video, 2011, DVD.

"All the World's a Stage." Season 3, Disc 5, *Scarecrow and Mrs. King.* May 12, 1986; Burbank: Warner Home Video, 2013, DVD.

"The Artful Dodger." Season 1, Disc 4, *Scarecrow and Mrs. King.* March 5, 1984; Burbank: Warner Home Video, 2010, DVD.

"Bad Timing." Season 4, Disc 3, *Scarecrow and Mrs. King.* February 6, 1987; Burbank: Warner Home Video, 2013, DVD.

Bennett, Tony, and Janet Woollacott. "The Moments of Bond." In *The James Bond Phenomenon: A Critical Reader,* 2d ed., edited by Christoph Lindner, 13–33. Manchester: Manchester University Press, 2009.

Biederman, Danny. *The Incredible World of Spy-Fi: Wild and Crazy Spy Gadgets, Props, and Artifacts from TV and the Movies.* San Francisco: Chronicle Books, 2004.

Britton, Wesley. *Spy Television.* Westport, CT: Praeger, 2004.

Brosnan, John. *James Bond in the Cinema.* New York: A.S. Barnes, 1972.

"Brunettes Are In." Season 2, Disc 2, *Scarecrow and Mrs. King.* November 12, 1984; Burbank: Warner Home Video, 2011, DVD.

Burlingame, Jon. *The Music of James Bond.* Oxford: Oxford University Press, 2012.

Chapman, James. *Licence to Thrill: A Cultural History of the James Bond Films.* London: I.B. Tauris, 2007.

"Charity Begins at Home." Season 2, Disc 1, *Scarecrow and Mrs. King.* October 29, 1984; Burbank: Warner Home Video, 2011, DVD.

"A Class Act." Season 2, Disc 2, *Scarecrow and Mrs. King.* December 3, 1984; Burbank: Warner Home Video, 2011, DVD.

"Dead Ringer." Season 1, Disc 4, *Scarecrow and Mrs. King.* February 6, 1984; Burbank: Warner Home Video, 2010, DVD.

Diamond, John M. *The CIA and the Culture of Failure: U.S. Intelligence from the End of the Cold War to the Invasion of Iraq.* Stanford: Stanford University Press, 2008.

"Do You Take This Spy?" Season 4, Disc 4, *Scarecrow and Mrs. King.* February 13, 1987; Burbank: Warner Home Video, 2013, DVD.

Dr. No. DVD. Directed by Terrence Young. 1962. Santa Monica: MGM Home Entertainment, 2007.

Earnest, David C., and James N. Rosenau. "The Spy Who Loved Globalization." *Foreign Policy* 120 (Sept.-Oct. 2000): 88–90.

"The Eyes Have It." Season 3, Disc 4, *Scarecrow and Mrs. King.* February 17, 1986; Warner Home Video, 2012, DVD.

"Fearless Dotty." Season 1, Disc 5, *Scarecrow and Mrs. King.* March 26, 1984; Burbank: Warner Home Video, 2010, DVD.

"The First Time." Season 1, Disc 1, *Scarecrow and Mrs. King.* October 3, 1983; Burbank: Warner Home Video, 2010, DVD.

Fleming, Ian. *You Only Live Twice.* London: Jonathan Cape and Ian Fleming Publications Ltd., 1964 and Las Vegas: Thomas & Mercer, 2012.

For Your Eyes Only. DVD. Directed by John Glen. 1981. Beverly Hills: Twentieth Century–Fox Home Entertainment LLC, 2012.

From Russia with Love. DVD. Directed by Terrence Young. 1963. Culver City, CA: Sony Pictures Home Entertainment, 2005.

Goldfinger. VHS. Directed by Guy Hamilton. 1964. Santa Monica: MGM/UA Home Video, 1995.

Hagopian, Kevin J. "Flint and Satyriasis: The Bond Parodies of the 1960s." In *Secret Agents: Popular Icons Beyond James Bond,* edited by Jeremy Packer, 21–52. New York: Peter Lang, 2009.

Hepburn, Allan. *Intrigue: Espionage and Culture.* New Haven: Yale University Press, 2005.

Hines, Claire. "'Entertainment for Men': Uncovering the *Playboy* Bond." In *The James Bond Phenomenon: A Critical Reader,* edited by Christoph Lindner, 89–105. Manchester: Manchester University Press, 2009.

"I Am Not Now, Nor Have I Ever Been ... a Spy." Season 1, Disc 3, *Scarecrow and Mrs. King.* January 30, 1984; Burbank: Warner Home Video, 2010, DVD.

James Bond Multimedia. "Gadgets." http://www.jamesbondmm.co.uk/gadgets/kgb-music-box-radio (accessed September 12, 2013).

Kackman, Michael. *Citizen Spy: Television, Espionage, and Cold War Culture.* Minneapolis: University of Minnesota Press, 2005.

Kelsey, Lynne. "Mystery in a Minor Key." Warner Bros. Television, Warner Bros. Inc. Shooting Final. January 9, 1987.

Laucht, Christoph. "Britannia Rules the Atom: The James Bond Phenomenon and Postwar British Nuclear Culture." *The Journal of Popular Culture* 46, no. 2 (2013): 358–77.

"The Legend of Das Geisterschloss." Season 2, Disc 1, *Scarecrow and Mrs. King.* October 22, 1984; Burbank: Warner Home Video, 2011, DVD.

"The Long Christmas Eve." Season 1, Disc 3, *Scarecrow and Mrs. King.* December 19, 1983; Burbank: Warner Home Video, 2010, DVD.

"A Lovely Little Affair." Season 3, Disc 1, *Scarecrow and Mrs. King.* September 23, 1985; Burbank: Warner Home Video, 2012, DVD.

"Magic Bus." Season 1, Disc 1, *Scarecrow and Mrs. King.* October 24, 1983; Burbank: Warner Home Video, 2010, DVD.

The Man with the Golden Gun. DVD. Directed by Guy Hamilton. 1974. Culver City, CA: Sony Pictures Home Entertainment, 2005.

MI-6: The Home of James Bond. "Allies: Q (Desmond Llewelyn)." http://www.mi6-hq.com/sections/allies/q.php3 (accessed September 12, 2013).

"Mission of Gold." Season 4, Disc 4, *Scarecrow and Mrs. King.* February 20, 1987; Burbank: Warner Home Video, 2013, DVD.

Moniot, Drew. "James Bond and America in the Sixties: An Investigation of the Formula Film in Popular Culture." *Journal of the University Film Association* 28, no. 3 (Summer 1976): 25–33.

Moore, Roger. *Bond on Bond: Reflections on 50 Years of James Bond Movies.* Guilford, CT: Lyons Press, 2012.

Morton, Greg. *Lifting a Foot Forward: A Lesson in Balance*. Glendora, CA: Morton Design Works, 2012.

Moss, Mark. *The Media and the Models of Masculinity*. Lanham, MD: Lexington, 2006.

Mulvihill, Jason. "The Golden Age of Bond: Creation of a Cold War Popular Hero (1962–1965) Part II." *International Journal of Instructional Media* 28, no. 4 (2001): 337–53.

"Need to Know." Season 4, Disc 2, *Scarecrow and Mrs. King*. December 5, 1986; Burbank: Warner Home Video, 2013, DVD.

Never Say Never Again. DVD. Directed by Irvin Kershner. 1983. Beverly, Hills, CA: Twentieth Century–Fox Home Entertainment LLC, 2009.

"Night Crawler." Season 4, Disc 2, *Scarecrow and Mrs. King*. October 31, 1986; Burbank: Warner Home Video, 2013, DVD.

Octopussy. DVD. Directed by John Glen. 1983. Beverly Hills: Twentieth Century–Fox Home Entertainment, 2007.

On Her Majesty's Secret Service. DVD. Directed by Peter Hunt. 1967. Santa Monica: MGM Home Entertainment, 2000.

"One Bear Dances, One Bear Doesn't." Season 3, Disc 3, *Scarecrow and Mrs. King*. January 6, 1986; Burbank: Warner Home Video, 2012, DVD.

"One Flew East." Season 4, Disc 4, *Scarecrow and Mrs. King*. February 27, 1987; Burbank: Warner Home Video, 2013, DVD.

"Over the Limit." Season 3, Disc 1, *Scarecrow and Mrs. King*. October 7, 1985; Burbank: Warner Home Video, 2012, DVD.

Owens, Craig N. "The Bond Market." In *Ian Fleming and James Bond: The Cultural Politics of 007*, edited by Edward P. Comentale, Stephen Watt, and Skip Willman, 107–28. Bloomington: Indiana University Press, 2005.

"Promises to Keep." Season 4, Disc 3, *Scarecrow and Mrs. King*. January 9, 1987; Burbank: Warner Home Video, 2013, DVD.

"A Relative Situation." Season 2, Disc 3, *Scarecrow and Mrs. King*. February 11, 1985; Burbank: Warner Home Video, 2011, DVD.

"Remembrance of Things Past." Season 1, Disc 3, *Scarecrow and Mrs. King*. January 9, 1984; Burbank: Warner Home Video, 2010, DVD.

Ropelewski, Tom. "Over the Limit." Warner Bros. Television, Warner Bros. Inc., Rev. Shooting Final, July 15, 1985.

"Santa's Got a Brand New Bag." Season 4, Disc 3, *Scarecrow and Mrs. King*. December 19, 1986; Burbank: Warner Home Video, 2013, DVD.

"Saved by the Bells." Season 1, Disc 2, *Scarecrow and Mrs. King*. November 28, 1983; Burbank: Warner Home Video, 2010, DVD.

Scarecrow and Mrs. King. Academy of Television Arts & Sciences. http://www.emmys.com/shows/scarecrow-and-mrs-king (accessed October 25, 2013).

Scarecrow and Mrs. King Forum. Episode Discussions. http://scarecrowandmrskingforum.yuku.com/forums/18/Episode-Discussions (accessed October 31, 2013).

"Service Above and Beyond." Season 1, Disc 2, *Scarecrow and Mrs. King*. November 21, 1983; Burbank: Warner Home Video, 2010, DVD.

Simon, Carly, and Marvin Hamlish. *The Spy Who Loved Me*. Los Angeles: EMI Records USA, 1977.

Smith, Jeff. "Creating a Bond Market: Selling John Barry's Soundtracks and Theme Songs." In *The James Bond Phenomenon: A Critical Reader*, 2d ed., edited by Christoph Linder, 136–52. Manchester: Manchester University Press, 2009.

SMK in London. http://www.zeemaps.com/SMK_in_London (accessed October 26, 2013).

The Spy Who Loved Me. DVD. Directed by Lewis Gilbert. 1977. Santa Monica: MGM Home Entertainment, 2007.

"Stemwinder: Part I." Season 4, Disc 1, *Scarecrow and Mrs. King*. November 19, 1986; Burbank: Warner Home Video, 2013, DVD.

"Suitable for Framing." Season 4, Disc 4, *Scarecrow and Mrs. King.* May 14, 1987; Burbank: Warner Home Video, 2013, DVD.

"Tail of the Dancing Weasel." Season 3, Disc 1, *Scarecrow and Mrs. King.* October 14, 1985; Burbank: Warner Home Video, 2012, DVD.

"The Three Faces of Emily." Season 2, Disc 3, *Scarecrow and Mrs. King.* December 31, 1984; Burbank: Warner Home Video, 2011, DVD.

"Unfinished Business." Season 4, Disc 1, *Scarecrow and Mrs. King.* October 3, 1986; Burbank: Warner Home Video, 2013, DVD.

A View to a Kill. DVD. Directed by John Glen. 1985. Beverly Hills: Twentieth Century–Fox Home Entertainment LLC, 2012.

"Vigilante Mothers." Season 2, Disc 5, *Scarecrow and Mrs. King.* May 13, 1985; Burbank: Warner Home Video, 2011, DVD.

"Welcome to America, Mr. Brand." Season 3, Disc 1, *Scarecrow and Mrs. King.* October 21, 1985; Burbank: Warner Home Video, 2012, DVD.

"We're Off to See the Wizard." Season 3, Disc 1, *Scarecrow and Mrs. King.* September 23, 1985; Burbank: Warner Home Video, 2012, DVD.

The Worldwide Guide to Movie Locations. Goldfinger Film Locations. http://www.movie-locations.com/movies/g/goldfinger.html (accessed October 26, 2013).

"The Wrong Way Home." Season 3, Disc 3, *Scarecrow and Mrs. King.* December 2, 1985; Burbank: Warner Home Video, 2012, DVD.

"You Only Die Twice." Season 2, Disc 4, *Scarecrow and Mrs. King.* April 1, 1985; Burbank: Warner Home Video, 2011, DVD.

You Only Live Twice. DVD. Directed by Lewis Gilbert. 1967. Beverly Hills: Twentieth Century–Fox Home Entertainment, 2007.

Part Three

Literature

Super-Spies Face the Collective Shadow of the Cold War in Matt Kindt's *Mind MGMT*

Hannah Means-Shannon

When Matt Kindt's comic series *Mind MGMT* debuted in 2012, it was highly anticipated as a spy-based fiction because of his earlier work in the genre such as *Super-Spies* and *2 Sisters*. The traumatic historical backdrop of the series is, ostensibly, the mid to late 20th century, following the careers of a core group of psychically super-powered secret government agents who eventually find themselves not so much obsolete as too dangerous to maintain in the field as their Cold War objectives become irrelevant over time. As Gennady Gerasimov said during the Reagan-Gorbachev summit in Moscow: "We are going to do something awful to you. We are going to deprive you of an enemy!"[1] Without programmed outlets for their training, Mind MGMT agents become increasingly dangerous pursuant to their own agendas.

Mind MGMT addresses the motivations of Cold War agencies and agents, their rationalization of extreme measures, and their subsequent psychological breakdowns when they are deprived of a definitive "other" against whom to pit their unusual skills. In particular, agent Henry Lyme represents the psychological dangers of Cold War attitudes whereas the journalist Meru's struggle to understand and accept the legacy of the Mind MGMT agency represents a modern perspective on an ambiguous, and perhaps still dangerous, legacy. For this reason, *Mind MGMT* is an overt response to the glamorization of secret agents in popular culture, a step-by-step breakdown of the myth of the idealized and self-confident super-spy.

Psychoanalyst Carl Jung's theories of the presence of "the shadow" as a representation of unconscious in conflict with the conscious mind have become commonplace in discussion of literature, film, and even graphic novels. However, in one of his final works, *The Undiscovered Self*, he also addressed the international state of tension brewing following the second World War and postulates

162

that the biggest danger the 20th century faced was the epidemic spread of what he called the "collective shadow."[2] This mass reaction of transference of one's own psychological shadow self onto others in a form of hysteria justifies any action without rational consideration or ethical analysis in a radical exemplar of the maxim, "the ends justify the means." Matt Kindt's Mind MGMT agents become the wasteland left behind by the rampant projection of the collective shadow, and picking up the pieces becomes a task for the younger generation, demonstrated through the characters Lyme and Meru respectively. Gaining true self-knowledge and addressing one's personal shadow side becomes the only method to protect the world at large from the highly destructive collective shadow syndrome continuing to affect the other agents of Mind MGMT.

The Collective Shadow and Its Legacy

Carl Jung's theories of the collective unconscious are still very much at work today in helping us analyze and understand the relationship between the rational consciousness and the unconscious psyche, often driven by very different instinctual patterns. In particular, engaging in aggressive behavior and identifying enemies often derives from projection of one's worst fears about oneself onto others, the projection of the "shadow."[3] But in Jung's consideration of international conflict, he noted that certain individuals were more inclined and adept at inducing a mass movement in the projection of the shadow onto entire groups of people or nations, enabling popular support for otherwise unethical behavior on the part of soldiers or governments.

He describes these key individuals, often the leaders of popular movements, thus: "Their mental state is that of a collectively excited group ruled by affective judgments and wish-fantasies. In a milieu of this kind, they are the adapted ones, and consequently they feel at home in it."[4] Jung also notes that "...despite their small number in comparison with the population as a whole, [they are] dangerous as sources of infection precisely because the so-called normal person possesses only a limited degree of self-knowledge."[5] The problem he describes is two-fold: the emergence of individuals capable of inspiring projecting behaviors in others, and also the degree to which "normal people" are easily led in this activity by individuals of influence.

The problem with unsuspecting members of society is that they are placed in a situation where they recognize the need for action and social change, perhaps because their way of life is threatened, but their own degree of self-knowledge inhibits responsible ethical behavior. They fail to recognize the danger of their own "shadow" and place all negative traits on offending groups. Jung explains,

"In accordance with the prevailing tendency of consciousness to seek the source of all ills in the outside world, the cry goes up for political and social changes which, it is supposed, would automatically solve the much deeper problem of split personality."[6] The danger is rife, especially in situations of international stress, and wars, both hot and cold, result. "None of us stands outside humanity's black collective shadow," Jung warns, and so, to a degree, individuals are responsible for the actions of mass movements or government decision-making.[7]

In post–Cold War society, these relics of uninhibited projection of the "shadow" still linger, and the after-effects of this excess continue to poison international relations and daily life for individuals encountering difference. Current commentators on Jung's concepts warn that, "In violence and oppression, in romantic projections, in the invisibility of current suffering, in the denial of current responsibility, we find the collective shadow."[8] The only solution, according to Jung, is unflinching self-analysis of one's own psychological state, motivations, and social behavior to help repair ingrained patterns of destructive social interaction. The individual "must know relentlessly how much good he can do, and what crimes he is capable of."[9]

Unhelpful, but all too common reactions to the legacy of the Cold War in Western cultures is similar to more archetypal reactions of society to the after-effects of the collective shadow. Typically, citizens take an attitude of denial, according to Kremer and Rothberg, seeking to "put the past behind us," and they follow this initial stage with "blanket amnesty to perpetrators," "self-righteous punishment of perpetrators," "scapegoating," "minimal acknowledgment of mistakes," and "spreading the blame" as we see in revisionist histories of Holocaust.[10] The last phase of denial reactions to the activity of the collective shadow is "rewriting of history" to entirely anneal the painful historical episodes from public memory. The results of shuffling off responsibility for the actions of individuals and nations can be disastrous since the same patterns are in danger of repeating themselves with even greater destructive impact. As Nhat Hanh, a Vietnamese poet and activist, commented on his own national tragedy, "The war is in us, but is also in everyone.... Everything is ready to explode, and we are all co-responsible."[11]

Meru the Truth-Seeker

Mind MGMT's first two collected volumes, containing serialized issues one through twelve, as well as extra material such as strips that only appeared online originally, are a highly interactive experience for readers because the narrative is not rendered in fully chronological order and information concerning key characters is fragmented and arranged in a way that encourages readers to construct a cohesive narrative around each character. Since the origin and function of the government agency Mind MGMT is essentially a mystery which journalist Meru is attempting to solve, her perspective becomes a point of identification for the reader.

She is, however, an unreliable source of identification, since she is initially unaware of her own past activity as a Mind MGMT agent and has had her memory of past encounters with the agency, and with the agent Henry, aka "Harry" Lyme, repeatedly wiped. In this way, the reader is actually privileged above Meru in constructing the narrative, nevertheless, since she is one of the most visible focal points of the narrative, and her reactions are "modern," representing a younger generation, she is an excellent subject for considering the negative psychological impact of the Cold War on the post-war world.

Meru is one of a few female agents present in *Mind MGMT*, but her presence particularly challenges an archetypal assessment of a wartime situation as a masculine domain. For instance, Jungian scholar Anthony Stevens asserts that "the cross-cultural evidence is overwhelming: war is a masculine problem. Women do not make war: men do."[12] It would be convenient to explain this by viewing Meru as an agent conscripted into war by superiors pursuing masculine drives toward aggression, but the presence of other female agents such as the Eraser, all of whom display aggressive tendencies in individualistic ways, contradicts this interpretation.

It is, however, possible that Meru's "difference" from other agents, a difference which is increasingly established throughout the narrative, and her function as something of an avenging angel seeking to redress the wrongs of imbalance concerning the projection of the collective shadow, does present her as more of a healing force than a destructive war-like presence in the world at large. Lyme's "vision" of her, describing "what I see in her," places her in the role of a "warrior princess"[13] in Eastern mythological terms, who fights for "truth." In this full-page spread she is depicted surrounded by banners, kneeling with a sabre, with red flowers in her hair and surrounding her, a reoccurring motif.[14] She may well represent, thematically, the healing powers of the psyche when in pursuit of self-knowledge, capable of restoring balance after a period of traumatic imbalance, even if the methods necessary to address radical deficits are at time radical in themselves.

Meru's journey into self-knowledge, however, is psychologically rocky to say the least, and as readers become aware of her own rewritten history, they also come to see the remarkably destructive impact of Mind MGMT on peoples' lives. At first the reader believes, like Meru, that the disorderly and poverty line existence that Meru faces as a writer is part of her choice in life. Kindt presents

Meru with a world-weary, haunted expression throughout these sequences when she feels she has been "drifting" through life.[15] Gradually it becomes clear that the effect of memory wiping has planted obsessions in her mind that keep her from moving on with her life. Her subconscious, essentially, continues to seek self-knowledge even while her conscious mind believes she has not yet begun to construct the narrative of the mysterious government agency connected to an "amnesia flight" occurrence, randomly destructive mental states in a village in Mexico, and an even more fateful and disturbing encounter with former Mind MGMT agents in Zanzibar. After an initial, revelatory meeting with Harry Lyme in which he narrates his own history as a Mind MGMT agent, and his connection to her life as her rescuer in childhood from a scene of devastation, Meru is once again "wiped," in a pattern of increasing mental deterioration for her.

Only when Lyme decides that she has become too involved to remain an "outsider" does she become an observer in a new mission for former Mind MGMT agents to escape assassination by rogue agents of their own. For Meru, she's back to the drawing board but can, at least, begin a journey into self-knowledge previously taken from her several times over. This is actually very dangerous for her psychologically, even while it contains the potential for healing since she's now part of a group formerly infected by transference of the collective shadow. The repercussions of their past actions make her a target, and she becomes increasingly likely to take their side regardless of their compromised ethics in the past. As she gets sucked in to surviving, and helping protect herself and others from rogue agents, she becomes part of the "in-group" that formerly transferred their shadow onto the "other" enemy forces, and her "shared paranoia promotes solidarity and prepares the group for effective action in its own defence."[16] Even though she tries to remain an "objective reporter," that's simply not possible, especially since her former instincts as a Mind MGMT agent begin to reveal themselves and make her a major asset to the new team in achieving their goals.[17] Her role as "successful author, now broke. Desperate for a story" becomes increasingly a sham, as she admits to the reader.[18]

The trajectory of the plot of the first two volumes of *Mind MGMT* relentlessly, though often circuitously, brings Meru closer to discovering personal truths about her own part in the collective shadow of the Cold War. Her abilities as a super-spy begin to emerge, but are at first patchy and unpredictable. The mental blocks in place that prevent her from achieving total recall of her past prevent her from confronting her personal shadow. The presence of Lyme is, however, essential to breaking down those blocks. As she says, "The more time I spend with Lyme ... I'm noticing inconsistencies ... in my own memory," which she describes as "...blind spots. Fuzzy spots."[19]

Meru still believes herself to be an outsider until the group achieves their new mission of locating the Mind MGMT school known as Shangri-la. There, a mystical library containing all "true" recorded history, unwiped and unaltered by the activities of Mind MGMT can offer her the self-knowledge she is gradually seeking from the mysterious Archivist who keeps the untainted records. Meru's encounter with this flood of information culminates in a panel that displays an unfolding image of possible selves fanned out through her streaming red hair, including a crying child and at least two princess-like figures.[20] Her motivations are, even then, mixed, since she believes she wants the truth about the agency, and about Lyme's life, and not necessarily about her own. She is tempted to flee this knowledge.

When she achieves full knowledge from the library, her encounter has implications far wider reaching than personal closure. She recognizes that she, too, was an agent who became too "dangerous" to keep in action, that her superpowers are so extensive that they are largely beyond measurement, and most painfully, that Lyme's amorality has been responsible for essentially contaminating her life at several junctures. Her "difference" from other agents is most fully established here because her future choices become of major importance to the future of the Mind MGMT legacy.

The experiences revealed in Meru's past are, however, consistent with the psychological trajectory of the choices that she makes in response to remembering them. She is prepared at last to hold Harry Lyme responsible for his humanitarian crimes, the impediments he has put in her way on her search for self-knowledge, and finally, to pronounce judgment on Mind MGMT as a whole. When she is capable of holding other agents responsible for their actions, she can hold herself responsible for her current choices. And her final choices at the close of volume two, to refuse to take sides between the two rival teams of agents, even though one seems more "other" than the one she has been supporting marks her development.

Rather than continuing in the transference of the shadow and continuing to promote the collective shadow cast by the Cold War, Meru distances herself as a fully-fledged individual. Her neutral position, however surprising to readers who may have come to see her as allied with "good guys" versus "bad guys," is an effective model of the attempt to restore balance between the conscious and unconscious mind through the centralizing position of the true "self" which encompasses both. By becoming non-partisan she moves from the position of a victim to a negotiating figure capable of brokering real peace in psychological terms. Lyme describes Meru as having "all of us in her" in the library at the end of Volume Two, a collective entity comprising all the agents and their powers, and this accompanies the return of all of her memory and her refusal to "pick sides."[21] She therefore may be a composite figure capable of taking on the responsibility of all the agents in their crimes and neutralizing the fallout from their actions. It remains to be seen how her role will develop along these lines in future installments of the series.

The Futurist

Duncan is a Mind MGMT agent who was a "late bloomer" according to his own reckoning, someone who used his talents in other realms, which caused him increasing boredom and a sense of purposelessness, and is the "Futurist" of the title of the second collected volume of the series.[22] By reading the minds of everyone around him within a five-mile radius, and collating the information, he can predict up to fifteen minutes into the future, enabling him to go unnoticed, unharmed, and to some extent, this renders him invulnerable. He explains to the reader, "What I can do is read the minds of everyone in close proximity to me. I can read their intentions. What they're about to do. I can take all of those thoughts around me and—mashing them together—I can predict what's going to happen. It's just like telling the future."[23]

Duncan might as well be referred to as an "invisible man" for these reasons. In his own words, in the prologue to the second volume, he explains, "Before we finish here, let me tell you my story. You see, I have to tell it now. And tell it in this order, or it won't work. You won't believe me and everything falls apart."[24] Duncan's strange explanation of where and how he must tell his story hints at a wider pattern in the discursive structure of Mind MGMT and hints that the manner of storytelling, in fragments and multiple perspectives, may well mirror his own perspective in life.

Is Duncan, in some way, an ordering structure to the series? It would explain the way the narrative jumps between perspectives, anticipates future actions and forms causal links between events. But more than that, Duncan is burdened with a heavy degree of self-knowledge that is different than Henry Lyme's but still a cause of extreme psychological stress. He believes that Mind MGMT saved him, since he was literally lying in a gutter having given up on existence when they found him, and yet, he eventually joins a team established by Lyme in the second volume of the series. He doesn't join enthusiastically, and Meru, Lyme, and other agents have to work for months to pin him down long enough to explain their need for him, however, once he joins, it is with a renewed sense of purpose.

Duncan initially believes in the good of the Mind MGMT agency, loses faith and direction, and then finds a degree of it again in this new team-up.

Meru's commentary on Duncan's initial "rescue" by Mind MGMT shows her burgeoning cynicism about whether a Cold War cause can save someone like Duncan: "The familiar Mind Management recruitment. Floating down like the hand of God to pluck the most beautiful flowers."[25] This line is significant because the flower imagery returns in the series, and is one of the few references that suggests the talents of these individuals could have served some other less violent purpose had they not been "plucked" away and altered through training. Even Duncan was a "flower" who, redirected, loses his way.

How does Duncan fit into the collective shadow framework that helps explain the legacy of the Cold War in Mind MGMT? Firstly, as a "late bloomer," he doesn't deal with childhood trauma associated with agent training, and immediately moves into an advisory role in the agency school. He is, in fact, someone keeping an eye on Lyme as his powers develop and a voice of caution. We are given little indication that Duncan has an explosive temper or is dangerous in the same way other agents can be, but there is a weariness about him that hints at his awareness of responsibility and fear for the future. When he is no longer with the agency, he creates a world around himself in which he tries to avoid routine and engages in challenging tasks to use his skills and keep life a little interesting for someone otherwise suffering from an extreme lack of engagement such as walking across a street in traffic with his eyes closed.[26] His personal shadow seems to consist of near-suicidal tendencies, a self-destructive urge, and the need for direction from his conscious life.

Since he can "predict" the future, he can alter its trajectory, but he rarely seems invasive in his techniques. In short, he is not a key figure in projecting the collective shadow onto others, though through working for the agency, he does allow them to do so and especially facilitates the school that is responsible for so much future destruction. Duncan is responsible by involvement, and particularly responsible for Lyme's destructive actions because he allows them. Duncan's passivity could be acknowledged as a crime purely because he has such a degree of self-knowledge. He is drawn to Meru, and wants her to know the truth about herself, perhaps because he suspects she can actually do something to influence the future, whereas he seems unable to do so. In that respect, too, he is a facilitator.

Duncan's legacy, though, is not one to easily brush aside. Though he is "saved" by Mind MGMT by being given a sense of purpose, Jungian analysis reminds us that "the most dreadful catastrophes occur when the moral complex forges an alliance with the shadow so as to justify us in perpetrating destructive acts of appalling malignity."[27] And Duncan's "moral complex" was certainly engaged by Mind MGMT during its period of activity to aid them in justifying extreme actions. He, too, needs to find a way to make reparations for his involvement.

The New Enemies

Two key characters act as opposing forces against the protagonists, or perhaps more rightly anti-heroes, of the Mind MGMT series, the Eraser and the Immortal. Significantly, both are depicted as Henry Lyme's schoolmates and therefore are introduced early in the narrative. They are consistently depicted in childhood as ideal agent material for Mind MGMT, capable of mastering the unsavory tasks set before the children such as self-harm in the case of the Immortal, and mind control in the case of the Eraser.[28] In this way, both the Immortal and the Eraser, like all child-trained Mind MGMT agents, could be seen as victims. Whether as "direct victims," "indirect victims" or "perpetrators" of violence associated with the Cold War, their youth places them in a vulnerable category implicating lasting psychological trauma however successful their training might be.[29]

Because the Immortal can mentally heal himself from inflicted wounds, he's an ideal combatant and so is sent into violent situations with equally violent results. It would be difficult not to view him as the darker aspect of the agency itself, their more aggressive feature. The Eraser, it would seem, could be a more neutral figure. By removing memory, she is capable of damage control for the agency. Because the narrative in the series is non-chronological, however, the reader views her activities as antagonistic early on, teaming up with the Immortal in an inexplicable vendetta against Meru. She at first wonders if they are "zombies" and then asks the bigger questions, "how they know her" and "why they won't kill her."[30]

In fact, if we see things from the perspective of the Eraser, she may be merely continuing the job she pursued for the agency. Meru wants to write a book about Mind MGMT and therefore must be silenced. We learn, however, as the series progresses, that the Eraser is possibly allied with the Immortal because she wishes to reactivate a team of agents without the governing forces of the agency to keep them in check. She and the Immortal, presumably, would become the de facto leaders of a new regime. Does she possess some degree of moral or ethical compass that would suggest her abilities as a leader? There is no evidence of this. She is consistently presented as a malignant force. This could be because her activity, consistently erasing the memories of "normal" people, takes away their self-knowledge. As such, she is acting as a perpetuator of the collective shadow, the spread of irrational and suggestible behavior. In her alliance with the Immortal, she seems to confirm her support for violent rule and domination of "normal" people for her own uncertain goals.

The role of the two "enemy" agents in Mind MGMT speaks to the wider conflicts within the series. They represent the past, as contemporaries of Lyme, and threaten a return to chaotic behavior in the future on the part of former agents. At one point, Lyme confronts them with the observation, "We need to stop all this. You're a product of a corrupt system. Like me."[31] Lyme realizes they are all an unusual combination of both obsolete and dangerous. In Jungian terms, there are two main types of conflict in society, "conflict within groups and conflict between groups."[32] When there is conflict within groups, there is "aggression they use against their own kind (which only occasionally results in injury or death)."[33] When there is conflict inspired by transference of the collective shadow, there is "the more lethal aggression they use against outsiders."[34] During the heyday of the Mind MGMT agency, all "normal" people were viewed as outsiders to the psychic agent group, and therefore justified as targets for "lethal aggression" with little real thought for the value of human life. In that paradigm, "insider" agents occupied a privileged position as allies. Once the Eraser and the Immortal set out to gather agents together again under their own leadership, however, all resistant or opposed agents become "outsiders" too, subject to lethal force.

Meru, for instance, is an outsider to the Eraser and Immortal, though one they would like to turn to their will, whereas Lyme and finally Duncan are targets for eradication. The Eraser and Immortal have reconstructed the projected shadow paradigm from their former Cold War days and are extending it, giving it a new lease on life. They could, essentially, set the whole paradigm of destruction in motion again if allowed to operate freely because they have never come to terms with their own shadow. They seem to operate without regulation, conscience, or an awareness of responsibility. It is useful to keep in mind that Mind MGMT made them that way, training them from childhood, and these "ideal" agents are the most direct legacy of the agencies aims and modes of operation. Without a Cold War enemy to combat, these agents have simply shifted their projected shadow onto other agents, following the archetypal pattern. If the shadow is done away with according to one group, it just "moves" to another and "the shadow will be projected onto other groups," making the projected shadow impossible to kill or destroy, essentially "immortal" in itself.[35]

This pattern may very well have been instilled in them through their childhood training, since the "enemy archetype" can be "built into the personal psyche in the form of a complex" and the two main sources for a developing complex are "cultural indoctrination" and "familial repression," which is kept in check by a "moral complex" instilled by familial lessons of guilt.[36] When the Eraser and the Immortal are trained by Mind MGMT, they receive both indoctrination regarding the "enemy" and also a form of familial instruction, but one devoid of moral consequences. Without necessary repressions and restraint, the shadow simply runs wild. The agents we see in the "modern day" of Meru's life in the narrative are examples of the shadow resurgent, simply transferred, and potentially immortal in its cycles of destruction. As Lyme says, "They can't be killed. They just evolve," and their evolution is the problem.[37]

The Propagandists

Other Mind MGMT agents display and utilize powers that play a significant role during the years of prime operation for Mind MGMT in the Cold War. The Ad Man and the twin Perrier sisters respectively represent the power of images and the power of words to suggest ideas and affiliations, as well as actions, to the masses of "normal" people being co-opted into the war. The Ad Man places ads next to key news items to do far more than damage control, but a virtual rewriting of history that aids in denial of destructive events connected with the agency and also suggests attitudes and associations that will help keep the home front engaged in opposition. He's involved in "instigations," but also "destabilization," and like Duncan, he's assured it is all "for the greater good."[38]

In scope, the Ad Man's powers may well rival Lyme's own in reaching vast numbers with a coercive message. When Lyme and Meru attempt to reach out to him in his memory-wiped state operating a highly successful ad agency, he gains recall of his former life, but is quickly taken out of play by the Immortal so that he cannot be drawn into an alliance with Lyme. It is a major loss to Lyme's plans, but this may indicate that in a shadow-war, propaganda is less helpful. The Ad Man has been taken out of play as a potential recruit for the Immortal, too, and this does disable the new shadow-based team from reaching as wide a populace as they might have hoped.

His activities in the past, though, have had devastating consequences in influencing "normal people." In Jungian terms, he is an archetypal propagandist, and "what makes such propaganda so devastating in its psychological consequences is that it can activate the archetype of the enemy, which may then be projected onto a designated out-group, in addition to the personal shadow."[39] Because the Ad Man is a product of the Mind MGMT educational system, his personal shadow side has been modified to create a specific enemy according to government guidelines, so when he projects it onto thousands of people, he takes away their ability to distinguish between enemy and friend, resulting in the "justification for the slaughter which ensues"[40] for both the Ad Man and his victims.

The Perrier sisters occupy a more nebulous realm of accountability because they create two mass-influencing novels on their own before agency work, a children's book, and a young adult novel, both of which spark unrest and riots among young people with ideas that "spread like an airborne virus."[41] Are the Perrier sisters simply anarchists with limited scope? They might have been had they not been drawn into agency service. Once working for Mind MGMT, they work alongside the Ad Man in words and pictures to create mass hysteria and governance. They have been modified in their direction of projecting their shadow, with more significant consequences for the world at large. They certainly are not blameless in taking away "self-knowledge" from the masses. They are, however, presented more sympathetically during the "modern day" of Meru's life, partly because they have become the victim of Mind MGMT when the agency decides they are too dangerous as a working unit and are separated. This separation results in their mental deterioration, and leads to the suicide of one sister.

The remaining Perrier sister regains the full faculties of both she and her twin as a result.[42] Her powers are still vast, and could potentially be used for shadow-projection and prompting conflict, but she quickly agrees to join Lyme's team against the Eraser and Immortal, proving that she's friendly toward taking responsibility and making some form of restitution for her actions in the past. She seems to have gained greater self-knowledge through the loss of her sister and becomes an asset in resisting a return to a destructive cycle. She is prepared to be "recruited" to join Lyme's new team, "if only to find out what's really going on."[43] Like Meru, being a truth-seeker suggests that she has become a positive figure.

The Guilty Man

Henry Lyme is as much an enigma at the heart of Mind MGMT as the agency itself. He is the definitive secret agent, and his origin story is one of the earliest told in the series in preference to other agents. He becomes Meru's goal and touchstone for the recovery of information, and of all the agents, he is the most burdened by the ambiguity of his actions in the past and the most uncertain of the corrective course of action in the future. He is defined for readers, eventually, by his guilt, a guilt which Meru suggests is the wrong kind of motivation at the conclusion of the second volume of the series.[44] As such, Lyme most fully represents the burden of responsibility for violence and destruction created during Cold War conflicts and espionage. He is the anti–James Bond of the series, and a constant source of interest for both Meru and the reader. For that reason, he is the most prone subject for psychological analysis but also the most resistant and complex figure in the narrative.

We learn that Lyme, like most agents of Mind MGMT, was conscripted as a child, but because his origin story is delivered early in the series, the reader is more likely to be shocked by his experiences in "training" by the agency as a child than they will be by later, similar stories featuring other agents. His struggle with self-harm or the harm of others, and depictions of his qualms gradually being drilled out of him, are disturbing to say the least and say as much about Mind MGMT as Lyme, but also make his propensity for destruction later even more of a contrast.[45] He explains his manipulation into an agent of war by Mind MGMT to Meru by saying, "It wasn't until near the end that I realized we weren't just experiments. We were being militarized."[46] Like other Mind MGMT agents, from the time of his recruitment, Lyme enters a period of "disruption," a psychological transition for young service men, but it is one from which Lyme never fully recovers since he never returns to a "normal" life.[47]

Lyme's abilities to quite easily influence the minds of those around him, however, make him a poster-boy for the powers of the agency, but also make the agency take note of the potential dangers he poses to themselves and others. Lyme is a personality quite dualistic in nature, extremely conscience-driven in some ways and prone to guilt, and extremely careless in others. These qualities humanize him for readers, but also keep him at a distance due to ethical reservations regarding his actions.

Lyme's gradual mental unraveling is, of course, the most dangerous aspect of his character, in tandem with his powers. He begins to wonder if anything is "real" including the love of his wife Natasha, or if he is "manufacturing" it.[48] Driven by the certainty that his wife and his young daughter are too "perfect" and therefore are largely the product of his own desire to make their lives perfect through mentally influencing them, Lyme unleashes his rage on surrounding minds. The events in Zanzibar are a science-fiction nightmare run rampant as Lyme turns the citizens of the city against one another in a murderous rampage. Unable to be certain of a reality outside of his own control, Lyme becomes incredibly destructive and his implosion wreaks havoc on such a massive humanitarian scale that the blast zone stands at the center of the *Mind MGMT* narrative as a singular instance of just why super-spies are a monstrous creation. As destructive as an atom bomb, as catastrophic to human life, Lyme's actions, which destroy even his own wife and child, send a final message to the Mind MGMT agency so unmistakable that they decommission the entire operation and "wipe" the minds of all former agents.

Even in childhood, Lyme exhibited the features that Jung refers to when discussing the dangers of mass hysteria at the hands of someone capable of directing the projection of the collective shadow. Around Lyme, all "normal" people become more than suggestible, but rather slaves to his power of will. For that reason, his projection of his own shadow becomes a universal thing. Everything becomes a "trigger" for Lyme, at first orders from the agency, and then personal whim and response. He is single-handedly capable of causing wars. Of course, he is also able to stop wars and redirect their outcome, for the most part, but that relies on his ability to focus and control his will. He is a magnified example of the "triggers" of war through projection on "other" parties of one's own fears. As Stevens says, "The 'causes' that historians attribute to wars may not really be causes at all, but merely the triggers that set them off."[49] In some ways, Lyme is the source and origin of wars, played out within his own personality and projected onto the world at large.

But what is it, exactly, that renders Lyme so dangerous other than his gargantuan super-power? Surely, he could also be the source of extremely beneficial outcomes for humanity if his own nature is sufficiently beneficent? In classic psychoanalytical fashion, one could look to his childhood. Two "great archetypal" systems of social interaction are established in childhood, one that is "concerned with attachment, affiliation, care-giving, care-receiving, and altruism" and the other that is "concerned with rank, status, discipline, law and order, territory and possessions, and warfare."[50] Like many Mind MGMT agents, Lyme is deprived of many childhood attachments, and so those ties to altruism may be weakened for him, but he manages to establish social ties to his wife and child nonetheless.

When Lyme begins to doubt those ties and feel alone, he falls back on the second system, based largely on the indoctrination of Mind MGMT, and a system that has tempered his skills. But without the first, the second breaks down too, and "law and order" cease to exist. In short, Lyme finds himself without any ordering psychological system and the events in Zanzibar reflect the unfettered activity of his own shadow side. Without the inhibiting, critical thinking of the conscious mind, the unconscious is set loose upon the world with devastating effect. And what the reader sees they may perceive to be barely human at all. Yet the rage and confusion that Lyme experiences is all too human. He turns outer reality into a mirror of his own inner turmoil at the hands of his personal shadow.

But there is life after Zanzibar, unfortunately, for Lyme. Unable to kill himself due to instilled psychological protocols to protect himself that he cannot circumvent, he becomes a symbol of extreme human despair. When the guilt he carries becomes too much to bear, he allows Meru to invade on his isolation, but unable to allow her to remember her past life, he continues to create destruction in her life through his selfish desire to speak to someone about his suffering. He's a weapon unable to de-weaponize himself, and so the pattern of destruction continues on a smaller scale in the life of a single individual, Meru. Though in some ways, the events at Zanzibar are long in the past, Meru is a survivor from the tragedy, and most certainly the representative of a Cold War legacy, a war child. It is unclear whether Lyme would have ever "done right" by Meru if he had not found himself pitted against a new foe, the rogue Mind MGMT agents attempting to regroup. He is either prepared for a big reveal in allowing Meru to finally write her book and tell the world about Mind MGMT, or he is aware that she is a convenient or even necessary asset to stop agents from working on the world for private gains.

Either way, Lyme allows Meru access to the library at Shangri-la, or at least buys time during which she reaches the "truth." He becomes the agent by which she finally reaches personal self-knowledge even though that knowledge will turn her against him. Lyme seems to have nothing to lose by doing this, since he is already suicidal and aware of his vast responsibility in projecting the collective shadow. It is possible, however, since the narrative never gives full revelation of the internal states of its characters, that Lyme realizes Meru's role in creating some form of potential harmony for humanity, a coming to terms with the past. Though he is not capable of achieving this restoration of balance himself, he may wish it for society, and certainly does not wish to contribute further to the projection of the shadow, hence his self-imposed exile in remote locations.

Lyme may represent a doomed, unredeemable past, but a self-aware past that is attempting to bring self-awareness to the current generation to prevent disasters on such a large scale from happening again. He does not wish for unsuspecting mentally cleansed agents to become the tools of projection and manipulation again, and so attempt to counter the actions of rogue agents. But in many ways, it is the least he can do considering his past crimes. It does assure the reader that Lyme is, in the most essential ways, still human. Of all the characters in Mind MGMT, Lyme has most demonstrably encountered the dangers of his own shadow writ large on society, and he refuses to take part in patterns of denial that would make his continued life more bearable. He prefers the "truth." In his reoccurring meetings with Meru, which he then wipes from her memory, he says, "Telling you everything ... does us both good," which could read as a coda for the entire *Mind MGMT* series.[51] Without Lyme, the truth would never be transmitted to Meru, who is a symbol of hope for the future.

Conclusion

Because the *Mind MGMT* series is still in development toward its thirty-six issue arc, questions remain regarding its engagement with and handling of the collective shadow as the legacy of the Cold War. It is however, significant to note that Matt Kindt originally constructed the first six issues of the series to stand alone as a narrative in case the series never reached completion.[52] The sixth issue ends with Meru locked in a cycle of memory loss at the hands of Lyme, but Lyme's reflection that Meru is, despite all, "changing" and perhaps recovering an ability to seize on the basics of Mind MGMT. This leaves open the possibility that she may yet write her book and recover self-knowledge. The sixth issue also confirms that Lyme is essentially unkillable in the face of the Immortal's best efforts because of his fail-safe self-protection program. At the end of the sixth issue, both Meru and Lyme are still at large, embedded with the tendencies and abilities that could carry them further into exposing Mind MGMT and resisting the attempts of the Immortal and the Eraser to terminate their involvement in future dealings.

Though Kindt allowed for the possibility that *Mind MGMT* might conclude after the sixth issue, it is also true that his original twelve-page proposal for a fifty-six-issue comic was accepted as a whole by Dark Horse before publication.[53] Kindt himself pared down the plans to a tighter thirty-six-issue arc. This suggests that the second volume as released was always intrinsic to his planning for the series and contains plenty of hints about what may be forthcoming for the series. If Duncan's governing structure is still influential, the fragmented, multi-perspective approach, we can expect for the themes of volume two to carry us onward however many surprises will still undoubtedly come our way. The projected total for the series only places the first two volumes at one third of the total narrative.

It is, nevertheless, possible to assess the psychological implications of the series so far and to place particular weight on the key character Meru's position at the conclusion of the twelfth issue, particularly in relation to other agents presented in the series. Having attained full knowledge of her identity, past, and the history of Mind MGMT, a "true past" that has not been rewritten, she has overcome tendencies toward denial, rationalization, and the renewed projection of the shadow. Why does she declare that Lyme is "making everything worse" and why does she easily evade the assertion from the Immortal that "we're on your side" in the twelfth issue?[54] Both agent teams, locked in mutual opposition, hope that she does not "pick a side" and further upset their balance.

Meru's choice to remove herself from the equation speaks volumes. It is possible that she sees the continued transference of shadow between both sides as a renewed danger for humanity and is struggling to come up with a more holistic solution to the problem of the Cold War legacy. Like Lyme after the disaster at Zanzibar, she has checked out of the conflict for the time being. But since she "contains" all the agents now, her decisions will be pivotal. As Stevens says, "Conflict is cooperation's shadow side" and by engaging in conflict, she is engaging the shadow.[55] She has impeded the pattern of memory erasure, halted the rewriting of history, and has looked in full at the devastation caused even by the instigation of good intentions.

Meru's disengagement from the shadow is the single most significant movement in the series so far, and suggests that if "normal" people were allowed full knowledge, as she has achieved, they too, would disengage from ongoing conflict and attempt the painful process of reconciling with the past. Writing her book and exposing Mind MGMT would be one way of accomplishing this within the framework of the *Mind MGMT* series, extending her hard-won knowledge to the unsuspecting world who are living in denial and consuming a version of manufactured history. *Mind MGMT* is a narrative about confronting the past, first and foremost, and we can expect self-knowledge to continue to be the key to unlocking this deeply psychological super-spy exploration of an archetypal wartime legacy.

Notes

1. Anthony Stevens, "Jungian Approach to Human Aggression With Special Emphasis on War," *Aggressive Behavior* 21 (1995): 10.

2. Carl Jung, *The Archetypes and the Collective Unconscious* (Princeton: Princeton University Press, 1990), 21.

3. Ibid.

4. Carl Jung, *The Undiscovered Self* (Princeton: Princeton University Press, 1990), 4.

5. Ibid.

6. Ibid., 45.

7. Ibid., 53.

8. Jürgen W. Kremer and Donald Rothberg, "Facing the Collective Shadow," *Revision* 22, no. 1.2 (1999): 2.

9. Carl Jung, *Memories, Dreams, Reflections* (New York: Pantheon, 1963), 330, quoted in Jürgen W. Kremer and Donald Rothberg, "Facing the Collective Shadow," *Revision* 22, no. 1.2 (1999):3.

10. Kremer and Rothberg, "Facing the Collective Shadow," 4.

11. Thich Njat Hanh, *Touching Peace* (Berkeley, CA: Parallax Press, 1992), 77–8, quoted in Jürgen W. Kremer and Donald Rothberg, "Facing the Collective Shadow," *Revision* 22, no.1:2 (1999): 4.

12. Stevens, "Jungian Approach," 5.

13. Matt Kindt, *Mind MGMT Volume One: The Manager* (Milwaukie, OR: Dark Horse Books, 2013), 73–74.

14. Ibid., 73.

15. Ibid., 17.

16. Stevens, "Jungian Approach," 10.

17. Matt Kindt, *Mind MGMT Volume Two: The Futurist* (Milwaukie, OR: Dark Horse Books, 2013), 61.

18. Ibid., 39.

19. Ibid., 77.

20. Ibid., 162.

21. Ibid., 161.

22. Ibid., 12.

23. Ibid., 11.

24. Ibid.
25. Ibid., 127.
26. Ibid., 115.
27. Stevens, "Jungian Approach," 9.
28. Kindt, *Mind MGMT Volume One*, 91.
29. Richard Williams, "The Psychosocial Consequences for Children of Mass Violence, Terrorism, and Disasters," *International Review of Psychiatry* 19.3 (2007): 264–5.
30. Kindt, *Mind MGMT Volume One*, 39.
31. Ibid., 131.
32. Stevens, "Jungian Approach," 7.
33. Ibid.
34. Ibid.
35. Ibid., 10.
36. Ibid., 8.
37. Kindt, *Mind MGMT Volume One*, 151.
38. Kindt, *Mind MGMT Volume Two*, 29.
39. Stevens, "Jungian Approach," 9.
40. Ibid.
41. Kindt, *Mind MGMT Volume One*, 60.
42. Kindt, *Mind MGMT Volume Two*, 51.
43. Ibid., 53.
44. Ibid., 166.
45. Kindt, *Mind MGMT Volume One*, 91–95.
46. Ibid., 95.
47. Alair MacLean, "The Cold War and Modern Memory: Veterans Reflects on Military Service," *Journal of Political and Military Sociology* 36.1 (2008): 105.
48. Kindt, *Mind MGMT Volume One*, 108.
49. Stevens, "Jungian Approach," 5.
50. Ibid., 7.
51. Kindt, *Mind MGMT Volume One*, 83.
52. Michael Carroll, "Interview: Matt Kindt, Writer and Artist for *Mind MGMT*," *Geeks of Doom*, June 28, 2012, http://www.geeksofdoom.com/2012/06/28/interview-matt-kindt-writer-and-artist-for-mind-mgmt.
53. Angela Jones, "WonderCon Interview: Matt Kindt, Creator of *Mind MGMT*," *Reading Realms*, April 9, 2013, http://www.readingrealms.com/2013/04/wondercon-interview-with-matt-kindt.html.
54. Kindt, *Mind MGMT Volume Two*, 166.
55. Stevens, "Jungian Approach," 6.

Bibliography

Carroll, Michael. "Interview: Matt Kindt, Writer and Artist for *Mind MGMT*." *Geeks of Doom*, June 28, 2012. http://www.geeksofdoom.com/2012/06/28/interview-matt-kindt-writer-and-artist-for-mind-mgmt.

Jones, Angela. "WonderCon Interview: Matt Kindt, Creator of *Mind MGMT*." *Reading Realms*, April 9, 2013. http://www.readingrealms.com/2013/04/wondercon-interview-with-matt-kindt.html.

Jung, Carl. *The Archetypes and the Collective Unconscious.* Princeton: Princeton University Press, 1990.

_____. *Memories, Dreams, Reflections.* New York: Pantheon, 1963. Quoted in Jürgen W. Kremer and Donald Rothberg, "Facing the Collective Shadow," *Revision* 22, no. 1.2 (1999): 3.

_____. *The Undiscovered Self.* Princeton: Princeton University Press, 1990.
Kindt, Matt. *Mind MGMT Volume One: The Manager.* Milwaukie, OR: Dark Horse Books, 2013.
_____. *Mind MGMT Volume Two: The Futurist.* Milwaukie, OR: Dark Horse Books, 2013.
Kremer, Jürgen W., and Donald Rothberg. "Facing the Collective Shadow." *Revision* 22 no. 1.2 (1999): 1–4.
MacLean, Alair. "The Cold War and Modern Memory: Veterans Reflect on Military Service." *Journal of Political and Military Sociology* 36.1 (2008): 103–130.
Nhat Hanh, Thich. *Touching Peace* (Berkeley, CA: Parallax Press, 1992), 77–8. Quoted in Jürgen W. Kremer and Donald Rothberg, "Facing the Collective Shadow," *Revision* 22, no. 1.2 (1999): 4.
Stevens, Anthony. "Jungian Approach to Human Aggression With Special Emphasis on War." *Aggressive Behavior* 21 (1995): 3–11.
Williams, Richard. "The Psychosocial Consequences for Children of Mass Violence, Terrorism, and Disasters." *International Review of Psychiatry* 19.3 (2007): 263–277.

Flirting with Bond

Or How I Created My
Sexy Female Secret Agent

K.A. Laity

The icon that is James Bond casts an enormous shadow over the genre of the secret agent thriller. Most writers have chosen to veer off into material and locations very different from those frequented by Fleming's hero, either into the ridiculousness of *In Like Flint* (1967, Gordon Douglas) or the grim humorlessness of the *Mission Impossible* franchise. Smiley's people in John le Carré's novels eschew the glamor while the Bourne movies have a resourceful hero who has no sense of style or identity. Films that try to capture the Bond feel more directly achieve it only through parody, like the Matt Helm or Austin Powers films. Sexual politics aside, when it comes to women, female action heroes like those played by Angelina Jolie in *Salt* (2010, Phillip Noyce) and *Mr. & Mrs. Smith* (2005, Doug Liman) are far too earnest to ever secure the same level of acclaim as 007.

Ars est celare artem, after all. It's Bond's aplomb that makes him stand out from the potentially unsavory nature of the work he does. John Le Carré describes the life of spies as "people who play cowboys and Indians to brighten their rotten lives."[1] As that anachronistic and culturally suspect division betrays, Bond benefited from a time that embraced a clear division of "good guys" and "bad guys" without a doubt as to who was whom.

To resurrect the fun of Bond in our less morally certain times, I decided to create a female secret agent. A woman in the Bond role offered a chance to examine the shifts in gender relations over the intervening years and whether the changes had been truly significant. The opportunity for doing so presented itself at the 2008 Northeast Writers Convention, better known as Necon or, more usually, Camp Necon. Longtime attendee and agent Lori Perkins announced that she was hopping on board the new ebook train to give it a whirl with a brand new company, Ravenous Romance. When the room full of horror writers rolled their eyes at this idea, Lori encouraged us to rethink the idea of romance for something edgier. Specifically, she was not ruling out horror (and in fact she went on to publish the zombie-themed romance anthology *Hungry for Your Love*, then started a separate horror line, Ravenous Shadows, a couple of years later—now sadly defunct after Perkins left the company for another start-up) and was eager to see other harder edged genres.

After selling a few short stories to Ravenous, I was encouraged to try writing a novel for them. My previous work had mostly been in the area of fairly literary fantastic. I wanted something light and fun, sexy but also gripping. I went back to an older idea: my very first novel in high school was about spies. The idea hadn't really left my mind since, and as I was writing pseudonymously, it seemed the perfect way to embody the slippery identity of a secret agent. There's just something romantic about the notion of the international *bon vivant* that I had absorbed from the Bond films—or at least the idea of the Bond films. I don't recall getting caught up in the franchise until Pierce Brosnan was tapped to play Fleming's hero. The '70s Bond films with Roger Moore mostly seemed too over the top and silly to my teenage self, though as a fan of *Remington Steele* (1982–1987), I could see the appeal of Brosnan.

It's funny how present the idea of Bond could be even without much in the way of direct experience. When I teach the idea of King Arthur in my medieval literature courses (my least favorite figure from the time period), I always spend a little time getting the students to demonstrate what they already "know" about Arthur, though most of them say they have never read any of the stories. What they know comes from the heady soup of popular culture: second hand references to the stories in films, cartoons and even products (don't forget King Arthur brand flour). Within minutes we have managed to come up with a good deal of information we "know" about King Arthur without reference to any primary materials. Bond has permeated our culture in much the same way: from the original novels, the films, the endless spoofs, and the extensions of the franchise from Kingsley Amis' revival novel to Charlie Higson's Young Bond series. People who've never read anything by Fleming or seen a Bond film, know that pretending to stroke a cat while speaking with an accent to "Mr. Bond" is the proper way to portray a villain. Even Fleming's biographer Andrew Lycett wrote, in his forward to the collection of scholarly essays examining *Ian Fleming & James Bond: The Cultural Politics of 007*, that "Bond is now a film-led phenomenon."[2]

When I began to sketch out the idea for my sexy secret agent, I modeled her name from one of the few women who could rival Bond's popularity in the field, Modesty Blaise. The name "Chastity Flame" was born first as a place-filler, but then I realized it was a case of "best thought, first thought." Not too surprisingly, Peter O'Donnell notes that his heroine came from a desire to join the genres of adventure and romance: "I had been intrigued by the idea bringing these two genres together by creating a woman who, though fully feminine, would be as good in combat and action as any male, if not better."[3] While O'Donnell's comic strip character (and to some extent the camp film version from 1966) inspired the name and the sense of fun inherent in this deadly weapon of a woman, Bond served as a more direct model. The adventures feature a good deal of humor, mostly offhand references to classic British comedy sketches, but never with the aim of spoofing the genre. Rather it was part of the self-assurance of the character to always see humor in a situation, even if death seemed the most likely outcome. Surely anyone in that line of work would develop a mordant sense of the surreal situations it put her into time and time again. I never wanted to satirize the genre per se, although I did make the effort to develop a signature drink for Chastity in keeping with Fleming's own decision.

To make the series as transgressive as the Bond books had been in their time, the novels feature a frankly sexual secret agent who happened to be female. Having a woman enjoy sex freely and vigorously seems to be the only barrier still offering some sense of the scandalous for modern readers, as the handwringing over the *Fifty Shades* books and the subsequent film version have demonstrated well. While recent research suggests the differences between genders have been vastly inflated[4] the frank sexuality of this secret agent offers an iconoclast image for the 21st century that nonetheless owes a great debt to Fleming's creation.

While the films stars that played the hero may be better known, Ian Fleming describes his agent precisely in *From Russia with Love*:

> Name: Bond, James. Height: 183cm, weight: 76 kilograms; slim build; eyes: blue; hair: black; scar down right cheek and on left shoulder; signs of plastic surgery on back of right hand; all-round athlete; expert pistol shot, boxer, knife-thrower; does not use disguises. Languages: French and German. Smokes heavily (NB: special cigarettes with three gold bands); vices: drink, but not to excess, and women. Not thought to accept bribes.[5]

The words of the antagonists are spare, pitched toward their own interests: identify him, know his dangers and skills, be aware he is not prone to excess or bribes. The rounded nature of his pursuits fits the mid–20th century time period in which he was born: boxing, a gentlemanly sport; knife-throwing, an almost carnivalesque one that also has the valuable factor of silence; and of course, pistol shooting, once again a rather gentlemanly type of shooting unlike a sharpshooter or machine gun thug. There's a touch of the dandy too, in his refusal to use disguises, his facility with the standard Continental languages, and of course in his special cigarettes with the three gold bands.

In contrast, the description of Bond from the photos included in the dossier in *From Russia with Love* have a great deal more romanticism which probably should be attributed to the author and not the thoughts of General G. as he reads it:

> It was a dark, clean-cut face, with a three-inch scar showing whitely down the sun-burned skin of the right cheek. The eyes were wide and level under straight rather long black brows. The hair was black, parted on the left, and carelessly brushed so that a thick black comma fell down over the right eyebrow. The longish straight nose ran down to a short upper lip below which was a wide and finely drawn but cruel mouth. The line of the jaw was straight and firm.[6]

The repetition of the word "straight" three times emphasizes the character of the agent "not thought to accept bribes" in any way, as if indeed it were a fundamental part of his physical makeup. The jet-black hair and "rather long" brows wouldn't be nearly as memorable if the hair did not fall across the brow in "a thick black comma"; it's a word that almost suggests a kind of whimsy at odds with the largely dour image we get from the other details. While Fleming based the appearance on Hoagy Carmichael (a debonair figure in the past who fits poorly with the modern metrosexual model), the ideal that comma of black hair fixes in the mind is completely timeless.

Also key are the details of the mouth. The "short upper lip" combined with the wider mouth below suggests an almost feminine appearance which Fleming is quickly at pains to dissuade. Though Bond's mouth is "wide and finely drawn" his creator adds that it is also "cruel" as must be a man in his line of work, though it also comes to define his sexual relationships as well, most of which have every bit of the brevity and cruelty of his hits. As General G. concludes after reading out this detailed dossier, "This man is a dangerous professional terrorist and spy," as far as the Soviets are concerned and not just condemned to die, but as the General adds in a sort of postscript to the order, "To be killed WITH IGNOMINY."[7] His very existence is something that offends their sensibilities.

A part of this is the ironic Englishness of the spy. As Vozdvishensky opines while they examine the information about Bond, "The English are not interested in heroes unless they are footballers or cricketers or jockeys," suggesting the British would not admire him because the British "do not like to think about war." As the secret war hero Fleming probably found it safer to put the words in Russian mouths, "after a war the names of their war heroes are forgotten as quickly as possible." However, one comrade suggests that by his peers he is not only known, but admired as "a lone wolf, but a good looking one."[8]

His attractiveness is not just the icing on the cake; it's an essential part of his acceptability as a hero, at least as far as Fleming was concerned. As Lycett puts it in the foreword to his biography of the writer, the work had been hampered by Fleming's deliberate and unconscious elusiveness: "he ... was a chameleon-like showman who presented the side of his character he thought people wanted to see,"[9] which left different people with considerably different impressions of the man himself. Not too surprisingly, the picture that gradually emerged from the greater access to correspondence and dueling sources not available to earlier biographers, was of

> a charming chancer who, dogged by the memory of an upright father killed in the Western Front in May 1917 and pushed by an ambitious and headstrong mother, had, by the time he was thirty, tried his hand at various careers—army officer, diplomat, journalist, banker and stockbroker—without ever finding his *métier*. War, however, proved his making, satisfying a powerful need to conform while providing unexpected outlets for his imaginative genius.[10]

Fleming, like his creation, needed to work as a "lone wolf" but with the approval, even admiration of his work by others. This shows in his seemingly cavalier attitude toward his own creation and its fame. Limelight, as Holly Golightly observed, could easily wreck one's complexion and Fleming appeared to delight in downplaying his reputation even though he had significant ambitions, as Lycett argues.[11] But serious heroes being "forgotten" Fleming is happy to put on a larkish attitude as if his deadly duties were no more serious than a football or cricket match, as he claimed in a 1963 interview Lycett quotes:

> James Bond is the author's pillow fantasy.... And fantasy isn't real life by definition. It's very much the Walter Mitty syndrome—the feverish dreams of the author of what he might have been—bang, bang, bang, kiss, kiss, that sort of stuff. It's what you would expect of an adolescent mind—which is what I happen to possess.[12]

Not being English and not needing to pretend to have only an "adolescent" mind, I have nevertheless taken a similarly larkish attitude toward my creation, although I, too, have been nursing some slightly more serious ambitions as well. But they had to be tied to a secret agent who embodied a sense of cultural cachet and tough attractiveness that fit the same impressive mold as James Bond. I made Chastity Flame as distinctive in her appearance as Fleming made his man, highlighting a few important characteristics that would be memorable without being too overwhelming. Her hair is golden brown with honeyed highlights and her eyes are amber. While Bond's appearance suggested a slightly menacing masculinity, I wanted to Chastity's appearance to suggest a modern view of femininity that nonetheless stood out from the bland Hollywood blondes used as window dressing in most mainstream films. As a horror movie fan, I've become bored with endless films stuffed with similarly bland "pretty" people whose deaths mean nothing because it's impossible to tell the actors apart. So Chastity needed brown hair not blonde, with natural highlights that accentuate the shade, which we only hear about through the appreciative words of others, and an unusual eye color that would not be forgotten.

Another aspect that reflected modern tastes was her mixed race background. Her father comes from Spain and her mother from the English countryside. I liked this mixture because it gave her a foot in two very different worlds and made her cosmopolitan upbringing in different nations also more suitable—and linked her to the similarly mixed race heritage of her first love interest, Damien Michelet, whose father is English while his mother is from the West Indies. Although we tend to think of Bond as every bit the quintessential English hero as his forebears like Bulldog Drummond, it's important to remember that his background, too, is more complicated, as the Ian Fleming site encapsulates it:

> Ian Fleming's James Bond was born in Zurich in the early 1920s to Andrew Bond of Glencoe and Monique Delacroix, from the Canton de Vaud in Switzerland. The family divided their time between a flat in Chelsea and a large house just outside Basel, which enabled James' fluency in French and German, as well as English. Tragically, both James' mother and father died in a climbing accident whilst on holiday in France when he was only eleven.[13]

I had Chastity's family based in Geneva when they were in Switzerland, more suitable to the academic mien her father maintains, although her parents we discover were also agents for the same secret organization. Unlike Bond's parents who die in a tragic accident, Chastity's parents are killed in a suspicious explosion that's believed to be tied to their work, but may indeed have been accomplished by a rival agent within the organization. She has been raised by the head of the organization, a woman known as "Monitor," in a much more directly supervised role than Bond received. This has not resulted in any sheltering. Like the "all-around athlete" Bond, Chastity has received a variety of training in weapons and hand-to-hand combat. She's accustomed to making the most of whatever she finds at hand or of relieving others of their weapons.

As a bit of whimsy, I found it amusing that the official Ian Fleming website sums up his family history by noting that "on the Fleming side, Ian Lancaster Fleming's family came from Scotland. His ancestors were crofters in Perthshire who moved to Dundee to look for work."[14] As if deliberately swimming against the Fleming stream I have a home in Dundee with my partner, although I also have a home I share with my brother in New York, managing the international spy lifestyle without any of the cloak and dagger aspects of it (although my publisher likes to refer to me jokingly as "Lady Fleming"). It is interesting that the latest film in the franchise made use of Scotland as the land of Bond's "ancestral home"[15]—a somewhat amusing grandiosity in this year before the Scottish vote on independence and in light of Fleming's own family background of crofters looking for work. His mother, Evelyn Beatrice St. Croix Rose, according to Lycett, would later "insist that her own family, 'the wild Roses,' were true Highlanders, unlike the parvenu Lowland Flemings, and would dress Ian and his brothers in Rose tartan kilts."[16] The film's use of the Highlands seems to fit the romantic notion of Scotland fueled more by American nostalgia by way of travel brochures rather than any reality the Flemings might have known.

Lycett also explains that for Fleming, "part of the fun was to pepper his prose with references to his friends, family and relations" and offering examples of how friends' names were appropriated and the amusing Jamaican incident from which Vesper Lynd's name and drink sprang.[17] Of course "Bond's himself, both in character and name" because "exotic things would happen to and around him but he would be a neutral figure,"[18] incongruously the same as the author of the *Field Guide to Birds of the West Indies*. When writing a series, the use of nearby inspirations for names proves immensely helpful on a practical level.

I admit to doing the same myself. I named Damien's sister after my friend and sometime publisher Adele, and offered cameos to some of my fellow writers in the second Chastity novel, *Lush Situation,* when my heroine goes to an erotic romance reading sponsored by the woman suspected of running a human trafficking ring. Her primary aim is reconnaissance, but she finds herself stirred by the writings and curious about the writers. Because she spends the second book trying to forget the man she fell for in the first, there's a lot of yearning. The writers offer a space for the heroine to explore that unusual feeling, but they also provide the practical aspect of giving her first hand information about the villain. Although Chastity is isolated by the nature of her work, it helps to give the impression of the real world around her.

Fleming might have appreciated this appropriation of popular culture as one of the aims of his own writing was to accurately represent the real world that Bond lives in. As Kerstin Jütting writes, "Those details, such as cars, weapons or locations, were more important to Fleming than the hero or the plot ... [saying] he would never write about things he had not seen himself."[19] In the films this has led to an almost absurd level of product placement that led the media to dub *Die Another Day* (2002, Lee Tamahori) "Buy Another Day"[20] but Fleming clearly wanted to show the world in which he lived—and indeed reveled—as well as all the finer things he enjoyed, part of what Lindner has described as, "an affluent life style based on brand-name consumerism, exotic travel and sexual conquest."[21]

While short of advertising dollars, I have not felt the need to fill the pages with product placement, but I do draw on popular culture to color the world in which Chastity lives. I also send her further and further abroad to make use of "exotic" locations and hope to send her even further afield in the future. Most of my use of popular culture is more subterranean and easy to miss. Because Chastity often uses pseudonyms while working I have to come up (and make sure to record) her aliases for the increasingly lengthy lists). In the first novel, I had her reading Graham Greene and using his character names to introduce herself to targets, only one of whom recognized them. In the second book, *Lush Situation*, I had fun playing with names of (mostly Belgian) beers, including having her call herself Amber Lambiek. More circumlocutory, her pseudonyms in *A Cut-Throat Business* come from character names in classic noir novels written by Dorothy B. Hughes' *In a Lonely Place*, Patricia Highsmith's Ripley novels and Elisabeth Sanxay Holding's *Net of Cobwebs*.

Perhaps the most indulgent popular culture appropriation was modeling my villain, the Norwegian mastermind Sven Wesenlund, on the late comedy genius Peter Cook. Cook had his own suave and debonair air as a young man that was perfectly *au courant* with Fleming's hero and even played a similar role in the cold war spy film *A Dandy in Aspic* (1968, Anthony Mann). His name came from a running gag that Cook carried out on BBC radio host Clive Bull's late night program, phoning in as "Sven," a lonely Norwegian fisherman. The surname came from beloved Norwegian comedian Rolv Wesenlund, who died in August 2013. For my fellow Peter Cook fanatics, there are loads of off-hand references to well-known Cook sketches, including the opening scene of the first novel in front of Paul Cézanne's painting *Les grandes baigneuses* in the National Gallery. British comedy fans will recognize the location from the Pete & Dud (Dudley Moore, Cook's frequent comedy partner in the 60s and 70s) Art Gallery sketch from *Not Only ... But Also*. I did my best to make sure that the winks were apparent only to those who were looking for them and did not interrupt the narrative. I have had people tell me that only on re-reading the book with that aim could they notice the references.

In keeping with Fleming's development of the signature Bond drink, the Vesper Lynd Martini in *Casino Royale*, I did create a Chastity Flame signature drink, although that was done nondiegetically for a cookbook put together by my publisher. I looked to Kingsley Amis' *Everyday Drinking* for inspiration where I was struck by his comment, "Never despise a drink because it is easy to make,"[22] so I tried to both mirror the style of Fleming's drink and keep the ingredients simple: two measures of gin, one of vodka and a dash of bitters with a lime garnish as I much prefer lime to lemon. Recommending brisk shaking to avoid dilution, I note that "it should be the color of Chastity's amber eyes and be rather lethal, but then again, so is its inspiration."[23] A fitting tribute to Bond and his creator, I hope.

The book series began life in the erotic romance genre, so the most transgressive aspect is the bold sexuality. We tend to think of Bond embodying retrograde notions of sexuality, but as Jeremy Black points out, Bond actually operates as "a forward thinking individual and modernizer, part of Fleming's portrayal that is sometimes lost, but that helped make Bond an attractive figure in the early 1960s. Style was not achieved at the expense of thought."[24] Black specifically refers to Bond's attitude toward homosexuality (far less retrograde than that displayed in the films) but it's interesting that one of the negative notes in a review for the original *Chastity Flame* was for her sexual encounter with another woman in Belgium. On the whole the frank sexuality self-selects an audience that welcomes it (one Amazon reviewer referred to the book as "Fifty Shades of Bond"), but the series has been moving away from its roots toward more direct thriller territory, as there's little overlap in audiences between erotic readers and thriller fans.

In this regard audiences don't seem to have changed a great deal. James Chapman sums up the prevailing attitudes toward Fleming's own erotic fantasies, an effort that was led by critic Bernard Bergonzi who detected

> "a strongly marked streak of voyeurism and sado-masochism in his books" and deplored the "complete lack of any ethical frame of reference." Bergonzi described the "erotic fantasies" of the books as "decidedly sinister," comparing Fleming to a "dirty-minded schoolboy."[25]

While the sex scenes once considered racy are far less transgressive than the ones in my own series, the fact remains that a lot of readers have a low tolerance for anything that does not match their own comfort levels and to reach a broad audience it is best not to stray too far beyond the bounds of the largest audience's agreed upon limits.

This doesn't only refer to sexual matters: Chapman also points to the fact that the "*Manchester Guardian* deplored 'the cult of luxury for its own sake.'"[26] For many people ostentatious consumerism can be a turn off, but as reality competition shows push instant fame and fortune as an achievable road to success in an increasingly divided economy, there seems to be a wide tolerance for aspirational narratives of wealth that will in all likelihood never be realized.

I put Chastity's home in Tavistock Square in Bloomsbury, an area I have often stayed while in London, especially when leading student tours. It's a challenge to find a region that has the same resonance as Bond's Chelsea. Any bohemian air Chelsea may have retained in Fleming's time has since evaporated with its escalating price tags; Bloomsbury has retained some of its literary charm because of its proximity to the University College London. As the real estate prices in the city continue to rise precipitously and even an august bureau like the *Financial Times* claims that "there's no point trying to live in London" because "the average London house price will rise 44 per cent by 2018,"[27] I have given up on the long-held dream of ever living there and content myself with visiting from time to time. But through the Chastity Flame books I can live the extravagant, globe-trotting life vicariously and I suspect my readers, like Mr. Fleming's, will continue to enjoy that world from quiet armchairs and the glowing screens of tablets and Kindles.

Notes

1. John le Carré, *The Spy Who Came in from the Cold* (London: Pan Books, 1964), 211.

2. Andrew Lycett, "Foreword," in *Ian Fleming & James Bond: The Cultural Politics of 007*, ed. Edward P. Comentale, Stephen Watt, and Skip Willman (Bloomington: Indiana University Press, 2005), viii.

3. Peter O'Donnell, "Girl Walking: The Real Modesty Blaise," *Crime Time*, n.d., http://www.crimetime.co.uk/features/modestyblaise.php.

4. Gery Karantzas, Celia Goncalves, Judith Feeney, and Marita McCabe, "Investigating Gender Differences in Romantic Relationships," *Family Relationships Quarterly* 18 (2011): 1–7.

5. Ian Fleming, *From Russia with Love* (1957; repr., London: Penguin, 2006), 67.

6. Ibid., 66.

7. Ibid., 70.

8. Ibid., 63–4.

9. Andrew Lycett, *Ian Fleming* (London: Phoenix, 1995), ix.

10. Ibid.

11. Ibid., 216–7.

12. Ibid., 220.

13. "Ian Fleming: The Official Website of Ian Fleming, Creator of James Bond and Chitty Chitty Bang Bang," *Ian Fleming*, n.d., http://www.ianfleming.com.

14. Ibid.

15. "James Bond 007," *James Bond Wiki*, n.d., http://jamesbond.wikia.com/wiki/James_Bond.

16. Lycett, *Ian Fleming*, 5.

17. Ibid., 222.

18. Ibid., 223.

19. Kerstin Jütting, *"Grow up, 007!" James Bond Over the Decades: Formula vs. Innovation* (München: GRIN Verlag, 2007), 5.

20. Samantha Felix and Laura Stampler, "The Evolution of James Bond Movie Product Placement," *Business Insider*, October 21, 2012, http://www.businessinsider.com/heres-how-james-bonds-relationship-with-product-placement-has-changed-2012–10.

21. Christoph Lindner, *The James Bond Phenomenon: A Critical Reader* (Manchester: Manchester University Press, 2003), 1.

22. Kingsley Amis, *Everyday Drinking* (London: Bloomsbury, 2009), 31.

23. C. Margery Kempe, "Drink the Chastity Flame," *C. Margery Kempe, Blog*, August 26, 2011, http://cmkempe.wordpress.com/2011/08/26/drink-the-chas/ (accessed August 26, 2011).

24. Jeremy Black, *The Politics of James Bond: From Fleming's Novels to the Big Screen* (Lincoln: University of Nebraska Press, 2005), 106.

25. James Chapman, *Licence to Thrill: A Cultural History of the James Bond Films* (New York: I.B. Tauris, 2009), 25.

26. Ibid.

27. Christian Oliver, "There's no point in living in London," *Financial Times*, October 4,

2013, http://www.ft.com/cms/s/0/caa96d96–2b9f–11e3–a1b7–00144feab7de.html#axzz2j D0Mq6Nq.

Bibliography

Amis, Kingsley. *Everyday Drinking: The Distilled Kingsley Amis.* London: Bloomsbury, 2009.
Black, Jeremy. *The Politics of James Bond: From Fleming's Novels to the Big Screen.* Lincoln: University of Nebraska Press, 2005.
Chapman, James. *Licence to Thrill: A Cultural History of the James Bond Films.* New York: I.B. Tauris, 2009.
Cork, John, and Bruce Scivally. *James Bond: The Legacy.* London: Boxtree, 2002.
Felix, Samantha and Laura Stampler. "The Evolution of James Bond Movie Product Placement." *Business Insider,* October 21, 2012. http://www.businessinsider.com/heres-how-james-bonds-relationship-with-product-placement-has-changed-2012–10.
Fleming, Ian. *From Russia with Love.* 1957. Reprint, London: Penguin, 2006.
"Ian Fleming: The Official Website of Ian Fleming, Creator of James Bond and Chitty Chitty Bang Bang." *Ian Fleming,* n.d. http://www.ianfleming.com.
Jütting, Kerstin. *"Grow up, 007!" James Bond Over the Decades: Formula vs. Innovation.* Müchen: GRIN Verlag, 2007.
Karantzas, Gery, Celia Goncalves, Judith Feeney and Marita McCabe. "Investigating Gender Differences in Romantic Relationships." *Family Relationships Quarterly* 18 (2011): 1–7.
Kempe, C. Margery. "Drink the Chastity Flame." *C. Margery Kempe Blog.* August 26, 2011. http://cmkempe.wordpres.com/2011/08/26/drink-the-chas.
Laity, K. A. *Chastity Flame.* Kildare, Ireland: Tirgearr, 2012.
_____. *A Cut-Throat Business: A Chastity Flame Adventure.* Kildare, Ireland: Tirgearr, 2013.
_____. *Lush Situation: A Chastity Flame Adventure.* Kildare, Ireland: Tirgearr, 2013.
Le Carré, John. *The Spy Who Came in from the Cold.* London: Pan Books, 1964.
Lindner, Christoph. *The James Bond Phenomenon: A Critical Reader.* Manchester: Manchester University Press, 2003.
Lisanti, Tom, and Louis Paul. *Film Fatales: Women in Espionage Films and Television, 1963–1973.* Jefferson, NC: McFarland, 2002.
Lycett, Andrew. "Foreword." In *Ian Fleming and James Bond: The Cultural Politics of 007,* edited by Edward P. Comentale, Stephen Watt, and Skip Willman, vii-x. Bloomington: Indiana University Press, 2005.
_____. *Ian Fleming.* London: Phoenix, 1995.
O'Donnell, Peter. "Girl Walking: The Real Modesty Blaise." *Crime Time* (n.d.), http://www.crimetime.co.uk/features/modestyblaise.php.
Oliver, Christian. "There's no point in living in London." *Financial Times,* October 4, 2013. http://www.ft.com/cms/s/0/caa96d96–2b9f–11e3–a1b7–00144feab7de.html#axzz2jD0M q6Nq.
Packer, Jeremy. *Secret Agents: Popular Icons Beyond James Bond.* New York: Peter Lang, 2009.
Tasker, Yvonne. *Spectacular Bodies: Gender, Genre and the Action Cinema.* New York: Routledge, 1993.
White, Rosie. *Violent Femmes: Women as Spies in Popular Culture.* New York: Routledge, 2007.
Woolf, M. "Ian Fleming's Enigmas and Variations." In *Spy Thrillers: From Buchan to le Carré,* edited by Clive Bloom, 86–99. New York: St. Martin's Press, 1990.

Part Four

Lifestyle

Modelling Bond
The Cultural Perception of James Bond on the Eve of the Eon Production Films

Edward Biddulph

A man dangles from a vertiginous cliff face, one hand gripping the meager hold of a jutting rock, the other reaching down to grab the arms of a blonde beauty pressed against the wall of a narrow ledge. The man is suitably attired in hard-wearing, but comfortable clothes: a Courtelle cotton shirt by Luvisca, and a pair of slacks in Abrelle, a Courtelle-blend fabric by Moore Johnston. Meet James Bond, licensed to model for Courtelle for Men, clothing designed, as the copywriter put it, for "a man's world."[1]

This advertisement was one of six that appeared in national newspapers in the U.K. during 1961. The advertisements followed a standard format, each showing a drawing of Bond in a dangerous, exotic or romantic situation and accompanied by text that linked what was regarded as a typically Bondian environment with the characteristics of the products that were being advertised. The writer or writers are unknown—presumably anonymous copywriters in Courtauld's marketing department—but the campaign evidently had Ian Fleming's approval. Each advertisement carried the statement that "James Bond is featured here with acknowledgements to Ian Fleming," and plugged the latest adventure, *Thunderball*. The advertisements are important documents for the study of the Bond phenomenon. They prefigure the significant role that the brand and iconography of James Bond has played in advertising over the past 50 years; James Bond has been used to sell perfumes, alcoholic drinks, toys, even tea bags, while actors who have played Bond have been employed as "brand ambassadors" for high-value goods, such as luxury cars and watches. In addition, the Courtelle campaign reveals that even before the Eon Productions film series commenced in 1962 with *Dr. No* (1962, Terence Young), James Bond had currency beyond the pages of Ian Fleming's novels as a cultural entity. No longer just a character in a series of books, Bond was by 1961 an aspirational figure who added value to products with which he was associated. This offers a glimpse of how James

Bond was perceived in cultural space before the film series drastically altered the popular view of him.

This essay will examine the Courtelle advertisements to identify traits taken from Fleming's novels and those introduced by copywriters, and assess the extent of other influences and the degree of divergence from Fleming's prototype. The essay will compare the 'Courtelle' Bond with contemporary depictions similarly uninformed by the Bond films, and contrast them with later representations to assess the impact of the film series on the expression of Bondian iconography. Finally, the essay will discuss the proposition that different Bonds have emerged as a result of ever-changing cultural environments.

Meet James Bond

DIPLOMATIC PASSPORT
0094567—BOND J.

The first of six advertisements was placed in the *Daily Express* in March 1961. With artwork by Richard Johnson, James Bond is shown facing the window of a city apartment carrying an unconscious woman (has she fainted or been knocked out?). Headlined "Diplomatic Passport 0094567-Bond J.," the copy by an unidentified copywriter reads:

> Where would you find James Bond? He's the man being hustled through U.S. Customs five minutes after the plane has touched down at Idlewild. He's the man driving the big grey Bentley (1933 4½ litre, Amherst-Villiers super-charger) that whispers past you on M.1. He's a lean dark man in the rough clothes of a sailor in a waterfront dive in Vladivostok. A man in white tie and tails at the Embassy reception. A man talking to a lovely girl in the smart cocktail bar overlooking Copacabana beach. James Bond, secret agent, taking the best of food, the finest wine, the loveliest women, the tops in clothes.[2]

The advertisement concludes with a description of what Bond is wearing: "a rugged 'Snowdon' sweater in 100% Courtelle by Byford," clothing that fits in "with James Bond's life."[3] The copywriter had turned to Ian Fleming's novels for inspiration. Bond's expeditious arrival at Idlewild (JFK International Airport) is lifted from *Live and Let Die*, in which Bond, carrying a passport with the same number as that used in the advertisement, has the "red carpet" treatment from the Department of Justice and thus bypasses the grind of Idlewild's Immigration and Customs.[4] The Bentley matches the description of the vehicle Bond drives in *Casino Royale*,[5] but there is no mention of the M1 motorway, which connects London and Leeds, in any of the novels. Indeed, Bond would barely have had the opportunity to use the road, as the first stretch of the motorway opened in November 1959.[6] The reference seems a curious one, but it is telling nonetheless. Headlines in the national newspapers published in late 1959, such as "I am the speed queen of the M1,"[7] "M1 death crash,"[8] and "Marples gets a scare on the M1,"[9] convey the thrill and danger of the early days of motorway travel. These are attributes that could be applied to Bond just as well, and the connection not only identifies the M1 as an ideal playground for Bond, but also reinforces the forward-looking, modern qualities perceived in them both. As for the remainder of the advertisement, the embassy reception, the Vladivostok waterfront, and the cocktail bar cannot be identified specifically in the novels published before 1961, but the copywriter may have drawn more generally on Bond's consumption of Martinis and champagne, passing references to diplomatic staff, and Fleming's descriptions of waterfront locations in Jamaica and elsewhere. The reference to Vladivostok, however, perhaps owes more to Somerset Maugham's *Ashenden* (1928). In it, the eponymous secret agent travels from New York to St. Petersburg via Vladivostok.[10]

The "Snowdon" sweater that Bond wears seems atypical of Bond's usual wardrobe, but there was a perceived connection in the marketed qualities of the fabric. Courtelle, a brand currently owned by Rowlinson Knitwear Ltd., is an acrylic fabric that was introduced in 1959 by Courtaulds Ltd., a U.K.-based textiles and chemicals company. Clothes made in the fabric were, as the advertisement claims, "easy to wear, easy to launder, distinguished to look at."[11] The emphasis was on comfort, durability, convenience, and style, traits that Courtelle's marketing team clearly felt was a good match for the fast-paced, physically and romantically active, and occasionally rough lifestyle of James Bond.

INFORM ALL AGENTS—BOND MUST DIE!

There was as much emphasis on these traits in the second advertisement, which was placed in the *Daily Express* in April 1961. The panel depicted Bond in the corridor of a train speeding through Europe. Artist Richard Johnson shows Bond about to enter a first-class carriage and rescue a woman—in fact Bond's supine companion from the previous advertisement—who is bound and gagged. The accompanying text reads:

> A quiet talk over the silver-gleaming dinner table in a Pall Mall club. This is Bond's life. Sudden death spilling from an alley in a Bucharest slum. This is Bond's life, too. James Bond (007), Special Agent. Unarmed combat workouts with a Commando sergeant in a basement in Whitehall; target practice with a Beretta .25 (you practise very carefully when your life one day might depend on your aim). See that arrogant

beauty at the tables, watching the croupier, risking a fortune? She hates you, Bond. Make her love you, that's an order.[12]

While the previous advertisement took aspects from *Casino Royale* and *Live and Let Die*, the second looked largely to *From Russia with Love*. The scene on the train immediately recalls Bond's journey on the Orient Express from Istanbul to Venice,[13] and the headline encapsulates the same notion of Bond as a top agent and figurehead for British intelligence, around which the Russian plot to compromise Bond revolves.[14] The arrogant beauty is a loose match for the novel's Bond girl, Tatiana Romanova; in the novel, Bond is ordered by his chief, M, to seduce Tatiana and fulfill her expectations.[15] The Pall Mall club could be Blades, at which Bond dines at M's invitation in *Moonraker*,[16] and the novel also contains a description of Bond practicing at a firing range.[17] The reference to unarmed combat workouts is not taken specifically from Fleming, though it may allude to Bond's interest in unarmed combat, as expressed in *Goldfinger* (he is compiling a manual of unarmed combat, called *Stay Alive!*).[18] The reference to murder in a Bucharest slum, however, seems to owe less to Fleming than scenes from classic film noir, such as the death of Harry Lime in a Viennese sewer in *The Third Man* (1949, Carol Reed).

As for Bond's clothing, the focus for this advertisement is on his trousers, which, made in Courtelle's Abrelle fabric, are "casual, but keep their crease; washable and need only the minimum of ironing."[19] As with its earlier advertisement, Courtelle's marketing team identified Bond as a character whose physical job demands casual clothes for comfort and style, made in a hard-wearing and low-maintenance fabric.

James Bond—Special Agent

The third advertisement was placed in the *Daily Express* in May 1961. Headlined simply "James Bond—Special Agent," the image showed Bond leaning out of his Bentley, firing his gun at a distant gunman hiding behind a tree. Bond's blonde companion sits in the passenger seat with a shocked expression on her face. The text reads:

How do you see James Bond? Panther-dark, silent, dangerous? The short snout of a Biretta [sic] .25 nuzzling his left arm-pit as his plane swings low over Tokyo? Sipping vodka Martini—ice-cold, stirred not shaken [sic]—on the fronded terrace of some distant sea-girt Government House? Near naked in a steaming swamp? Or pulling on a soft, cool shirt in his Chelsea flat with a soft, cool girl waiting in the big grey Bentley below...?[20]

The advertisement contains broad nods to Fleming. Government House and the steaming swamp allude to *Dr. No*,[21] and the Chelsea flat is taken from

From Russia with Love.[22] However, Fleming does not send Bond to Tokyo until *You Only Live Twice*, published in 1964, and the title of the advertisement (why not "secret agent" or "spy"?) would have brought to *Express* readers' minds *Dick Barton—Special Agent* (1946–1951). This was a highly popular radio serial broadcast on the BBC Light Programme in which the titular hero, a daring ex-commando, adventurer and freelance crime-buster, thwarted criminal master-minds, cheated death, rescued maidens, and saved England from destruction on a daily basis.[23] Another curiosity is the reference to Martinis "stirred, not shaken," which the copywriter took from *Dr. No* (though erroneously reversing Bond's stipulation for the perfect cocktail).[24] The advertisement shows that not only were Bond and the Martini synonymous by 1961, but that the phrase "shaken, not stirred" had escaped the pages of the novels as an independent expression and began to have resonance in popular culture before the film of *Dr. No*, which gave the phrase wider cultural penetration, was released in 1962. With the con-tinued emphasis on clothes that are "comfortable, rugged, and good-looking," James Bond is shown wearing a Courtelle shirt by Holyrood, which has "good looks, good washability."[25]

Death in the Caribbean

If May's advertisement began to loosen its bond with Fleming, the final three advertisements diverged further from the original source material. The fourth advertisement appeared in the *Daily Express* in September 1961. "Death in the Caribbean" depicts Bond, who wears Courtelle slacks in Abrelle by Moore Johnson ("lightweight, good-looking, keep their crease wonderfully"[26]), escaping from a boat and an advancing tough-looking individual armed with a machete. The text reads:

> Two of the others are dead, the third unconscious. But the cabin doors are beginning to give way under the battering of the men inside. And they are armed. Off you go, Bond. This is no time to die; the things you've learned must get back to England. Three-hundred yards to the shore in a racing crawl, take your luck with the sharks; you've come out of tougher spots.[27]

"M. Is Worried—Send for Bond!"

While the Caribbean setting and the swim through shark-infested waters recall *Live and Let Die*, the scene is not found in Fleming's novels. But even this vestigial trace of the source material is absent from the fifth advertisement, which was placed in the *Daily Mirror* in October 1961. The advertisement "M. Is Wor-ried—Send for Bond!" shows Bond hanging from a cliff edge, with one arm outstretched to reach his blonde companion trapped on a narrow ledge. Fortunately for Bond, he wears a Courtelle cotton shirt by Luvisca, which is "easy to wear, easy to wash."[28] The accompanying text reads:

> Why does James Bond survive? He knows fear—a crawling sensation at the pit of his stomach. But instinct overcomes numb fright and terror of vertigo (death awaits him below), as he hangs precariously to save a girl's life. Muscles tuned for danger— brain cool in the tightest corner—life too precious to surrender. A life where these things are important: black velvet—especially on the sunkissed skin of an exciting girl; the bubbling of his Bentley's exhaust in his wake.[29]

LADY WITH A LUGER

The final advertisement was published in the *Daily Express* in November 1961. Headlined "Lady with a Luger," it depicted Bond—in a bar and wearing a pair of Courtelle slacks—at the wrong end of a pointed pistol wielded by his blonde companion-turned-femme-fatale:

> Surprising how a gun barrel can glint even in the dim lights of an empty bar. A cold, grey, metallic glint. Surprising how she still looks lovely, apart from the cool rage in her soft brown eyes. This one you hadn't bargained for, Bond! And what's the next move? Sudden rush? Try a bluff? Wait it out and play it cool? There'll be a way. There always is.[30]

As with "Death in the Caribbean," the final two advertisements contain nothing but the broadest allusions to Fleming, and are consistent with a gradual divergence from not only the source material over the course of Courtauld's campaign, but tropes of espionage fiction. Compare, for example, the images in the final three, perhaps even four, advertisements with a fashion photograph published in May 1961 in the men's lifestyle magazine, *Man About Town*. Entitled "Secrets of an Agent," the photograph, taken by Terence Donovan, a pioneer of the "blow-up" school of photography, who brought a sophisticated, masculine, film-style look to fashion photography, shows the model Peter Anthony (who would audition for the role of Bond in 1961 and 1970 on the strength of such work[31]) in the foreground. He wears a sharp suit, a hat, and a shoulder holster. A man in the shadows hides behind a copy of the French newspaper *Le Figaro*.[32] Whereas this photograph encapsulates intrigue, suspense, and deception, the Courtelle advertisements emphasize more general traits of danger, action, physicality, and derring-do.

While Bond is recognizably Bond—his desire for cars, sex, and danger sets him apart from the "clubman heroes" of the past, such as Bulldog Drummond and Dick Barton—the scenarios have evolved to accommodate broader crime and adventure genres. Starring in such titles as *Gun Moll for Hire, Death Wore a Petticoat*, and *Sweethearts Vengeance*, the femme-fatale was a standard character of American pulp fiction published in the U.K. during the 1950s,[33] and she also appeared in Dick Barton's adventures, among them "Dick Barton—Wanted for Murder," in which a gangster's moll, Rusty, "whipped a revolver from her pocket and rammed it in Dick's stomach."[34] Escaping from tight spots in the nick of time was the very stuff of Dick Barton, Bulldog Drummond and others, and as if to underscore the connection with Bond's antecedents, "M. Is Worried—Send for Bond!" is literally a cliffhanger, a device with which every episode of *Dick Barton* traditionally ended.

Dressing Bond

The movement and physicality of the "Courtelle Bond" serve to epitomize the marketed qualities of the clothes he wears. Thus, the clothes are "comfortable, rugged, good-looking," "easy to wear, easy to launder," "easy to wash, easy to dry," can take "a beating."[35] Such hyper-masculine qualities conforms to popularly-held perceptions about how men choose—or once chose—their clothes. As Andrea Balestri and Marco Ricchetti note in their essay on the development of men's fashion, a man traditionally makes decisions when purchasing clothes on the grounds first of wearability, fit and comfort, then of the quality of the fabric, and only finally will he consider style (if at all).[36] Until 1970, when men's fashion embraced overt sexual display, accessories, and vivid colors, the selection of clothes was rigidly set by the expectations of occupation and status and concepts of appropriate attire.[37] The Courtelle range, introduced at the end of this period, emphasized this notion of appropriateness. The shirts, trousers and sweaters are Bond's work clothes, his uniform, designed for a man who is on the move and in the thick of the action, who requires free movement of his limbs to run, punch, and reach for a weapon, who does indeed occasionally takes a beating, and who, away from home and wife (in Bond's case, his housekeeper May), does not have the resources, knowledge or inclination to properly wash and iron his clothes. As the advertisements repeated, they were clothes "made for a man's world."[38] Valerie Steele reminds us that men have tended to take their fashion cues from sports stars, actors or pop stars, a list to which can be added James Bond. "Courtelle Bond" might be accommodated within the category of "rebel," one of two masculine styles that have guided male fashion over the course of the 20th century.[39] Certainly, the contrast with the Bond of Eon Production's films, who would unambiguously be identified as a "gentleman," the other prototype of masculinity, is clear.

When the first of Eon's Bond films, *Dr. No*, was released, U.S. audiences were invited to "meet the most extraordinary gentleman spy in all fiction," and posters underlined the epithet by showing an insouciant Bond dressed in a tuxedo or dinner-suit.[40] Though not making the same invitation, British posters nevertheless included the same image of Bond, which would have been enough to identify Bond as an upper class agent and "English gentleman," a view that to some extent conflicted with Fleming's own concept of James Bond, who had American origins—Fleming was partly inspired by the fiction of American pulp-fiction writers Raymond Chandler and Dashiell Hammett—and, in Fleming's words, was "very American in so many ways."[41] The dinner-suited Bond appeared on the British poster campaign for the next film, *From Russia with Love* (1963, Terence Young), and over time, the tuxedo has become an enduring element of Bondian iconography, featuring with few exceptions on poster campaigns throughout the Eon series, including the campaign of the most recent film, *Skyfall* (2012, Sam Mendes). In addition, the image of the dinner-suited Bond has been used on countless Bond-related products and promotional material, among them the James Bond 007 Secret Service board game made by Spears in 1965, "James Bond 007: Nightfire," a video game by Electronic Arts released in 2002, Omega watches advertised in conjunction with Bond films released from 1995 onwards, promotional bottles of Perrier water from 1995, a London Science Museum exhibition in 2002, and advertisements for the James Bond 007 range of fragrances introduced in 2012.

So synonymous is the tuxedo with James Bond that to see Bond in Courtelle's range of slacks, trousers, shirts and sweaters is disconcerting. For readers of the *Express*, however, "Courtelle Bond" was consistent with contemporaneous portrayals of Bond. Until 1962, the tuxedo had been little used in images of Bond. With the exception of *Casino Royale*, none of the artwork that featured on the covers of the Pan paperbacks published in the U.K. showed Bond in a dinner suit. Most did not even show Bond in a smart business or lounge suit, instead depicting Bond in a torn and open-necked shirt, for example the 1959 edition of *Live and Let Die*, with artwork by Sam Peffer, or more casual attire, such as the jeans and heavy-duty shirt he appears to be wearing on the cover of *Dr. No* (1958 edition, also by Sam Peffer).[42] Nor is Bond depicted in formal wear in artwork, mainly by Robb and occasionally Raymond Hawkey, that accompanied serializations of Fleming's novels in the *Daily Express* from 1956 onwards.[43] The comic strip adaptations of the novels by John McLusky that were published in the *Express* between July 1958 and December 1961 featured Bond in a dinner suit as the plot demanded, for example in casinos and at formal dinners,[44] but shown among the mass of panels depicting Bond in less formal wear, the dinner suit did not especially stand out. Fleming, meanwhile, described Bond's standard outfit as a dark-blue suit, Sea Island cotton shirt and black knitted tie.[45] Thus, *Express* readers would not have necessarily expected Bond to be dinner-suited in 1961, because the association had yet to be firmly established, reducing the chances of the dinner-suit image shaping popular perceptions of Bond or influencing advertisers, marketing teams or graphic artists. After 1962, the success of the Bond films, reinforced by massive poster campaigns, inevitably saturated cultural space with images of Bond in a tuxedo, and over time the image has come to dominate popular perceptions of the character.

James Brand

The Courtelle advertisements are remarkable because they reveal that by 1961—before the release of *Dr. No* the following year—James Bond had a sufficient degree of cultural weight to be used as an aspirational figure independent of Ian Fleming's novels. James Bond was no longer exclusively the cultural property of his creator. The advertisements marked the beginning of a phenomenon that saw Bond being co-opted to sell products that did not have strong associations with the novels or the films, but which were seen as carrying a certain "Bondian" quality. It is worth examining a few examples. In March 1965, shoe manufacturer Norvic published an advertisement in the *Daily Express* for "007 shoes," which were claimed to be designed for men "accustomed to the very best, like Bond," have a "man-of-the-world" look, and came in "ten impeccable Bond-worthy styles."[46] Bondian imagery was also used to advertise chocolate. Between 1968 and 2003, Cadbury ran a series of commercials in the U.K. that featured the "Milk Tray Man," a Bond-like figure who delivers boxes of chocolate to ladies by dramatic and thrilling means; in one commercial, he climbs onto the top of a train, grabs hold of the landing skids on a passing helicopter, drops down onto the roof of a house, finds the lady's bedroom and, unseen by the lady, deposits the box of chocolates and his calling card.[47] In 1980, Benson and Hedges ran a campaign for cigarettes which featured one-time Bond actor George Lazenby. One advertisement recreated the scene from the film of *On Her Majesty's Secret Service* (1969, Peter Hunt) in which Bond rescues a drowning Tracy from the sea, and another showed Lazenby on a Jamaican beach in scuba gear and armed with a harpoon gun. "Very James Bond," claimed the text.[48] James Bond has even been used to sell tea bags. In the 1980s, Brooke Bond tea merchants ran a number of TV commercials, which featured a chimpanzee (named Brooke Bond) dressed in a white dinner jacket and bow-tie. One commercial was set in a snowy landscape and featured a pursuit on skis, another placed Brooke Bond on the Orient Express, and a third showed the villain's lair and a shark tank.[49]

As disparate as these campaigns are, they show traits that link them with the Courtelle's series of advertisements. The campaigns of both Courtelle and Norvic, for example, trade on notions of style, comfort and sophistication. "Milk Tray Man" captures the same sense of resourcefulness and movement also evident in Courtelle Bond. Benson and Hedges Bond matches Courtelle Bond for ruggedness, toughness and masculinity. Brooke Bond, meanwhile, is plunged into the sort of danger and adventure that Courtelle Bond might enjoy. Inevitably, however, these campaigns were also influenced to lesser or greater extents by Eon's film series. The use as a brand of the code number, 007, largely absent from the Courtelle advertisements, reflects its increasing prominence on artwork after 1962, appearing, for example on Eon's film posters and paperback editions of Fleming's novels published by Pan between 1962 and 1963.[50] The Benson and Hedges' advertisements allude to *On Her Majesty's Secret Service* and *Dr. No*, the Tuxedo and scenarios of the Brooke Bond commercials are inspired by imagery of Sean Connery's Bond and scenes from *Thunderball* (1965, Terence Young), *From Russia with Love* and *The Spy Who Loved Me* (1977, Lewis Gilbert), while Milk Tray Man's calling card, which showed a figure in silhouette within a white dot surrounded by black, recalls the Bond films' gun-barrel sequence.

Bond Evolves

A comparison of the representations of James Bond in the various advertising campaigns provides glimpses into the evolution of James Bond, and highlights how the trajectory of that evolution has been restricted by the prevailing cultural environment. The mechanism by which culture evolves has long been the subject of debate,[51] but one promising area of research has been the concept of cultural selection, which equates aspects of cultural information with genes. Just as genes are subject to natural selection, whereby genetic information is transmitted through reproduction and has the potential to be selected and to spread, cultural traits—for instance, the idea of Bond's tuxedo, his vodka Martini "shaken, not stirred," or masculinity—are reproduced by being copied or imitated, and expressed on posters, advertisements, in films, by speech, or any other medium, and transmitted from one human mind to another. If selected, whether intentionally or through less deliberate means, these traits, or memes, become widespread and popular in the cultural environment.[52] Courtelle Bond emerged in an environment in which Eon's films were yet not in existence, and the perceptions of James Bond, at least in the U.K., were shaped by Fleming's novels and also by the *Daily Express* comic strip and illustrations accompanying serializations of Bond's adventures. It was also an environment in which precursors to Bond retained a degree of cultural currency; memories of Dick Barton and other earlier 20th-century adventurers remained strong. The traits or memes expressed in Courtelle Bond, such as the concept of Bond as "special agent," the emphasis on action and ruggedness, and the joy of motoring, had been inherited from these pre-existing forms of Bond and other heroes. Conversely, the memes that were to become dominant with the success of the film series, such as the tuxedo, the classic Bond pose, and the gun-barrel motif, and the use of Bond's code number, 007, as a logo and brand, were not available to be transmitted or else exerted a weak influence, and therefore could not be, or were unlikely to be, expressed in 1961. This cultural landscape was utterly transformed with the introduction and subsequent success of Eon's film series. Exposed for decades to Eon's epic, more science-fiction orientated plots and Bondian iconography (the gun-barrel motif, the 007 logo, the dinner-suited gentleman spy), advertisers have inevitably, and to an extent unintentionally, inherited the memes that have been expressed in the films or material inspired by the films. And as these traits or memes become more widespread and culturally prominent, they further increase their chances of being selected again, which in turn increases their dominance in the cultural "meme pool."

Returning to the Courtelle campaign, it has been suggested that over the course of the campaign, Courtelle Bond diverged from Fleming's character. Initially the advertisements followed Fleming's novels closely, using plot details and characteristics described in the books. As the campaign progressed, there was less reliance on the source material, and traits from other traditions, such as Dick Barton, film noir, and pre–Second World War spy fiction, appeared to have been incorporated into the advertisements. To explain this, it might be useful to think about the concept of speciation. In the natural world, speciation—a process whereby two species emerge through divergence from a common ancestor—requires an isolation event. If there is no event to divide a population, then interbreeding tends to pull any potentially diverging portion back to the single species.[53] Typically a species splits when part of a population becomes geographically isolated. It adapts to its new environment and evolves along a trajectory separate to that of the parent population. In cultural terms, new cultural "species" also emerge through geographical isolation (the differences between English in the U.S. and the U.K. is an obvious example). But other factors can be just as isolating, such as different social or work networks and the human mind itself. Without Ian Fleming's involvement in the Courtelle campaign, and in an environment created by the marketing team, Fleming's Bond was subject to different influences and ideas (for instance about perceptions of spies and heroes and the traditions of Courtauld's marketing) and was free to evolve along a separate trajectory to that of Fleming's Bond.

Conclusion

The Courtelle campaign of 1961 provides a unique window into how James Bond was perceived in popular culture. Courtelle Bond was rooted in Ian Fleming's novels, but the advertisements also showed how Bond was adapted to fit older literary and cinematic traditions, that of the resourceful, tough, somewhat rebellious, but yet incorruptible hero who springs into action to defeat crime capers. Bond was seen as a late development of the tradition that included Bulldog Drummond, Richard Hannay and Dick Barton. Some of the traits or memes that particularly characterized the early cinematic Bond, notably the sense of Bond as an English gentleman, and his tuxedo, were not well established in popular culture in 1961, and the clothes that Bond models do not conflict with contemporaneous perceptions; his slacks, casual shirts and sweater would not have been disconcerting to *Daily Express* readers. James Bond is constantly evolving, and over the course of the past 60 years, several Bonds have emerged and faded with the changing cultural environment. The Courtelle Bond of 1961 is just one Bond that has emerged and competed with others, ultimately giving way to the Bond of the cinema. That is not to diminish the significance of Courtelle Bond. The advertisements are testament to the enormous impact that Fleming's creation had on popular culture before the commencement of Eon's film series, and the role that Bond already had as an inspirational figure.

Acknowledgments

The brand name "Courtelle" is owned by Rowlinson Knitwear Ltd. I am grateful to Ken Edgar, Overseas Director of Rowlinson Knitwear Ltd., for granting me permission to reproduce the Courtelle advertisements.

Notes

1. Courtaulds Ltd., "Diplomatic Passport 0094567—Bond J.," *Daily Express*, March 28, 1961, p. 12.
2. Ibid.
3. Ibid.
4. Ian Fleming, *Live and Let Die* (London: Penguin, 2006), 1–11.
5. Ian Fleming, *Casino Royale* (London: Penguin, 2006), 35–6.
6. Nigel Perryman, *Fifties Britain: Post-war Life* (London: Bounty Books, 2006), 39.
7. "'I am the speed queen of the M1,'" *Daily Mirror*, November 13, 959, p. 11.
8. Patrick Mennem, "M1 Death Crash," *Daily Mirror*, November 7, 1959, p. 9.
9. Basil Cardew, "Marples gets a scare on the M1," *Daily Express*, November 3, 1959, p. 9.
10. Somerset Maugham, *Ashenden* (London: Vintage, 2000), 269.

11. "History," *Bluestar Fibres Company Limited*, 2009, http://www.bluestarfibres.com/page.php?path=history (accessed June 27, 2013).

12. Courtaulds Ltd., "'Inform All Agents—Bond Must Die!'" *Daily Express*, April 11, 1961, p. 9.

13. Ian Fleming, *From Russia with Love* (London: Penguin, 2006), 241–54.

14. Ibid., 60–71.

15. Ibid., 143.

16. Ian Fleming, *Moonraker* (London: Penguin, 2006), 54–65.

17. Ibid., 3–5.

18. Ian Fleming, *Goldfinger* (London: Penguin, 2006), 59.

19. Courtaulds Ltd., "'Inform All Agents—Bond Must Die!'" 9.

20. Courtaulds Ltd., "James Bond—Special Agent," *Daily Express*, May 10, 1961, p. 5.

21. Ian Fleming, *Dr. No* (London: Penguin, 2006), 63.

22. Fleming, *From Russia with Love*, 123.

23. Alex Hudson, "The Special Agent 'Killed' by the Archers," *BBC News*, July 15, 2010, http://www.bbc.co.uk/news/entertainment+arts-10634844 (accessed July 1, 2013).

24. Fleming, *Dr. No*, 208.

25. Courtaulds Ltd., "James Bond-Special Agent," p. 5.

26. Courtaulds Ltd., "Death in the Caribbean," *Daily Express*, September 14, 1961, p. 9.

27. Ibid.

28. Courtaulds Ltd., "'M. Is Worried-Send for Bond,'" *Daily Mirror*, October 17, 1961, p. 10.

29. Ibid.

30. Courtaulds Ltd., "Lady with a Luger," *Daily Express*, November 2, 1961, p. 7.

31. Edward Biddulph, "The Original Model Bond," *MI6: The Home of James Bond 007*, April 5, 2013, http://www.mi6-hq.com/sections/articles/history_dr_no_casting_peter_anthony.php3 (accessed July 4, 2013).

32. Terence Donovan, David Hillman, and Diana Donovan, *Terence Donovan* (London: Little, Brown, 2000).

33. Gary Lovisi, *Dames, Dolls and Delinquents: A Collector's Guide to Sexy Pulp Fiction Paperbacks* (Iola, WI: Krause, 2009), 121.

34. Geoffrey Webb and Edward J. Mason, *Dick Barton. Special Agent* (London: Contact, 1950), 32.

35. Courtaulds Ltd., "James Bond—Special Agent," p. 5; and Courtaulds Ltd., "Death in the Caribbean," p. 9.

36. Andrea Balestri and Marco Ricchoti, "Manufacturing Men's Wear: Masculine Identity in the Structure of the Fashion Industry," in *Material Man: Masculinity, Sexuality, Style*, ed. Giannino Malossi (New York: Harry N. Abrams, 2000), 56.

37. Valerie Steele, "Fashioning Men: The Role of Fashion in the Imagination of American Man," in *Material Man: Masculinity, Sexuality, Style*, ed. Giannino Malossi (New York: Harry N. Abrams, 2000), 81.

38. Courtaulds Ltd., "Death in the Caribbean," p. 9.

39. Steele, "Fashioning Men," 78.

40. Alastair Dougall, *James Bond: 50 Years of Movie Posters* (London: Dorling Kindersley Limited, 2012), 10–11.

41. Jack Fishman, "007 and Me, By Ian Fleming," in *For Bond Lovers Only*, ed. Sheldon Lane (London: Panther, 1965), 27.

42. Bazeer Flumore, "Sam Peffer Early Series," *Piz Gloria*, n.d., http://www.pizgloria.com/books.php?publisher=GREAT%20PAN&series=SAM%20PEFFER%20EARLY%20SERIES (accessed August 6, 2013).

43. For example, Ian Fleming, "The Tunnel of Death," *Daily Express*, March 31, 1957, p. 6.

44. For example, Ian Fleming, Anthony Hern, Henry Gammidge, and John McLusky, *Casino Royale* (London: Titan Books, 2005).

45. For example Fleming, *Moonraker*, 32; and Ian Fleming, *Diamonds Are Forever* (London: Penguin, 2006), 51.

46. Norvic Shoe Company Limited, "Norvic 007 Shoes Show the Kind of Man You Are," *Daily Express*, March 22, 1965, p. 8.

47. col2006ie, "Cadbury's Milk Tray U.K. TV Adverts, 1960s/1970s," *YouTube*, July 14, 2008, https://www.youtube.com/watch?v=THH8p21akrA (accessed August 7, 2013).

48. Charles Helfenstein, *The Making of On Her Majesty's Secret Service* (Frederick, MD: Spies Publishing, 2009), 272.

49. Jeffrey Reynolds, "007 Bond Brooke Bond," *YouTube*, September 16, 2012, https://www.youtube.com/watch?v=mHqoGswdXro (accessed August 7, 2013).

50. Dougall, 10–11; and Bazeer Flumore, "Sam Peffer Yellow 007 Series," *Piz Gloria*, n.d., http://www.pizgloria.com/books.php?publisher=GREAT%20PAN&series=SAM%20PEFFER%20YELLOW%20007%20SERIES (accessed August 8, 2013).

51. For example, Robert Boyd and Peter Richerson, *Culture and the Evolutionary Process* (Chicago: University of Chicago Press, 1985); and Daniel Dennett, *Darwin's Dangerous Idea: Evolution and the Meanings of Life* (London: Penguin, 1995).

52. Richard Dawkins, *The Selfish Gene,* 30th Anniversary Edition (Oxford: Oxford University Press, 2006), 189–201.

53. Jerry Coyne and H. Allen Orr, *Speciation* (Sunderland, MA: Sinauer Associates, 2004), 86.

Bibliography

Balestri, Andrea, and Marco Ricchoti. "Manufacturing Men's Wear: Masculine Identity in the Structure of the Fashion Industry." In *Material Man: Masculinity, Sexuality, Style*, edited by Giannino Malossi, 52–63. New York: Harry N. Abrams, 2000.

Biddulph, Edward. "The Original Model Bond." *MI6: The Home of James Bond 007*, April 5, 2013. http://www.mi6-hq.com/sections/articles/history_dr_no_casting_peter_anthony.php3 (accessed July 4, 2013).

Boyd, Robert, and Peter Richerson. *Culture and the Evolutionary Process.* Chicago: University of Chicago Press, 1985.

Cardew, Basil. "Marples gets a scare on the M1." *Daily Express*, November 3, 1959, p. 9.

Courtaulds Ltd. "Diplomatic Passport 0094567—Bond J." *Daily Express*, March 28, 1961, p. 12.

_____. "Inform All Agents—Bond Must Die!" *Daily Express*, April 11, 1961, p. 9.

_____. "James Bond—Special Agent." *Daily Express*, May 10, 1961, p. 5.

_____. "Death in the Caribbean." *Daily Express*, September 14, 1961, p. 9.

_____. "'M. Is Worried—Send for Bond.'" *Daily Mirror*, October 17, 1961, p. 10.

_____. "Lady with a Luger." *Daily Express*, November 2, 1961, p. 7.

Coyne, Jerry, and H. Allen Orr. *Speciation.* Sunderland, MA: Sinauer Associates, 2004.

Dawkins, Richard. *The Selfish Gene*, 30th Anniversary Edition. Oxford: Oxford University Press, 2006.

Dennett, Daniel. *Darwin's Dangerous Idea: Evolution and the Meanings of Life.* London: Penguin, 1995.

Donovan, Terence, David Hillman, and Diana Donovan. *Terence Donovan.* London: Little, Brown, 2000.

Dougall, Alastair. *James Bond: 50 Years of Movie Posters.* London: Dorling Kindersley Limited, 2012.

Fishman, Jack. "007 and Me, By Ian Fleming." In *For Bond Lovers Only*, edited by Sheldon Lane, 9–28. London: Panther, 1965.

Fleming, Ian. *Casino Royale*. London: Penguin, 2006.
_____. *Diamonds Are Forever*. London: Penguin, 2006.
_____. *Dr. No*. London: Penguin, 2006.
_____. *From Russia with Love*. London: Penguin, 2006.
_____. *Goldfinger*. London: Penguin, 2006.
_____. *Live and Let Die*. London: Penguin, 2006.
_____. *Moonraker*. London: Penguin, 2006.
_____. "The Tunnel of Death." *Daily Express*, March 31, 1957, p. 6.
Fleming, Ian, Anthony Hern, Henry Gammidge, and John McLusky. *Casino Royale*. London: Titan Books, 2005.
Flumore, Bazeer. *Piz Gloria*, n.d. http://www.pizgloria.com (accessed August 6, 2013).
Helfenstein, Charles. *The Making of On Her Majesty's Secret Service*. Frederick, MD: Spies Publishing, 2009.
"History." *Bluestar Fibres Company Limited*, 2009. http://www.bluestarfibres.com/page.php?path=history (accessed June 27, 2013).
Hudson, Alex. "The Special Agent 'Killed' by the Archers." *BBC News*, July 15, 2010. http://www.bbc.co.uk/news/entertainment+arts-10634844 (accessed July 1, 2013).
"'I am the speed queen of the M1.'" *Daily Mirror*, November 13, 1959, p. 11.
Lovisi, Gary. *Dames, Dolls and Delinquents: A Collector's Guide to Sexy Pulp Fiction Paperbacks*. Iola, WI: Krause, 2009.
Maugham, Somerset. *Ashenden*. London: Vintage, 2000.
Mennem, Patrick. "M1 Death Crash." *Daily Mirror*, November 7, 1959, p. 9.
Norvic Shoe Company Limited. "Norvic 007 Shoes Show the Kind of Man You Are." *Daily Express*, March 22, 1965, p. 8.
ol2006ie. "Cadbury's Milk Tray U.K. TV Adverts, 1960s/1970s." *YouTube*, July 14, 2008. https://www.youtube.com/watch?v=THH8p21akrA (accessed August 7, 2013).
Perryman, Nigel. *Fifties Britain: Post-War Life*. London: Bounty Books, 2006.
Reynolds, Jeffrey. "007 Bond Brooke Bond." *YouTube*, September 16, 2012. https://www.youtube.com/watch?v=mHqoGswdXro (accessed August 7, 2013).
Steele, Valerie. "Fashioning Men: The Role of Fashion in the Imagination of American Man." In *Material Man: Masculinity, Sexuality, Style*, edited by Giannino Malossi, 78–83. New York: Harry N. Abrams, 2000.
Webb, Geoffrey, and Edward J. Mason. *Dick Barton. Special Agent*. London: Contact, 1950.

Derek Flint, Matt Helm, and the Playboy Spy of the 1960s

BRIAN PATTON

The James Bond whom the world came to know through the enormously successful film series that was launched in 1962 is a "hero of modernization,"[1] in the words of Tony Bennett and Janet Woollacott, a figure very different in that regard from Ian Fleming's more old-school literary creation. As Adrian Turner remarks, 007's creator "was a creature of the 1920s who evoked 1930s values in the 1950s and became a phenomenon in the 1960s."[2] Although the Bond of the big screen remains a government man, an agent "on her majesty's secret service," he is clearly distinguished from the English establishment embodied by his superior, M, and his armorer, Q, in several ways: he is considerably younger than these authority figures and mildly rebellious in his attitude toward them; he is closely associated with cutting-edge technology, in the form of the latest high-end automobiles as well as the amazing gadgets of tomorrow: all those miniature devices for causing mayhem or discretely shadowing the enemy. Finally, the modernity of the Bond films is demonstrated by their "elaboration of a ... new set of gender identities"[3]—specifically, those of the sexually liberated "playboy" and his female counterpart in the series, the "Bond Girl." In 007's wake, the playboy spy became one of the most familiar and compelling figures of the 1960s, a defining embodiment of the period's modernity. The substantial box-office returns and world-wide cultural influence of the Bond film franchise by the middle of the decade encouraged a throng of hopeful imitators on both sides of the Atlantic and on large and small screens alike. Numbered among them were a handful of American film productions that offered, with varying degrees of irony, a series of stateside takes on the figure of the hip bachelor-spy: Fox's two Derek Flint films (*Our Man Flint* [1966, Daniel Mann] and *In Like Flint* [1967, Gordon Douglas]), Columbia's Matt Helm series (*The Silencers* [1966, Phil Karlson], *Murderer's Row* [1966, Henry Levin], *The Ambushers* [1967, Henry Levin] and *The Wrecking Crew* [1968, Phil Karlson]) and American International's Dr. Goldfoot films (*Dr. Goldfoot and the Bikini Machine*

[1965, Norman Taurog] and *Dr. Goldfoot and the Girl Bombs* [1966, Mario Bava]).[4] Demonstrating a self-reflexivity that had already begun to emerge within the Bond series itself, these movies replicate what had become the familiar formula of the 007 series, blending elements of the thriller, science fiction and comedy and featuring plots in which (usually) suave spies thwart grand conspiracies against a landscape littered with fantastic gadgets and beautiful, willing female companions. As ostensible parodies, they also magnify those signature features that define the Bond series, especially those that delineate the modern, 1960s man.

The many connections between the Bond franchise and Hugh Hefner's *Playboy* magazine, arguably the most important terrain on which notions of masculinity were reshaped in the postwar period, have been widely discussed. The connections begin with their roughly simultaneous debuts in 1953. According to Bill Osgerby, *Playboy* had taken note of a kindred spirit across the water as early as 1960: following a visit by Ian Fleming to its Chicago offices, the magazine ventured that "James Bond, if he were an actual person, would be a registered reader of *Playboy*."[5] Fleming himself appeared as the subject of a *Playboy* interview shortly before his death in 1964, by which time his Bond stories were appearing regularly and with much fanfare in Hefner's magazine; and, of course, regular photo features of the latest "Bond girls" coincided with the release of each new film. The films' producers in turn gave the February 1969 issue of *Playboy* a cameo appearance in *On Her Majesty's Secret Service* (1969, Peter Hunt) and made Bond a card-carrying member of the Playboy Club in *Diamonds Are Forever* (1971, Guy Hamilton). The Bond/*Playboy* connection was, clearly, a mutually agreeable marketing strategy, but it was rooted in a common project: the magazine, Ian Fleming's novels, and the films they inspired were all participating in the redefinition of manhood against a backdrop of more relaxed sexual mores and an ever expanding consumer culture. The masculine figure at the center of that project was the bachelor, who, in his new guise as the playboy, became a more prevalent and idealized figure than ever before—an embodiment of masculine liberation and modernization. As James Chapman notes, "There was an obvious similarity between Bond's attitude towards women and the *Playboy* ethos of easy, free, open sexuality."[6] There was also a connection—evident in the case of Bond, but much more so with his American cousins—between *Playboy's* celebration of the affluent male consumer who outfitted himself stylishly, demonstrated sophisticated taste in food and drink, and accessorized himself and his bachelor pad with the latest in technological gadgetry. Dwelling extensively on the spies' private lives, personal relationships, and taste in home décor, these American films embrace the *Playboy* "lifestyle" more fully than any of the Bond films do.

Work, Marriage and Conspicuous Consumption: From Postwar Man to Playboy

The postwar bachelor's identification with leisure, pleasure and consumption marks him as an emergent figure, a significant variation on the dominant masculine type of the day: the earnest breadwinner, the "man in the grey flannel suit." Bill Osgerby traces the origins of the postwar playboy back several decades, situating this redefinition of masculinity in the context of an emerging capitalist, consumer culture from the late nineteenth century to the present, and tracing a gradual reduction in the importance of responsibility, self-sacrifice and production in favor of a new emphasis on self-centeredness, pleasure-seeking, and consumption.[7] Until the early twentieth century, Osgerby notes, middle-class manhood was equated with producing things, an association most fully expressed in the nineteenth-century type of the "self-made man": a high-achieving entrepreneur who succeeds through hard work, good character and determination.[8] His life was characterized by a dedication to work and to the needs of his family: he was a provider, self-made but not self-indulgent. His successor in a postwar world far removed from the frontier spirit that energized this nineteenth-century type was the sober breadwinner who exemplified masculine maturity by donning a suit and bearing the tedium of the workaday world on behalf of his wife and children. Maturity, Barbara Ehrenreich contends, was *the* defining trait of postwar masculinity, one whose fundamental importance is hard to grasp from the other side of the transformative youth movements of the 1960s.[9] The breadwinner's marriage was a both sign of this maturity and the field within which it was to be proved from one hard-working day to the next.[10]

If the married man demonstrated his maturity by accepting the responsibilities of his socially-sanctioned roles—husband, father, provider, and weekend barbecue chef—the bachelor necessarily embodied a lesser version of manhood, a status confirmed by the word's etymology. "Bachelor" has, historically, conveyed a sense of irregularity, as in the phrase "a confirmed bachelor," a winking insinuation of homosexuality in more closeted times. More specifically, the word has long indicated incompleteness or insufficiency. According to the *Oxford English Dictionary*, "bachelor" has designated an unmarried man of marriageable age since at least the late fourteenth century,[11] but the word's undesirable connotations are made plain when this familiar meaning is situated amid its other roughly contemporary ones, all of which convey some sense of want: "a young knight, not old enough, or having too few vassals, to display his own banner"; "a junior or inferior member, or 'yeoman,' of a trade-guild, or City Company"; "one who has taken the first or lowest degree at a university, who is not yet a *master* of the Arts"; "an inexperienced person, a novice."[12] Historically, then, the bachelor was a deficient figure, defined by what he was not—or not *yet*. Thus, the conversion of the historically deficient bachelor into the newly contented playboy of the postwar period represents a fundamental change in the understanding of men in their relationship to marriage in very recent times. The word "playboy," in its familiar sense, has been in use only since the early nineteenth century,[13] and in wide circulation for a shorter period still: Osgerby suggests that the word came into its own during the hedonistic Jazz Age of the 1920s.[14] Clearly, "playboy" had a usefully evocative meaning by the time Hugh Hefner adopted it as the name of the magazine he launched in 1953, and Hefner's success with *Playboy* magazine has fixed the word's association with a stylish, self-indulgent and sexually liberated lifestyle for men.

While *Playboy* is generally thought of as the magazine that ushered pornography into mainstream American culture and brought the word "centerfold" into common usage, a look at any issue from the period under consideration here would indicate that *Playboy* was arguably far more interested in men than in women. The female semi-nude is a central presence only in a literal sense; the many images of men stylishly modeling a range of consumer goods—perhaps, but not necessarily in the presence of admiring women who approve of their choices—are arguably more indicative of the magazine's project: to fashion the ideal man through conspicuous consumption. As a men's magazine devoted in large measure to the rapidly shifting tides of men's fashion and lifestyle, *Playboy* catered to a reader seeking not only centerfolds, but also reassurance that his lapels were cut *à la mode* and that his bachelor pad, cocktails, and hi-fi selections would suitably impress. As Carrie Pitzulo has observed, *Playboy* magazine encouraged its readers to subject *themselves* to scrutiny at least as much as it invited their scrutiny of the monthly parade of Playmates:

> *Playboy* celebrated the fun-loving bachelor who knew how to match his belt to his shoes. The result was an objectified postwar man, a male reader whose appearance, home and lifestyle were newly scrutinized according to the particular standards of the urban playboy. Not just the Playmate, but the bachelor himself—albeit fully clothed—was put on display and offered up for critical evaluation in *Playboy*.[15]

Regular, full-page advertisements aimed at potential advertisers, but placed prominently in the sight of the magazine's readership in general, asked the question, "What sort of man reads *Playboy*?" The answers invariably emphasized the degree to which the playboy as envisioned by Hefner's magazine was an aspiring consumer for whom shopping and identity-formation were inseparable activities. In one typical example pitched toward the high-end automobile sector, the *Playboy* reader was described as "a young executive steering his way to success," often in the company of "a gorgeous model."[16] A leader of an "actionful life ... reflected in the automobiles he buys," the reader of *Playboy* is more likely than those of other magazines to purchase a convertible or a pricey foreign vehicle.[17] Another such ad, aimed at clothes-sellers, depicts "a confidently correct young man with a critical eye for appropriate ties," adding that "a higher percentage of PLAYBOY readers is concentrated in the style-conscious, young urban male market than that of *any* other magazine."[18] The ideal playboy as envisioned by *Playboy* magazine was an urban sophisticate, a man in easy possession of a sense of style admired by women and desired by the magazine's actual readers, presumably less ideal versions of the type, eager for the instruction the magazine and its advertisers provided in ample supply. Pitzulo describes *Playboy* as "one of the most sophisticated consumer magazines of the postwar years," whose "modern, hip look and high quality ... helped to legitimize its risqué nature."[19] However, the magazine's risqué nature itself served a legitimizing function in that it shielded the would-be playboy against any residual memory of the bachelor as an irregular figure and dispelled any doubts that might arise regarding the sexual orientation of an unmarried man with a keen interest in such traditionally feminine domains as fashion and grooming, cooking or interior design.

The Playboy-Spy

Both Derek Flint and Matt Helm clearly embody this new, self-centered and pleasure-seeking masculine ethos, and the hapless spies of the Dr. Goldfoot films are comic figures in part owing to their failure to do so. Sean Connery's Bond was first introduced in a moment of refined leisure, sporting a tuxedo at the baccarat table in *Dr. No* (1962, Terrence Young); both Flint and Helm make their first appearances in far more relaxed circumstances: asleep in their lavish beds. Derek Flint (James Coburn) exemplifies the playboy-as-sophisticate, the hip intellectual toward whom Hefner's magazine directed its interviews with important literary and political figures or its many articles and advertisements featuring jazz artists. Flint pursues pleasure through self-actualization: he is an amusingly remarkable polymath—an accomplished student of karate, isomerism and bull-fighting as well as languages ranging from Japanese to dolphin, a man who occasionally visits Moscow to teach ballet and humbly acknowledges that his various books on esoteric subjects, a year or so old now, are hopelessly out of date. Money is of no concern to him: he lives in luxurious style in a magnificent Manhattan penthouse and travels when and where he wishes in a private Lear jet. His interests, as he explains to Lloyd Cramden—his foil from the straight world of the suited and desk-bound—"are more personal than governmental,"[20] and it is only when Cramden is nearly killed by a poisoned dart intended for Flint himself that the suave spy agrees to redirect his interests in a governmental direction for a time—and then only on his own terms.

Matt Helm (Dean Martin) is similarly reluctant to heed his nation's call, and his self-indulgence is of a considerably more decadent kind. Although we see him working at his preferred occupation as a professional photographer, that work is never presented as more than a licentious form of play. When he is introduced in *The Silencers*, Helm is on a "semi-permanent leave"[21] from his duties with I.C.E. (Intelligence and Counter-Espionage) and keen to avoid any case that may interrupt his plans to travel to Acapulco with his lover/secretary, Lovey Kravezit—a name, surely, that requires no further comment. Although we see him working at his preferred occupation as a professional photographer, that work is never presented as more than a licentious form of play. Similar to Flint, Helm makes his debut asleep and dreaming in his luxurious, round bed in the bachelor pad that doubles as his photographer's studio. His distance from the world of real work is accentuated by the editing of this introductory sequence, which begins with Helm's supervisor at I.C.E., Macdonald, in his office commenting on Helm's semi-permanent leave, how much he is reportedly enjoying his present work, and his "rather peculiar ideas about keeping in shape,"[22] a line that cues a cut to the first shot of Helm in bed. The accompanying jaunty, percussive music of the boom-chick-a-boom variety indicates that some fun will begin here. The men's telephone conversation, which pulls Helm out of his amatory dreams, is depicted through cross-cutting, and the result is a sequence of sharply contrasting images as Macdonald tries to persuade Helm to take on a mission and Helm hopelessly attempts to convince his superior that, whatever the crisis, Matt Helm is not at home: Macdonald is dressed in a suit and seated at his desk with an American flag in the background, while Helm, barely awake, lies undressed beneath a rumpled bed-sheet.

The Playboy's Pad: Better Living Through Gadgetry

Flint and Helm are introduced into their respective series in their homes, amidst a décor that declares their credentials as leisured, masculine consumers. The nature of 007's home life is of little interest to the Bond series: of the six films released during the 1960s,[23] only the first, *Dr. No*, takes us briefly inside Bond's flat, and what it reveals there is affluence, taste and masculine elegance, but no especially remarkable detail. The scene is less interested in showcasing Bond's taste in home furnishings than in establishing his credentials as a nonchalant lady's man as he arrives home to find the first Bond girl, Sylvia Trench, practicing her putting while she awaits him in the bedroom. Derek Flint and Matt Helm's apartments also function as sites of seduction; however, they are not mere background. The fusion of traditional and modern elements in Flint's apartment, coupled with exotic pieces of art and other such signs of affluence and cultural sophistication, marks him as one of Hefner's men. Helm's bachelor pad in particular is a painstakingly staged spectacle of masculine leisure (arguably questionable) taste, and cutting-edge consumption, featuring in an extended set-piece whose function is to define him as the louche spy with the coolest gadgets. The carefully presented décor of Helm's apartment accords with his strong preference for play—and for work (if there must be work) that resembles play. Samples of his photography are displayed around the headboard: *faux* magazine covers (*Western Trails, Bait and Tackle,* and, most aptly, *Slaymate*), all featuring young women in pin-up poses. Those dreams interrupted by Macdonald's call, revealed in a series of inset images, involve romantic encounters with each of the scantily-clad women: pin-up photography, then, is quite *literally* his dream job. The second film in the series, *Murderers' Row,* provides a similarly appealing picture of Helm's preferred occupation, re-introducing him "at work" on a *Playboy*-style calendar with a January model whom he finds in his bed and a July model whose ingénue pose is called into question by her response to his suggestion of a "Spirit of '76" theme: "76? Are you kidding? I'm only a 44!"[24] The inseparability of Helm's business and pleasure is emphasized by the fact that he carries out this enjoyable labor in his state-of-the art fortress of fun. His working day begins with the push of a button on his headboard, which gently eases the motorized bed toward a wall whose sliding doors open to reveal a bathtub the size of a small swimming pool, full of suds and illuminated with a warm orange glow. The bed gradually tilts and Helm slides effortlessly into the water, where his secretary, Lovey Kravezit, awaits him with a morning kiss and a miniature bottle of whisky. A microphone lowered from the ceiling allows him to take a genial business call from the editor of *Slaymate* before he and Lovey emerge from the bath to be dried and dressed in matching robes by more hands-free, automated gadgets while yet another pours their coffee. Little wonder, then, that Helm seems determined to ignore Macdonald's telephone summons, which will force a leave from this occupation in favor of the more rigorous demands of life as a secret agent.

Even without the allusions to *Slaymate,* Helm's ultra-modern bachelor pad would suggest with particular clarity the series' indebtedness to *Playboy* magazine, since it is evidently modeled on a handful of highly popular *Playboy* features envisaging the ultimate playboy dwelling, a fantasy eventually realized in the construction of Hugh Hefner's own Playboy Mansion in Chicago and then, for wider consumption, in the modeling of his first Playboy Club on the design of his personal pleasure palace.[25] The earliest of these features comprised a pair of heavily illustrated articles appearing in the September and October 1956 issues entitled "*Playboy*'s Penthouse Apartment." A follow-up piece, "The Playboy Town House," appeared in May 1962, and introduced the rotating bed, the prototype of the one prominently featured in Helm's cocoon of self-indulgence.[26] All of these features affirm the superiority of the single man's existence to that of the man who has chosen marriage. The introduction to the first part of the "Penthouse" piece emphasized repeatedly the exclusivity of the playboy's domestic space: this is "a man's world," however many women might pass through it: "A man yearns for quarters of his own. More than a place to hang his hat, a man dreams of his own domain, a place that is exclusively his."[27] Instead of a wife to handle domestic duties, the perfect bachelor pad features the kind of ultramodern technology on view in Matt Helm's apartment, from the "ultrasonic dishwasher" that uses "inaudible hi-fi sound to eliminate manual washing" and the "touch-cool induction heating stove."[28] Minimizing domestic chores is only one function of the bachelor's gadget-filled home, though; a more important one is smoothing the pathway of seduction: a living-room cabinet "holds a built-in bar. This permits the canny bachelor to remain in the room while mixing a cool one for his intended quarry."[29] Similarly, "a self-timing rheostat ... will gradually and subtly dim the lights to fit the mood—as opposed to the harsh click of a light switch that plunges all into sudden darkness and may send the fair game fleeing."[30] The ultimate expression of the bachelor's easy command of his world and the "fair game" who may enter it, though, is in the control panel built into the headboard of his luxurious bed, where he will find "within easy reach ... silent mercury switches and a rheostat that control every light in the place and can subtly dim the bedroom lighting to just the right romantic level. Here, too are the switches which control the circuits for the front door and terrace window locks," and concealed within a storage cabinet is a telephone and an on/off switch, very much like the one Helm uses to temporarily banish Macdonald and the nation's business from his drowsy consciousness once again in the opening moments of *Murderers' Row*.[31] Later refinements brought still greater excess to this 1956 model: in defiance of linen departments everywhere, a round version of the bed was introduced in November 1959, with a motor added in May 1962, so that it could be rotated in a circular motion. "Without question," the editors gushed, the enhanced playboy bed of 1962, "a marvel of mechanical ingenuity," was "the Town House's single most dramatic piece of furniture."[32] The producers of the Matt Helm films have taken this already ludicrous contraption one step further: not even Hugh Hefner's designers saw the advantages of saving the playboy and, perhaps, his intended quarry, the minor bother of having to remove themselves from the bed before bathing.

"Whenever he needed a girl on the scene"

The envisioned penthouse and the later town house defined the architectural landscape on which the playboy was to exercise his freedom and indulge in his pleasure. Central to those pleasures, of course, was the company of women, whom the editors imagined passing through the bachelor's home with a frequency and impermanence comparable to those of the Playmates who featured each month in the magazine. "If the Playboy is defined by his singularity," says Beatriz Preciado, "the Playmate is pure multiplicity, ambiguity, and impermanence."[33] The steady supply of young, attractive and compliant female sexual partners that was such a familiar feature of the Bond films is not only repeated but amplified in all of these other film series; remarkably, the Bond films actually appear rather modest by comparison with their American cousins in this regard. Bond is a *serial* philanderer, dealing with multiple women at one time only in the films' promotional materials, but in these American films, sexually available women travel in numbers. *Dr. Goldfoot and the Bikini Machine* in particular presents a *Playboy* fantasy brought to (synthetic) life. As the matter is put in the film's title song, performed by The Supremes, the hero needs only to push a button in order for a beautiful, submissive girl to appear and fulfill his fantasies.[34] Dr. Goldfoot's contraption generates a dozen varieties of bikini-clad female robots whose various looks and personalities are determined by their maker, whose own style tends toward the smoking jackets favored by Hugh Hefner— a visual echo that lends an ironic twist to his employing these compliant robot– Playmates in a plot to seize the assets of affluent, single men.

Matt Helm occupies himself between cases as a pin-up photographer, and he occasionally finds himself surrounded, in not entirely professional circumstances, by the models who pose for him. The spying business in the Matt Helm series can also take on the appearance of a world imagined as a *Playboy* feature, as it does in *The Ambushers*, where Helm's labor at the I.C.E. Rehabilitation Center appears to consist solely of staged romantic encounters with attractive, young female trainees. In between Helm's stints behind the camera, his young secretary is always at hand to take dictation and receive his kisses at the same time. Not to be outdone, Derek Flint shares his Manhattan penthouse with four women, like a more discreet Hugh Hefner in a compact version of the famed Playboy Mansion. The number is reduced to a more modest three in the sequel, *In Like Flint*. When Flint's bemused superior, Lloyd Cramden, remarks to one of the women in the later film that he does not recognize her, she serenely replies, "No, we're new—all of us." Flint later explains that he is "trying to cut down," having experimented with five at one point and finding that number too much.[35] There is no tension or jealousy in evidence within the congested Flint household, though: each of the women seems perfectly contented, despite the fact that they clearly fill the role of domestic servants and secretaries—shaving Flint, selecting his clothes, and arranging his appointments. At one point in *Our Man Flint*, as he prepares to step on to the dance floor with one of his companions, Flint takes a sip of his cocktail and hands it to another without so much as a word or glance in her direction. Although the women are quite obviously Flint's live-in lovers, their shared penthouse is equally obviously *his* space, a more stylish version of the *Playboy* penthouse, whose décor is unequivocally masculine, whatever the number of women in temporary residence.

Not the Marrying Kind

For the bachelor-playboy, then, women are always at hand, but marriage is out of the question. Indeed, any constricting romantic claims on the playboy's liberty are unwelcome. *Playboy*'s fantasy apartment is the ideal seduction zone in part because it allows the button-pushing Don Juan to screen out any awkward calls from last night's date while tonight's is still a work in progress. The same inclination that gave the bachelor remote control over the mood-lighting and the temperature also placed within easy reach a handy on-off switch for the telephone, "so the jangling bell or, what's worse, a chatty call from the date of the night before, won't shatter the spell being woven."[36] Yet another bit of forward thinking resulted in the provision of a 1956-model telephone answering machine, so as to keep open the possibility that last night's date, however unwanted tonight, might yet remain an option for tomorrow. Like Flint's penthouse, Matt Helm's apartment is busy with women, but they are always merely passing through. In the closing moments of *Murderers' Row* a seemingly domestic *dénouement* pairing Matt Helm and the film's female star, Ann-Margaret, is overlaid with a Dean Martin recording of "I'm Not the Marrying Kind," a message repeated in various ways throughout the series as a whole.

Whenever marriage is discussed, the tone is ironic, as in the moment in *The Silencers* when Tina (Daliah Lavi), Helm's sometime partner-in-espionage (and in romance), does a double-take when he introduces her, during an undercover assignment, as "Mrs. Helm," or in *The Ambushers*, when Helm learns that he and another former lover and fellow spy, Sheila Sommers (Janice Rule), will have to pose as a couple: "What I don't do for my country," is the put-upon bachelor's response. *The Wrecking Crew* pairs Dean Martin with Sharon Tate in the thankless role of Freya Carlson, a female I.C.E. operative who demonstrates at virtually every moment the wisdom of Helm's preference for working without the encumbrance of a woman perpetually at his side. In the Flint films, the temporary nature of Flint's liaisons with his live-in companions is made explicit, another bit of evidence affirming Flint's credentials as the ultimate bachelor-playboy. In the sequel, when Cramden asks about Flint's former companions, Flint replies, as though he were stating the obvious, "Oh, they're married." Clearly feeling a generation or so out of his element, Cramden replies, "Ah, happily, I expect. Oh, naturally, why wouldn't they be? They certainly were well—um—well—um—prepared?"[37]—a remark that echoes Jules Archer's assertion in the pages of *Playboy* magazine in 1955 that "breaking-in" an unmarried woman was beneficial to her future husband.[38] The bachelor may have a role to play in the straight world of marriage, but he plays it from a comfortably free position outside marriage.

The Leering Camera and the "pleasure unit"

The romantic lessons of the bachelor-spy film are, thus, relatively straight-forward: marriage is the tender trap, but women are nonetheless to be enjoyed, often and in copious variety, as sexual partners—in accordance with the code endlessly reiterated within the pages of *Playboy*. The heterosexual male gaze licensed by *Playboy*'s photo features of its designated Playmates finds its cine-matic equivalent in a leering camera that similarly invites and satisfies that gaze in all of these films. To begin with the obvious, we might consider the Dr. Gold-foot films—an invitation to ogle is perhaps not a startling feature in films whose titles include the phrases "bikini machine" and "girl bombs." On his command, Dr. Goldfoot's principal *robot fatale*, Diane (Susan Hart), dutifully assumes a literally traffic-stopping pin-up pose for the benefit of her destined target, Todd Armstrong (Dwayne Hickman), but also, plainly, for the benefit of anyone in the audience who may have been wondering what physical marvels had been concealed by her trench coat. A leering cinematographic style is also a common feature of the Matt Helm films, which are marked by a preference for a hip-high camera placement where their female stars are concerned: for instance, Stella Stevens is introduced into *The Silencers* as klutzy Gail Hendricks in a strikingly composed close-up two-shot: her bottom, positioned in profile at the same height as the seated Helm's head, enters the frame well before the rest of her does. In *The Wrecking Crew*, similar treatment is afforded to *femme fatale* Linka Karensky (Elke Sommer), whose sensuous walks toward and away from the camera are given close and lingering attention via a hip-high framing, as is the more agitated hip-shaking of Helm's unwanted fellow agent, Freya Carlson (Sharon Tate) as she dances for his—and the viewers'—pleasure. By comparison, the cinematography in the Derek Flint films seems relatively restrained in this regard. Still, both of those films are heavily populated by partially-clad women, in fulfillment of the promises made by the promotional materials, and the pleasures of the gaze are openly winked at by way of a recurring joke in *Our Man Flint*: the non-conforming spy declines the government's authorized code book, preferring instead a personal cypher, "a mathematical progression: 40-26-36." Each time Flint begins to explain the basis of his code, his interlocutor (first Cramden and later a taxi driver) interrupts him by saying, "I can imagine what it's based on"[39]—as can the film's audience, unavoidably complicit in the joke.

There is considerable irony, then, in the sequence in *Our Man Flint* in which Flint rescues his companions as well as his erstwhile enemy, Gila, from the clutches of their Galaxy captors, who have conditioned them to serve as "pleasure units," tending to the desires of Galaxy's male employees in the facility's "Reward Room" during the men's off-duty hours. The journey from woman to pleasure unit is demonstrated when Gila is found by her Galaxy superiors to have failed in her task of eliminating Flint: she is to be subjected to hypnosis, branded, and then effectively given over into prostitution. The Reward Room is a hybrid of a Playboy club and Disneyland, a playground of masculine pleasure. "You'll love it,"[40] Gila assures Flint, moments before she asks him to brand her in order to disguise the fact that she has not been robbed of her personality and will via the conditioning process. As Gila, now known as Pleasure Unit 736, makes her way to the "Robing Room," Flint explores the waiting area, where men congregate and consume what is presumably some sort of mood-altering pill before entering their choice from a range of themed rooms—one looks like a mock-up of ancient Rome, while another features a wild 1960s dance party— where they will be greeted by hordes of eagerly awaiting pleasure units. Flint's liberation of the women is apparently to be understood in light of his steadfast dedication to the principles of individuality and non-conformity—principles he declares both prior to accepting his mission and at the moment of its climax. "You are not a pleasure unit,"[41] he commands each of the women, thereby freeing them from their hypnotically-induced slavery and releasing them from their various demeaning tasks: dancing with, massaging and passionately kissing strange men. The irony lies in the fact that they very plainly *are* "pleasure units." Freed from their hypnotic state, they may no longer be such for the older, more heavy-set men they abandon on the massage table or the dance floor, but they remain Flint's pleasure units, since they will presumably continue to dance with, massage and kiss *him*, and otherwise serve *his* pleasure. Furthermore, dressed for the remainder of the film in the enticing outfits their Galaxy masters had chosen for them, they continue to provide more vicarious forms of pleasure outside the contained world of the film's narrative for at least some members of the audience, who are unlikely to recall their names, which are rarely spoken and of little apparent importance: their role is to adorn Flint's perfect world.

Spy vs. Feminist

The obvious anti-feminism embodied by *Playboy* and echoed throughout the spy films of the 1960s and after has been widely discussed. Barbara Ehrenreich states a very familiar view when she asserts that "from the beginning *Playboy* loved women—large-breasted, long-legged young women, anyway—and hated wives."[42] There is much evidence to support this view, beginning with early opinion pieces like "Miss Gold-Digger of 1953" (December 1953) and "Open Season on Bachelors" (June 1954),[43] which, Carrie Pitzulo suggests, typify the misogynist attitude of the magazine in its early years. Such open attacks on marriage and wives were a tactic in the campaign to redefine bachelorhood as the preferred state for men. Pitzulo's reading of the magazine's vexed relationship with the women's movement is more nuanced than Ehrenreich's, though: she observes a marked shift in the early 1960s away from such transparent "antimarriage/antiwoman vitriol."[44] Noting that *Playboy*'s support for progressive political causes in general included financial support to the American Civil Liberties Union for the cause of women's rights and a role in funding day care for working mothers, Pitzulo suggests that *Playboy* embraced a particular vision of feminism that could be reconciled with its fondness for Playmates.[45] That vision was most famously articulated by Helen Gurley Brown, first in her best-selling 1962 book, *Sex and the Single Girl*, and subsequently in *Cosmopolitan* magazine, which came under her editorship in 1965 and assumed the "fun, fearless female" identity it maintains to the present day.[46] Brown's feminism "celebrated the traditional dance of heterosexual seduction, but also called for women's economic independence and sexual and reproductive freedom."[47] More radical forms of feminist challenge, however, especially in opposition to established standards of female beauty or the heterosexual norm, were clearly incompatible with Hefner's *Playboy* philosophy and could not be borne.[48]

Among these bachelor-spy films, the challenge of feminism is most directly addressed—albeit condescendingly and dismissively—in the second of the Derek Flint films, *In Like Flint*, in which Flint must counter a distorted reflection of the feminist movement of the time: a conspiracy of deluded women bent on world domination. The architects of the revolution are three middle-aged women, Miss Elisabeth, Miss Helena, and Miss Simone, whose wealth, power and influence stem from their prominence in the areas of women's cosmetics, fashion, magazines and communications. The insistence on the title "miss" is suggestive, though, undercutting their authority even before its fragility is demonstrated in the film's plot. The headquarters of their organization, Fabulous Face, is an island resort and spa to which unsuspecting women are lured for conditioning by way of rigid-hood hair dryers that double as brainwashing devices. These appliances, Miss Elisabeth informs Flint, have for many years been employed in beauty salons all over the world, insidiously planting the seeds of dissatisfaction in the minds of otherwise contented housewives: "Every time a woman went into a beauty shop, she came out a little bit more dissatisfied with a man's world. We've been busy, Mr. Flint. I think you'll find the contented housewife is a thing of the past."[49]

Miss Elisabeth's allusion to the discontented housewife clearly recalls Betty Friedan's ground-breaking 1963 book, *The Feminine Mystique*, and its powerful dissection of "the problem that has no name"—"a strange stirring, a sense of dissatisfaction, a yearning that women suffered in the middle of the twentieth century."[50] Friedan attributed this dissatisfaction not to insidious messages emanating from hair dryers but to the confining insufficiency of "the feminine mystique," a mystified, patriarchal notion of the feminine that naturalized exclusively domestic roles for women: "The mistake, says the mystique, the root of women's troubles in the past is that women envied men, women tried to be like men, instead of accepting their own nature, which can find fulfillment only in sexual passivity, male domination, and nurturing maternal love."[51] Flint, the film's arbiter of good sense, greets the women's pretensions to power with patronizing laughter, and implicitly invokes the "natural" maternal aspect of the feminine mystique in doing so. Granting, for the sake of argument, that the inherent superiority of woman will eventually result in power falling into their laps, he wonders aloud whether women will still have "laps" when they rule the world. Almost immediately, Flint's dismissive response to the faulty logic underlying the women's plot is proven correct, as their co-conspirator General Carter and his men burst in and reveal that the women have been his dupes from the start. From this point onwards, the erstwhile feminist revolutionaries readily embrace their traditional feminine roles, putting their sex appeal behind Flint's campaign and effectively bewildering and disarming Carter's men by way of a maneuver they call "Operation Smooch."[52]

Asserting the power of an eye-catching woman to disarm a man through her ability to attract and thereby distract him, the smooching combatants of *In Like Flint* advance a troublingly familiar argument about the relationship between women and power. A woman's pretension to a man's rightful possession of authority—the foolish aim of the misses Elisabeth, Helena, and Simone—is risible, but women do have an indirect and exclusively feminine means to power rooted in their biological difference and their ability to channel their sexual appeal to men. This was a power that *Playboy* magazine—ever wary of "Miss Gold-Digger of 1953"—was careful to eschew by favoring the wholesome, unthreatening "girl next-door" in a state of semi-nudity as the object of the bachelor's desire. The 1960s spy films, on the other hand, stage a series of contests between their masculine heroes and various specimens of the dangerously attractive *femme fatale* type. Examples are everywhere in these films, from Dr. Goldfoot's alluring robots and girl bombs to Matt Helm and Derek Flint's flesh-and-blood adversaries. The first of the Matt Helm films, *The Silencers*, begins with a partial striptease by Cyd Charisse as she lip-synchs over Vikki Carr's recording of the title song, whose lyrics imaginatively usurp the phallic power of the gun to serve a woman's seductive ends by transparently equating the desirable female body with a dangerous weapon: equipped with the vital statistics 22 and 38—numbers that simultaneously measure her astonishingly curvaceous frame and, less remarkably, the calibers of gun barrels and bullets—she herself becomes the eponymous "silencer."[53] The film's title actually has no bearing at all on the film itself other than by way of this connection between the silencer on a gun and the dangerously desirable woman, a type represented in *The Silencers* by Tina and in each of the subsequent films by Coco Duquette (Camilla Sparv in *Murderer's Row*), Francesca Madeiros (Senta Berger in *The Ambushers*), and Linka Karensky (Elke Sommer in *The Wrecking Crew*). The theme song and opening credits of *The Ambushers* similarly misidentify the film's title with a horde of bikini-clad dancers who will "get you in the sun" or "the shade" or wherever they please,[54] but whose role in the films ends when the credits do. The woman-as-bombshell cliché is made literal in *Dr. Goldfoot and the Girl Bombs*, in which the evil scientist's second generation of synthetic women are equipped with proximity fuses: "Just get too close and have too many right or wrong vibrations, and poof!—a wonderful explosion that destroys not only my girl bombs, but their victims as well."[55] Their revealing clothing (the gold *lamé* bikini is heavily favored) and tempting ways ensure that those "right or wrong vibrations" will be produced in virtually every case.

Spy vs. Teenager

The *femme fatale* is hardly a novel creature of the 1960s, but the iconography of these particular variations on the type—the newly revealing clothing styles, such as the mini-skirt and, above all, the bikini—is, arguably, revealing in more than just a literal sense, suggestive of a female sexuality whose wildness exceeds the bounds of the more sedate *Playboy* ideal. According to R.L. Rutsky, the bikini first was first introduced in 1946, mere days after headlines all over the world announced the first atomic test explosion in the Bikini Atoll. The association between the skimpy swimsuit's design and the atomic bomb appears, he suggests, "to have contributed to its *succès de scandale*, conveying a sense of 'explosive,' uncontrolled sexuality while nevertheless retaining the exotic and sexual connotations of life in the 'South Seas.'"[56] These connotations of a wild exoticism taken on by the wearer of the bikini are extended to youth culture in general in the glut of films and pop songs that turned the surfing subculture of the 1950s into a mainstream popular craze in the early 1960s, from *Gidget* (1959, Paul Wendkos) to *How to Stuff a Wild Bikini* (1965, William Asher) and from "Surfin' Bird" (1963, The Trashmen) to "Ride the Wild Surf" (1964, Jan and Dean). Rutsky contends that the appeal of the teen beach movies lay in "the attractiveness of nonconformist, irreverent, and anti-bourgeois attitudes cobbled together from elements of teenage culture, rock-and-roll, bohemian philosophy, and beat culture and mixed with a heavy dose of parody."[57] The culture on display in the surf movies (and music), in other words, offered an appealing taste of rebellion available specifically, exclusively, to the young.

The Dr. Goldfoot films, especially the first, all–American production, are indebted at least as much to American International Picture's (AIP) own Beach Party series as they are to the Bond films. The AIP series, launched in 1963 with the trend-setting *Beach Party* (1963, William Asher), brought the low-budget studio its greatest commercial success. *Dr. Goldfoot and the Bikini Machine* features a cast lifted directly from that ongoing series, including its young male star, Frankie Avalon, supporting actor Dwayne Hickman, and, in a succession of cameo appearances, Deborah Walley, Aron Kincaid, Annette Funicello, and Harvey Lembeck. The filmmakers clearly anticipate their core audience finding their way into this new variation on their familiar "beach" formula: Lembeck appears, to no purpose in this film's plot, in the costume of his recurring character in the Beach Party series—the motorcycling scoundrel, Eric Von Zipper—and Funicello's brief appearance is accompanied by a direct-to-camera double take on the part of both her and her usual co-star, Frankie Avalon. The film's end credits even include a message promoting AIP's *The Ghost in the Invisible Bikini* (1966, Don Weis), scheduled for release a few months later and featuring Dr. Goldfoot's principle robot-seductress, Susan Hart, in the title role. Thus, while the Dr. Goldfoot films nod toward the Bond films via, for instance, the titles' play on *Goldfinger* (1964, Guy Hamilton) and the unfortunate Todd Armstrong's designation as Agent 00½, "the Bikini Machine" and its shimmying, bikini-clad products gesture elsewhere, toward the contemporary surf movies produced by AIP and their imitators—and toward a new, distinctively raucous and zany youth culture.

The Bond films of the 1960s, following the lead of decidedly unhip author

Ian Fleming, generally steer clear of any direct acknowledgement of the decade's burgeoning youth culture. The one memorable exception occurs in *Goldfinger*, and the tone is unsympathetic. *Goldfinger* was released late in 1964, the year of "Beatlemania," in which the Liverpool quartet appeared for the first time in the U.S., most famously on *The Ed Sullivan Show*; made their film debut in *A Hard Day's Night* (1964, Richard Lester); and saw no fewer than seven long-playing albums cobbled together by their American label, Capitol. As Bond enjoys his time with Goldfinger's former companion, Jill Masterson (Shirley Eaton), he instructs her that "drinking Dom Pérignon '53 above a temperature of 38° Fahrenheit" is "as bad as listening to the Beatles without ear muffs,"[58] sounding very much like the curmudgeonly father of a young Beatles fan.

The Dr. Goldfoot films are obviously immersed in the youth culture that Bond disdains, but the Flint and Helm films also acknowledge more directly this new, rival notion of cool. As Bond's mildly grumpy allusion to the Beatles would suggest, the key indicators of this acknowledgement are the forms of music and dance on display. While the Bond themes of the 1960s often crept into the pop charts, their style tended toward the easy listening end of the spectrum, even in the case of "You Only Live Twice," whose singer, Nancy Sinatra, had one go-go booted foot planted firmly in the teen pop market. The Flint films mostly follow suit with their theme music and scores by Jerry Goldsmith, but the Helm films offer a more mixed assortment. Vikki Carr's performance of "The Silencers" bears some resemblance to the Bond themes, particularly Shirley Bassey's rendition of "Goldfinger," and the films' many musical cues feature Dean Martin's own recordings sharing space with instrumental music composed by the likes of Elmer Bernstein, Lalo Schifrin and Hugo Montenegro—the latter two familiar makers of the "easy" 1960s sound. The dialogue also abounds in worn, self-reflexive allusions to Dean Martin's fellow Rat Pack alumnus, Frank Sinatra, and rival crooner Perry Como. However, the Helm films also wade more determinedly into younger, hipper sounds, with Hugo Montenegro and Herbert Baker's upbeat theme for *The Ambushers* providing a suitable backdrop for the bikini-wearing dancers of that film's opening credits and the pounding 4/4 beat of the Boyce and Hart-penned "If You're Thinking What I'm Thinking" sounding entirely at home amidst the youth in the discotheque scene in *Murderers' Row*.

Groovy discotheque scenes simply do not feature in the Bond films, so there is no threat of 007 being drawn on to a dance floor where the distinctive jerking and shimmying dance moves of the decade are on display. That fate awaits poor Dean Martin as Matt Helm, though, in *Murderers' Row*, where, adding further insult and possible risk of injury, he is paired with a frantically gyrating Ann-Margret who is, and appears, half his age. While Suzie (Ann-Margret) cycles through a workout's worth of dance moves, a pained-looking and barely mobile Helm responds with a series of ironic comments and questions: "This is dancing?"; "You'll break something!"; "Don't you think we should be introduced first?"[59] His situation is not aided by the presence in the scene of Martin's teenaged son, one third of the performing band, Dino, Desi, and Billy, or the in-joke that has the younger Martin saying to the older one, "Hey, now you're swinging, Dad!" The hipster sense of "dad" is hard to hear in the moment, especially in light of Helm's subsequent comment about "the way they're wearing their hair nowadays."[60] James Coburn's Flint emerges from a go-go scene in *Our Man Flint* considerably less scathed, but there, too, the encounter between Flint's *Playboy*-flavored hipness and the younger, wilder version on display in Galaxy's ersatz dance club is not an easy one.

Conclusion

For a very brief period in the mid–1960s, the playboy spy emerged somewhere very near the center of Western conceptions of masculinity and modernity. A hybrid of an established popular type—the spy—and an emergent one—the bachelor-playboy—the 1960s bachelor-spy offers a revealing look at notions of manhood amidst changing understandings of work, leisure and consumption; marriage and bachelorhood; the growing presence of technologies of convenience; and the shifting sexual relations that brought the playboy into existence. While Bond is unquestionably at the focal point of this cultural moment, some of its more peripheral figures perhaps reveal its uncertain, transitional nature with particular clarity. The Bond, Flint and Helm films are all invested to some degree in notions of "cool" shaped in an earlier time and waning in the 1960s, giving way before the onslaught of newer and wilder forms of youth culture. *Playboy*, the self-appointed arbiter of stylish hipness in the 1950s, found itself struggling with the flourishing youth culture and clinging to its cocktails and tuxedos while much of the world began to slough off jackets and ties *en route* to sandals and beads. Carrie Pitzulo describes a conflict within the editorial offices of the magazine as the growing gulf between *Playboy*'s refined sense of style and the more relaxed cultures of youth became more apparent. Hefner apparently took exception to the inelegance of a February 1968 food feature accompanied by photographs of "two dashing couples erupting into a food fight," prompting an exchange of memos in which some of his editors expressed concerns that the magazine risked irrelevance.[61] Today, the very notion of the "playboy" seems a quaint relic, fixed in that postwar world out of which *Playboy* emerged, along with Bond and the numerous playboy spies who came in his wake. These American spy films—always more attuned to the masculine consumerist ethos upon which Hugh Hefner drew and that his magazine did so much to shape and communicate—also throw into relief the awkward but inevitable collision of yesterday's style and today's. Modernity and masculinity alike are targets no less shifting than the iconic image of 007 viewed through the barrel of a gun.

Notes

1. Tony Bennett and Janet Woollacott, "The Moments of Bond," in *The James Bond Phenomenon: A Critical Reader*, 2d ed., ed. Christoph Lindner (Manchester: Manchester University Press, 2009), 19.
2. Adrian Turner, *Adrian Turner on "Goldfinger"* (London: Bloomsbury, 1998), 55.
3. Bennett and Woollacott, "The Moments of Bond," 19.
4. The follow-up to *Dr. Goldfoot and the Bikini Machine* was actually produced in Italy, with joint American and Italian financing. Vincent Price reprised his role as the camp villain, Dr. Goldfoot, but the young agent out to foil his plot was played by Fabian, replacing Frankie Avalon, and the other key roles were filled by Italian actors, including Laura Antonelli and the popular Italian comedy duo Franco Franchi and Ciccio Ingrassia. The latter pair were given top billing in the Italian version of the film, *Le spie vengono dal semifreddo* ("The Spy Who Came in from the Semi-Cold").
5. "Playbill," *Playboy* (March 1960), 1, quoted in Bill Osgerby, *Playboys in Paradise: Masculinity, Youth and Leisure-style in Modern America* (Oxford: Berg, 2001), 159.
6. James Chapman, *Licence to Thrill: A Cultural History of the James Bond Films* (London: I.B. Tauris, 2007), 36.
7. Osgerby, *Playboys in Paradise*, 8–9.
8. Ibid., 19.
9. Barbara Ehrenreich, *The Hearts of Men: American Dreams and the Flight from Commitment* (Garden City, NY: Anchor Doubleday, 1983), 17.
10. Ibid., 19–20.
11. *Oxford English Dictionary*, 2d ed., s.v. "bachelor."
12. Ibid.
13. *Oxford English Dictionary*, 2d ed., s.v. "playboy."
14. Osgerby, *Bachelors in Paradise*, 35.
15. Carrie Pitzulo, *Bachelors and Bunnies: The Sexual Politics of Playboy* (Chicago: University of Chicago Press, 2011), 73.
16. "What Sort of Man Reads *Playboy*?" *Playboy*, April 1965, 63.
17. Ibid.
18. "What Sort of Man Reads *Playboy*?" *Playboy*, May 1962, 45.
19. Pitzulo, *Bachelors and Bunnies*, 78.
20. *Our Man Flint*, DVD, directed by Daniel Mann (1966; Beverly Hills: Twentieth Century–Fox Home Entertainment, 2002).
21. *The Silencers*, DVD, directed by Phil Karlson (1966; Culver City, CA: Sony Pictures Home Entertainment, 2005).
22. Ibid.
23. I am limiting my discussion here to the six films released by Eon Productions that featured Sean Connery (and, for one film, George Lazenby) in the title role. A seventh Bond film of the 1960s, *Casino Royale* (1967), was a barely coherent spoof released by another studio. It bears little resemblance to Fleming's novel or the film series that Eon Productions launched in 1962 with *Dr. No*.

24. *Murderers' Row*, DVD, directed by Henry Levin (1966; Culver City, CA: Sony Pictures Home Entertainment, 2005).

25. Beatriz Preciado, "Pornotopia," in *Cold War Hothouses: Inventing Postwar Culture, from Cockpit to Playboy*, ed. Beatriz Colomina, AnnMarie Brennan, and Jeannie Kim (New York: Princeton Architectural Press, 2004), 239, 252.

26. "*Playboy*'s Penthouse Apartment [I]," *Playboy*, September 1956, 53–60; "*Playboy*'s Penthouse Apartment [II]," *Playboy*, October 1956, 65–70; and "The Playboy Town House," *Playboy*, May 1962, 83–92, 105.

27. "*Playboy*'s Penthouse Apartment [I]," 54.

28. Ibid.

29. Ibid.

30. Ibid., 59.

31. *Playboy*'s Penthouse Apartment [II]," 68.

32. "The Playboy Town House," 92.

33. Preciado, "Pornotopia," 240.

34. *Dr. Goldfoot and the Bikini Machine*, DVD, directed by Norman Taurog (1965; Beverly Hills CA: TGG Direct/Twentieth Century–Fox Home Entertainment, 2012).

35. *In Like Flint*, DVD, directed by Gordon Douglas (1967; Beverly Hills: Twentieth Century–Fox Home Entertainment, 2002).

36. "*Playboy*'s Penthouse Apartment [I]," 59–60.

37. *In Like Flint.*

38. Jules Archer, "Don't Hate Yourself in the Morning," *Playboy* (August 1955), 21, quoted in Carrie Pitzulo, *Bachelors and Bunnies: The Sexual Politics of Playboy* (Chicago: University of Chicago Press, 2011), 25.

39. *Our Man Flint.*

40. Ibid.

41. Ibid.

42. Ehrenreich, *The Hearts of Men*, 42.

43. Bob Norman [Burt Zollo], "Miss Gold-Digger of 1953," *Playboy*, undated first issue [December 1953], 6–8; and Burt Zollo, "Open Season on Bachelors," *Playboy*, June 1954, 37–38.

44. Pitzulo, *Bachelors and Bunnies*, 24, 105; and see also Ehrenreich, *The Hearts of Men*, 42.

45. Pitzulo, *Bachelors and Bunnies*, 129.

46. Ibid.

47. Ibid., 127–29.

48. Ibid., 129.

49. *In Like Flint.*

50. Betty Friedan, *The Feminine Mystique* (1963; repr., New York: W.W. Norton, 2013), 9.

51. Ibid., 33.

52. *In Like Flint.*

53. *The Silencers.*

54. *The Ambushers*, DVD, directed by Henry Levin (1967: Culver City, CA: Sony Pictures Home Entertainment, 2005).

55. *Dr. Goldfoot and the Bikini Machine.*

56. R.L. Rutsky, "Surfing the Other: Ideology on the Beach," *Film Quarterly* 52, no. 4 (1999): 19.

57. Ibid., 13.

58. *Goldfinger*, DVD, directed by Guy Hamilton (1964; Beverly Hills: Twentieth Century–Fox Home Entertainment, 2006).

59. *Murderers' Row.*

60. Ibid.

61. Pitzulo, *Bachelors and Bunnies*, 99.

Bibliography

The Ambushers. DVD. Directed by Henry Levin. 1967; Culver City, CA: Sony Pictures Home Entertainment, 2005.

Archer, Jules. "Don't Hate Yourself in the Morning." *Playboy* (August 1955), 21. Quoted in Carrie Pitzulo, *Bachelors and Bunnies: The Sexual Politics of Playboy* (Chicago: University of Chicago Press, 2011).

Bennett, Tony, and Janet Woollacott. "The Moments of Bond." In *The James Bond Phenomenon: A Critical Reader*, 2d ed., edited by Christoph Lindner, 13–33. Manchester: Manchester University Press, 2009.

Chapman, James. *Licence to Thrill: A Cultural History of the James Bond Films.* London: I.B. Tauris, 2007.

Dr. Goldfoot and the Bikini Machine. DVD. Directed by Norman Taurog. 1965; Beverly Hills: TGG Direct/Twentieth Century–Fox Home Entertainment, 2012.

Dr. Goldfoot and the Girl Bombs. DVD. Directed by Mario Bava. 1966; Beverly Hills: TGG Direct/Twentieth Century–Fox Home Entertainment, 2012.

Dr. No. DVD. Directed by Terence Young. 1962; Beverly Hills: Twentieth Century–Fox Home Entertainment, 2006.

Ehrenreich, Barbara. *The Hearts of Men: American Dreams and the Flight from Commitment.* Garden City, NY: Anchor and Doubleday, 1983.

Friedan, Betty. *The Feminine Mystique.* 1963. Reprint, New York: W.W. Norton, 2013.

Goldfinger. DVD. Directed by Guy Hamilton. 1964; Beverly Hills: Twentieth Century–Fox Home Entertainment, 2006).

In Like Flint. DVD. Directed by Gordon Douglas. 1967; Beverly Hills: Twentieth Century–Fox Home Entertainment, 2002.

Murderers' Row. DVD. Directed by Henry Levin. 1966; Culver City, CA: Sony Pictures Home Entertainment, 2005.

Norman, Bob (Burt Zollo). "Miss Gold-Digger of 1953." *Playboy,* December 1953, 6–8.

Osgerby, Bill. *Playboys in Paradise: Masculinity, Youth and Leisure-style in Modern America.* Oxford: Berg, 2001.

Our Man Flint. DVD. Directed by Daniel Mann. 1966; Beverly Hills: Twentieth Century–Fox Home Entertainment, 2002.

Pitzulo, Carrie. *Bachelors and Bunnies: The Sexual Politics of Playboy.* Chicago: University of Chicago Press, 2011.

"The Playboy Town House." *Playboy,* May 1962, 83–92, 105.

"*Playboy*'s Penthouse Apartment [I]." *Playboy,* September 1956, 53–60.

"*Playboy*'s Penthouse Apartment [II]." *Playboy,* October 1956, 65–70.

Preciado, Beatriz. "Pornotopia." In *Cold War Hothouses: Inventing Postwar Culture from Cockpit to Playboy,* edited by Beatriz Colomina, AnnMarie Brennan and Jeannie Kim, 216–253. New York: Princeton Architectural Press, 2004.

Rutsky, R.L. "Surfing the Other: Ideology on the Beach." *Film Quarterly* 52.4 (1999): 12–23.

The Silencers. DVD. Directed by Phil Karlson. 1966; Culver City, CA: Sony Pictures Home Entertainment, 2005.

Turner, Adrian. *Adrian Turner on "Goldfinger."* Bloomsbury Movie Guides No. 2. London: Bloomsbury, 1998.

"What Sort of Man Reads *Playboy* ?" *Playboy,* April 1965.

"What Sort of Man Reads *Playboy* ?" *Playboy,* May 1962.

The Wrecking Crew. DVD. Directed by Phil Karlson. 1968; Culver City, CA: Sony Pictures Home Entertainment, 2005.

Zollo, Burt. "Open Season on Bachelors." *Playboy,* June 1954, 37–38.

Part Five

Reinterpretations

Archer
A Spy Parody for the Ears

IAN DAWE

Archer (2009–2014) is a remarkable animated spy/fantasy TV program first broadcast on the FX network in the U.S. Created by Adam Reed, it continues into its fifth, 13-episode season as of January 2014, and attracts a growing number of viewers in the U.S., numbering over 1.5 million per episode for much of Season 4.[1] The show features a cast of characters Sterling Archer, a superspy for the private spy service agency "International Secret Intelligence Service" (or, "ISIS"), headed by his mother, Malory. Other characters include his fellow agent and sometimes love interest, Lana Kane. Rounding out the corporate and office staff: comptroller Cyril Figgis; secretary Cheryl Tunt, who sometimes goes by the name Carol; HR director Pam Poovey; scientist "Doctor" Krieger; and analyst Ray Gillette, voiced by creator Adam Reed. The show mines familiar workplace comedy territory, with its accompanying sexual rivalries and banter, but this takes place in the environment of the superspy genre set in an unspecified mid–20th-century year, possibly the mid–1980s. Visually, the show has a highly "realistic" look, with painted 3D background and characters rendered based on life models, sometimes the voice actors themselves, with a great visual debt to 1960s genre comic books and animated series such as *Jonny Quest* (1964–1965).

Archer is clearly a parodic show, and one in the service of comedic ends. One of the strongest elements of the show's sense of parody comes from its use of, and arguable obsession with, sound. In a program with superspies jetting off on far-flung clandestine adventures and reporting to strong, influential political and business interests, there is an almost shocking lack of deference among the characters, particularly Archer himself. Unlike the programs that are the target of parody, where keen groups of young adventurers happily carry out missions in the service of stern-voiced authority figures, here the authorities are often presented as complete buffoons, such as recurring character Nikolai Jakov of the KGB, or the rapacious alcoholic narcissist, Malory Archer. The younger characters, epitomized by Sterling Archer himself, are universally skeptical of authority and constantly make wisecracks about their competence and character, questioning everything about most of their missions. The aural tone of the show—wisecracking agents with incompetent or egotistical supervisors—stands in stark contrast to the visual patina of mid-century espionage efficiency. *Archer* also extracts parody from the focus on inter-office personal dynamics, including workplace comedy clichés arising from sexual affairs, after-work visits to the pub, employee evaluations and random drug testing. The deliberate opposition of the mundane with the fantastic milieu is a clear and obvious element of the show's parodic sensibilities.

One of the elements that sets *Archer* apart from similarly parodic and satirical shows is its focus on the aural, including linguistics. Language and linguistic misunderstanding is, of course, a cornerstone of comedy and parody; one need only think of Abbot and Costello's "Who's on First" for example. Given that the visual aspects of the show are faithful to the target of parody (mid-century superspies), its aural elements seem to have been appropriated wholesale from a College-age comedy, in which the deliberate juxtaposition is one of the show's strongest and most consistent tools of oppositional parody. Furthermore, an examination of the linguistic aspects of *Archer* can lead to an understanding of the show's psychosexual and parodic peculiarities.

"That was ambiguously worded!" Archer's *Linguistic Focus*

In order to demonstrate *Archer*'s linguistic focus, it is necessary to examine some data. In *Archer* there appear to be three basic manifestations of language: (a) explicit mention of grammar, phrasing or wording; (b) mention of hearing loss or aural phenomena, including nonsensical verbal exclamations such as "Nooope!" and the characteristic "calling of names" that features in *Archer*, discussed in full below; and (c) reference to non–English languages. All episodes from Seasons 3 and 4 were watched and whenever an instance of any of those three phenomena occurred, it was noted. For example, if a witty turn of phrase such as a character mentioning phrasing occurred, the episode would get a mark in category "a." If characters discussed a foreign language, as, for example, in Season 4's "The Papal Chase," there is a discussion of which language is spoken by the Pope's Swiss Guards, that sort of occurrence would result in a note in category "c." And finally if the characters were exposed to loud gunfire or any other aural occurrence leading to hearing damage or loss, often accompanied on the show's soundtrack with a high pitched ringing, symbolizing tinnitus, this instance would be noticed in category "b." The data below presented in Table 1 represent summed scores for all three categories combined.

Table 13.1: Frequency of Linguistic References in Seasons 3 and 4 of *Archer*

	# of Episodes	Linguistic References (Mean #/per episode, +/ standard deviation of each data set)
Season 3	13	10.1 +/– 4.6
Season 4	13	11.4 +/– 2.4

The data presented in Table 13.1 indicate the frequency of linguistic or aural references in *Archer* as described above. It can clearly been seen that there is a significant amount of time spent on this linguistic issue, particularly for a program with episodes of only twenty minutes. By that measure, there is a linguistic reference in Season 3 approximately every two minutes of screen time, with one episode ("Space Race, Part II") having 21 references, or one per minute. Season 4 is comparable, with an average of 11.4 references per episode, with the individual episode frequencies more evenly weighted in terms of linguistic emphasis, thus the far lower standard deviation in the statistical means.

Some of these references include puns or ironic witticisms, such as Archer's line from "The Man from Jupiter" (Season 3, Episode 4), "I can't hear you over the sound of my giant throbbing erection."[2] Others take the form of Archer, quietly, to himself, mulling over the word, "cookiepuss" in Season 3, Episode 7. Or, characters creating new words to suit a peculiar situation, such as when Malory called Cheryl/Carol a "whorediot," which, she explains, is "a whore who dresses like an idiot."[3] Where it fits, foreign languages feature in the plot in several creative ways, such as in Season 3, Episode 10, "Crossing Over," where Archer asks, "What's Russian for 'Duh'?"[4] This pan-linguistic language use even extends to Archer having substantial dialogue scenes with a chicken in Season 3, Episode 9 or Cheryl/Carol's ocelot, Babu in Season 3, Episode 6. Many of the characters' insults directed at each other take a linguistic form. Malory, for example, chastises Ray for making a teeth sucking sound in Season 4, Episode 2, by saying, "If you want to keep those teeth, you won't suck them at me!"[5] Another link to sound is the frequent appearance of images of sonic waveforms on the monitor screens of ISIS when an exclusively aural telephone conversation is taking place. The waveforms appear to be generated in real-time, a technological achievement that would be remarkable for any time period prior to the late 1990s. This slight anachronistic touch appears to be in the service of highlighting the importance of sound, particularly speech, to the show.

The preoccupation with grammar and phrasing sometimes leads characters to yell out words like "Phrasing!" often when a particular turn of phrase uttered by one of the characters could be taken as a sexual reference, and such a reference is unwelcome, or the wonderfully telling line in Season 4, Episode 7, where Archer comments, with exasperation, "That was ambiguously worded!"[6] An effective and strong example of this thematic preoccupation appears in "Heart of Archness: Part II" (Season 3, Episode 2), where Archer is addressing Malay pirates using anthropologist Noah as his interpreter. Archer keeps uttering statements such as "You don't change horses in mid-stream."[7] Noah has to remind him that idiomatic expressions don't translate well to people without a shared cultural frame of reference. Archer struggles to make himself understood without the use of idioms, but ultimately breaks down, commenting on how often language makes use of idioms. The notion of Archer, posing as a pirate king, struggling to make himself understood is reasonably typical fare for a show that extracts comedy from awkward situations. The scene plays out effectively as comedy, before one realizes that these are two characters in a spyfi/superspy animated TV show having a long exchange about something very particularly anthropological and linguistic.

Other sonic devices are employed creatively by *Archer*. For example, the show uses drawn out pauses during dialogue to extend and reinforce comedic moments. This is a common enough tool in live-action comedy with deep roots in vaudeville, but other than occasionally being used in the Chuck Jones/Warner Brothers cartoons, one does not encounter prolonged silences in animation. This makes perfect technical sense: animation is labor-intensive and when combined with only 21 minutes per episode, one can understand how the creators would prefer not to spend resources adding silent passages to scenes that still require animation. But in the case of *Archer*, jokes are given the time to register, varying the pace of the show and sonically placing it closer to the world of live action.

Another signature device is bridging two scenes with dialogue, often a single word or line. Scenes may end with a question to which the answer is a yes or no, and then the next scene will begin with the dialogue "yes" or "no," spinning comedic effect from the juxtaposition of the answer to one question with another in a different context. This technique, once again rarely seen in animation, not only creates more jokes but blends the episodes together in a creative way that highlights the centrality of sound in their construction. Non-verbal sound, or any other kind of sound, seems to form the basis of the communication between all of the characters in *Archer*. Their desire to be heard and make themselves heard assumes a primacy that can be interpreted as psychological, in addition to comic.

Being Heard: Archer's Demands

Any viewer of *Archer* is likely to be struck by the way characters call to each other in an urgent, insistent way. This comes up particularly in the relationship between Archer and Lana, but others participate in the calling as well. In almost every episode, often several times, Archer will call out for Lana even though she is in close proximity in an increasingly urgent "Lana. Lana! LANA!!," which Lana responds with an exasperated "WHAT?!" This signature trope is itself parodied as the series goes on, with Cheryl, Pam and even Malory Archer going through similar exercises with each other. For example, in Episode 11 of Season 4, Lana points out to Malory how silly Pam looks dressed as a nun by pointing to her and rhetorically asking:

> MALORY. Pam?
> PAM. What?
> LANA. Pam?
> PAM. (Responds again.) What?
> ARCHER. (Observes the conversation and spontaneously yells) Pam!
> PAM. (Shouts her signature line.) What?!
> ARCHER. (Responds, chuckling bemusedly.) I don't know. What are we doing?[8]

Clearly, it is very important in this show for characters to be heard. However, it also seems to be important that characters not be heard too quickly by the listener, bringing up themes of power, demand, control and psychological repression.

In order to understand this theme, we must examine one of the models of childhood development, Lacan's "mirror stage." Lacan describes three states of perception that humans move through in the normal course of their development, the Real, the Imaginary and the Symbolic.[9] The "Real" is simply that, reality, unaffected by language or culture or any other artifice. Lacan proposes that we humans experience this reality only as infants. Further experience of the "Real" is impossible because of the consequences of adult development. "The Real hence would be whatever is beyond, behind or beneath phenomenal appearances accessible to the direct experiences of first person awareness."[10] The "Imaginary" is experienced during the mirror stage, when we humans become aware that there is a physical body associated with our their existence and that it is different from the one our their mothers posses. The mirror stage is characterized by two main features pertinent to our discussion: the fragmented body and the state of demand. Passage from this mirror stage to an adolescent and later adult stage is made possible by the acquisition of language, because it is language that gives structure to the "Symbolic" world and which obliges us to enter into a state of submission to its order, termed the "Symbolic Order." In particular,

Lacan refers to the order of the law of the father, a symbolic statement implying, among other things, a submission to the patriarchy.[11]

The difference between demand, which is experienced in the mirror stage with the Imaginary, and desire, experienced in adulthood upon entry into the Symbolic, is subtle but significant in the analysis of Archer. In psychological terms, "demand" is the urgent cry of an individual to an "other" (in some models, this is the "mother") to satisfy their every need. But demand, by its nature, calls upon the other for needs that cannot be fulfilled. Lacan writes, "In this way, demand annuls the particularity of everything that can be granted, by transmuting it into a proof of love, and the very satisfaction demand obtains for need are debased to the point of being no more than the crushing brought on by the demand for love...."[12] Archer's demands for every manner of thing (guns, women, alcohol, money) can be read simply as an extension of his unquenchable thirst for love. Passage from the mirror stage into the next stage of maturity transmutes "demand" into "desire." Lacan's differentiation between demand and desire is simply that desire is what remains when need is subtracted from demand.[13] This equation implies inherently that desire will not be fulfilled, and it emerges from the imposition of limits, or order, on the universal demands of one in the mirror stage.

These limitations, symbolized by the law of language and the order it imposes on the imaginary manifested in the mirror stage, require an understanding and appreciation of aural phenomena to be respected. In psychological and sexual terms, what this means is that in the adult stage there are things we can't have, but we still want. We call this "desire" and it is distinct from "demand," which characterizes the mirror stage. In the desire stage we may desire something but we know we cannot have it, therefore the desire remains unfulfilled but motivational. In the mirror stage, the individual simply demands. It does not realize that there are things it cannot have.

The fragmented body comes about due to the difference between the body we see in the mirror and the body we have been told we posses. It is a product of cognitive dissonance between idealization and reality, and the solution to that dissonance is often to "fragment" or fetishize certain body parts. This might be eyes, legs, hair, breasts: whichever is most able to satisfy the illusory demands of the psyche.

Sterling Archer is trapped in the mirror stage because he cannot adequately acquire language. This is reflected in his narcissistic body worship (his hair, for example) and his state of demand. Archer in fact exhibits all the classic qualities of a child in the mirror stage. He does not yearn, or pine, or desire. He demands and takes, and his demand is ultimately always for love. For Archer, getting something is as easy as reaching out and taking it. Even, and acquires through perhaps especially, attention. Thus, we have his urgent calling out, combined with his fetishism combined with his ego.

Archer is, in truth, calling out for his mother, or whatever symbolic authority he puts in his mother's place, but either way he is acting on a childish demand rather than an adult desire. Archer's desperate need to be at the center of attention in almost every situation is a function of his desperate need to be heard. Interestingly, it is "given" that Archer will be seen, as with all other members of the ISIS team. His preoccupation with his appearance, not to mention the phallic extension of his cars, seems to indicate a healthy, if indeed overdeveloped, ego. But this is an illusion when examined closely, because all of this is a symptom of Archer's obsession with his own fragmented body. For, the worst scenario imaginable is one in which he cannot be heard. It becomes doubly ironic that his hearing is quite possibly his weakest physical attribute, but it is that specific weakness which gives us an important window into the character's psychology.

In the theoretical Lacanian framework, the order is generally imposed by the father.[14] Significantly, Sterling Archer has no father on the show, and this search for a father figure (emotional or biological) is an absolutely central aspect of his character. His mother, Malory, has a sexual history that is densely populated and with a wide variety of candidates. Almost every age-appropriate male that appears on the show is suggested as Archer's potential father, including Jakov of the KGB, Len Drexler of a competing espionage organization called "ODIN" (that name is itself a paternal reference) and the one character who Archer would welcome as a father figure, actor Burt Reynolds. The show spends a great deal of time exploring Archer's personal history, including several flashbacks to his distant, abusive mother and his valet, Woodhouse, who helped raise him and continues to serve him. Flashback scenes reveal a younger Malory who has no time for the child–Archer, because she is an agent of espionage herself, and completely self-absorbed. The adult Archer has nothing but contempt for his mother and chafes under the control she continues to exercise over his life while simultaneously choosing to remain under her control and enjoying the freedom and power that comes along with her sanction. Unlike other ISIS employees, Archer has freedom to indulge in sexually or chemically irresponsible behavior that he exploits at every opportunity. Other members of the ISIS team eventually abuse Malory's occasionally indulgent management style, such as Ray Gillette's abuse of the corporate credit card for enjoying fine dining in "Heart of Archness: Part II" but not the same degree as Archer. This is because they, unlike Sterling himself, have moved from the mirror stage and have learned to submit to the order presented. They do not need to call out in order to be heard, because they have moved from demand to desire.

Hearing Damage, Arrested Development and the Fragmented Body

Archer, unlike so many shows of its type, goes out of its way to highlight the noises caused by guns and explosions and the damage that can be inflicted upon a human being in close proximity. In the Season 3 three-part opening episodes titled "Heart of Archness," Archer, Lana, anthropologist Noah and veteran agent Rip Riley are trapped in a small cell in the dungeon of a South Pacific pirate fortress. A bomb is dropped into the cell and explodes. The show's soundtrack reduces to muted thuds combined with the characteristic "ringing" sounds of tinnitus. Though the characters recover, this is only one of several instances in this show where the theme of hearing loss is examined. Archer himself occasionally comments on it, admitting that he has to "sleep with a fan on" to combat the debilitating effects of tinnitus from which he continues to suffer as a result of his work.

To focus on hearing loss is a curious dramatic choice, as characters are thrown long distances, shot, stabbed, cut, have their clothing burned off in explosions, and undergo all manner of physical abuse. Hearing loss is the only health issue, other than Ray's paralysis and Archer's two-episode bout with cancer, which any character seems to chronically suffer from. Acknowledgement of *any* long-term health effects of the "superspy" lifestyle is exceptional in the genre. One could imagine, for example, James Bond undergoing treatment for liver failure, certainly a wide variety of sexually transmitted diseases, lingering effects of metabolic poisons and even radiation sickness. The genre demands that its heroes be superhuman, therefore Bond always emerges unscathed. Daniel Craig's bumps and bruises in *Casino Royale* (2006, Martin Campbell) aside, he recovers from defibrillation in record time, missing only one hand of poker and a drink.) *Archer* follows this pattern with the exceptions noted above, but the overarching theme is that of hearing loss.

There are several possible interpretations of this motif. One could simply be that, of the chronic health consequences of the lifestyle, hearing loss is the easiest to depict in an animated show, where soundtrack work can be completed in much less time than changes to character animation and so on. There is, however, a curious psychological/linguistic interpretation that may be illuminating for this discussion.

When Archer complains of the repeated insults to his hearing, it provides a glimpse into his inner psycho-sexual trauma. Perhaps Archer wants to hear and join the Symbolic Order provided by language, which would, after all, ultimately lead to him assuming the dominant masculine position and allow him to speak from authority. But each time his hearing undergoes physical trauma, he is driven further back into the pre-language state of infancy, back to his mother's arms in front of the mirror, only able to see the black-haired, square-jawed well-muscled superspy.

In the mirror stage, one is faced with the dichotomy of appreciating the "real" reflection, or the true appearance of the body versus the "ideal" body of the imagination, reinforced very often by parental sentiment ("What a lovely little boy you are," etc.). The ego, which develops partially as a mechanism to retain elements of the imagined identity following the encounter with the real, but it is defined by external forces and perhaps is even situated externally.[15] "The ego ... [is] a repository for the projected desires and fantasies of larger others: the child's image is a receptacle for his/her parents' dreams and wishes, with his/her body image being always-already overwritten by signifiers flowing from the libidinal economies of other speaking beings."[16] Note that "speaking" is an essential part of this ego reinforcement, and the essential tool for the formation of an ego that complements and overcomes the mirror stage identity.

In response to the difference, particularly in terms of childhood, between a clumsy physical reality and an idealized adult identity, termed by Lacan the "Ideal-I," the experience of the "fragmented body" emerges.[17] The fragmented body comes about due to the difference between the body we see in the mirror and the body we have been told we posses. This fragmentation results from at once idealization of the physical and fetishization of those bodily parts that are the focus of a parents' attention on an infant (mouth, anus, penis, vagina, hair), and identification with the means of suturing all of those together into a coherent whole, namely the reconstitution of the infant/mother bond.[18] In adulthood, the bodily fragmentation. It is a product of cognitive dissonance between idealization and reality, and the solution to that dissonance is often to "fragment" or fetishize certain body parts. This might be eyes, legs, hair, breasts: whichever is most able to satisfy the illusory demands of the psyche. This is reflected, for example, in his narcissistic body worship (his hair, for example) and impulses that owe more to demand than desire and his state of demand. But this is an illusion when examined closely, because all of this is a symptom of Archer's obsession with his own fragmented body.

The style of this animated program is by its nature given to producing "idealized" images. This is traditional in the cartoon medium, to represent idealized or exaggerated bodies. In *Archer*, even the characters such as Pam, whose body type falls slightly off the norm for animated cartoon images, particularly of women, are drawn to an ideal rather than to reality. Archer himself is rendered in absolutely flawless masculine terms, and is seen in the nude on several occasions (such as the episodes "Legs," Season 4, Episode 3 and even the pilot episode, "Mole Hunt"), showing his perfectly developed muscles and perfectly proportioned frame. Archer himself has an ego that produces for him, if anything, an even more perfectly aligned physical presence than the one drawn by the animators. The significance of Archer's image of physical perfection in a fetishistic and fragmented way for this discussion is that it once again positions Archer somewhere in Lacan's mirror stage, lacking the complete transformation into an adult that has awareness of their own physical flaws and respects their contours, who has accepted limitations in the world that are imposed from without. He has not been able to progress from this due to the one physical flaw the show acknowledges: his hearing loss. It becomes doubly ironic that his hearing is quite possibly his weakest physical attribute, but it is that specific weakness which gives us an important window into the character's psychology. This enormously ironic lack on Archer's part provides us with an important window into his peculiar psychological development, particularly in terms of his power relationships.

Due to his being trapped in the mirror stage through the neglect of his mother and his hearing loss, Archer's only public identity is in fact a gestalt, created as a response to that control and abuse. The one aspect of Archer that is not a part of his mother's artificial gestalt is his speech, which becomes his only method of expressing his true, private identity. What he says and how he chooses to say it leads into the world of carnival, where barriers between what is considered infantile and what is considered adult and refined melt away.

High and Low: Archer and the Parodic Carnival

"Holy Shitsnacks!"—Pam Poovey[19]

Having established a central role for language and sound in *Archer*, the final logical question to ask is what the characters choose to say. For the most part, other than expository dialogue, characters on *Archer* exhibit a "low" or "marketplace" speech associated with college-age youth or, historically and culturally rooted in the carnivalesque as described by Bakhtin.[20] For Bakhtin, carnival involves a short or long-term celebration in which cultural norms are upended in a number of different, but related ways.[21] Stam recognizes these as including "the valorization of Eros"; "a perspective on language which valorizes the obscene"; "celebrating the grotesque, excessive body and the 'orifices' and 'protrubances' of the 'lower bodily stratum'"; and finally "a rejection of social decorum."[22] All the characters in *Archer* engage in speech patterns that are fiercely obscene and preoccupied with sexual and other bodily functions that one would ordinarily keep out of polite conversation. In other words, the ISIS offices function as a sort of "carnival" in which the values espoused by Bakhtin are celebrated at the expense of considerations of decorum. In Jarry's *Ubu Roi*, for example, the play begins with a king emerging on stage and proclaiming, loudly and proudly, "*Shitter!*"[23] Archer himself mirrors this in Season 4, Episode 8 by calling out "*Mierde!*" when a mission near the Mexico/U.S. border does not go as planned. The deliberate ironic contrast between appearance and speech here is employed often by *Archer* in the service of its own parodic ends.

"Splooosh" is an often used term on *Archer*. Used primarily by Pam, this apparently refers specifically to vaginal fluids brought about by arousal. In "Heart of Archness: Part II" (Season 3, Episode 2) the group is admiring a former ISIS Agent, the ruggedly handsome Rip Riley. Both Pam and Cheryl exclaim, "Sploosh!" Ray, a male homosexual character, adds, "And whatever my equivalent would be. I guess, sploosh."[24] This term meets some, if not all, of the criteria set out above for carnivalesque language, in the most explicit way possible. But this theme of carnival at ISIS goes beyond sexual innuendo. Consider, for example, the preoccupation with food and drink and celebration, primarily involving Pam, but Archer himself is constantly drinking a wide variety of liquors, enjoying the sensual stimulation. Malory, by contrast, always drinks the same drink but never appears to be enjoying it. For her, the constant flow of scotch and ice seems to take the form of medication. Malory's alcoholism is so advanced that in the Season 3 finale, "Space Race," she is seen on a spacecraft drawing alternatively from a bag of isopropanol and a bag of orange-flavored drink in order to satisfy her craving. Food also takes center stage, in "Heart of Archness," when the character Bilbo, an overweight computer technician, complains that delaying his lunch in order to search for a missing agent will ruin his meatball sub sandwich, making it "congeal into a big blob of shit,"[25] a phrase that is as evocative of the carnivalesque as one could imagine. Consider, as well, how much action takes place in bathrooms and in varying states of undress or compromising physical situations. Lana and Cyril are discovered by Malory having sex in his office, in Season 4, Episode 5, when Archer and Malory are drawn to the sound of Lana's voice saying, "Yes." In a sonic sign, Archer interprets her affirmative response as an answer to a question he is asking, rather than a sensual exclamation. Pam, seems to enjoy mixing sex and food and is often seen with food and drink either in hand or imploring her co-workers to join her in happy hour, often at the beginning of an episode. Just as importantly for the true carnival, Pam is not embarrassed by either her appetites or her weight and is quite confident in her sexual and consumptive abilities for any number of intoxicants. A somewhat ironic observation of this is found in several episodes towards the end of Season 3, where Archer and Pam have a recurring sexual relationship, and Archer is astounded by Pam's expertise.

Superspy films and media, particularly James Bond, have always celebrated some aspects of the carnivalesque in terms of their language, with the so-called "Bond Girl" names ("Pussy Galore"), Bond's peculiar tastes in drink, and his periodic witticisms. The difference with *Archer* seems to be one of intensity and frequency, particularly in the linguistic and aural realm. Bond may tease, as he does in *Octopussy* (1983, John Glen), for example, his opponent at a casino game for using "loaded" dice by using understated English wit, "I'll just use your ... lucky dice,"[26] but he doesn't swear as openly as Archer, nor does he go into detail about his injuries on those rare occasions when he is injured. *Archer* characters use a specifically juvenile collection of phrases in the course of their day, such as "Oh my *God*" or "Come *on*" (emphasis added), which one would never encounter in a Bond film. This suits the carnivalesque environment of *Archer* perfectly, and highlights a difference between it and the Bond text.

　　Parody is deeply concerned with the relationship between the original text and that of the parodic text. To use one of Hutcheon's definitions, parody "is a form of imitation, but imitation characterized by ironic inversion, not always at the expense of the parodied text."[27] At its most obvious, *Archer* inverts many of the Bond archetypes: British is transposed to American and government agencies become private companies, but *Archer* exaggerates for effect many of the Bond tropes. For example, while Bond is a womanizer who enjoys a drink, Archer is an aggressive sexual interloper who is constantly drunk. The difference between *Archer* and the Bond archetype is simply in tone and language, with ironic critical distance. Whereas Bond may leave the bed of a woman with whom he has carried on some kind of affair, and the woman will sigh as he leaves on a knowing wink, Archer leaves women crying and guilt-ridden while he pours himself another drink and tells them to calm down. Archer is a completely self-absorbed sexual predator with no sense of shame or decorum whatsoever. Bond may be a womanizer, but he at least has some semblance of good manners.

　　This critical distance that *Archer* exhibits from the Bond image is essentially based on language associated with behavior. Although Archer is from an aristocratic background, in flashbacks throughout the series, his childhood spent in private schools with the always-present manservant, Woodhouse he has inherited none of the "higher" linguistic habits one might expect to be produced by that environment. In other words, he speaks the "low" or "marketplace" speech of the carnival, as does every other member of the ISIS team with the occasional exception of Malory. In relation to previous observations regarding Archer's lack of facility with language and its Lacanian/Freudian implications, the carnivalesque and specifically childish nature of his speech can be read as a conscious choice on his part to reclaim, clumsily and without strategy, some part of his identity. After all, it is only Malory who ever seems to note or comment upon any carnivalesque speech and activity taking place in the ISIS office, as she appears to be the only character affected by its presence. Archer's specific use of terms and his creation of, or at least his complicity in, carnivalesque speech patterns are an assertive, if childish, response to his mother's metaphorical theft of his linguistic capacity. While Archer's behavior might be akin to Bond's superficially, his language and his attitude create the ironic distance necessary for parody.

Archer, finally, shows an unvarnished, vulgar version of Bond that is grotesque yet finds us in the state of "knowing smile" that Hutcheon identifies as the result of a one sort of parody.[28] The linguistic conventions and preoccupations of *Archer*, and all their implications for the psychological development of the main character and the sonic tenor of the show, have a distinct and psychologically potent parodic sensibility. Given that the ears are the most direct vehicle for delivering that sensibility, along with the actions being portrayed, *Archer* is, very much, a spy parody for the ears.

Notes

1. Amanda Kondolojy, "Thursday Cable Ratings: 'Swamp People' Wins Night + 'Archer,' NBA Basketball, 'Ridiculousness,' 'Chasing Tail' & More," *Zap2it*, April 12, 2013, http://tvbythenumbers.zap2it.com/2013/04/12/thursday-cable-ratings-swamp-people-wins-night-archer-nba-basketball-ridiculousnesschasing-tail-more/177495/.

2. *Archer*, "The Man from Jupiter," Season 3, Episode 4, FX, January 19, 2012, written/created by Adam Reed. Directed by Adam Reed.

3. *Archer*, "Space Race: Part II," Season 3, Episode 13, FX, March 22, 2012, written/created by Adam Reed. Directed by Adam Reed.

4. *Archer*, "Crossing Over," Season 3, Episode 10, FX, March 1, 2012, written/created by Adam Reed. Directed by Adam Reed.

5. *Archer*, "The Wind Cries Mary," Season 4, Episode 2, FX, January 24, 2013, written/created by Adam Reed and Chris Provenzano. Directed by Bryan Fordney.

6. *Archer*, "Live and Let Dine," Season 4, Episode 7, FX, February 28, 2013, written/created by Adam Reed. Directed by Bryan Fordney.

7. *Archer*, "Heart of Archness: Part II," Season 3, Episode 2, FX, September 22, 2011, written/created by Adam Reed. Directed by Adam Reed.

8. *Archer*, "The Papal Chase," FX, March 28, 2013, written by Eric Sims (story) and Adam Reed (teleplay), created by Adam Reed. Directed by Bryan Fordney.

9. Dino Felluga, "Modules on Lacan: On Psychosexual Development." *Introductory Guide to Critical Theory*, January 31, 2011, Purdue University. http://www.cla.purdue.edu/english/theory/psychoanalysis/lacandevelop.html

10. Adrian Johnston, "Jacques Lacan," *The Stanford Encyclopedia of Philosophy* (Summer 2013 Edition), Edward N. Zalta, ed., http://plato.stanford.edu/archives/sum2013/entries/lacan/.

11. Susan Hayward, *Cinema Studies: The Key Concepts,* 3d ed. (London: Routledge, 2006), 318.

12. Jacques Lacan, *Écrits: The First Complete Edition in English,* trans. Bruce Fink (New York: W.W. Norton, 2006), 580.

13. Ibid.

14. Ibid.

15. Ibid.
16. Johnston, "Jacques Lacan."
17. Felluga, "Modules on Lacan."
18. Lacan, *Écrits,* 693.
19. Pam says this in many episodes: it is a recurring joke. It was first seen in the episode "Training Day," *Archer* Season 1, Episode 2, FX, January 14, 2010, written/created by Adam Reed. Directed by Mack Williams.
20. Robert Stam, *Subversive Pleasures: Bakhtin, Cultural Criticism and Film* (Baltimore: Johns Hopkins University Press, 1989), 93.
21. Ibid.
22. Ibid., 93–94.
23. Alfred Jarry, *Ubu Roi.* trans. Beverly Keith and G. (Gershon) Legman (Mineola, NY: Dover, 2003).
24. *Archer,* "Heart of Archness: Part II."
25. Ibid.
26. *Octopussy,* DVD, directed by John Glen (1983; Beverly Hills: Twentieth Century–Fox Home Entertainment, 2007).
27. Linda Hutcheon, *A Theory of Parody: The Teachings of Twentieth-Century Art Forms* (Urbana: University of Illinois Press, 2000), 6.
28. Ibid., 64.

Bibliography

Archer. "Blood Ferlin," Season 3, Episode 9. Written/created by Adam Reed. Directed by Adam Reed. FX, February 23, 2012.

_____. "Un Chein Tangerine," Season 4, Episode 10. Written by Adam Reed and Mike Arnold. Created by Adam Reed. Directed by Bryan Fordney. FX, March 21, 2013.

_____. "Coyote Lovely," Season 4, Episode 8. Written/created by Adam Reed. Directed by Bryan Fordney. FX, March 7, 2013.

_____. "Crossing Over," Season 3, Episode 10. Written/created by Adam Reed. Directed by Adam Reed. FX, March 1, 2012.

_____. "Drift Problem," Season 3, Episode 7. Written/created by Adam Reed. Directed by Adam Reed. FX, February 9, 2012.

_____. "A Going Concern," Season 2, Episode 2. Written/created by Adam Reed. Directed by Adam Reed. FX, February 3, 2011.

_____. "Heart of Archness: Part I," Season 3, Episode 1. Written/created by Adam Reed Directed by Adam Reed. FX, September 15, 2011.

_____. "Heart of Archness: Part II," Season 3, Episode 2. Written/created by Adam Reed. Directed by Adam Reed. FX, September 22, 2011.

_____. "Heart of Archness: Part III," Season 3, Episode 3. Written/created by Adam Reed. Directed by Adam Reed. FX, September 29, 2011.

_____. "The Limited," Season 3, Episode 6. Written/created by Adam Reed. Directed by Adam Reed. FX, February 2, 2012.

_____. "Live and Let Dine," Season 4, Episode 7. Written/created by Adam Reed. Directed by Bryan Fordney. FX, February 28, 2013.

_____. "The Man from Jupiter," Season 3, Episode 4. Written/created by Adam Reed. Directed by Adam Reed. FX, January 19, 2012.

_____. "Mole Hunt," Season 1, Episode 1. Written/created by Adam Reed. Directed by Mark Williams. FX, January 14, 2010.

_____. "The Papal Chase," Season 4, Episode 11. Written by Eric Sims (story) and Adam Reed (teleplay). Created by Adam Reed. Directed by Bryan Fordney. FX, March 28, 2013.

_____. "Space Race: Part I," Season 3, Episode 12. Written/created by Adam Reed. Directed by Adam Reed. FX, March 15, 2012.

_____. "Space Race: Part II," Season 3, Episode 13. Written/created by Adam Reed. Directed by Adam Reed. FX, March 22, 2012.

_____. "Training Day," Season 1, Episode 2. Written/created by Adam Reed. Directed by Mack Williams. FX, January 14, 2010.

_____. "Viscous Coupling," Season 4, Episode 5. Written/created by Adam Reed. Directed by Adam Reed. FX, February 14, 2013.

_____. "The Wind Cries Mary," Season 4, Episode 2. Written/created by Adam Reed and Chris Provenzano. Directed by Bryan Fordney. FX, January 24, 2013.

Felluga, Dino. "Modules on Lacan: On Psychosexual Development." *Introductory Guide to Critical Theory.* January 31, 2011, Purdue University. http://www.cla.purdue.edu/english/theory/psychoanalysis/lacandevelop.html.

Hayward, Susan. *Cinema Studies: The Key Concepts,* 3d ed. London: Routledge, 2006.

Hutcheon, Linda. *A Theory of Parody: The Teachings of Twentieth-Century Art Forms.* Urbana: University of Illinois Press, 2000.

Jarry, Alfred. *Ubu Roi.* Translated by Beverly Keith and G. (Gershon) Legman. Mineola, NY: Dover, 2003.

Johnston, Adrian. "Jacques Lacan." *The Stanford Encyclopedia of Philosophy,* ed. Edward N. Zalta (Summer 2013 Edition), http://plato.stanford.edu/archives/sun2013/entries/lacan/.

Kondolojy, Amanda. "Thursday Cable Ratings: 'Swamp People' Wins Night + 'Archer,' NBA Basketball, 'Ridiculousness,' 'Chasing Tail' & More" *Zap2it,* April 12, 2013. http://tvbythenumbers.zap2it.com/2013/04/12/thursday-cable-ratings-swamp-people-wins-night-archer-nba-basketball-ridiculousnesschasing-tail-more/177495.

Kristeva, Julia. *Powers of Horror: An Essay on Abjection.* Translated by Leon S. Roudiez. New York: Columbia University Press, 1982.

Lacan, Jacques. *Écrits: The First Complete Edition in English.* Translated by Bruce Fink. New York: W.W. Norton, 2006.

Octopussy. DVD. Directed by John Glen. 1983; Beverly Hills: Twentieth Century–Fox Home Entertainment, 2007.

Stam, Robert. *Subversive Pleasures: Bakhtin, Cultural Criticism, and Film.* Baltimore: Johns Hopkins University Press, 1989.

"Sometimes the old ways are the best"

Ret-Conning in James Bond Video Games

James Fleury

The cinematic James Bond franchise has long attempted to reconcile the past and present. From George Lazenby's observation in *On Her Majesty's Secret Service* (1969, Peter Hunt) that "[t]his never happened to the other fellow" to Pierce Brosnan's (re)use of retired gadgetry in *Die Another Day* (2002, Lee Tamahori), the initial twenty films in the series were comfortable in creating an elastic continuity that combined nostalgia and innovation.[1] *Casino Royale* (2006, Martin Campbell), however, functioned as a reboot that introduced Daniel Craig as a version of Bond new to his "00" status. Despite this apparent renunciation of established continuity, the series has been careful to not outright abandon its legacy.

In fact, 2012 represented a shared return and departure for the franchise as it celebrated its fiftieth anniversary. Among the accompanying fanfare was a new Blu-ray anthology and even an appearance at London's Summer Olympics featuring Craig, as 007, escorting Queen Elizabeth II to the opening ceremony. The consequent awareness helped the actor's latest installment, *Skyfall* (2012, Sam Mendes), earn over one billion U.S. dollars at the worldwide box office by the year's end. Thematically linking all of these elements is a reconciliation of the old and the new. *Skyfall*, for instance, remains spatiotemporally rooted in the present while concerning itself narratively, iconographically, and conceptually with the notion that "sometimes the old ways are the best."[2]

This phrase extends to *007 Legends* (2012, Activision),[3] a first-person shooter (FPS) video game developed by Eurocom and published by Activision for PlayStation 3, Xbox 360, Wii U, and PC. Released in North America just weeks before the theatrical debut of *Skyfall*, *007 Legends* adopts the anniversary's chronological synthesis to celebrate the character's filmic exploits by placing

Craig's incarnation in missions based on films in which he did not originally star, including *Goldfinger* (1964, Guy Hamilton), *On Her Majesty's Secret Service*, *Moonraker* (1979, Lewis Gilbert), *Licence to Kill* (1989, John Glen), and *Die Another Day*.[4] Whereas *Skyfall* received a great deal of critical acclaim, such as Roger Ebert's proclamation that it "triumphantly reinvents 007,"[5] audiences and critics declared the game an insult to the character, with *IGN*'s Tristan Ogilvie calling it "an abhorrent 'tribute' to the history of the British super spy that doesn't just take liberties—it takes the piss."[6] As such vitriol demonstrates, *007 Legends* speaks to the contested positioning of the Bond games vis-à-vis the Bond films, particularly at a time of shifting media trends in which horizontally integrated conglomerates are promoting a drive towards transmediated brand cohesion.

Cinematic and Ludic Convergence

007 Legends raises issues central to analyses of the multi-faceted connection between video games and film. This examination of the game and other interactive titles set within the James Bond cinematic universe does not subscribe to the exclusivity of either narratology, the centrality of story, or ludology, the field of game studies that privileges play; rather, it follows Harrison Gish's position of moving beyond this discursive debate in favor of "understanding how video games function digitally, interactively, spatially, temporally, and culturally."[7] To understand the functions of the Bond games in relation to the character's films, the project's focus rests on the problematic aspects produced by textual and industrial convergence.

Games adapted from films, such as those inspired by the screen adventures of 007, generally exemplify this problematization. In their introduction to *ScreenPlay: Cinema/Videogames/Interfaces*, Geoff King and Tania Krzywinska note, "The boundary between cinema and videogames often appears to be a permeable one, with movements both ways between one medium and the other."[8] Narrative, aesthetic, and platform permeability have frequently characterized this relationship. Gaming elements are evident in films as varied as *Run Lola Run* (1998, Tom Tykwer)[9] and *Inception* (2010, Christopher Nolan),[10] and filmic tropes appear in an array of games, including the cutscenes (or "cinematics") of *Final Fantasy VII* (1997, Sony Computer Entertainment of America) and the use of motion-captured actors in *L.A. Noire* (2011, Rockstar Games).[11] These examples support King and Krzywinska's claim that "[t]he interface between cinema and games extends well beyond the direct spin-off or industrial convergence."[12] Stylistically and narratively, adoption and adaptation occur between these media in an exchange supported through the industrial convergence to which King and Krzywinska refer. Warner Communications's 1976 purchase of Atari serves as the earliest instance of a media conglomerate acquiring a game company,[13] a practice that intensified through the continued consolidation of the entertainment business. As Stefan Hall[14] and Jamie Russell have highlighted, however, the relationship between video game companies and film studios has "sometimes led to an incredible amount of antagonism,"[15] with criticism lobbied against both films based on video games and video games based on films. This analysis of *007 Legends* rests on the sometimes-antagonistic corporate relationship as well as the extensive interfacing between cinema and interactive media. Combining these approaches allows for an examination of the Bond films and games in terms of both their textual and industrial convergence and how this convergence affects interpretations of the 007 enterprise as a whole.

Bond Games as Paratexts

Although James Bond scholarship has predominantly privileged the Fleming novels or the EON-produced films, some scholars have written on various aspects of the character's video game entries. This multiplatform attentiveness is likely due to there being no central Bondian textual corpus against which other texts are compared, such as the primacy of the Sir Arthur Conan Doyle books in work on Sherlock Holmes or the films in studies of *Star Wars*. Within many franchises, though, there has been, until relatively recently, a lack of academic attention paid to the peripherals, or what Jonathan Gray refers to as "paratexts."[16] Ancillary products, as he notes, have tended to be ignored within critical circles as independent sites of meaning, save for typically denigrating analyses like Stephen Kline's "Limits to the Imagination: Marketing and Children's Culture."[17] As early as 1987, the cultural studies project of Tony Bennett and Janet Woollacott's *Bond and Beyond: The Political Career of a Popular Hero* went "beyond the Bond novels and films to take account of the broader range of texts and coded objects through which the figure of Bond has been put into circulation as a popular hero."[18] Bennett and Woollacott's articulation of Bond as a mobile signifier among an amalgamation of sources[19] precedes more recent explorations of the rich intertextual meanings within the character's video games such as their production and reception history,[20] their limitations of characterization,[21] and the particular influence of *GoldenEye 007* (1997, Nintendo).[22]

This writing on Bond video games underscores an emphasis on paratexts among contemporary approaches to adaptations involving convergent media. Gray claims that critics like Kline have traditionally held "the film or television program as the center of the textual interaction and the only source of authentic textuality while peripherals ... are seen as tacked on to the film or program in a cynical attempt to squeeze yet more money out of a successful product."[23] Prior academic indifference to paratexts appears to be not far removed from the film studios' conventional understanding of peripherals as mere promotional extensions intended to direct consumers to a more expensive, and implicitly more important, central product.[24] Convergence within the entertainment industry has challenged this textual privileging, as conglomerates have embraced the synergistic principles of transmedia storytelling by which their various media holdings can carry the narrative of an intellectual property across multiple platforms. David Thorburn and Henry Jenkins offer a contrast to the restrictive specificity of earlier studies by advocating a decentralized approach to material adapted from film or television texts in recognition of the industry's consolidation.[25] This position acknowledges that the so-called "peripherals" occupy, as Gray argues, a "constitutive role in the production, development, and expansion of the text,"[26] especially in moments like the present that call for a shift in how media is understood. Bond scholarship, therefore, should continue to consider the intertexual relations that the franchise's games and other paratexts create.

Conned, Ret-Conned

While James Bond has featured in over twenty games, arguably none have cast as long a shadow as 1997's *GoldenEye 007* for the Nintendo 64. A FPS from Bond's perspective, the title immerses players in the narrative of *GoldenEye* (1995, Martin Campbell), which introduced Pierce Brosnan as the fifth actor to portray the character. *GoldenEye 007* is unique among licensed games in that its release did not coincide with that of the cinematic text on which it is based. Trevor Elkington explains that, because the sales of a licensed game are predicated on a film or television program's promotional awareness, games of this type "are rushed out the door, with most being pushed to ship simultaneously with the release date of the film."[27] Synergistic exploitation, however, is often detrimental to their development and ultimate reception because Hollywood film productions are typically completed within one year to eighteen months whereas most games are in development for two years. This scheduling conflict leaves game developers having to either "remain faithful to the film production schedule and shorten their development cycle, or ship a game potentially months after the marketing campaign for the film is over."[28] Aided by this longer period of development, *GoldenEye 007* became the standard against which later Bond games have been ranked. In Gray's terminology, the game has served as an "entryway paratext"[29] in that it has determined some audiences' understanding of 007, especially within the video game medium.

The determinant paratextuality of *GoldenEye 007* is evident across the narrative and formal elements of the character's subsequent games. As Hall and David McGowan point out, these later titles have worked to imitate the game's formula, including adopting its FPS generic conventions and inclusion of a split-screen, multiplayer "deathmatch" mode.[30] Structurally, *GoldenEye 007*'s levels do not just retell the same story as its cinematic counterpart but rather "constantly alter the narrative of the film by rearranging, expanding, and adding plot elements."[31] The "Silo" mission, for example, tasks the player with infiltrating a Soviet missile facility in 1991, an otherwise unseen period between the film's 1986 opening sequence and its remaining diegesis set in 1995. While Hall mentions that the game's un-lockable "Aztec" and "Egyptian" levels are comprised of components from Roger Moore's tenure as 007,[32] he is not concerned with how these stages go beyond mere rearrangement or expansion in their rewriting of the Bond franchise. "Aztec" adapts a sequence from *Moonraker* but replaces Moore with Brosnan, whose Bond must thwart the launch of Hugo Drax's space shuttle. Because the bonus levels bear no narrative connection to the remainder of the game aside from featuring the same main character, it is unclear if their events constitute what in comic books is known as "ret-conning," or the act of creating a retroactive continuity that supersedes previous continuities,[33] Displacement such as this nonetheless has become a staple of Bond games.

Along with ret-conning, many elements of *GoldenEye 007* have been exploited to appeal to players' nostalgia. In 2004, Electronic Arts (EA) released *GoldenEye: Rogue Agent*, a game, intended, as Hall says, to "cash in on the popularity of the original *GoldenEye 007* release."[34] Despite its name, *GoldenEye: Rogue Agent* has nothing to do with either the 1995 film or the 1997 game. Instead, in another case of confounding continuity, players take on the role of disgraced MI6 agent "GoldenEye," who, after losing his right eye at the hands of Dr. No, receives a golden, computer-enhanced replacement. This rogue agent pursues vengeance by partnering with Bond villains Auric Goldfinger and Francisco Scaramanga and traveling to recognizable locations from the films, including Crab Key from *Dr. No* (1962, Terrence Young) and Scaramanga's island lair featured in *The Man with the Golden Gun* (1974, Guy Hamilton). Bond, meanwhile, only briefly appears as a non-playable character within the game's opening training simulation and quickly "dies" due to GoldenEye's recklessness. The game's misleading title made clear that *GoldenEye* was no longer just the name of the seventeenth Bond film; *GoldenEye* had become its own brand.

This exploitation of name recognition and ret-conning was EA's method of continuing to produce Bond games while the direction of the film series was in limbo. At the time, MGM, the franchise's studio, was undergoing financial upheaval, which resulted in a four-year gap between Bond films and a change in actors. A transition also took place with the games when, in 2006, Activision assumed the 007 license in an agreement that was supposed to last until 2014. EA reportedly was looking to leave the movie-game business, one in which Activision had found success with their best-selling *Spider-Man* games.[35]

Even with the change in license-holders and despite the reboot of the film franchise, Activision continued to mine nostalgia for the *GoldenEye* brand through further ret-conning. *GoldenEye 007* for the Nintendo Wii initially followed its namesake's practice of having an exclusive release on a Nintendo home console, but to maximize sales, it was also upgraded to high-definition in 2011 for Sony's PlayStation 3 and Microsoft's Xbox 360 as *GoldenEye 007 Reloaded*. This title is simultaneously an adaptation of the 1995 film and an update of the 1997 game, and like the current films, it attempts to synthesize the old and the new.

The game narratively rewrites the original *GoldenEye* film by modernizing its setting and substituting Daniel Craig for Pierce Brosnan. Because of Craig's presence, the world of the game is aesthetically and tonally aligned with his films, such as its menus and cutscenes adopting the same graphical interface featured throughout *Quantum of Solace* (2008, Marc Forster) as well as an overall de-emphasis of the franchise's more fantastical qualities. This realignment signals a revision of the pre-reboot cinematic continuity, by which the story events of the *GoldenEye* film are modified for the Craig era. The promotional materials call attention to the game's lineage, as shown in the announcement trailer that debuted at the 2010 Electronic Entertainment Expo (E3). Opening with a series of shots showing different groups of men and women seated at a boardroom table, a voice from off-screen dramatically reveals, "Let's say, after thirteen years of game innovation, a new *GoldenEye* game is coming up."[36] The trailer then presents a highlight reel, scored to the same iteration of "The James Bond Theme" that had accompanied *Casino Royale*'s theatrical trailers. This musical association and the advertisement's foregrounding of Craig's voice, likeness, and name homogenize the *GoldenEye* experience as distinctly his, an idea that *007 Legends* extends across the James Bond cinematic collection.

A View to a Disappointment

The critical and commercial failure of *007 Legends* appears surprising considering that it continued the narrative rewriting of the well-received *GoldenEye 007*.[37] At the time of its announcement in April 2012, fans, such as members of the discussion forums at Bond fansite *MI6*, exclaimed that the concept of *007 Legends* struck them as "awesome" and "interesting."[38] They speculated about what it would be like to inhabit the spaces of classic Bond films, especially since most of the included titles had not yet been adapted into video games.[39] Although not explicitly stated, this initial interest may have emanated from the press release's announcement that the game "features an original, overarching storyline tying together six classic Bond movies, concluding with ... *Skyfall*."[40] This implied that the game was to connect a film from each of the six Bond actors within a cohesive story.

Despite the warm response to the game's announcement, fan sentiment quickly turned hostile once it became clear that only Craig's version of the character would feature across each of the film-based missions. One Bond fan on *MI6* even said, "I take that back!" after having earlier proclaimed that it sounded "like the best bond [*sic*] game Activision has made!"[41] Together with this negative audience reaction, harsh reviews contributed to the game's abysmal financial performance. On January 20, 2013, after three months on the market, global sales for *007 Legends* accounted for approximately 300,000 units across all video game consoles[42]; by comparison, *Call of Duty: Black Ops II* (2012, Activision) moved 6,000,000 copies in its first week alone on only the Xbox 360.[43] Considering that Activision released both games for the 2012 holiday season, the comparison is appropriate. Numerous reviews underscore this connection, such as Ogilvie's reference to *007 Legends* as both "a poor man's *Call of Duty*" and "*Call of Duty: Bond Ops*."[44] Even with its adoption of tried-and-true tropes from Bond's interactive legacy as well as components of Activision's flagship FPS series, the narratively and ludically recombinant *007 Legends* did not live up to the potential of its name.

The critical and audience mauling that greeted the game arguably contributed to its commercial failure. "While game reviews are subjective," Elkington argues, they "do offer a sense of the perceived quality of particular games."[45] Furthermore, Geoffrey Zatkin noted at the 2012 Game Developers Conference a direct correlation between video game sales and the scores compiled by review aggregator *Metacritic*. In 2011, the games that scored a "ninety" or above (out of a possible "one-hundred") on the site sold an average of 700,000 units in three months, whereas the games that ranked "fifty" or below moved only 30,000 copies.[46] With "generally unfavorable reviews," *007 Legends* earned a Metascore of "forty-one."[47] On December 7, 2012, a little more than one month after the release of *007 Legends*, Activision closed the game's developer, Eurocom. At the time, Eurocom explained, "Since 2008, there has been a steep decline in the sales of Console [*sic*] and PC games, which has led to a severe contraction in the number of new games being commissioned."[48] A month later, Activision had pulled all of its Bond games from digital download services like Steam before it was confirmed that the publisher had terminated its rights to the Bond license before they were due to expire in 2014.[49] What exactly is to account, then, for the colossal failure of *007 Legends*?

Never Say Continuity Again

One of the major grievances critics and fans expressed with *007 Legends* is its confusing approach to the cinematic storyline. This argument holds that the franchise's continuity collapses on itself by transposing Daniel Craig within modernized versions of older films. Opening with the pre-title sequence from *Skyfall*, the tenuous narrative thread of *007 Legends* emanates from the moment in which Bond is drowning after having been shot off a train outside of Istanbul. As his life flashes before his eyes, 007 recalls five earlier, unrelated missions, each of which is provided with no narrative context. Player engagement begins with an adaptation of *Goldfinger*, with Bond fuzzily awaking to find Jill Masterson's gold-painted corpse displayed on his hotel-room bed. To assert its placement within the Craig period, the game revises this iconic moment from the 1964 film by immediately instructing the player to answer Bond's smartphone. The remainder of the *Goldfinger* mission largely adheres faithfully to its referent's storyline, as Bond infiltrates Auric Goldfinger's Swiss headquarters before teaming with Felix Leiter of the C.I.A. to halt the villain's raid on Fort Knox and ultimately triumphing when Goldfinger fires a revolver aboard an aircraft and is pulled out of a ruptured cabin window. Unlike the film, which follows this climactic struggle with Bond (Sean Connery) and Pussy Galore (Honor Blackman) having parachuted to safety, the level abruptly cuts to black after Goldfinger's death and transitions to the diegetic present, where the drowning 007 reminisces about the events of *On Her Majesty's Secret Service*. While the game may offer a narrative resolution to each of its missions, the memories themselves are not resolved. In other words, the missions follow a non-contextual structure in which their individual plots are completed without providing any linkage to what follows. Each of the adapted films remains a revised memory meant to take the place of the original text.

The revisionism of *Casino Royale*, intended to erase the memory of the previous films, contradicts the logic of *007 Legends'*s mnemonic plot device. Although, as James Chapman points out, "*Die Another Day* had been the biggest-grossing Bond to date and a radical change to the formula might risk alienating fans who preferred their Bonds full of spectacle and CGI (computer-generated imagery),"[50] the Bond creative team felt that *Die Another Day* had signaled an over-reliance on gadgetry, such as an invisible Aston Martin Vanquish. Veteran franchise producer Michael G. Wilson explained that *Casino Royale* was intended as a return to a more "basic Bond"[51] devoid of the over-the-top traits that had come to characterize the series. Given this back-to-basics approach, it appears all the more incongruent that the *Moonraker* mission of *007 Legends* features Craig's Bond wielding lasers aboard a space station.

In fact, the game selectively chooses what portions of the films it wishes to retain and what portions to rewrite, which creates further continuity conundrums. Because the *On Her Majesty's Secret Service* levels follow the same fundamental plot of the film, it is confusing that Craig's Bond marries Tracy di Vicenzo; the tragic loss of Vesper Lynd (Eva Green) in *Casino Royale*, after all, causes him so much grief that it sets in motion the plot of *Quantum of Solace*. The mission's final cutscene, in which the villainous Ernst Stavro Blofeld kills Tracy, accentuates this disparity by concluding with dialogue directly borrowed from *Casino Royale*. As the newlywed Bond tearfully mourns the loss of his bride, the disembodied voice of M (Judi Dench) laments, "Sometimes, we're so focused on our enemies that we forget to watch our friends."[52] Originally delivered by M following Vesper's death, the line is presented here with an echoing filter to suggest its status as a memory. Furthermore, the line appears to have been rerecorded for the game, as Dench's delivery subtly differs from that heard in the film. This line, then, represents both an auditory and narrative deviation from the Craig films.

Not only does this type of narrative disjunction problematize the cinematic canon, changes are made to the main characters that ultimately reorient Bond's relationships. These characters are portrayed by new and reprising actors alike; the *Die Another Day* mission, for instance, features Toby Stephens returning as Gustav Graves while Halle Berry's Jinx now carries the likeness of Gabriela Montaraz with the voice of Madalena Alberto. More surprising is the *Goldfinger* and *Licence to Kill* levels' casting of Demetri Goritsas as Felix Leiter, a character played by Jeffrey Wright in the first two Craig films. As such, the game rewrites elements of both the original continuity and the rebooted storyline as well. In its drive to recreate memorable Bond moments, *007 Legends* fails to account for the inconsistencies it creates in both cinematic timelines.

The critical and commercial failure of *007 Legends*, though, cannot be blamed solely on its continuity issues. The character's appearances in many media, such as the novels, have been plagued by these problems. Beginning with 1968's *Colonel Sun* by Kingsley Amis (under the pseudonym "Robert Markham"), various writers have carried on the adventures of Ian Fleming's original character within a continuity separate from the EON films. *Solo* (2013) author William Boyd, for one, acknowledges the existence of "a disconnect between the film Bond and the literary Bond, which is their contemporaneity."[53] This temporal divide has encouraged the novels and films to take on different thematic and contextual concerns: "While the novels remain rooted in the social and political context of the 1950s," Chapman argues, "the films have responded to changing industrial and cultural circumstances in order to maintain their position at the forefront of popular film culture."[54] In reference to Activision's *GoldenEye 007*, David McGowan claims that its "ambiguous status as an adaptation and/or remake is indicative of the problematic continuity of the franchise as a whole."[55] Despite the chronic discord that these authors underscore, some media reconciliation has taken place within the Bond brand.

Andy Lane and Paul Simpson explain in *The Bond Files: An Unofficial Guide to the World's Greatest Secret Agent* that extreme lengths sometimes have been required in the negotiation between print and screen. The film *Licence to Kill* draws inspiration from several Fleming stories, including *Live and Let Die* (1954) and the short story "The Hildebrand Rarity" (1960). To incorporate them into the novels' continuity, series continuation author John Gardner's novelization alters the film's events, in which Bond (Timothy Dalton) pursues revenge after his ally Felix Leiter (David Hedison) suffers the death of his wife (Priscilla Barnes) and the dismemberment of his legs. Because Leiter had already sustained the same injury in the original *Live and Let Die* novel, the character loses an artificial leg in the *Licence to Kill* novelization,[56] thereby subsuming the canonicity of the film franchise. That Leiter in the *Licence to Kill* mission of *007 Legends* exhibits no visible damage whatsoever to his lower half further complicates this incident and raises the issue of textual primacy in light of continuity changes.

In terms of the films, *Skyfall* manages to obliterate any sense of cohesive continuity established by the reboot pairing of *Casino Royale* and *Quantum of Solace*, the shared presence of Judi Dench as M in both the Brosnan and Craig eras notwithstanding. In particular, *Skyfall* features Bond driving his Aston Martin DB5, a car that Craig's version of 007 had won in a poker game in *Casino Royale*; *Skyfall*'s DB5, meanwhile, is supposedly the Q-Branch model from *Goldfinger*, with its ejector seat and headlight-mounted machine guns. Similar inconsistencies, though, have long been overlooked in the Bond films. As Joey Esposito notes, "Bond has avoided continuity for decades. Different actors have taken on the role time and again without a strict continuity other than some recurring characters, but that's totally accepted by viewers. We just sort of recognize it as a collective anthology of Bond's greatest tales."[57] No wonder fans have theorized that the films can be interpreted as loosely connected stories of multiple 007s, with each new actor portraying a different character who has assumed the name "James Bond."[58]

Any interpretation of the character is perhaps best understood in the sense of multiplicity. Another storytelling technique lifted from comic books,[59] a medium in which several unrelated stories featuring the same character appear each month, multiplicity relies on the conceit of separate but simultaneous narrative universes. Roberta Pearson and William Uricchio have posited that all versions of Batman are legitimate when accepting that multiplicity allows for various, competing readings to coexist, even though, like Bond, the character's "identity has fluctuated over time and across media as multiple authors and fan communities competed over his definition."[60] As this distinction suggests, multiplicity is a product of and for authors and fans alike. Recent film installments of long-running franchises, such as *Star Trek* (2009, J.J. Abrams) and *Evil Dead* (2013, Fede Alvarez), have adopted this concept to both re-imagine and continue their established narrative worlds by combining elements from the original and the revised continuities. Doing so respects longtime fans' attachment to canon while also providing a starting point for audiences unfamiliar with the series. Applied to 007, the idea of multiplicity holds that several James Bond universes can exist within different but parallel continuities. The disparate timelines of the novels, films, video games, and other media all abide by individual rules and codes, yet each series is acceptable on its own terms. At the same time, these distinctions call into question the practice of one medium displacing the continuity of another through ret-conning, as is the effect of *007 Legends* on the films.

Not explicitly embracing multiplicity points to the game's true shortcoming: a lack of synergy within the James Bond brand. Rob Matthews, *007 Legends*'s Product Manager at Eurocom, explained that Danjaq, the rights-holder of the Bond films, dictated its problematic narrative structure.[61] This control of intellectual property (IP) is to be expected, given Elkington's explanation that "[f]ilm and television license-owners ... largely [dictate] the course of game development, treating video games more or less like traditional ancillaries."[62] While Activision's 2010 remake of *GoldenEye 007* attempts to both embrace and rewrite the character's video game history, the corporate logic of *007 Legends*'s transplanting of Daniel Craig within classic Bond stories suggests a deliberate effort on the part of Danjaq to solidify the current actor's presence as not only the definitive Bond of the present time but also the definitive Bond of all-time.

Craig's presence illustrates the claim that many of the problems with licensed games result from the competing interests of multiple parties. Specifically, the game has no clear sense of a target audience. Its appeals to nostalgia appear aimed at long-time Bond franchise followers, while the game's modernization and inclusion of Craig indicate an appeal to younger fans of the more recent films and FPS titles like those within the *Call of Duty* series. By casting too wide a net, this multi-demographic approach ultimately alienates everyone, as veteran fans will be disenchanted with the rewriting of the older films whereas newcomers will be confused by the game's absence of contextualization. As Elkington argues, this type of audience antagonization "underscores the idea that media convergence, despite its apparent ability to smooth over differences in media actually" reveals that "the different goals of the various license-sharers stand in direct conflict, even contradiction to each other, so that not only do they sacrifice consistency and continuity, they effectively achieve negative synergy."[63] Despite the harmonious celebration of the old and the new during the Bond films' fiftieth anniversary, the synergistic cacophony of *007 Legends* represents the need for change.

Towards a Transmediated James Bond

The shifting landscape of the licensed gaming market suggests remedies for the James Bond franchise's negative synergy. Derek Johnson describes licensing as a Post-Fordist practice by which IP owners strike temporary partnerships with independently subcontracted licensees.[64] As with other licensing arrangements, the right to produce a game associated with a film is traditionally the product of a transaction between the film studio and the highest-bidding game company; conglomerated horizontal integration, though, has encouraged film studios to consolidate and take on a more constitute role in the video game development of their IP. Changes, though, have taken place in the world of licensed games. On the one hand, the rise of inexpensive mobile games has led the Walt Disney Company's Disney Interactive division to invest less in console-based adaptations in favor of games made for smart phones and tablets.[65] On the other hand, the company's *Disney Infinity* (2013, Disney Interactive) creates a universe presented through not only console and handheld video games but also figurines and mobile and web applications.

Multiplatform projects like *Disney Infinity* might suggest the transmedia direction in which Bond's interactive titles could move. Transmedia storytelling, as outlined by Henry Jenkins, involves a narrative that "unfolds across multiple media platforms, with each new text making a distinctive and valuable contribution to the whole."[66] Such an approach to Bond would require meaningful engagement among its different media appearances instead of games like *007 Legends* adding nothing new to the films from which they are adapted. Not only does the game rewrite the narratives of five pre–Craig films, *007 Legends* also fails to distinctively and valuably contribute to *Skyfall*, whose two levels were released as downloadable content after the film's theatrical debut. These levels, rather than expanding the story through transmedia, merely retell its pre-credits motorcycle chase and Shanghai skyscraper sequence while also restricting the storyline by abruptly concluding after the latter set-piece, one that occurs less than halfway through the film's running time. Unlike 1997's *GoldenEye 007*, *007 Legends* fails at even direct adaptation. "While virtually every Bond video game since *GoldenEye 007* has attempted to replicate that game's degree of success," Hall argues, "designers looking to the future of Bond need to be extremely cognizant of the history of the character, now spread across the media trifecta of novels, films, and video games."[67] Despite this trifecta, Bond remains a specifically multimedia franchise that has yet to undertake the transmedia approach of other brands like *The Matrix* (1999–2003, Larry and Andy Wachowski), *Riddick* (2000–2013, David Twohy), or the *Batman: Arkham* series (2009–2013, Warner Bros. Interactive Entertainment).

As the example of *Licence to Kill*'s novelization demonstrates, the Bond franchise's practicing of transmedia storytelling techniques has only generated further continuity questions. The Bond video games, especially, have adopted these methods. With the foregrounding of the "007" moniker assuring consumers of their legitimacy within the brand, *007: Nightfire* (2002, Electronic Arts), *007: Everything or Nothing* (2003–2004, Electronic Arts), and *007: Blood Stone* (2010, Activision) all tell original stories and are, as of this writing, the franchise's most current examples of games attempting to incorporate transmedia properties. *007: Nightfire*, featuring the likeness of Pierce Brosnan, and *007: Blood Stone*, starring Daniel Craig, are each set within their respective cinematic continuities. The latter title, for instance, takes place after the events of *Quantum of Solace* and before those of the then-unproduced *Skyfall*, with M (Judi Dench) and Tanner (Rory Kinnear) assisting Bond in a quest to retrieve stolen biochemical weaponry. Because *007: Blood Stone* and *007: Nightfire*'s episodic nature does not add to the films in any noticeable manner, these games do not appear to adequately qualify as transmedia. *007: Everything or Nothing*, by contrast, betrays its transmedia premise in another manner altogether. The first game to include both the likeness and voice of a Bond actor, *007: Everything or Nothing* stars Brosnan in a story that combines concepts from his films with those of Roger Moore. While it features Dench as M and John Cleese as Q, the game places Bond in conflict with Jaws (Richard Kiel) from *The Spy Who Loved Me* (1977, Lewis Gilbert) and *Moonraker* as well as Nikolai Diavolo (Willem Dafoe), a former KGB associate of *A View to a Kill*'s (1985, John Glen) Max Zorin (Christopher Walken). As suggested by the "An Old Friend" title of the level in which the player first interacts with Jaws and by Bond's pun that he and Zorin "once played bridge together,"[68] the game posits that Brosnan's incarnation of the character had previously interacted with these villains from the Moore period. The game had potential to lay the foundation for a transmedia experience whose narrative could have carried across the video games and the Brosnan films. Instead, it and 1997's *GoldenEye 007* demonstrate that, even before *007 Legends*, the Bond franchise was more interested in exchanging continuity than extending it.

The closest to transmedia storytelling Bond has come never even made it to audiences. Original VHS copies released in 1998 of *Tomorrow Never Dies* (1997, Roger Spottiswoode) feature Desmond Llewellyn's Q delivering an advertisement for a video game titled *Tomorrow Never Dies: The Mission Continues.* Beginning "where the film ends,"[69] it was to feature Bond investigating Satoshi Isagura, a character shown briefly in the terrorist arms bazaar of the film's opening sequence. The game, which was being developed by MGM Interactive, the in-house software unit of MGM Studios, was shelved when EA picked up the 007 license and outsourced development to BlackOps Entertainment. In 1999, EA released *Tomorrow Never Dies* for the Sony PlayStation, which, like most licensed titles, simply walks players through the plot of the film. This early and aborted experiment of narrative extension would be an appropriate avenue for future Bond games to take.

The collapse of *007 Legends* could lead to a transmedia approach to the James Bond franchise. Writing in 2002, the year of the cinematic 007's fortieth anniversary and the release of *Star Wars Episode II: Attack of the Clones* (2002, George Lucas), Lane and Simpson note that the *Star Wars* brand "is centrally co-ordinated, with the projects ... all referring to each other and feeding off a coherent continuity, each created by talented people writing with care and with respect, if not love. With Bond the various projects are certainly written with respect and love, but there is little care, no coherence, and the central quality assurance appears to be missing."[70] With Activision no longer holding the rights to produce 007 games, it would be appropriate for Sony, the current distributor of the Bond films, to acquire the gaming license. Sony's conglomerated structure has already allowed it to synergistically leverage its latest incarnation of the *Spider-Man* film franchise for transmedia storytelling purposes through films, websites, and video games, even as Marvel's retaining of the character's non-cinematic rights has restricted the extent of this transmediation.[71] Perhaps, then, the reason behind the distinct continuities of Bond's films and literature is not textually determined but rather one of legality and contractual limitations. Future paratextual examinations might consider licensing issues, especially the negotiations between Ian Fleming Publications's literary rights and Danjaq's cinematic properties. Synergy among the brand, whether across multiple media or just in terms of the games and films, could encourage a greater level of narrative and aesthetic cohesion as well as the level of care, coherence, and quality that could make future James Bond video games truly legendary.

Notes

1. This project is not concerned with the two "unofficial" Bond films, *Casino Royale* (1967, Ken Hughes, John Houston, et. al.) and *Never Say Never Again* (1983, Irvin Kershner) that exist in separate continuities altogether.

2. *Skyfall*, Blu-ray, directed by Sam Mendes (2012: Beverly Hills: Twentieth Century FX Home Entertainment, 2013). Beyond Eve Moneypenny's (Naomi Harris) delivery of this line to 007 while he shaves with a cutthroat razor, *Skyfall* relies narratively, generically, and thematically on nostalgia. The reincorporates, for instance, several tropes of previous Bond adventures that had been absent from the Craig era, including not just characters like Moneypenny and Q (Ben Whishaw) but also a more humorous tone. In doing so, this reincorporation instills a sense of nostalgia for the franchise's history while also updating its conventions for contemporary audiences.

3. When referencing video games, I parenthetically include the name of the North American publisher and year of release.

4. The particular films featured in the game are a curious collection. Although *Goldfinger* and *On Her Majesty's Secret Service* are praised among Bond-film aficionados, *Licence to Kill* is problematic, and neither *Moonraker* nor *Die Another Day* represent the franchise's creative zenith. These films, while not chosen for their narrative strengths or the high esteem they hold among fans, were likely selected because none, until *007 Legends*, had yet been adapted into a video game employing three-dimensional graphics.

5. Roger Ebert, "Skyfall," *RogerEbert.com*, November 7, 2012, http://rogerebert.suntimes.com/apps/pbcs.dll/article?AID=/20121107/REVIEWS/121109990 (accessed November 7, 2012).

6. Tristan Ogilvie, "007 Legends Review," *IGN*, October 16, 2012, http://www.ign.com/articles/2012/10/16/007-legends-review (accessed October 17, 2012).

7. Harrison Gish, "Media Boundaries and Bullet Time: A *Hard Boiled* Fan Plays *Stranglehold*," *Mediascape: UCLA's Journal of Cinema and Media Studies* (Winter 2012), http://www.tft.ucla.edu/mediascape/Winter2012_MediaBoundaries.html (accessed January 10, 2013.

8. Geoff King and Tanya Krzywinska, "Introduction: Cinema/Videogames/Interfaces," in *Screenplay: Cinema/Videogames/Interfaces,* ed. Geoff King and Tanya Krzywinska (New York: Wallflower Press, 2002), 1.

9. See Margit Grieb, "Run Lara Run," in King and Krzywinska, *Screenplay,* 157–170.

10. Henry Jenkins, "No, You Do Not Have to Be a Gamer to Like Inception!" *Confessions of an Aca-Fan: The Official Weblog of Henry Jenkins*, August 8, 2010, http://henryjenkins.org/2010/08/no_you_do_not_have_to_be_a_gam.html (accessed September 21, 2013.

11. Evan Narcisse, "L.A. Noire Becomes First Video Game Ever Featured at Tribeca Film Festival," *Time*, March 29, 2011, http://techland.time.com/2011/03/29/l-a-norie-becomes-first-video-game-ever-featured-at-tribeca-film-festival/ (accessed September 15, 2013). The film noir-influenced *L.A. Noire* features MotionScan technology to capture vividly detailed expressions from its actors. Its cinematic qualities are so emphatic that, in 2011, the title was the first game to be chosen as an official selection at the Tribeca Film Festival.

12. King and Krzywinska, "Introduction," 2.

13. Jamie Russell, *Generation Xbox: How Videogames Invaded Hollywood* (East Sussex: Yellow Ant, 2012), 6.

14. See Stefan Hall, "'You've Seen the Movie, Now Play the Video Game': Recoding the Cinematic in Digital Media and Virtual Culture" (PhD diss., Bowling Green State University, 2011); and Stefan Hall, "Shaken, Stirred, Pixellated: Video Gaming as Bond," in *The James Bond Phenomenon: A Critical Reader*, 2d ed., ed. Christoph Lindner (Manchester: Manchester University Press, 2009), 312–330. While components of the latter work appear in Hall's subsequently completed dissertation, the content differs slightly. Because of its 2009 publication,

"Shaken, Stirred, Pixellated" does not discuss the 2010 version of *GoldenEye 007*, for example.

15. Russell, *Generation Xbox*, 206.

16. Jonathan Gray, *Show Sold Separately: Promos, Spoilers, and Other Media Paratexts* (New York: New York University Press, 2010), 6.

17. Ibid., 177.

18. Tony Bennett and Janet Woollacott, *Bond and Beyond: The Political Career of a Popular Hero* (New York: Methuen, 1987), 1.

19. Ibid., 6.

20. See Kevin D. Impellizeri, "Use Your Joystick, 007: Video Games and the Interactive Bond Experience," in *James Bond in World and Popular Culture: The Films Are Not Enough*, 2d ed., ed. Robert G. Weiner, B. Lynn Whitfield, and Jack Becker (Newcastle upon Tyne: Cambridge Scholars, 2011), 7–22.

21. See Abe Stein and Matthew Weise, "All Bang Bang, No Kiss Kiss? The Bond Figure and Video Games," in Weiner, Whitfield, and Becker, *James Bond in World and Popular Culture*, 23–39.

22. See Hall, "'You've Seen the Movie, Now Play the Video Game';" Hall, "Shaken, Stirred, Pixellated"; and David McGowan, "Some of This Happened to the Other Fellow: Remaking *GoldenEye 007* with Daniel Craig," in *Game On, Hollywood!: Essays on the Intersection of Video Games and Cinema*, ed. Gretchen Papazian and Joseph Michael Sommers (Jefferson, NC: McFarland, 2013), 115–128.

23. Gray, *Show Sold Separately*, 177.

24. Russell, *Generation Xbox*, 207.

25. David Thorburn and Henry Jenkins, "Introduction: Toward an Aesthetics of Transition," in *Rethinking Media Change: The Aesthetics of Transition*, ed. David Thorburn and Henry Jenkins (Cambridge, MA: MIT, 2004), 11.

26. Gray, *Show Sold Separately*, 175.

27. Trevor Elkington, "Too Many Cooks: Media Convergence and Self-Defeating Adaptations," in *The Video Game Theory Reader 2*, ed. Bernard Perron and Mark J.P. Wolf (New York: Routledge, 2009), 224.

28. Ibid., 225.

29. Gray, *Show Sold Separately*, 23.

30. See Hall, "'You've Seen the Movie, Now Play the Video Game'"; Hall, "Shaken, Stirred, Pixellated"; and McGowan, "Some of This Happened to the Other Fellow."

31. Hall, "Shaken, Stirred, Pixellated," 322.

32. Hall, "'You've Seen the Movie, Now Play the Video Game,'" 159–160.

33. Tyler Weaver, *Comics for Film, Games, and Animation: Using Comics to Construct Your Transmedia Storyworld* (New York: Focal Press, 2013), 200.

34. Hall, "Shaken, Stirred, Pixellated," 324.

35. "EA's Lost Casino Royale Game," *MI6: The Home of James Bond 007*, May 26, 2010, http://www.mi6-hq.com/sections/articles/gaming_ea_casino_royale_lost.php3 (accessed January 13, 2013).

36. IGN, "GoldenEye 007 Wii Trailer—E3 2010," *YouTube*, June 15, 2010, http://www.youtube.com/watch?v=o3KqiZr-AjI (accessed May 14, 2013).

37. "GoldenEye 007 for Wii Reviews," *Metacritic*, November 2, 2010, http://www.metacritic.com/game/wii/goldeneye-007 (accessed September 15, 2013).

38. "007 Legends Announced," *MI6 Community*, page 1, http://www.mi6community.com/index.php?p=/discussion/2931/007-legends-announced/p1 (accessed May 26, 2012).

39. The exceptions are *Goldfinger*, which was adapted into the text adventure title *James Bond 007: Goldfinger* (1986, Mindscape), and *Licence to Kill*, whose video game, *007: Licence to Kill* (1989, Domark), features a variety of levels presented from an overhead perspective.

40. "Experience James Bond's Most Iconic and Intense Missions as the World's Top Under-

cover Agent in 007 Legends," *Activision*, April 18, 2012, http://investor.activision.com/releasedetail.cfm?releaseID=665255 (accessed May 26, 2012).

41. "007 Legends Announced," page 5.

42. "James Bond 007: Legends," *VGChartz*, http://www.vgchartz.com/game/71065/james-bond-007-legends/Global/ (accessed January 20, 2013).

43. "Call of Duty: Black Ops II," *VGChartz*, http://www.vgchartz.com/game/70716/call-of-duty-black-ops-ii/Global/ (accessed January 20, 2013).

44. Ogilvie, "007 Legends Review." For more reviews that discuss the links between *007 Legends* and the *Call of Duty* games, see Leif Johnson, "007 Legends Review," *GameSpot*, October 24, 2012, http://www.gamespot.com/reviews/007-legends-review/1900–6398807/ (accessed January 27, 2014); and Will Porter, "007 Legends Review," *Eurogamer.net*, October 19, 2012, http://www.eurogamer.net/articles/2012–10-19–007-legends-review (accessed January 27, 2014).

45. Elkington, "Too Many Cooks," 216.

46. Dale North, "GDC: How Important Review Scores Are to Games Sales," *Destructoid*, March 9, 2012, http://www.destructoid.com/gdc-how-important-review-scores-are-to-games-sales-223570.phtml (accessed January 20, 2013).

47. "007 Legends," *Metacritic*, http://www.metacritic.com/game/playstation-3/007-legends (accessed January 20, 2013).

48. Wesley Yin-Poole, "James Bond Developer Eurocom Makes Staff Redundant, Ceases Trading," *Eurogamer.net*, December 7, 2012, http://www.eurogamer.net/articles/2012–12-07-james-bond-developer-eurocom-makes-remaining-staff-redundant-ceases-trading (accessed January 7, 2013).

49. "Game Over for Activision," *MI6*, January 7, 2013, http://www.mi6-hq-com/sections/articles/gaming_activision_game_over.php3 (accessed January 7, 2013).

50. James Chapman, *Licence to Thrill: A Cultural History of the James Bond Films*, 2d ed. (New York: I.B. Tauris, 2007), 241.

51. Ibid.

52. "On Her Majesty's Secret Service," *007 Legends*, developed by Eurocom (2012; Los Angeles: Activision, 2012), Sony PlayStation 3.

53. Matilda Battersby, "William Boyd on Debut Play Longing—And Why Daniel Craig Isn't Right for His James Bond," *The Independent*, February 27, 2013, http://www.independent.co.uk/arts-entertainment/theatre-dance/features/william-boyd-on-debut-play-longing--and-why-daniel-craig-isnt-right-for-his-james-bond-8512909.html (accessed September 15, 2013).

54. Chapman, *Licence to Thrill*, 48.

55. McGowan, "Some of This Happened to the Other Fellow," 116.

56. Andy Lane and Paul Simpson, *The Bond Files: An Unofficial Guide to the World's Greatest Secret Agent, Expanded and Updated* (London: Virgin, 2002), 248.

57. Joey Esposito, "Hero Worship: The 007 Approach to Continuity," *IGN*, October 26, 2012, http://www.ign.com/articles/2012/10/26/hero-worship-the-007-approach-to-continuity (accessed October 26, 2012).

58. Luke Reilly, "Could 007 Legends Prove an Old James Bond Fan Theory Right?" *IGN*, April 22, 2012, http://www.ign.com/articles/2012/04/23/could-007-legends-prove-an-old-james-bond-fan-theory-right (accessed September 15, 2013).

59. Weaver, *Comics for Film, Games, and Animation*, 169.

60. William Uricchio and Robert E. Pearson, "I'm Not Fooled by That Cheap Disguise," in *The Many Lives of the Batman: Critical Approaches to a Superhero and his Media*, ed. William Uricchio and Roberta E. Pearson (New York: Routledge, 1991), 183.

61. Erik Norris, "Making 007 Legends, Pt. 1—Inception," *Crave Online*, September 10, 2012, http://www.craveonline.com/gaming/articles/195687-making-007-legends-pt-1-inception (accessed January 13, 2013).

62. Elkington, "Too Many Cooks," 222.

63. Ibid., 214–215.

64. Derek Johnson, *Media Franchising: Creative License and Collaboration in the Culture Industries* (New York: New York University Press, 2013), Kindle edition.

65. Ben Fritz, "Disney Unveils Plans to Revive Its Video Game Business," *Los Angeles Times*, January 15, 2013, http://articles.latimes.com/2013/jan/15/entertainment/al-et-ct-disney-infinity-20130115 (accessed September 14, 2013).

66. Henry Jenkins, *Convergence Culture: Where Old and New Media Collide* (New York: New York University Press, 2006), 97–98.

67. Hall, "Shaken, Stirred, Pixellated," 327.

68. In *A View to a Kill*, Zorin falls to his death while fighting Bond atop the Golden Gate Bridge.

69. Promotional spot for *Tomorrow Never Dies: The Mission Continue* (Unreleased, MGM Interactive), featured on *Tomorrow Never Dies*, VHS, directed by Roger Spottiswoode (1997; Santa Monica: MGM Home Entertainment, 1998).

70. Lane and Simpson, *The Bond Files*, 2.

71. More precisely, the narrative of the video game *The Amazing Spider-Man* (2012) continues that of its cinematic namesake, and the story of the 2014 interactive sequel details events that occur parallel to those featured in the second film. Despite this transmedia approach, however, the film sequel includes a version of the character The Rhino that differs from that of the initial game, signifying a revision of continuity that, ironically, is not dissimilar from that in the Bond series.

Bibliography

Battersby, Matilda. "William Boyd on Debut Play Longing—And Why Daniel Craig Isn't Right for His James Bond." *The Independent*. February 27, 2013. http://www.independent.co.uk/arts-entertainment/theatre-dance/features/william-boyd-on-debut-play-longing--and-why-daniel-craig-isnt-right-for-his-james-bond-8512909.html (accessed September 15, 2013).

Bennett, Tony, and Janet Woollacott. *Bond and Beyond: The Political Career of a Popular Hero*. New York: Methuen, 1987.

"Call of Duty: Black Ops II." *VGChartz*. http://www.vgchartz.com/game/70716/call-of-duty-black-ops-ii/Global/ (accessed January 20, 2013).

Chapman, James. *Licence to Thrill: A Cultural History of the James Bond Films*, 2d ed. New York: I.B. Tauris, 2007.

"007 Legends." *Metacritic*. http://www.metacritic.com/game/playstation-3/007-legends (accessed January 20, 2013).

"007 Legends Announced." *MI6 Community*. http://www.mi6community.com/index.php?p=/discussion/2931/007-legends-announced/p1 (accessed May 26, 2012).

"EA's Lost *Casino Royale* Game." *MI6: The Home of James Bond 007*. May 26, 2010. http://www.mi6-hq.com/sections/articles/gaming_ea_casino_royale_lost.php3 (accessed January 13, 2013).

Ebert, Roger. "Skyfall." *RogerEbertwww*. November 7, 2012. http://rogerebert.suntimes.com/apps/pbcs.dll/article?AID=/20121107/REVIEWS/121109990 (accessed November 7, 2012).

Elkington, Trevor. "Too Many Cooks: Media Convergence and Self-Defeating Adaptations." In *The Video Game Theory Reader 2*, edited by Bernard Perron and Mark J.P. Wolf, 213–235. New York: Routledge, 2009.

Esposito, Joey. "Hero Worship: The 007 Approach to Continuity." *IGN*. October 26, 2012. http://www.ign.com/articles/2012/10/26/hero-worship-the-007-approach-to-continuity (accessed October 26, 2012).

"Experience James Bond's Most Iconic and Intense Missions as the World's Top Undercover Agent in 007 Legends." *Activision*. April 18, 2012. http://investor.activision.com/releasedetail.cfm?ReleaseID=665255 (accessed May 26, 2012).

Fritz, Ben. "Disney Unveils Plans to Revive Its Video Game Business." *Los Angeles Times*. January 15, 2013. http://articles.latimes.com/2013/jan/15/entertainment/la-et-ct-disney-infinity-20130115 (accessed September 14, 2013).

"Game Over for Activision." *MI6: The Home of James Bond 007*. January 7, 2013. http://www.mi6-hq.com/sections/articles/gaming_activision_game_over.php3 (accessed January 7, 2013).

Gish, Harrison. "Media Boundaries and Bullet Time: A *Hard Boiled* Fan Plays *Stranglehold*." *Mediascape: UCLA's Journal of Cinema and Media Studies* (Winter 2012). http://www.tft.ucla.edu/mediascape/Winter2012_MediaBoundaries.html (accessed January 10, 2013).

"GoldenEye 007 for Wii Reviews." *Metacritic*. November 2, 2010. http://www.metacritic.com/game/wii/goldeneye-007 (accessed September 15, 2013).

Gray, Jonathan. *Show Sold Separately: Promos, Spoilers, and Other Media Paratexts*. New York: New York University Press, 2010. Kindle edition.·

Grieb, Margit. "Run Lara Run." In *Screenplay: Cinema/Videogames/Interfaces*, edited by Geoff King and Tanya Krzywinska, 157–170. New York: Wallflower Press, 2002.

Hall, Stefan. "Shaken, Stirred, Pixellated: Video Gaming as Bond." In *The James Bond Phenomenon: A Critical Reader*, 2d ed., edited by Christoph Lindner, 312–330. Manchester: Manchester University Press, 2009.

_____. "'You've Seen the Movie, Now Play the Video Game': Recoding the Cinematic in Digital Media and Virtual Culture." PhD diss., Bowling Green State University, 2011.

IGN. "GoldenEye 007 Wii Trailer—E3 2010." *YouTube*. June 15, 2010. http://www.youtube.com/watch?v=o3KqiZr-AjI (accessed May 14, 2013).

Impellizeri, Kevin D. "Use Your Joystick, 007: Video Games and the Interactive Bond Experience." In *James Bond in World and Popular Culture: The Films Are Not Enough*, 2d ed., edited by Robert G. Weiner, B. Lynn Whitfield, and Jack Becker, 7–22. Newcastle-upon-Tyne: Cambridge Scholars, 2011.

"James Bond 007: Legends." *VGChartz*. http://www.vgchartz.com/game/71065/james-bond-007-legends/Global/ (accessed January 20, 2013).

Jenkins, Henry. *Convergence Culture: Where Old and New Media Collide*. New York: New York University Press, 2006.

_____. "No, You Do Not Have to Be a Gamer to Like Inception!" *Confessions of an Aca-Fan: The Official Weblog of Henry Jenkins*. August 8, 2010. http://henryjenkins.org/2010/08/no_you_do_not_have_to_be_a_gam.html (accessed September 21, 2013).

Johnson, Derek. *Media Franchising: Creative License and Collaboration in the Culture Industries*. New York: New York University Press, 2013. Kindle edition.

Johnson, Leif. "007 Legends Review." *GameSpot*. October 24, 2012. http://www.gamespot.com/reviews/007-legends-review/1900-6398807/ (accessed January 27, 2014).

King, Geoff, and Tanya Krzywinska. "Introduction: Cinema/Videogames/Interfaces." In *Screenplay: Cinema/Videogames/Interfaces*, edited by Geoff King and Tanya Krzywinska, 1–32. New York: Wallflower Press, 2002.

Lane, Andy, and Paul Simpson. *The Bond Files: An Unofficial Guide to the World's Greatest Secret Agent, Expanded and Updated*. London: Virgin, 2002.

McGowan, David. "Some of This Happened to the Other Fellow: Remaking *GoldenEye 007* with Daniel Craig." In *Game On, Hollywood!: Essays on the Intersection of Video Games and Cinema*, edited by Gretchen Papazian and Joseph Michael Sommers, 115–128. Jefferson, NC: McFarland, 2013.

Narcisse, Evan. "L.A. Noire Becomes First Video Game Ever Featured at Tribeca Film Festival." *Time*. March 29, 2011. http://techland.time.com/2011/03/29/l-a-noire-becomes-first-video-game-ever-featured-at-tribeca-film-festival/ (accessed September 15, 2013).

Norris, Erik. "Making 007: Legends, Pt. 1—Inception." *Crave Online.* September 10, 2012. http://www.craveonline.com/gaming/articles/195687-making-007-legends-pt-1-inception (accessed January 13, 2013).

North, Dale. "GDC: How Important Review Scores Are to Game Sales." *Destructoid.* March 9, 2012. http://www.destructoid.com/gdc-how-important-review-scores-are-to-game-sales-223570.phtml (accessed January 20, 2013).

Ogilvie, Tristan. "007 Legends Review." *IGN.* October 16, 2012. http://www.ign.com/articles/2012/10/16/007-legends-review (accessed October 17, 2012).

Porter, Will. "007 Legends Review." *Eurogamer.net.* October 19, 2012. http://www.eurogamer.net/articles/2012-10-19-007-legends-review (accessed January 27, 2014).

Reilly, Luke. "Could 007 Legends Prove an Old James Bond Fan Theory Right?" *IGN.* April 22, 2012. http://www.ign.com/articles/2012/04/23/could-007-legends-prove-an-old-james-bond-fan-theory-right (accessed September 15, 2013).

Russell, Jamie. *Generation Xbox: How Videogames Invaded Hollywood.* East Sussex: Yellow Ant, 2012.

Stein, Abe, and Matthew Weise. "All Bang Bang, No Kiss Kiss?: The Bond Figure and Video Games." In *James Bond in World and Popular Culture: The Films Are Not Enough,* 2d ed., edited by Robert G. Weiner, B. Lynn Whitfield, and Jack Becker, 23–39. Newcastle-upon-Tyne: Cambridge Scholars, 2011.

Thorburn, David, and Henry Jenkins. "Introduction: Toward an Aesthetics of Transition." In *Rethinking Media Change: The Aesthetics of Transition,* edited by David Thorburn and Henry Jenkins, 1–16. Cambridge: MIT Press, 2004.

Uricchio, William and Roberta E. Pearson. "I'm Not Fooled by That Cheap Disguise." In *The Many Lives of the Batman: Critical Approaches to a Superhero and His Media,* edited by William Uricchio and Roberta E. Pearson, 182–213. New York: Routledge, 1991.

Weaver, Tyler. *Comics for Film, Games, and Animation: Using Comics to Construct Your Transmedia Storyworld.* New York: Focal Press, 2013.

Yin-Poole, Wesley. "James Bond Developer Eurocom Makes Staff Redundant, Ceases Trading." *Eurogamer.net.* December 7, 2012. http://www.eurogamer.net/articles/2012-12-07-james-bond-developer-eurocom-makes-remaining-staff-redundant-ceases-trading (accessed January 7, 2013).

Afterword

Trevor Sewell

I can still remember hearing the 007 theme for the first time as if it were yesterday. It seemed to somehow sum up everything that was cool about instrumental music in the 1960s. I was very young then but looking back with the benefit of hindsight it was so much more than that! It encapsulated the glamor, style and aspirations of the '60s transforming the previous world, which had been well defined by film noir and populated by downtrodden Philip Marlowe–type characters and replacing them with an altogether new type of hero. Enter James Bond.

The Bond theme was really my first introduction to the music of the spy genre and it was instrumental (no pun intended) in inspiring me years later to look back, discover and engage with many of its predecessors.

This trip into the past ignited my interest in the music of 1960s instrumental acts such as The Ventures, The Safaris and Duane Eddy, all of whom could conjure up vivid images in my imagination with just a few simple echoed guitar notes. I soon realized the musical relationship between the parallel worlds of spies and private eyes and I was hooked.

My first hearing the opening guitar riff of the original James Bond theme, years before I had even considered playing myself, had a profound effect on me. When I finally did begin to teach myself guitar the James Bond theme was high on my list of priorities and my first band (age 13) used to incorporate a section of it into a jam that we would often embark upon in the middle of other completely unrelated songs. I loved the guitar sound and it was so iconic that you could play the opening motif and be mentally and instantly transported into the wonderful world of Bond. This John Barry arrangement had brought the spy genre into a new world, a world that one could aspire to be a part of instead of the one inhabited by the stereotypical Cold War, white Macintosh-wearing spies of the previous era.

Many years later I would record an instrumental with the band I was playing with at the time The Revillos for EMI Records in the U.K. The track "ZX7" paid more than a passing nod to that great John Barry 007 arrangement. It was then that I promised myself that one day I would compose a full album of instrumental pieces and inflict it on the unsuspecting world.

Little did I know it would be more than twenty years later when I would finally get my chance to realize my ambition.

In 2011 with the advent of digital recording systems that even Q could have been proud of, the dream had finally become reality as it was now possible to create albums up to master standards in small home studios.

The first track I recorded for the project was called "The Big Sleep" inspired by the film noir movie of the same name which starred Humphrey Bogart as the acid-tongued Philip Marlowe. My track went on to make the final nominees list at the 2011 Hollywood Music In Media Awards at the Kodak Complex in Los Angeles. I took this as a good sign and consequently spent pretty much the next six weeks doing little else but writing and working on the other tracks for the album. It was a very enjoyable time for me as it was indeed "a true labor of love."

My thoughts turned to the Cold War period with my research revealing The Bridge of Spies (Glienicke Bridge), which immediately triggered ideas for creating a musical representation of the stark environment that I imagined, where spies, hostages and political prisoners from either side of the Iron Curtain were routinely swapped between the years of 1952 and 1986. The mood of the track was intended to be cold, stark and merciless entwined with an air of mistrust and business as usual.

When recording the track I found it necessary to try and keep the imaginary image foremost in my mind in order that the cold detached attitude of the track could be performed appropriately, almost like a kind of method acting. I also wanted the track to sound more contemporary so I employed a midi guitar system to create new textures while staying true to the genre. There is certainly a very retro feel to the track but it also draws on influences from much later works.

The Bond franchise initially established its presence with a film that contained excitement adventure, humor, glamor and a totally new type of hero. Consequently it's easy to see why we loved James Bond then, when he first appeared in *Dr. No* and why, 50 years on, the Bond franchise is still at the top of its genre. I couldn't have completed the album without at least a nod to the impact that those few guitar notes so personifying the very spirit of Bond had had on me all those years ago making the Barry treatment and arrangement, in my humble opinion one of the most iconic tracks of all time.

I once again revisited my preoccupation with the Barry arrangement of the 007 theme and created what is intended as a tribute to the music that originally inspired my own album, *Surf, Spies and Film Noir*. My "Mission Improbable" track is very upbeat and intended to represent the more glamorous, ever confident aspects of a Bond-inspired superspy who, although constantly in danger, is never phased and is ultimately always in control. This spy unlike his film noir counterparts has a penchant for the high life, speaks several languages, inhabits casinos and is constantly surrounded by beautiful women.

I know which spy I would rather be.

I was very happy to be asked to write the afterword to this fine book, which bears testament to a genre very close to my own heart and thank Michele for affording me the opportunity while further applauding her vision in compiling this fascinating collection of essays.

Trevor Sewell is a multi-award–winning British musician, composer and producer. He also lectures in interactive media design at Northumbria University, one of the U.K.'s most respected educational establishments.

About the Contributors

Thomas M. **Barrett** is a professor of history at St. Mary's College of Maryland. He has published on the history of the North Caucasus, the Cossacks, and Russian themes in American entertainment. He is writing a book on the image of Russians and East Europeans in American popular culture.

Michael **Baskett** is an associate professor of film studies in the Department of Film and Media Studies at the University of Kansas where he teaches courses in East Asian cinema and film history. He is the author of *The Attractive Empire: Transnational Film Culture in Imperial Japan* (University of Hawaii Press, 2008). He is at work on a book-length manuscript on Japanese film culture in Cold War Asia.

Edward **Biddulph** is the author of *Licence to Cook* (lulu.com, 2010), a cookbook inspired by food described in the James Bond books. He writes "James Bond Memes," a blog which explores the ideas behind Ian Fleming's writing and the Bond films, and he has published other Bond-related articles in journals, magazines and on-line.

Michele **Brittany** is an independent scholar who actively supports several popular culture organizations in a variety of capacities, including serving as book review editor for the *Journal of Graphic Novels and Comics*, North American news correspondent for *Comics Forum*, and West Coast correspondent for *Bleeding Cool*. She is the James Bond, Espionage and Eurospy Area Chair for the Southwest Popular/American Association's annual conference.

Ian **Dawe** received an M.A. in film studies from the University of Exeter. He has published and presented academic articles about the works of Alan Moore, Harvey Pekar and Greg the Bunny. He has taught film studies, world cinema, anthropology, and introduction to comics studies at Selkirk College in Nelson, British Columbia, Canada, as well as delivering workshops in comics studies for Self Design High.

Nicholas **Diak** holds an M.A. from the University of Washington and is an independent scholar of Italian genre films, exploitation films, and neofolk/martial-industrial music. He presents annually at the SW PCA/ACA conference and posts his scholarly essays at his blog at http://www.heiligetod.com.

James **Fleury** is a Ph.D. student in cinema and media studies at UCLA. He has taught courses in Le Moyne College's departments of English and Communication and Film Studies. A Bond fan since childhood, his other research interests include tie-in video games, superhero franchising, and D.I.Y. YouTube culture.

K. A. **Laity** is an award-winning author whose bibliography is chock full of short stories, humor pieces, plays and essays, both scholarly and popular. She spent the 2011–2012 academic year in Galway, Ireland, where she was a Fulbright Fellow in digital humanities at NUIG. She teaches medieval literature, film, gender studies, new media and popular culture at the College of Saint Rose.

Hannah **Means-Shannon** is a comics scholar and journalist who has contributed articles to the *Journal of Graphic Novels and Comics, Studies in Comics, The International Journal of Comic Art,* and several anthology collections. She is editor-in-chief at the popular culture news site *Bleeding Cool.*

Christine D. **Myers** teaches European history at Monmouth College in Illinois. Along with her ongoing research in the history of higher education, she researches the filming locations in *Scarecrow and Mrs. King* and has led students in the same project, with multiple conference papers resulting from it.

Ipshita **Nath** is a graduate student at the Centre for English Studies, School of Language, Literature and Cultural Studies, Jawaharal Nehru University, Delhi. Her research interests come under the rubric of cultural studies, though she has an abiding fondness for the textual mythologies of Shakespeare, Milton, Byron and nineteenth-century British and American novelists.

Fernando Gabriel **Pagnoni Berns** teaches on American horror cinemas and Euro horror at the Universidad de Buenos Aires (UBA), Facultad de Filosofía y Letras (Argentina). He has published articles in *Imagofagia, Stichomythia, Anagnórisis, Lindes* and *UpStage Journal,* among others, as well as essays in a variety of edited collections.

Brian **Patton** teaches English and film studies at King's University College at Western University, London, Canada. His research interests include postwar British literature and culture, spy fiction and film, and comics and graphic narratives.

Anubhav **Pradhan** is a student of literatures in English, in Jamia Millia Islamia's M.Phil degree course in English literature and an assistant professor in the Department of English, Bharati College, University of Delhi. He is interested in the production, conception and dissemination of cultural artifacts.

John **Vohlidka** is an assistant professor of history at Gannon University. He specializes in early modern European history, with special emphasis on Tudor-Stuart history and the Reformation. He also lectures on a variety of topics such as comics and culture, post-atomic Japan, and the history of the future.

Cynthia W. **Walker** is an associate professor and chair of the Department of Communications and Media Culture at St. Peter's University in Jersey City, New Jersey, where she teaches public relations and marketing, media literacy, gender and communication, film, animation, broadcast studies, scriptwriting and research writing.

Index